# Family Welfare

**Recent Titles in**
**Contributions in Family Studies**

Revolutions in Americans' Lives: A Demographic Perspective on the History of
Americans, Their Families, and Their Society
*Robert V. Wells*

Three Different Worlds: Women, Men, and Children in an Industrializing
Community
*Frances Abrahamer Rothstein*

Family and Work: Comparative Convergences
*Merlin B. Brinkerhoff, editor*

Child-Rearing and Reform: A Study of the Nobility in Eighteenth-Century
Poland
*Bogna Lorence-Kot*

Parent-Child Interaction in Transition
*George Kurian, editor*

The Dutch Gentry, 1500–1650: Family, Faith, and Fortune
*Sherrin Marshall*

Migrants in Europe: The Role of Family, Labor, and Politics
*Hans Christian Buechler and Judith-Maria Buechler, editors*

A History of Marriage Systems
*G. Robina Quale*

Feeding Infants in Four Societies: Causes and Consequences of Mothers' Choices
*Beverly Winikoff, Mary Ann Castle, Virginia Hight Laukaran, editors*

The Reconstruction of Family Policy
*Elaine A. Anderson and Richard C. Hula, editors*

Family, Justice, and Delinquency
*Brenda Geiger and Michael Fischer*

Fathers as Primary Caregivers
*Brenda Geiger*

# Family Welfare

*Gender, Property, and Inheritance since the Seventeenth Century*

## EDITED BY DAVID R. GREEN
## AND ALASTAIR OWENS

Contributions in Family Studies, Number 18

**Westport, Connecticut**
**London**

**Library of Congress Cataloging-in-Publication Data**

Family welfare : gender, property, and inheritance since the seventeenth century / edited by David R. Green and Alastair Owens.
    p.  cm. — (Contributions in family studies, ISSN 0147–1023 ; no. 18)
  Includes bibliographical references and index.
  ISBN 0–313–32328–3
    1. Land tenure—Europe—History—Congresses.  2. Inheritance and succession—Europe—History—Congresses.  3. Family—Europe—History—Congresses.  4. Sex role—Europe—History—Congresses.  I. Green, David R., 1954–  II. Owens, Alastair, 1971–  III. Series.
HD584.F34  2004
306.3′2—dc22    2004004783

British Library Cataloguing in Publication Data is available.

Library of Congress Catalog Card Number: 2004004783
ISBN: 0–313–32328–3
ISSN: 0147–1023

First published in 2004

Praeger Publishers, 88 Post Road West, Westport, CT 06881
An imprint of Greenwood Publishing Group, Inc.
www.praeger.com

Printed in the United States of America

The paper used in this book complies with the Permanent Paper Standard issued by the National Information Standards Organization (Z39.48–1984).

10  9  8  7  6  5  4  3  2  1

# Contents

# Illustrations

## FIGURES

## APPENDICES

# Preface

The origins of this book lie in a conference session organized by the editors at the third European Social Science History Conference, held at the Vrije Universiteit in Amsterdam, The Netherlands, April 12–15, 2000. The session brought together a selection of papers that dealt with the themes of wealth, gender, and welfare across a range of historical and geographical settings. Most of the papers that were given in that session appear as chapters in this volume, alongside studies of others who presented their work in different strands of the conference or who have a keen interest in the historical relationships between gender, property, and family strategies. We must thank the organizers of the European Social Science History Conference and, specifically, Marco van Leeuwen and Lynn Hollen Lees, convenors of the network of which the session was a part, for their support in enabling what has become an extraordinarily fruitful exchange of ideas and perspectives. The biannual European Social Science History Conference has quickly become a leading international meeting for historians and social scientists and a festival of intellectual exchange. We hope that this book stands as an example of the success of that conference in stimulating high-quality, international comparative historical scholarship.

Editing a book with contributors working in several different countries across two continents has been both a pleasure and a challenge. We are very grateful to our contributors for responding so efficiently and with such good humor to our frequent requests for information. We would also like to thank Marie-Pierre Arrizabalaga for her excellent translation of Rose Duroux's contribution to the book and Caterina Pizzigoni and Robert Dennehy for their careful translation of Sandro Guzzi-Heeb's chapter. We are grateful to Ed Oliver of the Department of Geography at Queen Mary, University of London, for drawing the maps and diagrams that appear in various chapters. Thanks also to Ralph Guite for help with Latin translations. We are also very grateful to the production team at Greenwood Press, and especially Michael Hermann and Cynthia Harris, for their help, patience, and encouragement in completing this book. As the chapters that follow demonstrate, support and assistance frequently comes most readily from those who are "nearest and dearest"—we are especially indebted to Hilary, Julie, and William for putting up with the distractions that completing this volume entailed.

# CHAPTER 1

# Introduction: Family Welfare and the Welfare Family

*David R. Green and Alastair Owens*

Few words are used as widely and, arguably, as inconsistently as *welfare* and the *family*. Few concepts are as closely related as the two. What do we understand by the term *welfare*? Who is in need of assistance and why? How can the family be defined? What roles do families play and what strategies do they adopt in the provision of welfare? How does gender influence that provision? Raising these questions leads to others. How does welfare provided by the family relate to other sources of assistance? What functions do institutions play, including the market, in providing support? These are the main questions that underpin the chapters in this book.

In raising these questions our aim is to open up fresh perspectives on the provision of welfare by moving the focus of attention beyond the state and voluntary sectors and away from definitions of need based on notions of material poverty. In pursuing this aim, it is our belief that the study of welfare provision in the past has been unnecessarily restrictive. The historiographical obsession with the rise of the welfare state and the narrow definition of welfare as provision for the poor has for too long constrained our understanding of the variety of forms of assistance and support, some direct and others indirect, provided by a balance of the state, the voluntary sector, the market, kin, and the family. Part of the reason for this historiographical preoccupation with the state is the fact that written sources for the study of welfare are typically generated when needy individuals come into contact with formal welfare agencies. As Michel Foucault has argued, the observations, descriptions, and classifications of the poor that emerged from this contact constituted a "normalizing gaze" that defined those in need in relation to specific categories of relief—in short to be defined as a "case" and to be corrected, classified, and provided for accordingly.[1] Any history of welfare based solely on studying the poor defined in this way will only capture those who came into contact with these disciplinary reforming agencies. When need is defined more broadly, as we suggest below, it is clear that those who would normally be considered poor were by no means all, or indeed anywhere near a majority, of those who actually depended on one form of assistance or another.

This book demonstrates that for many social groups, including those with property, family and kin formed an important pivot around which the provision of welfare took place. However, this is not to deny the complex ways in which the family interacted with other institutions and agencies of provision—the law, the market, the state, and the voluntary sector. Rather, our approach has been to consider the family not as a closed demographic unit, but as a transactional nexus involved in a mixed economy of welfare. In this manner, although unusual in its focus on the provisions made for those with property, this book is a contribution to the wider realm of scholarship that seeks to understand the intricate ways in which welfare operated in the past.

This introduction concentrates on the relationships between welfare, institutions, and the family, taking account of the ways in which gender relations in particular influenced the provision of assistance and the transfer of resources. In doing so it explores, first, the way in which welfare needs and wants can be defined and raises the suggestion that the history of welfare should not consider provision just for those who were poor. It then examines the historiography of the welfare state, taking account of the move away from Whiggish explanations of its origins to a more nuanced understanding of the varieties of assistance made by societies in the past. Next we focus attention on the role of the family, arguing that we need to understand its welfare function in terms of transactions between individual members and between the family and wider networks of kin and community. This, in turn, raises issues relating to the strategies families adopted over the life course to provide for their members. One of the crucial considerations in these strategies was the role of gender, an issue that informs discussion throughout the book. What role did women play in the transmission of family resources? How were they provided for? And what was the impact of wider economic changes on their situation? While we cannot hope to provide all the answers, by posing such questions we can, at least, try to open up new avenues to a broader understanding of welfare.[2]

## WELFARE FOR WHOM?

Welfare has traditionally been interpreted as provision for those in need, typically the poor. However, it is clear that need takes many forms, ranging from basic human requirements of food, warmth, and shelter to more relative wants and desires that allow individuals to participate more fully in social life. In practice any distinction between absolute needs and relative wants is difficult to uphold.[3] Indeed, we would argue that a broad definition of welfare is required that addresses issues of social want related to status as well as absolute need related to survival. Leaving aside moral questions about those who are more or less deserving of support, this broader approach argues that welfare is as important for the rich as it is for the poor.

It is clear, for example, that irrespective of income or social status, at certain times in the life course, such as during childhood, widowhood, or old age, even those with access to means might have had difficulty making provision for their own well-being and therefore would have had to seek support from elsewhere, be it family, kin, community, charity, or the state. Children, for example, required provision over and above the care and nurture necessary for their mere survival. At various points during the life course, notably at the time of their marriage and possibly the establishment of a separate household, individuals may also have required or received significant amounts of assistance in the form of gifts or money. At the same time, the elderly, whether poor or not, also required care and assistance. Similarly, in most historical societies the needs of women have often been regarded as different from those of men. Middle-class women, for example, required the means to sustain their respectable status without the necessity of taking paid employment, while for men the same did not hold true. Although not "needy" in the sense of being poor, unless they could provide an independent income for themselves, such individuals required some form of provision to maintain their social stranding. Viewed in these broad terms, welfare rights and wants were as much defined by life course position, gender, and social status as they were by any notion of absolute need.

Welfare also serves a purpose for those individuals and institutions that provide support. In this context, the relationship established in the process of giving and receiving between donors and recipients is as important as the nature of provision itself. In anthropology and sociology, the giving of the gift is interpreted not merely as the one-way flow of resources but rather as an exchange of rights, obligations, and expectations between the parties involved.[4] The acts of giving and receiving in this sense help to reproduce moral, social, and political structures and hierarchies.[5]

## HISTORIOGRAPHIES OF WELFARE: THE BRITISH CASE

Until recently, histories of welfare in western liberal democracies, particularly the United Kingdom, have typically focused on the origins or rise of the welfare state.[6] Such accounts present an image of the growing importance of increasing state provision as part of a beneficent process of modernization. From the cradle to the grave, it became the state's role to provide for its citizens. In turn, it is argued that the rise of a more or less comprehensive system of secular state provision was paralleled by the relative decline of other forms of welfare based on charity, philanthropy, and the family. This was supposedly true in relation to various forms of provision, from housing and health to pensions and social security. In all these arenas the state came to play a dominant role. For most postwar historians all roads appeared to lead inexorably toward ever increasing state involvement in welfare provision.

More recently, such linear accounts have been questioned from two directions. First, the ending of the liberal postwar political consensus and the rise of the New Right on both sides of the Atlantic has cast doubts on the need and desirability for the state to be so deeply involved in the provision of welfare. This debate has focused on attempts to alter the balance of provision and responsibility away from the state and toward the family and the individual via the mechanism of the market. Second, historians themselves have begun to rethink the nature and chronology of the welfare state, arguing that its apparent rise has obscured the extent to which welfare provision in the past, as well as the present, has depended on a balance between statutory provision, voluntary efforts, the market, and informal assistance from families, kin, and community. This complex arena of provision has been described as the "mixed economy of welfare."[7]

In the British context Jane Lewis has remarked that "rather than seeing the story of the modern welfare state as a simple movement from individualism to collectivism and ever increasing amounts of (benevolent) state intervention, it is more accurate to see Britain as always having had a mixed economy of welfare."[8] In England and Wales in the 1890s, for example, only 2.6 percent of the population was in receipt of poor relief, an indication of the importance of other sources of assistance.[9] In poor urban communities family, kin, and community were individually and collectively crucial sources of welfare.[10] Higher up the social strata, skilled workers flocked in the thousands to buy Samuel Smiles's *Self Help*, published in 1859, joined friendly societies, subscribed to burial clubs, and contributed to a myriad of other schemes to protect themselves against the contingencies of life.[11] Middle-class widows bought life assurance and spinsters invested in annuities as a means of providing for themselves in old age—in effect a form of insurance against living too long.[12] In short, there has always been a veritable patchwork of provision made by people in all social strata to meet the risks inherent in life. Moreover, this mixed economy of welfare was commonplace in countries on both sides of the Atlantic.[13] In the rush to explain the rise of the welfare state, however, such informal and individualistic sources of support have largely been ignored, and it is only relatively recently that accounts, including the chapters here, have started to redress the balance.[14]

## THE MIXED ECONOMY OF WELFARE

The mixed economy of welfare, mentioned earlier, is a key concept that lies at the heart of several recent attempts to broaden our understanding of welfare provision. It serves to remind us that the history of welfare is not only about the prevalence of one type of provision over another, of, say, the importance of the state over the family or vice versa, but rather about the shifting balance between a range of different sources of support. Just as the family was not always the first resort for those in need, so too were institutions such as the workhouse or orphanage not necessarily the last port of call for the desperate. There is, as Peregrine Horden has remarked, no "hierarchy of resort"—any form of provision may be called upon in virtually any permutation.[15]

While it is possible to distinguish among the state, the market, the voluntary sector, and informal mechanisms of support, as shown in Figure 1.1, in practice these informal and formal sources of welfare blur and overlap in ways that make it difficult to impose any clear-cut boundaries on their respective fields of action. Nevertheless, it is still useful to consider each of these categories separately in order to understand the specific ways they are involved in the provision of welfare.

### The State

It is important here to distinguish between, on the one hand, the direct role of the state as a welfare provider and, on the other, the indirect way

**Figure 1.1**
**The Mixed Economy of Welfare**

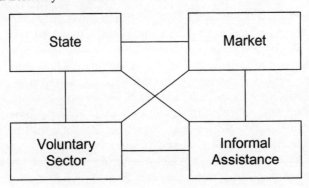

it operates through the redistributive and regulatory functions that provide the framework within which other institutions and agencies operate. As a source of provision, the classic welfare state provides a range of assistance and support from education and health to social security and pensions. However, it is perhaps through its redistributive and regulatory functions that it plays a more fundamental role in the provision of welfare, particularly for those with property. Indirectly, it affects the provision of welfare through the redistribution of income via taxation. It provides incentives for saving and to a greater or lesser degree regulates the financial markets in which such activities take place. Similarly, it is responsible for establishing the legal framework within which transfers of property over the life course take place: setting rules of guardianship, establishing rights in marriage and divorce, and regulating inheritance. The Napoleonic Civil Code introduced in France in 1804 is a good example of how the state can intervene by establishing clear rules for the partition of property. As Gérard Béaur and Rose Duroux show in their chapters in this volume, such a regulatory framework provided only a normative system for the transmission of property between individuals and across generations, honored sometimes more in the breach than the observance of customs. Nevertheless, it demonstrates clearly the very public way that the state attempted to impose a vision of welfare in the private sphere of family property transmission.

### The Market

As a source of welfare provision, as opposed merely to the satisfaction of preferences, the market plays two roles. First, it is itself an instrument for the provision of specific types of assistance, such as the life assurance schemes and widows' funds in eighteenth-century Germany discussed in Eve Rosenhaft's chapter. Paying into these types of savings funds represented a way of pooling risk and tapping into financial expertise. The market, however, also played a second role, providing a mechanism by which individuals and families could provide and accumulate resources. So, for example, in his chapter that considers areas of France where partible division of property at death prevailed, Gérard Béaur argues that land sales were used by relatives to even out the value of different portions of inheritance. David Sabean has also pointed out how similar mechanisms operated in Germany.[16] In this sense, recourse to the market should not necessarily be seen in isolation but rather as part of a wider strategy of providing welfare for those relatives with a share in inherited property.[17] Both examples demonstrate how the market could be used as a means of providing welfare in very different contexts.

In the context of welfare provision, entering the market inevitably involved taking risks, and problems often arose when this entailed the use of another's property, such as occurred when guardians sought to use the assets of their wards. As Ann Ighe shows in her chapter, this was an issue that troubled reformers of the law of guardianship in late-nineteenth-century Sweden. It is clear, however, that when the benefits outweighed the risks, the market offered a potentially rewarding and accessible mechanism for fashioning welfare strategies.

## The Voluntary Sector

Unlike the state provision of welfare predicated on a set of rights, voluntary provision was based on criteria that defined suitable objects of charity and as such depended to a much greater degree on the altruistic motives of the donor. In addition, however, the act of giving was also implicated in the process of social reproduction.[18] While the objectives of charity focused on provision for the vulnerable, they also served to maintain and reproduce structures of authority and deference. Contrasting the role of voluntary charity with compulsory poor relief, the Reverend Thomas Chalmers argued in the *Christian and Civic Economy of Large Towns* that it was only through the charitable actions of "private Christians, each acting separately, and in secret" that harmonious class relations could be sustained.[19] The dual functions of charity are also highlighted by Anne McCants in her chapter discussing the eighteenth-century Amsterdam municipal orphanage. In the process of providing care for orphaned children, it also shored up the economically vulnerable bourgeois family by removing elsewhere the financial burden of care.

## Informal Assistance

Informal assistance that stretches out from the family to encompass friends, neighbors, kin, and the wider community comprises the fourth element in the mixed economy of welfare. For many, this kind of support has been particularly neglected in comparison with provision by the state and the voluntary sector, though, as Jane Lewis has remarked, the latter two have frequently sought to buttress the former, especially the role of the family in the provision of care.[20] What perhaps distinguishes informal assistance from other forms is the element of reciprocity among those involved, although it is important not to exaggerate the influence of warmth over calculation. Arguably, reciprocity is likely to be strongest between family members among whom bonds of affection are closest and trust best developed. It is important, though, to be aware of the limitations of family care imposed by demographic circumstances and economic capacity. In poor communities, both urban and rural, where few if any families could protect themselves against risk stemming from ill health, unemployment, or the other blows that fate could deal, mutual aid could act as a form of social insurance against the future. On such occasions the help of kin, neighbors, and friends was critical, as Michael Young and Peter Wilmott showed in *Family and Kinship in East London,* a classic study of working-class family relationships and mutual aid.[21] We should not necessarily see such forms of generosity purely in terms of the poor. Across the life course it is clear, as the chapters in this book demonstrate, that informal assistance was an important source of welfare for those with property. As Sandro Guzzi-Heeb's chapter shows, many a son and daughter received a helping hand from wealthy relatives and rich patrons in establishing a career or in making a good match.

## FAMILY, HOUSEHOLD, AND KIN

While the family is neither the exclusive provider of assistance nor necessarily the first port of call for those in need, it is often the pivot around which the mixed economy of welfare revolves. As Michelle Perrot has recently argued, the family was "civil society's invisible hand: [it] was both nest and nexus."[22] It was the nest in the sense of being the primary unit of biological reproduction and the nexus in the sense that it was also the primary unit of social reproduction. Through marriage it was the link between individuals and wider society; through nurture and descent it was the means by which various forms of capital—both material and symbolic—were transferred between and across generations.

From Frederic Le Play onward, demographers have searched for—and apparently found—various distinctive family types that more or less correspond to particular geographical regions, patterns of marriage, and systems of property transmission. Whether there are two models as John Hajnal suggests, three, as suggested by Le Play, or four, as Peter Laslett argues, is not important here.[23] Of greater significance is the criticism that such a demographic approach focuses on fixed types of family structures and ignores the dynamic nature of family and household formation that inevitably stems from the aging process.[24] As André Burguèires and François Lebrun have argued, "the chief feature of the traditional European family was its instability, the successive blows dealt it by death: the loss of infants . . . and the frequent ending of marriages, by a husband's or wife's death."[25] Under such circumstances, families experienced continuous change as members aged, died, or moved away, each of these occasions changing the family dynamics and providing opportunities for renegotiating positions, altering power relations, and transforming authority structures within the household.

Appreciating the impact of these life-course changes is crucial in understanding the transactional dynamics of family provision. Rather than seeing the family as a static demographic unit, our approach here is to treat it as a more dynamic social entity, engaged in a set of welfare transactions characterized by consensus as well as conflict. Such transactions were guided by considerations of love, affection, and duty—what Avner Offer has called the economics of regard—as well as other power relations and cultural expectations.[26] The family was subject to the language of hierarchy and dependency, and authority and obedience.[27] The pooling of contributions and liabilities and decisions regarding the redistribution of resources were often subject to negotiations and struggle. Differences in age, gender, and status frequently resulted in complex and sometimes competing interests and motivations among family members. As such, common strategies and solidarity cannot be assumed.[28] As Tamara Hareven has pointed out, "collective family strategies, although uniform on the surface, were never simple and streamlined in reality."[29]

The ways in which gender and age affected the power relationships that shaped family strategies of welfare is illustrated in several chapters in this book. Marsha Rose's chapter demonstrates that patriarchal assumptions about appropriate gender roles generated conflicts around the different ways in which daughters and sons of elite families inherited wealth. Hermann Zeitlhofer's chapter shows how such power relations were never static. The aging process and shifts in status always served to alter the balance of power among family members, as his study of retirement amongst peasant households in Bohemia demonstrates.

Important as it was, the family was not the sole source of assistance. Either by marriage or descent, all families were part of a broader set of kinship relations that structured their actions and provided a reservoir of relatives and a network through which sets of reciprocities and claims were activated. Such wider kinship connections provided important transactional linkages and have been shown to have been crucial sources of support, particularly in situations of rapid social change. Michael Anderson's study of mid-nineteenth-century Preston, for example, demonstrated how kinship contacts helped structure residential choices of urban migrants.[30] Clearly, the nature of kinship and the obligations that it entails in relation to the provision of welfare have varied over time and among societies. Nevertheless, as David Sabean has suggested in the German context, "although it [kinship] is constructed in the give and take of daily life, in the end it offers a system of patterned expectations, a coherent set of constraints, and an arena in which claims and obligations can be negotiated with strategic intent and greater or lesser degrees of tactical finesse."[31] These claims and obligations are well illustrated in Sandro Guzzi-Heeb's contribution to the book on elite families in Alpine communities, in which he demonstrates how kinship alliances forged through both marriage and descent were crucial for the provision of a range of support for individuals and families over several generations.

However, while kinship provided a system that structured expectations and behavior, the degree to which individuals fulfilled their roles is a matter for investigation rather than assumption. Kinship might have provided the structure but did not necessarily indicate capacity nor guarantee agency. Often the provision of family welfare involved transactions with the wider community. In this context, spatial proximity and residential stability were crucial. In nineteenth-century London, for example, Ellen Ross has shown how neighbors frequently acted as surrogate kin, looking after children and taking them in if their parents died.[32] Similar surrogate or affective kinship support based on proximity has also been commented on in more contemporary societies. Carol Stack's study of survival strategies in contemporary poor, black urban communities, for example, makes the point that personal kin networks comprised those people who were socially recognized as having reciprocal responsibilities, frequently based not on cognatic relationships but on spatial proximity.[33] In both these examples, spatial proximity was crucial in providing the capacity to lend support, but residential stability was essential because without personal knowledge and trust that services rendered would in due course be reciprocated, individuals would have been less keen to offer assistance.

## FAMILY WELFARE STRATEGIES

Focusing on families, households, kin, and community as sources of support draws attention to the relationship between risk and strategy. In the context of welfare, Paul Johnson has identified the main risks as those associated with health, the life course, economic circumstances, and environmental conditions. He suggests that the function of all welfare systems is either to reduce exposure to these risks or to diversify the risk burden by spreading the costs of support.[34] By strategy we mean the various actions taken by families to cope with such risks and achieve goals.[35] This approach emphasizes how families actively make decisions governing membership, welfare, migration, employment, and consumption, often in the face of structural barriers arising from external circumstances.

Broadly speaking, two types of strategy can be distinguished that families and households adopted to minimize risk and maximize welfare. These refer, first, to demographic behavior that, depending on economic circumstances, aims either to increase or decrease the number of heirs, and, second, to the transactional decisions made relating to the provision of resources. Jack Goody has drawn attention to the first in his discussion of comparative heirship strategies.[36] In situations where heirs were in short supply, particularly when infant mortality was high, strategies could have been followed to increase their number, including polygamy and having more children. The problem with this was that family security was also a question of balancing resources against demand, and any actions that increased household size without a parallel increase in wealth potentially reduced long-term security for its members.

If security was less of a problem than maintaining the viability of the estate, other strategic choices could be made, either by limiting the number of children, and therefore potential heirs, or by reducing their claims on the estate itself. These strategies could be achieved in a variety of ways: by placing children in service, as Peter Laslett has pointed out was common practice in early modern England; by encouraging emigration; or by promoting celibacy.[37] Rose Duroux's chapter on the relationships between migration and heirship in the High Auvergne provides a case study of the demographic nature of family strategy. She shows how emigration was used as a way of ensuring long-term economic viability of the household farm by reducing the number of potential claimants and by tapping into additional sources of wealth external to the region. In a similar way, David Siddle has shown how emigration in late-eighteenth-century Savoy, an area also characterized by impartible forms of inheritance, was a way of releasing individuals for long periods of time and allowing them access to wider economic opportunities. In turn, such migrants provided additional cash income and remittances for families, including large dowries for noninheriting siblings.[38] In both cases, migration was a vital component in ensuring long-term patrimonial success.

The second type of transactional strategies are, if anything, more complex and refer to the various ways in which resources are transferred within and between families and generations. Inheritance was the most important form of transmission, though marriage settlements, *inter vivos* gifts, and retirement contracts were also significant points in the life course at which resources were transferred. These forms of transfer, notably inheritance, are discussed in several of the chapters that follow.

Less well known, however, are the processes by which decisions regarding transfers were made. Raising this issue poses important questions about the way in which systems of allocation and exchange can be theorized. Karl Polanyi famously argued that over the course of the eighteenth and nineteenth centuries there was a disembedding of economic relations from their social context, a process that lay at the heart of the "great transformation" that underpinned the coming of the self-regulating market.[39] Crucially, the "embedded" sphere of private social relations within the family was increasingly distinguished from the "disembedded" public sphere of economic transactions. Even if never completely realized in practice, at an ideological level the family came to be regarded as the antithesis of the market—an institution founded upon the bonds of love and affection rather than the cold and calculative rules of market-based exchange.[40] While this separation of public and private has been widely questioned, especially by gender historians, it remains the case that patterns of exchange and assistance that occur within and through family and kinship networks do call for a different theoretical perspective.[41] As Douglass North has noted, "economic historians have not even begun to account for such nonmarket allocative systems, and until they do, they can say very little about societies in which markets had very limited allocative effects."[42]

One way of theorizing these forms of family and kinship exchange is to use Avner Offer's notion of the "economy of regard."[43] Offer argues that Polanyi's "great transformation" remains incomplete because in many areas of life, transfer and exchange take the form of gifts underpinned by a strong reciprocal impetus. Interaction and exchange is therefore driven by the pursuit of regard that is shaped, among other things, by intimacy, respect, reputation, status, power, love, kinship, friendship, and sociability. It is not a form of transaction that can easily be reckoned in monetary terms. Offer suggests that this "economy of regard operates whenever incentives are affected by personal relations."[44] As he notes, such systems of allocation are central to the functioning of households and families, which should be regarded as the "well-spring of regard," but also permeate other forms of exchange where people work in small groups or negotiate face to face.[45] Offer's account of this alternative economy is particularly attentive to questions of family welfare provision. He notes, for example, the significance of gifts of money from parents to their children at various stages in the life course, such as at marriage and death. Such transfers of wealth are, it is argued, designed to elicit regard from offspring but also generate reciprocal "welfare gifts" such as loyalty and the provision of care in old age. As Offer also notes, "beyond the nuclear family, gifting fulfills some of the functions of insurance, financial and welfare systems."[46] His account therefore offers a compelling framework with which to understand the provision of welfare in transactional families. Nevertheless, it is important to recognize that not all forms of provision and assistance were necessarily embedded in the social relations of regard or reciprocity. Just as Polanyi's disembedding process was never complete, so the family and household were never entirely shielded from the ravages of market exchange. Many individuals and families were forced to grapple with impersonal markets and private institutions in order to realize welfare ambitions and cement the bonds of regard that were supposedly priceless.

Beyond these conceptual questions, the idea of a family or household strategy also raises difficult methodological issues. In order to understand a strategy it is necessary to know not only the motives but also the limitations, options, and decision-making process of those involved. First, we need to consider how strategies were modified by broader institutional, cultural, social, and economic circumstances. Family and individual strategies operated within specific historical contexts of cultural constraints, shifting opportunities, and environmental limitations, and it is important not to exaggerate the extent of individual freedom. In relation to cultural constraints on behavior, Pierre Bourdieu's concept of *habitus*—a set of practices that are reproduced through use and that collectively can be defined as "a system of schemes structuring every decision without ever becoming completely and systematically explicit"—is of help.[47] In this way, although individuals might have made independent decisions regarding provision for children and relatives, in practice their choices were constrained by expectations placed on them by the cultural context in which they operated. A good example of this is Alastair Owens's discussion of male inheritance practices in nineteenth-century Stockport, which, he argues, were strongly influenced by bourgeois notions of a husband's role in ensuring that his family was well provided for in the case of his death. Failure to act in an appropriate manner, he suggests, would have rendered such men open to criticism.[48] At the same time, of course, it is equally important not to assume that individuals were totally constrained by the circumstances in which they found themselves. Affection, favoritism, and emotions often directed the flow of resources regardless of cultural expectations and custom.

Second, in terms of shifting opportunities, it is clear that not all family members were equally capable of undertaking strategic actions. This was particularly true for women and children, not to mention those who, in leading a more hand-to-mouth existence, had neither the capacity to forecast nor the ability to design strategies to overcome risk.[49] Nor should we assume that family members necessarily agreed on specific strategies. Far from it. Critics of the concept have pointed out how an emphasis on family strategy can obscure internal differences and imply consensus where none exists.[50] An emphasis on strategy, therefore, inevitably raises questions relating to power relations and access to resources within the family. Finally, we need to be mindful of how external circumstances might also affect the capacity to think and act strategically, a point raised in Rose Duroux's chapter in relation to the impact of economic downturn on family inheritance practices.

## FAMILY WELFARE: STRATEGIES AND THE LIFE COURSE

It is often true, as Jan Kok has pointed out, that most historical sources are silent on these topics and therefore historians are generally restricted to inferring strategy from behavioral outcomes. However, one way in which we can explore how welfare strategies were shaped by broader institutional, cultural, social, and economic contexts and how they unfolded and altered over time is to consider them within the context of the family life course.[51] In family and social history, as well as in the field of sociology, the life course approach has become increasingly popular as a means by which to understand the temporal dynamism of human actions and social processes.[52] By paying attention to different stages in the life course we can begin to identify the forms of assistance and support that families sought to provide as individuals' biological and social circumstances altered. Rather than offering a potentially misleading picture of family welfare that might be gained from taking a cross-sectional approach, consideration of the life course discloses the dynamic nature of family strategies. It allows an understanding of how actions taken at one moment in someone's life were often closely related to those that took place at another.

Of course, such an approach is not without its limits. One significant problem is that the concept of a life course can suggest a uniformity and coherence to individual and family behavior that did not exist. It cannot be assumed that any given strategy promoted the collective good of all family members. Certainly, the chapters that appear in this book pay particular attention to the uneven impact of family strategies and the disputes and contradictions that often characterized them, especially in relation to gender. The problem of riding roughshod over these differences really arises, however, only when the concept of a life course is used in a mechanistic way. In sketching out the life course of family welfare below, the aim is not to suggest a definitive model of behavior to which all families necessarily conformed. Rather, the intention is to show how different welfare priorities came into play at different moments in the life course and to examine the way in which forms of assistance, care, and support could be delivered in relation to such priorities. In this way, the chapters in the book deal with pivotal moments in the life course, notably marriage, divorce, retirement, old age, and death.

The transmission of resources at these different moments could be achieved through a variety of means, used singly or in combination, including dowries, retirement contracts, inheritance, life insurance, divorce settlements, and guardianship. While some of these activities depended on the "economics of regard" that underpinned family relationships, others relied on market processes or legal conventions with which to redistribute wealth. Consideration of such welfare provision over the life course therefore brings into consideration the way in which the state, the market, the voluntary sector, and informal assistance—the mixed economy of welfare—came together and overlapped in providing individuals and families with the means by which to reproduce their ways of life.

## Marriage

Marriage was a pivotal moment in the creation of new families and the extension of kinship links. It was also an important occasion for the transmission of property and the provision of services. Whether exchanges of wealth took place formally through the existence of marriage contracts stipulating the transfer of resources and possibly services, or less formally through the ways in which families related by marriage formed strategic kinship alliances, marriage was a fundamental moment in the provision of family welfare.

In relation to exchanges, what is of most interest here is not so much the forms that marriage took but rather the relationship between marriage and the circulation of property. In this context it is important to recognize that marriage was one of several points in the life course when property was passed over.[53] However, it was often the case that exchanges made at these points of transmission could be altered depending on circumstances. For example, revision clauses in marriage contracts often allowed children who had already been endowed with family property to claim a share of the estate when their parents died. Of course, once a contract had been agreed, other claims on family property might have taken precedence. In this way, dowry and inheritance, marriage contract, and testament were closely related.[54]

Marriage contracts differed significantly among countries, regions, classes, and over time, but until "affective individualism," as Lawrence Stone has called it, replaced calculation and contract by love and affection, marriages between wealthy individuals often included contractual agreements relating to a wife's and husband's separate and communal property.[55] In England, for example, from the late sixteenth century, marriage contracts frequently included provisions made for women's "sole and separate estate" through which they retained use and control over property brought to the marriage.[56] In French regions where systems of *régime dotal* existed, wives administered their own property while the dowry was transferred to the husband. As Michelle Perrot has noted, in such circumstances, the liquid wealth brought to the marriage by women was crucial to the extent that "when dowry payments fell into arrears, husbands turned accountants and scrutinized their in-laws' books."[57] In some parts of France, such as those explored in the chapter by Rose Duroux, men brought liquid wealth while women brought land to the marriage. Elsewhere, contracts distinguished between property held by each individual prior to the marriage and that which had been accumulated jointly, an issue that Kirsti Niskanen explores in her chapter dealing with the division of wealth at the point of divorce in early-twentieth-century Sweden. Clearly, the variety of arrangements regarding property rights in marriage contracts is far more complex than just those touched on here, although each demonstrates the way in which property, marriage, and family welfare were closely related.

As well as the flow of land and liquid wealth between individual families and across the generations, marriage also could entail obligations to provide support, such as lodging, food, and maintenance for one or both parents. Retirement arrangements, such as those discussed in chapter 4 by Hermann Zeitlhofer, were often included in marriage contracts in return for the transmission of property to sons or daughters.[58] This was particularly true in regions where complex households prevailed in which co-residence of the stem family was the norm and where there was a relatively late age of marriage.

In a strategic sense, marriage also presented an opportunity for forging alliances and establishing kinship linkages. This issue is developed in chapter 5 by Sandro Guzzi-Heeb in relation to the construction of kinship networks and the flow of property and position in Alpine communities. Through marriage and descent, elite families created networks of kin in which the fortunes of any individual depended on the actions of others. The family estate was therefore considered to belong more to the collective set of kin than solely to the head of the family. Both the law and customary practice provided relatives with a set of opportunities to interfere and influence individual destinies, including the choice of marriage partners and inheritance, both of which were closely linked. In relation to marriage, women, in particular, played an important role in maintaining this fluid system of property transfer and the transmission of offices.

### Retirement

As a social transition between the worlds of work and nonwork, retirement was—and still is—a crucial stage in the life course.[59] Before the availability of adequate institutional support in old age, individuals made their own more-or-less formal arrangements for care in later life.[60] In the United States, for example, close to half of retired men aged over 64 in 1880 lived with their children or other relatives.[61] In making this choice, as Shakespeare's King Lear found to his cost, new patterns of inequality could be created and authority transformed.

One common way of arranging retirement was the strategic use of property by aging parents to ensure that their offspring would provide support later in life. Retirement contracts usually made between parents and children, though sometimes also with other kin or non-kin, provide a good example of how this functioned. In Galicia, northwestern Spain, female control over property and familial authority provided older women with the power to negotiate retirement contracts, usually with one of their children, but sometimes with friends or other relatives. Such contracts appeared in various forms: in conditions stipulated in a dowry, in bequests to a favored child, through the provision of gifts, or in a will.[62] Although less concerned with the gendered implications of retirement, in chapter 4 Hermann Zeitlhofer examines the importance of such contracts for farm households in South Bohemia between 1640 and 1840. This chapter is particularly concerned with the ways in which headship succession and retirement formed part of a wider strategy of family welfare provision. Rather than passing their property over after death, parents transferred their property step by step in return for care in old age. Contracts outlining respective obligations were common and covered the rights of parents, children, and often noninheriting siblings. Such contracts usually expressed a preference for sons over daughters, increasingly so as the eighteenth century wore on, but there were also occasions when they were negotiated with non-kin. Couples who retired often lived in a separate house and continued to farm a small plot while cottagers with less property tended to live in the same house as their successor.

A different way of making provision in old age in more urban and commercial societies was to resort to the financial markets through investment in life assurance. This is the subject matter of Eve Rosenhaft's chapter on widows' funds in eighteenth-century Germany. The transition from trades to the professions and the shift of work away from the home to an office or workshop transformed gender roles and redefined the nature of the family. Bourgeois women were excluded from the possibility of earning an income and instead came to rely more on their husbands' earnings. When they were widowed, which in effect normally represented their retirement from participating in the paid economy, the threat of penury was real and immediate. To counter this threat, widows' funds were established to provide for women after the death of their husbands. The family promoted by these widows' funds was a new kind of patriarchal family in which women's economic agency had no place. The issue that emerged, however, was whether or not women could participate in the funds in their own right rather than just as recipients of pensions upon widowhood. Demand from women for these financial services resulted in significant institutional change and the emergence of actuarially self-conscious schemes that extended well beyond widows' funds.

### Guardianship

Like retirement, which indicated a shift in power relations among family members, being a minor and guardian respectively also implied a clear hierarchy of authority based on social as well as biological age. Minors consisted of two groups of dependants: children, who by virtue of their age could not provide for themselves, and others who because of actual or imputed incapacity were thought to be similarly disadvantaged. Women, because of legal restrictions and cultural expectations, often fell into this second category. Just as minority status defined the condition of dependency, so the institution of guardianship also defined who was considered suitable to act *in loco parentis*, notably fathers, brothers, husbands, and other male relatives and kin. In this sense, the institution of guardianship was highly gendered. The complex ways in which gender, guardianship, and market exchange interacted is well illustrated by changes in the legal framework, and three chapters in particular explore this theme, albeit it in very diverse ways.

In the situation discussed by Robert Beachy in his chapter on Germany between 1680 and 1830, the spread of commercial activity prompted legal changes in gender guardianship. This legal custom shielded a married woman's property from her husband's control. Assigned the legal status of a dependant and placed under the guardianship of a man, generally not a husband, a woman was technically unable to sign enforceable contracts without her guardian's permission, which significantly restricted her commercial activities.[63] However, this economic incapacity also allowed some to exploit their dependent status by evading financial liability for debts incurred. In cases of insolvency, the rules of gender guardianship stated that women could not be sued and could therefore protect their property from creditors. As long-distance trade and commerce expanded and as impersonal relationships of trust grew in importance, this situation became increasingly anachronistic. The repeal of gender guardianship laws in the first half of the nineteenth century represented a type of legal emancipation for single women, who gained formal economic independence. At the same time its repeal intensified the subjection of married women because it then placed their property under the control of their husbands. With the elimination of gender guardianship, in effect, a woman's creditors could sue her husband for his wife's debts and thereby make claims more easily on a married woman's marriage portion.

The complex ways in which gender and guardianship altered in relation to changing market relations is also central to Ann Ighe's chapter on guardianship in eighteenth- and nineteenth-century Sweden. Guardianship was designed to protect the property of minors until they came of age, but in doing so it limited their freedom to participate in the market economy. Women were deemed always to be minors until they married. Guardians were either one of the parents, usually the father, or were appointed by a court, in which case they were usually male kin. Once married, women were assumed to be legally dependent on their husbands. In an age of growing bourgeois individualism, such gendered restrictions on economic activity were called into question. As women participated more actively in the urban and commercial economy, so their legal status as dependants contrasted sharply with their personal freedom as independent economic actors. This growing rift between their legal and economic status resulted in pressures to change the laws, and in the early twentieth century guardianship was reformed to remove the restrictions on women.

Finally, the financial burdens involved in guardianship over children are examined in an institutional setting in Ann McCants's chapter on Amsterdam's municipal orphanage in the eighteenth century. Providing for children was an expensive process, and in the case of orphans these costs could be a huge burden on relatives and their families. The reluctance of bourgeois families to take on the financial responsibility of caring for their orphaned relatives encouraged the establishment of a municipal orphanage as part of a set of strategies to secure familial resources. The orphanage, therefore, took on the role of guardian in place of relatives. It did not absolve families from their financial obligations concerning orphaned relatives, but it nevertheless contributed to their ability to preserve family property and transmit wealth from one generation to the next without the potential drain of having to support additional numbers of children.

## Divorce

A critical moment when family welfare strategies are likely to be disrupted is the point at which relationships between key members of the family unit come to an end, either through divorce or death. As we shall consider later, the death of an individual was a particularly important stage in a family's life-course trajectory, where new welfare strategies were fashioned and implemented. However, the termination of relationships as a result of divorce was of growing significance over the period covered by this book, especially from the late nineteenth century.[64] In terms of family strategies, divorce poses an interesting case because, unlike death, it is not a life-course event that, at least in the early stages of a union, is likely to be predicted. The breakup of a marriage therefore can seriously disrupt long-term strategic ambitions, with profound consequences for the social, economic, and emotional well-being of family members. The dissolution of a marriage requires that partners make some kind of settlement with regard to the care and maintenance of the children and, especially in the case of women, agree on an allowance for the wife as well as a division of the property.[65]

As the civil death of a relationship, divorce by its nature and consequences had profound implications for the welfare of family members, particularly women. As Mavis Maclean and Lenore Weitzman have remarked, the settlement of property upon divorce discloses "the underlying issues of dependency and power, individualism and collectivity in the family."[66] This is particularly important in the way that the division of family assets has traditionally benefited men more than women, because the contribution of household labor to family property—usually performed by women—has not been valued in the same way as the breadwinning formal economic activity of men. Furthermore, the embedded social and cultural expectations about the role of women in families has often meant that the burden of support and care for children after the divorce has fallen upon the mother.[67] For Jack Goody this economic hardship and the associated problems of providing appropriate welfare for children is one result of the decline of the dowry system across Europe in the later nineteenth century. The disappearance of such arrangements gave women no claim to property received or accumulated before marriage.[68]

Whatever the causes of this apparent inequality, it is clear that divorce poses a number of welfare needs, especially where there are minority children. Some of these themes are explored in this volume by Kirsti Niskanen, who examines the ambivalent effect of the reform of marriage and divorce law upon women in Sweden. Under the new marriage laws of 1921, women were more likely to initiate divorce proceedings in the knowledge that their rights to property were stronger. Women who brought their own property to a marriage were generally in a better situation than those who did not. The new law strengthened their position further and also recognized that women's work in the home had an intrinsic value for the household. However, despite this formal equality, in practice, patriarchal discourses tended to define women's rights to own and manage property. This meant that the economic burden of providing for children in the case of divorces fell more heavily on the woman than the man. This important insight reveals the power of ideology and everyday experience in shaping economic relations and discloses the essential mutability of the law as a medium through which property relations were regulated.

### Inheritance

As death has always been a certainty, inheritance and succession are processes that have long been recognized as important to the social reproduction of propertied families. In most historical societies family members have, almost without exception, been the main recipients of inheritance.[69] As Jean-Baptiste Pisano has demonstrated, the study of property transmission at death provides a valuable insight into the "geography of family relations."[70] In a tradition of scholarship stretching back to the work of Friedrich Engels, historians, anthropologists, and others have recognized that despite a bewildering array of practices "inheritance laws and customs are a fundamental part of family strategies."[71]

A key issue relating to inheritance and the family is the apparent tension between patrimony—the preservation of dynastic estates—and provision—the material support of all family dependants.[72] Where patrimony dominates, inheritance strategies are characterized by unigeniture—the transmission of property to a single family heir—which, in practice, usually equates to primogeniture—the transmission of property to the firstborn or eldest surviving heir. In most cases, primogeniture fell on the male line. Such inheritance strategies are highly impartible, but they preserve the unity of the family estate. Where the support of dependants is the focus of inheritance strategies, then the transmission of property to multiple family heirs and often partibility (the equal treatment of heirs) dominate transmission practices. Such strategies can be more egalitarian but often result in the division and fragmentation of family property rather than its preservation. According to Goody, it is these "contradictory pulls towards the equal treatment of offspring . . . and the preservation of the estate" that are at the heart of understanding family inheritance strategies.[73]

The exact conditions under which patrimony or provision became the dominant inheritance strategy have defied easy identification. As Jeffery Longhofer has remarked, "similar inheritance practices have been found in association with a diverse array of social formations. Likewise, dissimilar practices have been found in association with similar social formations."[74] Understanding why different groups of people in different times and in different geographical locations have pursued one or the other of these two main strategies has been a major preoccupation for researchers.[75] It is clear, however, that the pursuit of particular strategies is contingent upon complex constellations of social, economic, demographic, legal, and cultural conditions that inform inheritance practices in any given time and place. Therefore, as Edward P. Thompson perceptively noticed, a full understanding of the nature of family inheritance can really be gained only through an investigation of the wider social and economic "grid" within which property transmission takes place.[76]

In the face of these complexities, studies of inheritance often fail to move beyond the simple reconstruction of patterns of bequests in order to consider the strategic role of property transmission in fulfilling broader social and economic goals. A particular obsession hinges around the distinctions between partible and impartible inheritance. However, according to one recent study, "to make a radical and structural contrast between the inegalitarian character of some customs (those allowing for the right of primogeniture or the choice of a principal heir) and the egalitarian ideal of others (which imposed division between all entitled persons) would be to disregard their common ambivalence, which inevitably surfaced in practice."[77] In chapter 2, Gérard Béaur demonstrates how this dichotomy can be misleading, especially if the wider life-course strategies, of which inheritance was only one element, are not considered alongside the devolution of property at death. In the context of pre-Revolutionary France, Béaur questions the distinctions between partible and impartible inheritance systems. By comparing such systems in a variety of different *pays*, he demonstrates the way in which families pursued a variety of strategies to ensure that all children were provided for in some way and the productivity of family property was not compromised by excessive subdivision. In impartible *pays* he points to the significance of *inter vivos* gifts— especially marriage settlements—as well as compensatory payments made by heirs to nonheirs as a strategy for ensuring that cadets (the youngest offspring who were not the designated heir to the family estate) received an interest in family property. In the regions of France where partible inheritance was practiced, he shows how siblings frequently entered into a series of market and nonmarket exchanges to help prevent the breakup of the family estate. His argument is that in order to understand inheritance as a family strategy it is necessary to look forward as well as backward in the life course to examine longer-term patterns of transmission and exchange. His chapter is also a good illustration of the everyday flexibility of apparently rigid legal frameworks and customs, as well as a demonstration of the significance of the market as a means by which family strategies could be achieved.

While Béaur's chapter is illustrative of a genre of inheritance studies that have been concerned with issues of family strategy, discussion of such property transmission has rarely been couched in terms of welfare. It is, however, possible to consider inheritance as a welfare mechanism in a variety of ways. The conclusion that Gregory Hanlon and Elspeth Carruthers drew from their study of inheritance practices in seventeenth-century France could apply with the same degree of force to provision-oriented inheritance practices in many other contexts: "property transmission through the will . . . follows several logical routes directed, in the first instance towards the maintenance of the aged and the dependent, then with children with some concern for equality, and finally toward a measure of reward and punishment to keep a moral and social order intact."[78]

The support of spouses and dependants through the provision of a secure place to live, a regular income, care, maintenance, and education was the immediate goal of many inheritance strategies and came before any division of family property.[79] The final devolution of estate usually took place only after the children no longer had dependent status—when they married or reached their age of majority—at which point they were supplied with capital for new family formation.[80] Yet even at this point it is important to note the welfare functions that the division of family wealth fulfilled: a theme captured by the French phrase *les placer des enfants*. For sons the receipt of an inheritance often provided land and status or paved the way into a trade or profession. For female inheritors the provision of such capital either provided them with the means by which to sustain a degree of independence, or it supplied a suitable portion of cash for a dowry. In this way, inheritance initiated a new phase of the life course and reproduced the key social institution of marriage with its assumption that women became dependent on their husbands.

Gender played a key role in the functioning of these inheritance-based welfare systems. Indeed, the different experiences and roles of men and women in the property-transmission process is a key theme in inheritance. While the picture presented has often been one of inequalities, where females have been subordinate to patriarchal family structures, the essays in this book demonstrate the complex and variable situations that women occupied in relation to inheritance strategies. In her chapter on inheritance and migration in the High Auvergne in the eighteenth and nineteenth centuries, Rose Duroux discusses how women tended to inherit family property in preference to men. In this economically marginal region, younger single men often migrated to Spain, usually on a seasonal basis, in order to secure funds to support the complex stem-family households back home. Women, on the other hand, remained at home and frequently inherited the household property. In turn, cash-rich returning male migrants tended to marry land-rich women in a strategy that ensured the economic viability of family units. In this way inheritance and migration collectively played pivotal and mutually reinforcing roles.

In a different context, Marsha Rose's chapter explores the significance of affective perceptions of gender in structuring inheritance among elite families in the United States, taking the Rockefellers and Binghams as case studies. Despite superficial differences in the transmission of property, in practice both families pursued male primogeniture. Female heirs were considered as individuals to be provided for rather than as providers themselves, and this affected not only the amount of property they received, which in the case of Edith Rockefeller was substantially less than her brothers, but also the way that the capital was supplied, such as through the trust fund that was supplied for Edith but administered by male members of the family. As such, gender inequalities permeated the transmission of both material resources and cultural capital. In the course of time this created tensions and conflicts within each family.

In a variety of ways, therefore, the transmission of resources through inheritance represents an important strategic response by families to ensuring the well-being of their members and securing their reproduction as a stable and economically viable social entity. Viewed in the context of the life course, however, inheritance was but one element in the strategic transmission of resources.[81] Furthermore, even where states imposed strict rules of inheritance, there was always considerable latitude for fashioning welfare strategies through property transmission, and such processes reveal the flexibility of family welfare mechanisms across the life course.

## CONCLUSION

In this introduction we have tried to suggest that the history of welfare must adopt a wider perspective than simply provision for the poor. We have argued that it should encompass the study of those who possessed property as much as those who did not. In making this claim, we have suggested that it is necessary to take into account the complex interdependence of different sources of welfare. The family and its relationships with the market, the state, and the voluntary sector have been highlighted as the key nexus around which welfare in the past was organized. Finally, we have also suggested that gender relations are crucial in understanding the operation of these systems of provision.

While the earlier discussion has set out some of the key themes of the book and raised a number of conceptual issues, the chapters that follow grapple with the complexities of family-welfare provision in a variety of historical and geographical contexts. Individual chapters incorporate case studies from western Europe and the United States and cover the period from the seventeenth to the twentieth century. They exhibit a variety of scales of analysis, from microhistorical studies of individual families to broader discussions of institutional change, and a range of different methodological approaches, including detailed family reconstitution. The book is loosely divided into two sections, the first focusing specifically on the family and the second on various institutional arrangements that underpinned the family's role. In the first section issues relating to inheritance, marriage, retirement, and gifting are explored in the context of gender and kinship relationships. In the second, individual chapters concentrate more on the institutional and legal contexts of welfare relating to guardianship, life assurance, charity, and divorce. This book as a whole emphasizes that if we are to appreciate the various ways that welfare is provided in human societies, we must search not for any single path to provision nor for any hierarchy of resort. We must focus our attention instead on the relationships among different sources of provision and different groups in society. In doing so we recognize that at various points in their lives all human beings rely on others for their own welfare.

## NOTES

We are grateful to Hilary Guite and Bernard Harris for their comments on an earlier version of this chapter.

1. Michel Foucault, *Discipline and Punish: the Birth of the Prison* (Harmondsworth: Penguin, 1977), esp. 170–94. See also Mitchell Dean, *The Constitution of Poverty: Towards a Genealogy of Liberal Governance* (London: Routledge, 1991).

2. For a wider discussion of the relationships between gender and the welfare state see Ann Orloff, "Gender and the Social Rights of Citizenship: The Comparative Analysis of Gender Relations and Welfare States," *American Sociological Review* 58 (1993): 303–28 and Ann Orloff, "Gender in the Welfare State," *Annual Review of Sociology* 22 (1996): 51–78.

3. For further discussion of distinctions between "wants" and "needs" in relation to the welfare state, see Norman Barry, *Welfare* (Buckingham: Open University Press, 1999), 122–24.

4. The classic work on gift giving is Marcel Mauss, *The Gift* (London: Routledge, 1990; first published as *Essai dur le Don,* 1925). See also Alvin Gouldner, "The Norm of Reciprocity: A Preliminary Statement," *American Sociological Review* 25 (1960): 161–78.

5. For a general discussion of the relationships between welfare and social reproduction, see Robert Pinker, *The Idea of Welfare* (London: Heinemann, 1979), 46–60.

6. Such historiographies talk of the "rise," the "growth," or the "emergence" of the welfare state. In the context of Great Britain see, for example, Maurice Bruce, *The Coming of the Welfare State* (London, Batsford, 1961); Derek Fraser, *The Evolution of the British Welfare State* (London: Macmillan, 1973); and David Roberts, *The Victorian Origins of the British Welfare State* (New Haven, Yale University Press, 1960). For a critique of this approach see Geoffrey Finlayson, *Citizen, State, and Social Welfare in Britain 1830–1990* (Oxford: Clarendon Press, 1994). More recent historiographies of the British welfare state have recognized the need to extend the scope of discussion to incorporate other forms of provision, notably from the voluntary sector. See, for example, Bernard Harris, *The Origins of the British Welfare State: Society, State, and Social Welfare in England and Wales, 1800–1950* (Houndsmills: Macmillan, 2004); Keith Laybourn, *The Evolution of British Social Policy and the Welfare State* (Keele: Keele University Press, 1995); and Pat Thane, *Foundations of the Welfare State* (London: Longman, 1996). For international comparisons of welfare states see, for example, Douglas E. Ashford, *The Emergence of the Welfare States* (Oxford: Basil Blackwell, 1986).

7. This phrase, first used in connection with social policy, was brought to historians' attention by Finlayson, *Citizen, State, and Social Welfare*, 6.

8. Jane Lewis, "Family Provision of Health and Welfare in the Mixed Economy of Care in the Late Nineteenth and Twentieth Centures," *Social History of Medicine* 8 (1995): 1. This point echoes Finlayson, *Citizen, State, and Social Welfare*.

9. Paul Johnson, "Risk, Redistribution and Social Welfare in Britain from the Poor Law to Beveridge," in *Charity, Self-interest and Welfare in the English Past*, ed. Martin Daunton (London: University College London Press, 1996), 244. Johnson suggests that this low figure reflected in particular the importance of private forms of assistance.

10. See, for example, Michael Anderson, *Family Structure in Nineteenth-Century Lancashire* (Cambridge: Cambridge University Press, 1971); Marguerite W. Dupree, *Family Structure in the Staffordshire Potteries, 1840–1880* (Oxford: Oxford University Press, 1995); and Ellen Ross, "Survival Networks: Womens' Neighbourhood Sharing in London before World War I," *History Workshop Journal* 15 (1983): 4–27.

11. See, for example, Geoffrey Crossick, *An Artisan Elite in Victorian Society* (London: Croom Helm, 1978), esp. 134–98.

12. David R. Green, "Independent Women, Wealth and Wills in Nineteenth-Century London," in *Urban Fortunes: Property and Inheritance in the Town, 1700–1900*, ed. Jon Stobart and Alastair Owens (Aldershot: Ashgate, 2000), 212–14.

13. Michael Katz and Christoph Sachsse, eds., *The Mixed Economy of Social Welfare: Public/Private Relations in England, Germany and the United States, the 1870s to the 1930s* (Baden-Baden: Nomos, 1996) and Marco van Leeuwen, "Histories of Risk and Welfare in Europe during the Eighteenth and Nineteenth Centuries," in *Health Care and Poor Relief in Eighteenth and Nineteenth-Century Europe*, ed. Ole Peter Grell, Andrew Cunningham, and Robert Jütte (Aldershot: Ashgate, 2002), 40–43.

14. There is a rapidly growing literature on this topic. See, for example, Hugh Cunningham and Joanna Innes, eds., *Charity, Philanthropy and Reform: From the 1690s to 1850* (Basingstoke: Macmillan, 1998); Martin Daunton, ed., *Charity, Self-Interest and Welfare in the English Past* (London: University College Press, 1996); Peregrine Horden and Richard J. Smith, eds., *The Locus of Care: Families, Communities, Institutions and the Provision of Welfare Since Antiquity* (London: Routledge,

1998); Alan Kidd, "Civil Society or the State? Recent Approaches to the History of Voluntary Welfare," *Journal of Historical Sociology* 15 (2002): 328–42; and John Offer, "Idealist Thought, Social Policy and the Rediscovery of Informal Care," *British Journal of Sociology* 50 (1999): 467–88.

15. Peregrine Horden, "Household Care and Informal Networks: Comparisons and Continuities from Antiquity to the Present," in Horden and Smith, *The Locus of Care*, 27–28.

16. David W. Sabean, *Property, Production and Family in Neckarhausen, 1700–1870* (Cambridge: Cambridge University Press, 1992).

17. Pier P. Viazzo and Katherine A. Lynch, "Anthropology, Family History, and the Concept of Strategy," *International Review of Social History* 47 (2002): 444–45.

18. Barbara Laslett and Johanna Brenner, "Gender and Social Reproduction: Historical Perspectives," *Annual Review of Sociology* 15 (1989): 381–404.

19. Thomas Chalmers, *The Christian and Civic Economy of Large Towns,* vol. 1 (Glasgow: Chalmers and Collins, 1821), 276.

20. Lewis, "Family provision of health and welfare," 4–16.

21. Michael Young and Peter Wilmott, *Family and Kinship in East London* (Harmondsworth: Penguin, 1962).

22. Michelle Perrot and Anne Martin-Fugier, "The Actors," in *A History of Private Life: From the Great Fires of Revolution to the Great War,* ed. Michelle Perrot (London: Belknap Press, 1990), 97.

23. The history of family forms is extensive. See John Hajnal, "European Marriage Patterns in Perspective," in *Population in History,* ed. David Glass and David Eversley (London: Edward Arnold, 1965), 101–43 and Peter Laslett and Richard Wall, eds., *Household and Family in Past Time* (London: Cambridge University Press, 1972).

24. This point is discussed further in David I. Kertzer and Peter Laslett, eds., *Aging in the Past: Demography, Society and Old Age* (Berkeley: University of California Press, 1995), esp. 375–77.

25. André Burguière and François Lebrun, "The One Hundred and One Families of Europe," in *A History of the Family: Volume II, The Impact of Modernity,* ed. André Burguière, Christiane Klapisch-Zuber, Martine Segalen, and Françoise Zonabend (Cambridge: Polity, 1996), 15.

26. Avner Offer, "Between the Gift and the Market: The Economy of Regard," *Economic History Review* L (1997): 450–76.

27. Olivia Harris, "Households and Their Boundaries," *History Workshop Journal* 13 (1982): 150 and Laurence Fontaine and Jürgen Schlumbohm, "Household Strategies for Survival: An Introduction," *International Review of Social History* 45, supplement 8 (2000): 5.

28. Roger Friedland and Alexander F. Robertson, eds., *Beyond the Marketplace: Rethinking Economy and Society* (New York: Aldine de Gruyter, 1990), 13–14 and Henk de Haan, *In the Shadow of the Tree: Kinship, Property and Inheritance Among Farm Families* (Amsterdam: Het Spinhuis, 1994), 19.

29. Tamara Hareven, "A Complex Relationship: Family Strategies and the Processes of Economic and Social Change," in Friedland and Robertson, eds., *Beyond the Marketplace,* 237.

30. Anderson, *Family Structure in Nineteenth-Century Lancashire,* 56–64. See also Lynn Lees, *Exiles of Erin: Irish Migrants in Victorian London* (Manchester: Manches-

ter University Press, 1979), 131–33 and David R. Green and Alan Parton, "Slums and Slum Life in Victorian England: London and Birmingham at Mid Century," in *Slums*, ed. Martin Gaskell (Leicester: Leicester University Press, 1990), 81–82.

31. David W. Sabean, *Kinship in Neckarhausen 1700–1870* (Cambridge: Cambridge University Press, 1998), xxvi.

32. Ross, "Survival Networks: Womens' Neighbourhood Sharing in London before World War I." Margeurite Dupree arrives at similar conclusions in her study of mid-nineteenth-century working-class communities in the Staffordshire Potteries. See Dupree, *Family Structure*, 271–345.

33. Carol Stack, *All Our Kin: Strategies for Survival in a Black Community* (New York: Harper Collins, 1974).

34. Paul Johnson, "Risk, Redistribution and Social Welfare in Britain From the Poor Law to Beveridge," in Daunton, *Charity, Self-Interest and Welfare*, 226–30.

35. Phyllis Moen and Elaine Wethington, "The Concept of Family Adaptive Strategies," *Annual Review of Sociology* 18 (1992): 234. There is an extensive literature on the nature of household strategies. See Hareven, "A Complex Relationship," 215–44.

36. Jack Goody, "Strategies of Heirship," *Comparative Studies in Society and History* 15 (1973): 3–20.

37. Peter Laslett, "Introduction: The History of the Family," in Laslett and Wall, *Household and Family*, 56–58; Peter Laslett, "Mean Household Size in England Since the Sixteenth Century," in Laslett and Wall, *Household and Family*, 151–52.

38. David Siddle, "Migration as a Strategy of Accumulation: Social and Economic Change in Eighteenth-Century Savoy," *Economic History Review* L (1997): 1–20.

39. Karl Polanyi, *The Great Transformation* (Boston: Beacon Press, 1957; originally published New York: Farrar and Rinehart, 1944).

40. Geoffrey R. Searle, *Morality and the Market in Victorian Britain* (Oxford: Clarendon Press, 1998) and Leonore Davidoff and Catherine Hall, *Family Fortunes: Men and Women of the English Middle Class, 1780–1950* (London: Hutchinson, 1987).

41. For critiques of the "separate spheres thesis" see Amanda Vickery, "Golden Age to Separate Spheres? A Review of the Categories and Chronology of English Women's History," *The Historical Journal* 36 (1993): 383–414 and Robert B. Shoemaker and Mary Vincent, eds., *Gender and History in Western Europe* (London: Arnold, 1998).

42. Douglass North, "Markets and Other Allocation Systems in History: The Challenge of Karl Polanyi," *Journal of Economic History* 6 (1997): 706.

43. Offer, "Between the Gift and the Market."

44. Offer, "Between the Gift and the Market," 471.

45. Offer, "Between the Gift and the Market," 458, 471.

46. Offer, "Between the Gift and the Market," 457.

47. Pierre Bourdieu, "Marriage Strategies as Strategies of Reproduction," in *Family and Society: Selections from the Annales Economies, Societes, Civilisations*, ed. Robert Forster and Orest Ranum (London: Johns Hopkins Press, 1976), 119.

48. Alastair Owens, "Property, Gender and the Life Course: Inheritance and Family Welfare Provision in Early Nineteenth-Century England," *Social History* 26 (2001): 299–317.

49. Fontaine and Schlumbohm, "Household Strategies for Survival," 11.

50. Viazzo and Lynch, "Anthropology, Family History, and the Concept of Strategy," 449.

51. Jan Kok, "The Challenge of Strategy: A Comment," *International Review of Social History* 47 (2002): 473–77.

52. The literature on the life course is considerable. Among historians the work of Tamara Hareven has been especially significant: Tamara K. Hareven, "Cycles, Courses, and Cohorts: Reflections on Theoretical and Methodological Approaches to the Historical Study of Family Development," *Journal of Social History* 12 (1978): 97–109; Tamara K. Hareven, ed., *Transitions: Family and the Life Course in Historical Perspective* (New York: Academic Press, 1978); Tamara K. Hareven, *Family Time and Industrial Time* (Cambridge: Cambridge University Press, 1982); Tamara K. Hareven, "The Impact of the Historical Study of the Family and the Life Course Paradigm on Sociology," *Comparative Social Research* 2 (supplement) (1996): 185–205; and Tamara K. Hareven, *Families, History and Social Change: Life-Course and Cross-Cultural Perspectives* (Boulder, CO: Westview Press, 1999). More generally, see John A. Clausen, *The Life Course: a Sociological Perspective* (New York: Prentice Hall, 1986).

53. Jack Goody, "Inheritance, Property and Women: Some Comparative Considerations," in *Family and Inheritance: Rural Society in Western Europe 1200–1800*, ed. Jack Goody, Joan Thirsk, and Edward P. Thompson (Cambridge: Cambridge University Press, 1976), 15.

54. See, for example, Emmanuel Le Roy Ladurie, "Family Structures and Inheritance Customs in Sixteenth-Century France," in Goody, Thirsk, and Thompson, *Family and Inheritance*, 48.

55. Lawrence Stone, *The Family, Sex and Marriage in England 1500–1800* (Harmondsworth: Penguin, 1979), 165.

56. The variety of types of settlement is discussed in Amy Erickson, *Women and Property in Early Modern England* (London: Routledge, 1993), esp. 102–55.

57. Perrot and Martin-Fugier, "The Actors," 140. For the significance of dowries in general see Jack Goody, "Dowry and the Rights of Women to Property," in *Property Relations: Renewing the Anthropological Tradition*, ed. Chris Hann (Cambridge: Cambridge University Press, 1998), 201–13.

58. Goody, "Inheritance, Property and Women," 22. See also Allyson Poska, "Gender, Property and Retirement Strategies in Early Modern Northwestern Spain," *Journal of Family History* 25 (2000): 313–25.

59. Angela M. O'Rand and John C. Henretta, *Age and Inequality: Diverse Pathways Through Later Life* (Boulder, Colo.: Westview Press, 1999).

60. See, in particular, the chapters in Kertzer and Laslett, *Aging in the Past*.

61. Dora L. Costa, "The Evolution of Retirement: Summary of a Research Project," *American Economic History Review* 88 (1998): 234.

62. Poska, "Gender, Property and Retirement," 316–17.

63. For a discussion of gender and the decline of guardianship in Sweden see the chapter in this volume by Ann Ighe.

64. Roderick Phillips, *Untying the Knot: A Short History of Divorce* (Cambridge: Cambridge University Press, 1991), 224–26. For a particularly thorough discussion of the changing legal regulation of divorce and accompanying shifts in social and

cultural attitudes to it in an English context, see Lawrence Stone, *Road to Divorce: England, 1530–1987* (Oxford: Oxford University Press, 1990).

65. For a discussion of divorce and its implications for wives and other family members, see Goody, "Dowry and the Rights of Women," 206–12.

66. Mavis Maclean and Lenore J. Weitzman, "Introduction to the Issues," in *Economic Consequences of Divorce: The International Perspective*, ed. Lenore J. Weitzman and Mavis Maclean (Oxford: Clarendon Press, 1992), 9.

67. See, for example, Lenore J. Weitzman, "Marital Property: Its Transformation and Division in the United States," in Weitzman and Maclean, *Economic Consequences of Divorce*, 85–142.

68. Goody, "Dowry and the Rights of Women," 206–13.

69. For exceptions see Goody, "Strategies of Heirship," 3–20.

70. Jean-Baptiste Pisano, "Wills as a Geography of Family Relations," in *The Art of Communication: Proceedings of the 8th International Conference of the Association for History and Computing, Graz, Austria, August 24–27, 1993*, ed. Gerhard Jaritz, Ingo Kropac, and Peter Teibenbacher (Graz: Akademische Druck-u Verlangsanstalt, 1995), 150–63.

71. Jack Goody, "Introduction," in Goody, Thirsk, and Thompson, *Family and Inheritance*, 1. The seminal work by Engels on the family is: Friedrich Engels, *The Origins of the Family, Private Property and the State* (London: Lawrence and Wishart, 1972, originally published 1885).

72. Toby Ditz, *Property and Kinship: Inheritance in Early Connecticut 1750–1820* (Princeton, N.J.: Princeton University Press, 1986), 26–34.

73. Goody, "Introduction," 3. This point is also emphasized by Burguière and Lebrun, "The One Hundred and One Families," 66.

74. Jeffery Longhofer, "Toward a Political Economy of Inheritance: Community and Household Among the Mennonites," *Theory and Society* 22 (1993): 338.

75. See, *inter alia*, H. John Habakkuk, "Family Structure and Economic Change in Nineteenth-Century Europe," *Journal of Economic History* 15 (1955): 1–12; Liam Kennedy, "Farm Succession in Modern Ireland: Elements of a Theory of Inheritance," *Economic History Review* XLIV (1991): 477–99; Longhofer, "Toward a political economy of inheritance"; David Siddle, "Inheritance and Lineage Development in Peasant Society," *Continuity and Change* 1 (1986): 333–61; and Edward P. Thompson, "The Grid of Inheritance: A Comment" in Goody, Thompson, and Thirsk, *Family and Inheritance*, 328–60.

76. Thompson, "The Grid of Inheritance."

77. Burguière and Lebrun, "The One Hundred and One Families," 66.

78. Gregory Hanlon and Elspeth Carruthers, "Wills, Inheritance and the Moral Order in Seventeenth-Century Agenais," *Journal of Family History* 15 (1990): 158. Other studies emphasizing some of the welfare functions of inheritance within families include Ann McCrum, "Inheritance and the Family: The Scottish Urban Experience in the 1820s," in Stobart and Owens, *Urban Fortunes*, 149–71; and Maria Ågren, "Caring for the Widowed Spouse. On the Use of Wills in Northern Sweden, 1750–1915," unpublished paper.

79. Owens, "Property, Gender and the Life Course."

80. Robert J. Morris, "The Middle Class and the Property Cycle During the

Industrial Revolution," in *The Search for Wealth and Stability: Essays in Social and Economic History Presented to M. W. Flinn*, ed. T. Christopher Smout (Basingstoke: Macmillan, 1979), 91–93 and Owens, "Property, Gender and the Life Course," 306–7, 313–17.

81. Janet Finch and Lynn Wallis, "Death, Inheritance and the Life Course," in *The Sociology of Death*, ed. David Clark (Oxford: Blackwell, 1993), 50–68. More generally, see Janet Finch and Jennifer Mason, *Passing On: Kinship and Inheritance in England* (London: Routledge, 2000).

# CHAPTER 2

# Land Transmission and Inheritance Practices in France During the *ancien régime:* Differences of Degree or Kind?

*Gérard Béaur*

## INTRODUCTION

Before the Revolution in France there were several different ways to hand down real estate to one's heirs.[1] For well over 20 years, French historians have been attempting to describe and understand these different land-transmission strategies. At least three somewhat contradictory and seemingly incompatible aims have been identified that shaped families' attempts to pass on real estate to the next generation: the need to provide a settlement for as many heirs as possible; the desire to establish a provision for the family head in old age; and, finally, the wish to maintain the family farm as a viable economic unit.[2] These three priorities frequently involved making difficult economic choices in the context of traditional rules and customs of inheritance.

In large parts of France, but especially in the south, specific legal customs or the rules of Roman law shaped inheritance practices. Land was generally passed to a single heir, usually the elder son, or, more rarely, to an elder daughter. This inheritance strategy, the so-called impartible system of transmission, has been of particular interest to scholars who have sought to understand its social and economic functions in early modern French society.[3] Frédéric Le Play, who first drew attention to it in the mid-nineteenth century, argued that this form of inheritance should be regarded as a moral "ideal."[4] It preserved the integrity of the estates, maintained the stability of households, and encouraged family cohesion.

According to Le Play, the Civil Code established by the Revolution which, through its emphasis on partible inheritance strategies made possible the partition of land, was a disaster for France's agricultural economy and society. He argued that as well as leading to the partition of productive land, it generated household and family instability. Indeed, the effects of the Civil Code on inheritance were such that it came to be stigmatized as a "land hashing-machine" (*la machine à hacher le sol*) and is even argued by some to have been the principal reason for the fall in the birth rate in nineteenth-century France.[5] Today this view is widely questioned. However, even if historians and anthropologists have since avoided Le Play's moralizing tone, they have usually concluded that the partible inheritance system entailed the parceling of land, which in turn led to farms becoming uneconomic. It is frequently argued that such farms were too small to enable improvements in agricultural productivity.[6]

In contrast to the historiographical celebration of France's pre-Revolutionary impartible inheritance systems, much less is known about those parts of the country where partible inheritance involving a more equal transmission of property among heirs was favored. There are several reasons for this lack of interest. First, it is argued that such property transmissions were economically regressive as they retarded agricultural improvement and competitiveness. Second, historians have questioned the seeming irrationality of such a system. Would peasants really have been unconcerned by the fate of their children and have divided their land among their heirs in such a way that it would make the farm unproductive and incapable of supporting a beneficiary and his or her family?[7] Finally, partible systems of inheritance have arguably been less well studied by historians because they are more difficult to analyze. The continual dispersion of plots and the large number of transactions that occurred after the initial transmission of property through inheritance makes it difficult to follow the perpetual disaggregation and reconstitution of farms and the subsequent movement of heirs. In contrast, it is obvious that in impartible inheritance regions, farms would remain virtually unchanged over generations, and each household head would likely have been the direct successor of his or her parents. It is therefore no great methodological feat to observe the transmission of land from father to son (or, occasionally, daughter) over decades and even centuries. As a result, there is a wealth of knowledge of impartible inheritance practices in areas such as the Massif Central, Basse-Provence, and, above all, the Pyrénées.[8] By comparison, very little is known about inheritance systems in partible regions such as Normandy, Île-de-France, or Poitou.

However, it would be inaccurate to think that the partible inheritance systems that predominated in these *pays* were in some way exceptional. Geographically speaking, the equal sharing of land among heirs predominated in France, especially in the north.[9] Nevertheless, it is important to recognize that there was not one but several different partible property transmission models that varied from one region to another. Some systems of transmission were more partible than others, particularly with respect to gender; many daughters inherited property under different conditions than sons. This adds an important dimension to understanding the operation of partible inheritance systems in France and forms a key focus of the discussion below.

This chapter concerns itself with three key questions relating to the operation of partible inheritance systems in pre-Revolutionary France. First, how egalitarian were the various partible inheritance systems? Second, to what extent were they really that different from the impartible inheritance systems that dominated the south of the country? Last, by way of conclusion, were they as socially and economically irrational as most historians usually argue?

## PARTIBLE INHERITANCE SYSTEMS: DIFFERENCES OF DEGREE?

According to Jean Yver, a number of different partible inheritance systems were practiced in northern France during the *ancien régime*.[10] Although based on the partible principle of dividing estates among all heirs, these systems often deviated from a strictly egalitarian property transmission. Three main variations of the partible inheritance model can be identified: gendered partibility, "optional" partibility, and strict equality.

### Gendered Partibility

The first commonly practiced strategy involved sharing land among sons rather than all heirs. At the beginning of the eighteenth century, this system predominated in Normandy, in northwestern France (with the exception of the pays de Caux). It could also be found at the other end of the country in Franche-Comté and in adjacent areas to the east, such as the Val de Saône.[11] Daughters had no rights to family lands, but their share of the estate usually came in the form of a dowry. This gendered strategy of property transmission limited the breakup of the farm and was reinforced by the common practice of sons remaining as joint tenants to avoid the fragmentation of landholding into uneconomic units. There were, however, differences in practice between the partible inheritance regions of northwestern France and those in the east of the country. In Franche-Comté, as Bernard Derouet has explained, the main aim of property transmission was to preserve the integrity of the household, and therefore the logic of the system was similar to that in regions where impartible inheritance predominated. There was little that was partible about such an inheritance system: sons kept the land undivided for as long as they could, while daughters usually received none of the estate. Even after the Revolution, in Franche-Comté the property transmission system continued to favor sons. In Normandy the principle of partibility and of "real division" of lands among sons, as opposed to the retention of "divided" estate under joint tenancy, was more deeply embedded; the system moved toward a clearer egalitarian sharing of estate for males and females as soon as the French Revolution made it more difficult to disregard daughters.

### "Optional" Partibility

In many parts of France it was virtually impossible to make a will that gave more land to one heir than to another. However, a second widely practiced variation of the partible system involved favoring one or several children by providing them with an *inter vivos* gift of money or land prior to death. In various regions of France it was common for each child to be given family property when he or she married and settled. Through this strategy it was possible to provide certain heirs with advantages over others. Shares of estate granted to one child or several children at marriage could often be more important than what he, she, or they could expect to obtain after their parents' death. In terms of preserving the principle of partibility, the key issue was whether the endowed heirs were required to return what they had received when their parents died. Sometimes property would be given as a dowry, as was frequently the case in Poitou, whereas on other occasions the gift was intended as an advance on the legacy that would eventually follow the death of a parent. The rules and customs that governed this practice were complex and varied, not least because some *inter vivos* gifts took the form of movable property that was not treated in the same way as land. The discussion here focuses on what happened to land.

In some cases, heirs were not bound to bring any gifts of land received as a dowry back into the settlement of estate at the death of a parent. In such instances, the system for transmitting property over the life course was far from partible, even if the final inheritance settlement appeared to treat each heir equally. In other cases, however, such as in central France, especially in the Île-de-France and the surrounding regions, those who had received *inter vivos* gifts from the estate had a choice: either they kept what they had received but renounced their rights to exclusive ownership, or they gave it back and took an equal share of the property after redistribution. In such cases various outcomes were possible. The system could produce an *impartible* inheritance outcome if the share of property that had been given as a lifetime gift to a favored heir was greater than the equal share the legatee would normally have received upon the parents' death. The outcome could obviously be *partible* if the advance made to the heir was smaller than the shares distributed at death. In such cases the transmission of property that occurred with the death of the parent equalized the distribution of estate. This "trick" was used to prevent the excessive subdivision of landholding. Moreover, it enabled heirs who had been given gifts in advance of their parents' death to retain their land without breaking the sacrosanct principle of equality.

### Strict Equality

The third partible inheritance strategy was more rigidly egalitarian. Even if heirs received an *inter vivos* gift, such as a dowry, when they married, they were required to give it back upon the death of their parents. Alternatively the gift would be taken into account at the moment of the sharing. This partible inheritance strategy had four variants. First, in some regions family property would be divided into as many parts as there were heirs. Second, there were regions where heirs were given portions of land that were strictly equal in size, although clearly, the productive value of equal-sized plots could vary. Who got what was decided by drawing lots or, alternatively, plots would be distributed giving priority to the eldest heir. Third, in certain areas heirs would receive their legacy partly as land and partly as money (the *soultes*). Money was given to ensure that all gifts were equal in value, even if some heirs received more land than others. Finally, in other regions heirs received either land *or* the equivalent in money.

These ways of passing on land were most common in the west of France: in Anjou, Poitou and, particularly, Brittany. In this latter region, especially in the pays bigouden, all four variants were practiced.[12] It is not difficult to appreciate, however, that the consequences of the various strategies were radically different. The first led to the subdivision and parceling out of family lands, which, in the context of a growing population, ultimately caused difficulties for farming. Subdivision forced peasants to travel between scattered fields, thereby wasting considerable time and effort. Fragmentation of lands also meant that many farms became too small to support even the basic subsistence requirements of households. The second and the third variants of partible inheritance had fewer dramatic effects, but they too did not prevent the splitting up of the farm and its substitution by several smaller units. The fourth variant protected the farm from excessive division as long as the household head had enough money to compensate those who did not take part in the distribution of land. As this was rarely the case, it is likely that the practice of such an inheritance system created credit relations between children. It also left little capital for improvement and investment. However, this was an inheritance system that prioritized equality of treatment for all heirs—male or female—over family patrimony.

## PARTIBLE AND IMPARTIBLE INHERITANCE
## SYSTEMS: DEGREES OF DIFFERENCE?

### Who Got What? The Fate of Heirs

In impartible inheritance regions sons were given priority. In Livradois, for example, 79 percent of heirs were males and only 21 percent females.[13] Similarly, in eighteenth-century Morvan, when the exploitation of wood for the Paris region began and when, as a result, the inheritance system became impartible, males were the favored heirs. Among a sample of 56 marriages deeds, 46 were concluded in favor of sons and only 7 in favor of daughters. Six of these daughters had no brother.[14] However, in regions where there was considerable emigration, women played an important role in the transmission and preservation of family wealth and frequently inherited the land. As Rose Duroux shows in her chapter in this book and elsewhere, in nineteenth-century Cantal there were as many heiresses as there were heirs.[15] In the Pyrénées widows were also active in maintaining family property. Among agricultural communities, they often became the household head until their son was old enough to manage the farm.[16] And finally, it should be noted that the experiences of *cadets* (the younger, non-inheriting male children) and *cadettes* (the younger, noninheriting female children) were rarely that different. Offspring who were not heir to the estate were treated similarly, regardless of gender.

How different was the situation in partible inheritance regions? Where joint tenancy was the rule each heir retained an equal right to family lands. In theory, this prevented the lands from being divided. But how long did this last? In many cases, the preservation of cohesive landed estates became a priority for heirs. While marriage and the birth of children created more potential claims on shares of estate, celibacy, death, emigration, and the giving away of property often ensured that land slowly returned to a small number of people. This had the effect of preserving the integrity of family estates, and more often than not it was sons rather than daughters who profited. In seventeenth-century Morvan, for example, while some children left their parents' farm long before the father's and mother's death, others stayed, usually sons, and ensured that the land remained undivided.[17] In this way, the outcomes of the property transmission strategies practiced in these regions were not radically different from those of the impartible *pays*.

In the regions where some heirs received *inter vivos* gifts in advance of their parents' death, the situation is less clear. Did parents really exclude or favor certain children through this practice, or were all heirs required to return gifts to the estate for equal redistribution? Jerome Viret, in his work on the Île-de-France, suggested that parents never excluded or favored a child.[18] Indeed, here as elsewhere, they gave land, money, and movables (such as livestock) to sons upon marriage so that they could establish themselves in farming or a trade. However, the gifts themselves were frequently relatively small in value and certainly less than the size of the anticipated legacy at the parents' death. This strategy militated against specific heirs retaining an oversized share of family property. It provided an incentive to pool the estate so that all heirs could receive larger units of property distributed on an equal basis. Where this predominated, since at least the seventeenth century it was common practice that each heir received an equal share of the estate.

But was sharing always absolutely equal? In his study of the large farmers of the Île-de-France, Jean-Marc Moriceau has shown that daughters and sons rarely received equal shares of the family estate when their father died.[19] The situation was also unequal at marriage. One child, preferably a son, was given the right to lease the family land along with farming implements and other resources. The remaining sons might be established on other farms or enter a different trade or profession. Daughters, in contrast, never received land but were instead given a dowry. In these parts of France, it was common for farmers' sons to marry farmers' daughters. Economically this was a good match: the husband brought the right to lease land and the resources and implements to farm it, and the wife brought ready capital in the form of a dowry. As Jean-Marc Moriceau and Gilles Postel-Vinay demonstrate, this strategy was practiced by the Chartier family and many others who farmed in the plaine de France, close to Paris.[20] The *pepinierists* (*marchands d'arbres*—sellers of young trees for gardens), who successfully farmed smaller plots of land near Paris, followed a similar strategy, and it is likely that the wine growers of the Paris region adopted comparable tactics.[21]

In fact, it was quite common for sons to receive the buildings, tools, equipment, and other resources that were attached to the family farm in preference to daughters. It was certainly the case in the Val de Saône from the middle of the eighteenth century, where a son received the *pourprix* (the farm buildings, tools, and equipment) by will. This was in spite of the fact that females had recently gained the right to inherit land on the same basis as males, either by a will or by a marriage deed.[22] Even in Brittany, where strictly partible inheritance was practiced, one child remained on the family farm, kept the buildings, and retained the farming implements and machinery. In fact, the inheritance system practiced here was not really a partible one. The successor to the family farm was more often a son than a daughter. According to Martine Segalen's research on the pays bigouden, in southwestern Brittany, in 123 different cases of inheritance, sons succeeded to the family farm on 75 occasions compared with 48 for women. The heir that succeeded to the farm was required to compensate his brothers and sisters for their share in the estate.[23] Therefore, being heir to the family farm was not always an advantage, and, in fact, it could be an intolerable financial burden to indemnify one's co-heirs.

In many, though not all, cases, the situation in these partible inheritance regions was not radically different to the impartible inheritance *pays;* even under a seemingly egalitarian system, daughters often ended up being excluded from the inheritance of landed property. While this was not always disadvantageous, it is clear that such inheritance strategies were gendered: sons received gifts of land; daughters received money and little else.[24] Moreover, in regions where female heirs did take an equal share of the landed estate, it was more common for daughters to be the sellers of plots to their co-heirs, rather than the purchasers. This was therefore a partible inheritance system that created gender inequalities among the co-heirs.[25]

Nevertheless, there were still important differences between partible and impartible inheritance regions. In partible regions daughters nearly always received a theoretically equal share of the estate; in the impartible *pays*, daughters, along with any brothers who were not the designated heir of the estate, generally received only a *légitime*. This was usually a small legacy, often in the form of a cash gift, that was frequently left unpaid. While it is clear that daughters fared badly when it came to inheritance in impartible regions of France, it should not be assumed that the position of female heirs in partible regions was significantly better. As discussed earlier, it was not always the case that estates were divided equally. Farm buildings and the agricultural *capital d'exploitation* were generally left to sons, as was the right to lease land. Finally, it was common that daughters who inherited land received inferior plots that were often geographically separated from the nucleus of the farm. Alternatively, daughters might receive holdings acquired by their parents that were not part of the original family patrimony.[26]

### Inheritance, Family Strategies, and the Life Cycle

Ultimately, analysis of the devolution and division of estate upon the death of a property owner reveals only part of the process of land transmission in partible inheritance regions. The key issue is what happened to the property after it had been shared out. When the parents died nothing was really settled. Once the formal legal division of property had been completed, heirs frequently embarked upon a series of sales, exchanges, and leases. Some legatees bought the shares of their fellow heirs, initiating a complex process of land transfers and allowing the establishment of new households and estates. Other children cashed in their inheritance and moved away or perhaps entered a new trade. This is precisely the reason why it is so difficult for historians to understand fully land transmission in partible inheritance regions. The subdivision of land that was a feature of egalitarian inheritance systems was partially compensated for by an unrelenting reconsolidation of plots through a family-centered system of market exchange. In this way inheritance was just one part of a wider set of social and economic strategies that individuals and families engaged in over the course of their lives.

It is often misleading to focus excessively on the division of family property that occurred with inheritance. The study of land transmission in Normandy at the start of the nineteenth century has revealed that the problems arising from subdivision of estate were not as acute as have often been thought. The dilemmas of sharing really came into play only when families had several children and where the land was substantial enough for division to significantly affect its value. In such cases the consolidation of the property in fewer hands was obviously more desirable. In Normandy the issue of sharing arose in only 30 percent of a sample of successions examined in Livarot and in 50 percent of another sample in Domfront. Sharing became a problem in those cases because there was both more than one heir to the estate and a significant amount of property to divide.[27]

It is tempting to imagine that the buying and selling of plots took place on the open market but that exchanges between family members were often negotiated at preferential rates. Unfortunately, there is little evidence that enables the reconstruction of this process. The example of Vernon in Normandy suggests that the peasants sold to and bought from one another without any real consideration of affinity.[28] The goal here was not to reconstitute exactly the original farm but to reaccumulate land into a larger unit, whatever the origin of plots gathered in this way. At the end of this process only a few heirs remained as landholders, and as a result the situation was similar to that which might be found in impartible inheritance regions. However, the key difference was that the farm did not remain the same from one generation to another; a new farm was produced as a result of the series of market-based land exchanges. A second difference was that unlike the situation in impartible inheritance regions, the transmission of land was not a sudden and exceptional life-course event, settled by marriage deed or will.[29] As we have seen, while gifts of property by will or at marriage were not uncommon in partible inheritance regions, they were moments in a series of property exchanges that stretched across and beyond the lifetime of any landowner.

In partible inheritance systems, therefore, the transmission of land was a perpetual cyclical process. A series of contracts and economic relationships were entered into at various stages across the family life course. Often starting at marriage, loans, gifts, and advances on estates were made by the parental generation to their children. Formal inheritance occurred with the death of the parents, which usually led to the division of property, but also, sometimes, to heirs declining their share of the estate. This process preceded a succession of sales, resales, auctions, exchanges, and leases among heirs and with the wider community.[30] In the partible regions of France, therefore, inheritance and succession were not shock events that threw the social and economic strategies of families into sudden disarray. Instead, they were long, drawn-out, and often carefully negotiated processes that initiated as many social and economic opportunities as they did constraints. It is clear, therefore, that marriage and death were not the only important moments in the family life course when property transmission took place.[31]

The issues raised by this analysis also pose questions about the relationship between inheritance and land accumulation. In impartible inheritance regions, it is widely known that heirs to estates rarely married heiresses. In Augerolles in the Livradois region of the Massif Central, only 3 percent of unions were marriages between an heir and an heiress.[32] This demonstrates that the priority in such regions was not to accumulate wealth through the joining of estates. The aim of most family strategies (including inheritance) was not to produce larger farms but to maintain the existing property structure and to protect what were called *maisons*. Usually an heir or an heiress married a nonheiress or a nonheir who brought a dowry to the partnership. It should be recalled that heirs were far more numerous than heiresses, except in certain regions such as the pays Basque where, by custom, the eldest child, male or female, inherited the estate.[33] Elsewhere the daughter became heiress only when there was no son or when the male heir was unable to take on the farm. Most women, as well as many men, in impartible inheritance regions were therefore excluded from the inheritance of land. Sometimes a nonheir with a dowry would marry a nonheiress with a dowry, just as happened in partible inheritance regions. Children without dowries fared the worst and had little chance of ever being married. Women in such a situation remained spinsters throughout their lives and often became a servant of their brother who had become the heir to the family. Alternatively, they could leave the household in order to find work elsewhere.

In partible inheritance regions the situation was, of course, different. All children received some land or some money to establish themselves. Many left the family farm but frequently did not move far from the village. One brother or sister would inevitably stay in the household. All heirs were free to marry—an event that usually meant the joining of resources from two families, as each partner brought his or her inheritance into the union. This provided the means for the foundation of a new household and the basis upon which the future accumulation of property could take place. In fact, the accumulation of property was a priority in order to allow land sharing among the couple's own children and to avoid pauperization.[34] The sale and purchase of land was a normal feature of family strategies, and therefore no farm was ever the same as that passed on from the previous generation.

The result was that property owners were often very active in local land markets. As was the case among the winegrowers in the Maintenons region of Beauce near Paris, peasant agriculturists purchased and sold plots of land to one another throughout their lives in preparation for the settling of their children.[35] Such strategies made good economic sense. According to their income and family priorities, property owners tried to adapt the resources that they had at their disposal to their needs. As a couple grew older, this strategy of accumulation eventually gave way to one of dispossession. This began with the transmission of property upon the marriage of children, and it culminated with death, when, as we have seen, the estate would finally be divided among the surviving heirs.[36]

## CONCLUSION: THE "RATIONALITY" OF PARTIBLE AND IMPARTIBLE SYSTEMS OF INHERITANCE

Following Frédéric Le Play, it is often assumed that impartible inheritance systems were the most economically rational and efficient.[37] While such systems may have prevented the excessive subdivision of land, the evidence to support a claim of greater economic efficiency is sketchy. Indeed, it was, in fact, within the partible inheritance regions of France—such as on the plains near Paris—that capitalist agriculture was most clearly expanding during this period. How could this be? In Brittany, it seems indeed obvious that the parceling up of the farms over the generations must have led to a progressive but ineluctable impoverishment of households. However, in other regions this was less true, and it can even be argued that capitalist agriculture benefited from precisely the subdivision and recombination of land made possible under conditions of partible inheritance.[38] In Burgundy many farmers succeeded in accumulating land throughout their lives.[39] Similarly, in the Île-de-France farmers were generally becoming more wealthy, even if they were regularly sharing their property among their children.[40]

As Bernard Derouet argued, the main difference between partible and impartible inheritance systems was that the former usually occurred in a society characterized by a high level of mobility of land and people, while the latter system was most often found in regions where there was greater stability.[41] On these grounds he claimed that societies that favored equal sharing among heirs were not irrational, but instead followed a different kind of rationality. The key goal—and, indeed, the central principle of any partible inheritance system—was not to pass on a complete farm from generation to generation but to give some property to everyone, even though it was well known that nobody, or virtually nobody, would receive enough land to making a viable living.[42] Unlike in impartible inheritance regions, a gift of property was not seen as a form of total provision; rather, it was viewed as a type of venture capital, a resource that could help in establishing a household and earning a living. As a result, heirs were forced to enter either the land market to rent additional plots or farms, or they sold their labor power by working on other people's holdings. All things considered, the priority was not land itself, but maintaining the ties with and among kin. These ties were the real strength of the family.[43] In short, it is clear that equal sharing, which was a feature of partible inheritance systems, did not necessarily hinder the economic viability of farms. The key was the capacity to lease other lands as well as the use of land itself as a source of capital.

A closer look at the situation in Brittany also highlights some of the relationships between economic development and the prevailing inheritance system. Nadine Vivier's study of Finistère, in Brittany, has revealed a north-south split in levels of economic development that corresponds with the patterns of farm transmission.[44] While the whole of Brittany was a partible inheritance region, transmission of the land varied in ways described in previous sections of this chapter. In the north a rigidly egalitarian system operated so that all children acquired equal shares in the family lands. In this part of the region the price of land was higher, and agriculture was generally more commercialized than elsewhere. In the south, the sales, exchanges, leases, compensations, and so on that accompanied inheritance tended to lead to the reversion of lands into the hands of a single heir. Here, the price of land was lower, and agriculture was less commercialized. In understanding these patterns of economic development it is difficult to establish cause and effect. Did the division of land that was a feature of strict partible inheritance push land prices up and thereby stimulate the economy? Or did high land prices and a commercialized local economy encourage the division of estate among all heirs? The situation is further complicated by the fact that the relationship appears to be inverted *within* south Brittany, between Morbihan in the east, which had a more commercialized economy and yet little subdivision of estates, and Finistère in the west, where the situation was the opposite.

The logic of the partible inheritance system favored a society that was more individualistic, and in this sense it is hardly surprising that levels of economic development tended to be greater than in impartible regions, where land ownership went unchanged from one generation to another.[45] Indeed, from this standpoint the claim that impartible inheritance systems were the most economically rational seems overstated. An unequal property transmission system "fossilized" the land structure. The farm hardly changed for generations, and its operation was often characterized by routine rather than improvement and innovation. Such a system provided little incentive for the commercialization of agriculture through the sale of products on the market. In short, it encouraged self-subsistence and immobility for those who inherited land. It is surely no coincidence that the regions where agriculture was most overtly capitalist were also those where partible inheritance was practiced, even if the central problem of recognizing cause and effect remains.[46]

People in both partible and impartible inheritance regions had to cope with a world where land was scarce and people were numerous. To resolve this problem, they pursued different strategies that had different priorities. In impartible inheritance regions the main goal was to preserve, at whatever cost, a property large enough to retain its viability. Families were also keen to maintain the structure, shape, and form of the property so that it resembled that which had been passed down from the previous generation. In partible inheritance regions, on the other hand, the aim was to provide an opportunity for each child to make his or her way in life through a gift of an equal share of the estate. In impartible regions the heir was appointed; in partible *pays* the heir (or heirs) emerged from the events of life. While these different systems of inheritance produced inequalities among heirs, particularly between sons and daughters, they nevertheless fulfilled important social and economic goals. The historiography of French inheritance practices has for too long been preoccupied by the distinction between partible and impartible systems of property transmission. This chapter has shown that a more refined approach is needed, where the transfers of land that occur with the death of a parent are seen within the context of wider patterns of transmission and exchange and within the broader social and economic strategies of families. Only then will it be possible to understand the ways in which birth order and gender shaped the exercise of power and distribution of resources within landowning families.

## NOTES

1. Jean Yver, *Essai de géographie coutumière: Egalité entre héritiers et exclusion des enfants dotés* (Paris: Sirey, 1966); Emmanuel Le Roy Ladurie, "Système de la coutume: structures familiales et coutumes d'héritage en France au XVIe siècle," *Annales Economies, Sociétés, Civilisations* XXVII (1972): 825–46.

2. Rolande Bonnain, Gérard Bouchard, and Joseph Goy, eds., *Transmettre, hériter, succéder: La reproduction familiale en milieu rural, France-Québec, XVIIIe–XXe siècles* (Lyon-Paris-Villeurbanne: Presses Universitaires de Lyon, 1992); Gérard Bouchard, John A. Dickinson, and Joseph Goy, eds., *Les exclus de la terre en France et au Québec, XVIIe–XXe siècles: La reproduction familiale dans la différence* (Sillery: Septentrion, 1998); Gérard Bouchard and Joseph Goy, eds., *Famille, économie et société rurale en contexte d'urbanisation (17e–20e siècle)* (Chicoutimi-Paris: SOREP– Ecole des Hautes Etudes en Sciences Sociales, 1991); and Gérard Bouchard, Joseph Goy, and Anne-Lise Head-König, eds., *Problèmes de la transmission des exploitations*

*agricoles (XVIIIe–XXe siècles): Nécessités économiques et pratiques juridiques* (Rome: Ecole Française de Rome, 1998).

3. Georges Augustins and Rolande Bonnain, *Les Baronnies des Pyrénées, vol. 1: Maisons, mode de vie, société* (Paris: Ed. de l'Ecole des Hautes Etudes en Sciences Sociales, 1982); Georges Augustins, Rolande Bonnain, Yves Péron, and Gilles Sautter, *Les Baronnies des Pyrénées, vol. 2: Maisons, espace, famille* (Paris: Ed. de l'Ecole des Hautes Etudes en Sciences Sociales, 1986); Elisabeth Claverie and Pierre Lamaison, *L'impossible mariage: Violence et parenté en Gévaudan XVIIe, XVIIIe, XIXe siècles* (Paris: Hachette, 1982); Alain Collomp, *La Maison du père: Famille et village en Haute-Provence aux XVIIe et XVIIIe siècles* (Paris: Presses Universitaires de France, 1983); and Elie Pélaquier, *De la Maison du Père à la maison commune: Saint-Victor-de-la-Coste, en Languedoc rhodanien (1661–1789)* (Montpellier: Publications de l'Université Paul-Valéry-Montpellier III, 1996).

4. Frédéric Le Play, *La réforme sociale* (Paris: H. Plon, 1864) and Frédéric Le Play, *L'organisation de la famille selon le vrai modèle signalé par l'histoire de toutes les races et de tous les temps* (Paris: Téqui, 1871).

5. Gérard Béaur, *Histoire agraire de la France au XVIIIe siècle: Inerties et changements dans les campagnes françaises entre 1715 et 1815* (Paris: SEDES, 2000) and Paul-André Rosental, "Pratiques successorales et fécondité: L'effet du Code civil," *Economie et Prévision* 100–101 (1991): 231–38.

6. This interpretation of partible inheritance has been discussed by Joseph Goy, "Transmission successorale et paysannerie pendant la Révolution française: Un grand malentendu," *Etudes Rurales* 110–12 (1988): 45–56.

7. Bernard Derouet, "La transmission égalitaire du patrimoine dans la France rurale (XVIe–XIXe siècles): Nouvelles perspectives de recherches," in *Familia, Casa y Trabajo: Historia de la Familia*, ed. F. Chacon Jimenez (Murcia: Universidad de Murcia, 1997), 73–95.

8. See, for example, Marie-Pierre Arrizabalaga, "Famille, succession, émigration au Pays-basque au XIXe siècle: Etude des pratiques successorales et des comportements migratoires au sein des familles basques," (Ph.D. diss., Ecole des Hautes Etudes en Sciences Sociales, Paris, 1998); Rolande Bonnain, "Droit écrit, coutume pyrénéenne et pratiques successorales dans les Baronnies, 1769–1836," in Augustins et al., *Les Baronnies des Pyrénées, vol. 2*, 157–77; Antoinette Fauve-Chamoux, "Les structures familiales au pays des familles-souches: Esparros," *Annales Economies, Sociétés, Civilisations* XXXIX (1984): 513–28; Antoinette Fauve-Chamoux, "Les frontières de l'autorégulation paysanne: Croissance et famille-souche," *Revue de la Bibliothèque nationale* 50 (1993): 38–47; and Anne Zink, *L'héritier de la maison: Géographie coutumière du Sud-Ouest de la France sous l'Ancien Régime* (Paris: Ecole des Hautes Etudes en Sciences Sociales, 1993).

9. Yver, *Essai de géographie coutumière*.

10. Ibid.

11. On Normandy see Yver, *Essai de géographie coutumière*, 91–109; for the Franche-Comté see Bernard Derouet, "Le partage des frères: Héritage masculin et reproduction sociale en Franche-Comté aux XVIIIe et XIXe siècles," *Annales Economies, Sociétés, Civilisations* XLVIII (1993): 453–74; for the Vale de Saône see Philippe Gonod, "Les modalités du partage égalitaire: L'exemple du val de Saône aux XVIIIe et XIXe siècles," *Etudes Rurales* 137 (1995): 73–87.

12. Martine Segalen, *Quinze générations de Bas-Bretons: Parenté et société dans le pays bigouden Sud, 1720–1980* (Paris: Presses Universitaires de France, 1985), 81.

13. Bernard Brunel, *Le Vouloir vivre et la force des choses: Augerolles en Livradois-Forez du XVIIe au XIXe siècle* (Clermont-Ferrand: Université Blaise-Pascal, Institut d'études du Massif Central, 1992), 317.

14. Francine Rolley, "Reproduction familiale et changements économiques: L'exclusion dans le Morvan du nord, XVIIe–XVIIIe siècles," in Bouchard, Dickinson and Goy, *Les exclus de la terre en France et au Québec*, 133–57.

15. Rose Duroux, "La noria des exclus: Stratégie chez les migrants auvergnats en Espagne (XIXe siècle)," in Bouchard, Dickinson and Goy, *Les exclus de la terre en France et au Québec*, 96–113. See also Rose Duroux's chapter in this volume.

16. Antoinette Fauve-Chamoux, "Stratégies individuelles et politiques de reproduction familiale: Le perpétuel ajustement intergénérationnel des destins migratoires à Esparros (XVIIe–XXe siècles)," in *Marchés, Migrations et Transmission (XVIIIe–XXe siècles). Les stratégies familiales dans les espaces français, canadiens et suisse*, ed. Luigi Lorenzetti, Anne-Lise Head-König, and Joseph Goy (Bern: Petre Lang, 2004).

17. Rolley, "Reproduction familiale et changements économiques."

18. Jérôme-Luther Viret, "Valeurs et parenté: L'exemple d'Ecouen et de Villiers-le-Bel (1560–1685)" (Ph.D. diss., Université de Paris X-Nanterre, 1998).

19. Jean-Marc Moriceau, *Les Fermiers de l'Île-de-France: Ascension d'un patronat agricole (XVe–XVIIIe siècles)* (Paris: Fayard, 1994).

20. Jean-Marc Moriceau and Gilles Postel-Vinay, *Ferme, entreprise, famille: Grande exploitation et changements agricoles, les Chartier (XVIIe–XIXe siècles)* (Paris: Ecole des Hautes Etudes en Sciences Sociales, 1992).

21. Michel Traversat, *Les pépinières: Etude sur les jardins français et sur les jardiniers et les pépiniéristes* (Ph.D. diss., Ecole des Hautes Etudes en Sciences Sociales, Paris, 2001).

22. Gonod, "Les modalités du partage égalitaire."

23. Segalen, *Quinze générations de Bas-Bretons*, 106.

24. Tiphaine Barthelemy de Saizieu, "Partages égalitaires en Basse-Bretagne," *Terrains* 4 (1985): 42–49.

25. Ibid.

26. Marie-Claude Pingaud, "Partage égalitaire et destins des lignées," *Annales de démographie Historique* 84 (1995): 17–33.

27. Gérard Béaur, "Land Accumulation, Life-Course and Inequalities among Generations in Eighteenth-Century France: The Winegrowers from the Chartres Region," *The History of the Family* 3 (1998): 285–302.

28. Jean-Pierre Bardet, Gérard Béaur, and Jacques Renard, "Marché foncier et exclusion en normandie: Premiers résultats d'une enquête sur la région de Vernon dans la seconde moitié du XVIIIe siècle," in Bouchard, Dickinson, and Goy, *Les exclus de la terre en France et au Québec*, 193–202.

29. Gérard Béaur, "La transmission des exploitations: Logiques et stratégies. Quelques réflexions sur un processus obscur," in Bouchard, Goy, and Head-König, *Problèmes de la transmission des exploitations agricoles*, 109–16.

30. Béaur, *Histoire agraire de la France*, 45 and Pingaud, "Partage égalitaire et destins des lignées." For the situation in Germany see also David W. Sabean,

*Property, Production and Family in Neckarhausen 1700–1870* (Cambridge: Cambridge University Press, 1990).

31. Segalen, *Quinze générations de Bas-Bretons*, 90.

32. Brunel, *Le Vouloir vivre et la force des choses*, 315.

33. Arrizabalaga, "Famille, succession, émigration au Pays-basque."

34. Tiphaine Barthelemy de Saizieu, "Pratiques successorales et mobilité sociale: Exemples bretons," in Bouchard and Goy, *Famille, économie et société rurale*, 57–66.

35. Gérard Béaur, *Le marché foncier à la veille de la Révolution: Les mouvements de propriété beaucerons dans les régions de Maintenon et de Janville de 1761 à 1790* (Paris: Ecole des Hautes Etudes en Sciences Sociales, 1984).

36. Gérard Béaur, "Investissement foncier, épargne et cycle de vie dans le Pays chartrain au XVIIIe siècle," *Histoire et Mesure* VI (1991): 275–88 and Béaur, "Land Accumulation, Life-Course and Inequalities." See also the studies of the larger farmers, where this strategy is particularly evident: Moriceau, *Les Fermiers de l'Île-de-France* and Moriceau and Postel-Vinay, *Ferme, entreprise, famille*.

37. Le Play, *La réforme sociale* and Le Play, *L'organisation de la famille*.

38. Segalen, *Quinze générations de Bas-Bretons*, 110–12.

39. Marie-Claude Pingaud, *Paysans en Bourgogne: Les gens de Minot* (Paris: Flammarion, 1978), 125.

40. Moriceau, *Les Fermiers de l'Île-de-France*.

41. Bernard Derouet, "Pratiques successorales et rapport à la terre: Les sociétés paysannes d'Ancien Régime," *Annales Economies, Sociétés, Civilisations* XLIV (1989): 173–206.

42. Bernard Derouet, "La transmission égalitaire du patrimoine."

43. Barthelemy de Saizieu, "Partages égalitaires en Basse-Bretagne."

44. Nadine Vivier, "La transmission des patrimoines en Bretagne au XIXe siècle," in *Familles, terre, marchés: Logiques économiques et stratégies dans les milieux ruraux (XVIIe–XXe siècles)*, ed. Gérard Béaur, Christian Dessureault, and Joseph Goy (Rennes: Presses Universitaires Rennes II, 2004).

45. Bernard Derouet, "Transmettre la terre: Origines et inflexions récentes d'une problématique de la différence," *Histoire et Sociétés Rurales* 2 (1994): 33–67.

46. Barthelemy de Saizieu, "Partages égalitaires en Basse-Bretagne."

# CHAPTER 3

# Emigration, Gender, and Inheritance: A Case Study of the High Auvergne, 1700–1900

*Rose Duroux*

## INTRODUCTION

This chapter explores the relationships between migration, inheritance, and gender in the context of mountain communities in southern France. In such communities, families followed a strategy of single inheritance (unigeniture), stressing the importance of the family "house" and the transmission of the family property to one child, preferably the firstborn son (male primogeniture), as in Béarn and the Baronnies, but also the firstborn son or daughter (male or female primogeniture), as in the Basque country.[1] In this context, single inheritance necessitated the cohabitation of the parents and the selected child with his or her family, and perhaps unmarried siblings as well, thus forming a household structure known as the stem family.[2] Because of these traditional inheritance practices and limited economic opportunities in such rather poor, isolated, mountain regions, property owners encouraged the temporary migration of noninheriting children to other parts of France or permanent emigration to Spain and North America.

These strategies operated in eighteenth- and nineteenth-century Cantal, which was a hilly, cattle-raising region in the former High Auvergne in the Massif Central. In this region small property owners often worked on the land themselves and generally allowed only one child to marry into the family household.[3] As income was low and cash scarce, they developed strategies to protect the family house and secure single inheritance, thereby transmitting both house and property to one child. In doing so they avoided the need to divide landholdings and partition the estate to such an extent as to threaten the economic viability of the household. Among these strategies, families favored male migration to Spain and female unigeniture. The former strategy allowed men to save sufficient money to marry heiresses, and the latter allowed the heiresses themselves to use their husbands' dowry to compensate their noninheriting siblings. In this way both house and property remained undivided and viable for the parents, the selected child and family, and the unmarried siblings.

Property owners in the High Auvergne encouraged migration to Spain as a way of coping with the burden of heavy taxes and the consequences of demographic increase that collectively threatened economic survival and traditional patterns of inheritance. In the eighteenth and nineteenth centuries, some 10,000 men from the High Auvergne migrated back and forth from the rural districts of western Cantal to Spain. From the mid-nineteenth century destinations began to diversify within France and abroad, and from then on migration to Spain became an elite activity that Cantal men considered only if it paid off. As a consequence, the number of migrants declined significantly from about 3,000 in 1850 to a few hundred in 1900.[4] Until that point, emigration to Spain was both a necessity and an asset for Cantal families and provided men and women alike with the necessary means to keep the family house and property intact and under the control of one child. As will be demonstrated, those who did not follow this traditional pattern of migration were excluded from inheritance and marriage. In this way, male migration, female inheritance, and heiresses' marriage with returning migrants combined to form a closely interlinked system of welfare that encompassed not just individual heirs but entire households. This welfare system is the focus of the chapter.

The analysis is based on detailed family reconstitution of stem families originating from a small number of villages including Crandelles, Saint-Paul-des-Landes, Ytrac, La Ségalassière, and Pers, all of which were affected by long-distance migration (see Figure 3.1). Civil records of births, marriages and deaths, and notarial records, along with private archives provided by individual families and genealogists, are the main sources of evidence.[5] Using this information it was possible to reconstitute seven families or "houses" for which the data are particularly rich. The experiences of these families—Nicques, Messac, Rigou, Sanhes, Oustalniol, Montin-Bas, and Nosières—over two centuries form the empirical core around which this chapter is based.

## HOUSES IN THE HIGH AUVERGNE

As in many regions in southern France, Cantal families followed inheritance practices that resulted in the transmission of the family house and property to one heir, the aim of which was to keep the estate intact from one generation to the next.[6] As Diane Gervais argues, "property was con-

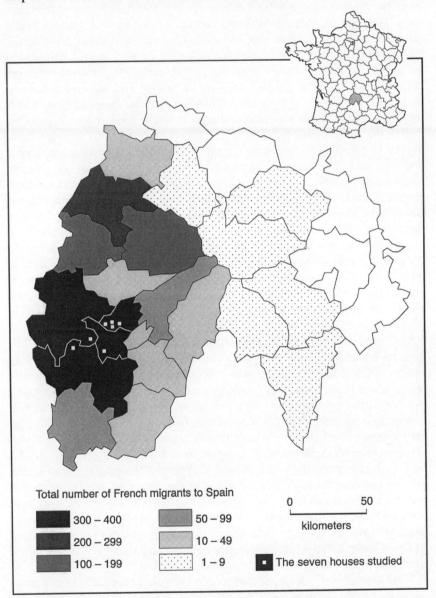

**Figure 3.1**
**Map of Cantal and the Location of the Seven Houses**

Total number of French migrants to Spain

- 300 – 400
- 200 – 299
- 100 – 199
- 50 – 99
- 10 – 49
- 1 – 9
- The seven houses studied

0      50
kilometers

sidered as an entity which had to survive intact through generations and whose owner saw himself as the transmitter of the property he was responsible for."[7] However, in the eighteenth and nineteenth centuries changing economic and demographic conditions meant that Cantal property owners adopted new practices that in effect benefited women rather than men. The heir or, more commonly, heiress settled into the family house with his or her spouse in accordance with a clause normally written in the marriage contract, which stated that he or she would inherit the greater share of the parents' property. The household would therefore comprise the parental couple, the heir or heiress and his or her spouse, and other members of the stem family. Parents and heirs entered into a legally binding "contract of association" that specified single inheritance within the stem-family household. In this contract, the heir or heiress also agreed to compensate his or her unmarried siblings with a cash dowry at specific dates. Brothers and sisters who had married before the selected heir received a dowry and generally approved a clause in their own marriage contracts in which they renounced their shares of the inheritance. Those who married after the heir or heiress were duly provided with a dowry and also expressly renounced their claims to the inheritance in their marriage contracts. Therefore, the only ones to remain at home were the donors, the heir or heiress, his or her family, and other unmarried relatives, such as brothers, sisters, uncles, and aunts.[8] The household therefore effectively functioned as a stem family. What was important was that each child was settled comfortably, enjoying the same status as his or her parents.

This type of contract prevailed almost intact even after the Civil Code became effective. Testaments were exceptional, other than for departing emigrants, and land partition was correspondingly rare. Over time, contracts turned into customary arrangements where donations and partitions occurred regardless of any marriage agreements that children signed before their parents' death. Notaries were used to establish land and property values except in cases where family members disagreed. In such instances other officials were called upon to adjudicate between the parties involved. However, the value of land was generally underestimated, usually by between 30 to 70 percent. This was a common practice aimed at reducing inheritance taxes and the size of compensation to which siblings were entitled for their share of the inheritance. Although lawsuits were rare, settlements were sometimes disputed after the donating parents' death.[9] Generally speaking, these strategies secured stability, single inheritance, and the continuation of propertied families.

Migration played an important role in the selection of an heir. Considering that male siblings migrated to and from Spain annually, the choice of the heir or heiress was dependent not only upon the relationship with his or her parents, but also upon his or her absences and personal motivations. One set of questions that needs to be asked, therefore, is the extent to which exclusion of men from inheritance was the result of emigration and the prevalence of female succession the result of sons' absences. Using longitudinal analysis from 1700 until 1900, this chapter explores trends in inheritance practices relating, first, to the selection of the heir or heiress and, second, to the destiny of those who were excluded from inheritance.

## THE SUCCESSOR

### Female Inheritance

In the course of the eighteenth and nineteenth centuries, inheritance practices changed in line with patterns of migration.[10] This had particular importance for women because, in the absence of sons, who had migrated to Spain, daughters often inherited the family house and property. Not infrequently they married men who had returned from Spain with enough money to provide a cash dowry. With this sum heiresses could compensate their noninheriting siblings, thereby preventing the subdivision of the family house and property among surviving descendants. This pattern is well illustrated by the experiences of the seven selected families in western Cantal between 1700 and 1900.

Table 3.1 and Figure 3.2, which summarize the evidence contained in the family reconstitution, illustrate two main points. First, 32 of the 53

**Table 3.1**
**Heiresses and Heirs among the Seven Houses**

|  | Heiresses | | | Heirs | | |
|---|---|---|---|---|---|---|
|  | Number | Length of ownership (years) | Average length of ownership (years) | Number | Length of ownership (years) | Average length of ownership (years) |
| Nicques | 5 | 134 | 26.8 | 3 | 66 | 22.0 |
| Messac | 4 | 113 | 28.2 | 3 | 87 | 29.0 |
| Rigou | 4 | 125 | 31.2 | 3 | 75 | 25.0 |
| Sanhes | 5 | 126 | 25.2 | 3 | 74 | 24.6 |
| Oustalniol | 5 | 114 | 22.8 | 3 | 86 | 28.6 |
| Montin-Bas | 3 | 70 | 23.3 | 4 | 130 | 32.5 |
| Nozières | 6 | 141 | 23.5 | 2 | 59 | 29.5 |
| Total | 32 | 823 | 25.7 | 21 | 577 | 27.5 |

Source: This table is based on the family reconstitution described in the text and summarized in Appendixes 3.1–3.7.

**Figure 3.2**
**Inheritance and Succession in the Seven Houses**

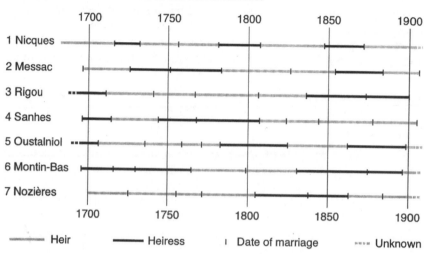

heirs, equivalent to more than 60 percent of cases, were women. The Rigou house illustrates this point well: between 1711 and 1836 all 4 heirs were women (Appendix 3.3). In the Nozières house, 6 out of the 8 heirs were women who, over a 200-year period, collectively held property for 141 years (Appendix 3.7). Nor were these trends exceptional as other families reproduced similar patterns: female inheritance also prevailed in the Malbert house in the Saint-Santin-Cantalès and Mirandes houses in Sauvat. From 1795, 5 women were also in charge of property transmission in the Chabannes house in Méallet.

Second, women were propertied household heads for longer than men: the 32 heiresses owned the family house and property for a cumulative total of 823 years compared with 577 years for the 21 male heirs. However, on average the length of ownership was shorter for women than men: 25.7 compared with 27.5 years, respectively. In part, this can be explained by women's shorter life expectancy of 62.9 years compared with 68.9 years for men, the result of successive pregnancies and hard physical labor on the farm.

With the exception of the Basque country, where women also had greater opportunities to inherit the family house and property, this pattern of female inheritance is almost unheard of elsewhere in the Pyrénées and in the Alps, not to mention the rest of France.[11] In so acquiring property and the capacity to control the family business, women also acquired authority and leadership and allowed men the liberty to migrate to Spain, secure in the knowledge that the family house and property would remain intact. In those houses where temporary migration took place several times a year, therefore, female inheritance served both as compensation for and encouragement of male migration.

### Male or Female Primogeniture

With some exceptions, male and female primogeniture prevailed in western Cantal throughout the eighteenth and nineteenth centuries. However, because it was impossible to determine how some 19 household heads selected their heirs, any conclusions drawn from these data must be treated with caution. Nevertheless, families sometimes opted for male primogeniture, transmitting the family house and property to their first-born son, and in a few cases chose their heirs from among younger sons or daughters. Of the 43 successions for which reconstitution was possible, 22 household heads chose their firstborn as the heir, 17 of which were daughters and the remainder sons. By contrast, 4 left the family house and property to a younger child, one of whom was a daughter and the remaining 3, sons. Only 2 household heads chose the youngest of their children as their heir. The analysis of the Sanhes house over 8 generations highlights this situation: in 6 of the 10 cases the chosen heir was the firstborn child (Appendix 3.4). In the Rigou house, household heads almost always alternated their choice of heirs, selecting either the firstborn or *cadet* male or female heirs (Appendix 3.3).

There were usually sound reasons in those relatively rare cases when a younger child or another relative inherited the family property. First and most obviously, firstborn male and female inheritance was impossible when household heads had no descendant. For example, Jeanne-Marie Cruèghe transferred her property to her husband, who had temporarily migrated to Spain, while Justine Oustalniol and Joseph Vidal transmitted their house to their nephew. Second, underage orphans could not inherit until they reached adulthood. In this case, the law allowed temporary ownership by a "regent," usually a relative, such as an uncle or aunt, who was responsible for the family business and household. Third, unexpected mortality sometimes disrupted succession practices, thereby forcing parents to change their choice of heirs. For example, the first two *cadets* of the Nicques family, who were the logical heirs after their older sister opted for a religious life, were assassinated in Spain. Fourth, succession was the result of unexplainable family choices. One couple, Géraud and Julie Vermemouze, settled in Julie's house (the third-born child of the family) when she inherited the house and property of another member of the Vermemouze family who was "an original cousin at odds with the family."[12] Finally, families agreed to heiresses' marriages even though they were barely old enough to marry. Out of necessity, the two eldest daughters of the Nicques house were forced to marry young: one was 12-year-old Jeanne Pélissier and the other, 13-year-old Jeanne-Marie Cruèghe. Heirs also sometimes married young. However, both situations were rare given that the average age at marriage in the seven selected houses was 21.5 years for heiresses and 27.3 years for heirs.

Just as migration was an important factor influencing the pattern of inheritance, so too did it affect the age at which individuals inherited property, though often in contrasting ways. In general, both heiresses and heirs married at a younger age than their siblings. Cantal household heads, who had on average 6 children, generally tried to select an heir in order to secure single inheritance and encouraged the others to work temporarily in Spain or remain single in the village.[13] Sons-in-law who had amassed a dowry married even later. In the village of Crandelles, daughters-in-law married when they were 21.9 years old and sons-in-law when they were 30.1 years old. Nor did land ownership appear to hinder emigration. On the contrary: out of the 21 heirs, 10 were migrants who had worked in Spain temporarily before marriage, and out of the 32 heiresses, 20 married local men who had previously migrated and who had since returned to the village with savings. What the data clearly highlight is that marriage with migrants was common and was probably arranged early in the heirs' life, as appeared to have been the case in the marriage of two of the Nicques heiresses, who were 12 and 13 years old, respectively. Of the 53 cases identified in the data, 30 marriages were encouraged because of the money that migrants had saved while in Spain and that allowed them to amass a dowry that could be used to compensate those siblings and others who did not inherit property.

## SIBLINGS' MARRIAGE

### The Decision to Marry

Marriage depended on many parameters, one of the most important of which was men's willingness to migrate and their capacity to save enough money to marry. It was also dependent on having enough resources to support a family, and in this respect migrants had greater chances than others to marry and settle as property owners. Using family reconstitution, Table 3.2 outlines the marital situation for the majority of children who did not inherit property. Besides the 43 heirs, there were also 191 noninheriting sons and daughters to marry out. The issue was the extent to which their chances of finding a spouse were influenced by the fact that they could not expect to receive the family house or property. Of the 93 noninheriting daughters, 43 got married, of which at least 14 married men who had migrated to Spain.[14] Among the 50 remaining daughters, 7 became nuns and 43 remained single, many of whom stayed in the parental home. We can therefore conclude that while some women could consider marriage only to a returning migrant after receiving their com-

Table 3.2
Marital Status of the Noninheriting Children

|            | Married | Single | Total |
|------------|---------|--------|-------|
| Daughters  | 43      | 50     | 93    |
| Sons       | 34      | 64     | 98    |
| Total      | 77      | 114    | 191   |

Source: See Table 3.1.

Table 3.3
Marital Status of the Noninheriting Males

|             | Married | Single | Total |
|-------------|---------|--------|-------|
| Migrants    | 21      | 22     | 43    |
| Nonmigrants | 13      | 42     | 55    |
| Total       | 34      | 64     | 98    |

Source: See Table 3.1.

pensation for the inheritance, there was little choice for those without access to property but to remain single.

Among the 98 noninheriting sons, Table 3.3 shows that 55 were nonmigrants and 43 had lived and worked in Spain and returned to the village with their savings. Almost half the male migrants (21) married, and the other half (22) remained single. In comparison, among the 55 nonmigrants only 13 married and 42 remained single, suggesting that temporary migration was a precondition for marriage in the village because without the money made in Spain, they had little chance of gaining access to land. There was little money circulating in the village and inheritance shares were small, so without personal savings and the heirs' compensation, they found it difficult to get married. This explains why less than a quarter of nonmigrants married while 39 of the others remained single (probably in the family house) and 3 opted for a religious life.

For the 114 who remained unmarried out of the total of 234 single individuals who remained single, one may wonder whether this situation was the result of fate, necessity, or culture. Studies of celibacy have shown that it could have a number of benefits for the heir and subsequent generations. These included the labor inputs made by unmarried siblings to the household farm economy, the encouragement it provided for migrating siblings to donate their seasonal savings to the household, and the prestige, not to mention the cash, that arose from having an unmarried relative who had decided to become a priest.[15]

We should not overestimate the significance of family members entering the church. On the one hand, in terms of numbers, religious siblings— three priests and seven nuns—were hardly significant in the overall scale of things. While there are some examples of families in which religious siblings were more common, such as the sixth generation of the Nicques house, where two women became nuns and one man a bishop, it is important not to overstate their significance (Appendix 3.1). Having said that, however, religious siblings were also found in other families studied here, such as in the Sanhes household, which included the famous Cardinal Saliège, the relative of male migrants from the region who had settled temporarily in Madrid (Appendix 3.4). On the other hand, for those unmarried siblings who wished to avoid celibacy, had no desire to enter the church, or were less willing to provide family services within the household, migration to Spain remained an option.

Finally, a number of migrating siblings who did not marry into a house as heirs or as sons-in-law tended to refuse to return to the village. Men and women in Cantal shared similar goals relating to access to property, status, and marriage in the village. Unless their savings allowed them to settle in a new house or live off their income in the village, this group often preferred to stay abroad. The only reason that justified their return to the village was the acquisition of property and the status that it guaranteed. If after years of work in Spain they could not marry in the village and settle comfortably as property owners or as heiresses' spouses, they generally remained abroad.

Attitudes of these noninheriting siblings toward their share of the family property varied. In several cases notary records and especially consular records comprised documents signed by noninheriting siblings who, from their residence in Spain, sold or donated their shares of the family inheritance. However, noninheriting siblings were also aware of their rights to property, which they not infrequently used to demand compensation in return for relinquishing their claim to an inheritance. Occasionally, permanent emigrants sold their inheritance shares to a third party after their parents' death, especially if they considered they had been treated unfairly by the family, thereby denouncing the family agreement, which underestimated the value of the inheritance and of the siblings' compensations. One instance of this is contained in a letter which Jean Carles sent from Madrid to his sister who inherited the house, and her husband, Géraud Réveilhac, a former day laborer who had temporarily migrated to Castille in Spain and who had made money in business prior to marriage. In the letter to his sister of December 6, 1806, he explained that he had just left hospital and was forced to beg. He asked her to send him 200 francs, or at least 150 francs, as an early and partial payment for his share of the inheritance in order to help him overcome his difficulties. Otherwise, he warned his sister he would sell his inheritance, a course of action that he would reluctantly take if forced to do so.[16] His request had two meanings: one material, related to money, and the other cultural, related to inheritance. In this context, noninheriting siblings were conscious of their property rights and status, both of which could be used to negotiate compensation in the knowledge that it was economically dangerous and culturally shameful to sell their share of the inheritance outside the family.

## THE MESSAC HOUSE, 1700–1900: A CASE STUDY OF ENDOGAMY AND HOMOGAMY

Family reconstitution allows us to examine these general processes in more depth, focusing on individual households. In this case, the Messac household, outlined in Appendix 3.2, provides an excellent case study of the way in which inheritance, migration, and welfare operated over seven generations between 1700 and 1900.

Of the first generation, it was possible to trace only the heir who had three sons, all of whom migrated to Spain temporarily to work for the Chinchón Company, established in the town of Chinchón in Madrid province and run by emigrants from Cantal.[17] All three returned to settle in Cantal: Pierre, the firstborn son, inherited his parents' family house and property and married the daughter of a man who had temporarily migrated to Spain; Raymond, the second-born son, married the heiress of the Nicques house (Appendix 3.1); and, Géraud, the third son, married the heiress of the Rigou house (Appendix 3.3).

The third generation of the Messac house included 10 children. All 4 *cadet* sons who had migrated to work for the Chinchón Company later returned from Spain and married heiresses. While all sons returned to live comfortably in Cantal, it was at times difficult to settle all the daughters, most notably Marguerite, the firstborn daughter, and Marie, the fifth-born, both of whom remained single. Jeanne-Marie, the second-born daughter, married the heir of the Leyritz house, a family of emigrants from Crandelles. Marie-Anne, the third-born daughter, married the heir of the Cornet house, a family of emigrants from Teissières-de-Cornet. Jeanne-Marie, the fourth-born daughter, inherited the family house and married a man who had lived in Spain for a while and returned to the village with his savings. Marie-Rose, the sixth-born daughter, married the heir of the Puech house in Crandelles, a family whose members temporarily worked for the Chinchón Company. Noël and Jean-Ambroise-Noël, the seventh- and eighth-born sons, also married the heiresses from the Puech house. Jean-Baptiste, the ninth-born son, married the heiress of the Rigou house (Appendix 3.3) who was, in fact, his first cousin (Géraud's daughter).

Finally, like most of his siblings, Géraud, the tenth-born son, married an heiress of a family of emigrants from Bac in Saint-Paul-des-Landes.

Little is known about the fourth generation of the Messac house. Indeed, none of the five sons migrated to Spain and, from the evidence that remains, none appeared to have married. Two of the three daughters also remained single. Finally, the sixth-born daughter inherited the house and married a local migrant who had worked for the Chinchón Company. The fifth generation consisted of only two people: Amédée, the firstborn son, and Marie, the second-born daughter. Amédée, who inherited the house, had earlier migrated to Madrid where, together with another relative, he opened a bakery with Jules Laveissière, whom Marie had married and who was heir of the Bourret house in Crandelles.[18] In this case the close interrelationships between migration, enterprise, and family were clear.

In the sixth generation of the Messac house, there were six daughters, three of whom married temporary migrants. Adèle, the firstborn, married a coppersmith merchant from Lesparre, a man who had never lived in Spain. No information was found on Marie-Antoinette, the second-born, and Victorine, the sixth-born daughter. Félicie, the third-born, married Frédéric Vermenouze, originating from a nonpropertied family, but who was probably a temporary migrant to Spain. Joséphine, the fourth-born daughter, died at a young age, and Marie-Louise, the fifth-born, who inherited the family house, married Firmin Mager, a temporary migrant to Spain. The single daughter of the seventh generation married a migrant to Lillo, in the province of Toledo.

This detailed family reconstitution highlights patterns of female inheritance and male migration outlined earlier. All Messac heirs who had temporarily lived in Spain were able to return to the village with sufficient savings to provide a dowry. In this way they could marry into a propertied family and maintain their status in the community. Correspondingly, heiresses married Cantal men who had also temporarily migrated to Spain and returned to the village with sufficient savings to compensate the noninheriting siblings. As for those who were excluded, the men temporarily migrated to Spain to save enough money to settle comfortably as property owners in the village. All had ties with the Chinchón Company or other profitable businesses in Spain. This system not only secured economic stability and status for heirs, heiresses, and their spouses, but also allowed returning male migrants to settle in the village even if they did not inherit property or marry heiresses. Celibacy commonly awaited those women who did not inherit and could not marry returning migrants. For the whole system to work, men had to migrate: they were the only ones able to work in Spain and save sufficient money, which, on their return, recirculated within the village. Temporary migration was therefore perceived to be the only way to inherit and marry an heir or an heiress. If families

were unable to provide a dowry to each of the children, men and women
were forced to remain single in the family house or emigrate permanently.

Besides inheritance patterns, there were many lineage links between
families from one generation to the next and between Cantal and Spain.
The fifth generation of the Messac house, in which many heirs and *cadets*
intermarried with those from other households and associated in businesses with Cantal men, best demonstrates trends of marital endogamy
and homogamy. There were discrepancies at times from one generation
to the next. Indeed, among the third generation of the Messac house, 8 out
of 10 descendants were comfortably settled. Two daughters remained single, and all the sons who had temporarily migrated to Spain returned
with their savings and married heiresses. By contrast, in the fourth generation it appears that none of the children established himself or herself
in Cantal. The only exception was the heiress who married a temporary
migrant who had made enough money to restore the family's fortunes.
As none of her siblings had migrated to Spain, none were able to amass
a dowry, and therefore none managed to marry into a propertied family.

Why was the fourth generation thus unable to settle comfortably? In
part the answer lies in less-favorable economic conditions. From the middle of the eighteenth until the middle of the nineteenth century, heirs' and
heiresses' spouses often originated from the same houses, from related
houses, or from associated houses. These were the golden years, when
migration from Cantal to Spain was lucrative. There were, however, low
points that were not necessarily connected to family failures but linked
more to the transitional period of the late eighteenth and early nineteenth
century characterized by wars between France and Spain, most notably
between 1808 and 1814. Migration to Spain had probably slowed even
before 1808, when minor conflicts between France and Spain began. Yet
many soon found their way back to Spain, especially the agricultural day
laborers from Crandelles who were faithful traders in the region around
Madrid and Toledo. Family and business ties, as well as intermarriages,
were the key factors to explain such trends.

## CONCLUSION

This study has demonstrated the clear links that existed between migration, inheritance, and welfare that encompassed not only those who
inherited directly but also those who benefited in other ways, notably
through compensation in return for renouncing their share of the family
wealth. Because the household economy of Cantal was family based and
therefore evolved within lineage networks, life chances for children differed from the start, not merely among families with different amounts of
wealth but also among heirs who inherited the family house and those
who did not. Noninheriting descendants from wealthy houses received

sufficient compensation for their share of the inheritance, higher than was needed to invest in a prosperous commercial business, such as the Chinchón Company. This compensation amounted to the dowry that noble families gathered to settle their *cadet* sons as army officers and that other families used in similar fashion to establish their children in different occupations. For noninheriting daughters, the dowry provided an opportunity to negotiate advantageous marriages, often with men who had migrated and thereby amassed a degree of wealth. By contrast, those who received much smaller compensation found economic success, not to mention marriage itself, more elusive.

In the case of the High Auvergne, migration was the crux around which the system revolved. In a resource-poor economy, it allowed men to amass sufficient income from external sources and on their return, through marriage, to ensure continuity of the family enterprise. In the absence of men, women often took on responsibility for the household, in return for which they were chosen to inherit the family house and property. Migration, therefore, allowed women the opportunity to acquire wealth through inheritance and thereby to secure an advantageous marriage. Furthermore, an heiress's marriage with a returning migrant provided noninheriting siblings with the cash necessary to collect a dowry and marry out, the goal being to secure them status within a propertied household and keep the house and land intact and viable. Compensation for noninheriting members of the household, therefore, also depended directly on the nexus of migration and inheritance. Wealth accumulated while in Spain was probably smaller than the value of their inheritance share and was therefore less than that inherited by the main heir. However, the analysis of family reconstitution showed that even though unmarried *cadets* remained in the family house and worked on the property as laborers, as potential heirs they nevertheless enjoyed a higher status than that of a day laborer. Families tried to compensate *cadets* by encouraging them to migrate to Spain and financing their settlement as businessmen there. On their return they also endeavored to settle their descendants comfortably, secured others with a decent retirement, and reduced economic uncertainties for all as well as they could. These aspirations were not necessarily different from other French families during the period, but the strategies used to achieve these objectives differed, depending on local economic circumstances, and in the case of the High Auvergne resulted in an explicitly gendered pattern of inheritance. Indeed, female single inheritance and male temporary migration to Spain functioned together to prevent partition while at the same time sustain cultural continuity and economic stability.

**Key to Appendices 3.1–3.7**

Appendices 3.1–3.7 show patterns of succession in the seven houses studied.
Note: The first row gives the approximate date of marriage. Children are listed
according to their birth rank.

| | Heiress | | Heir |
|---|---|---|---|

|  |  |
|---|---|
| ▲ | Heir |
| △ | Son |
| ● | Heiress |
| ○ | Daughter |
| ⟨ | Migrant to Spain |
| ⟩ | Migrant spouse to Spain |
| ☿ | Nephew |
| ■ | Nun or priest |
| † | died young |

Appendix 3.1
The Nicques House: Mas Marty, Crandelles

| 1682 | 1716 | 1732 | 1756 | 1781 | 1807 | 1847 | 1871 |
|---|---|---|---|---|---|---|---|
| Marie GRANDCAM 1658–1745 | Antoine PELISSIER 1686–1738 | Jeanne PELISSIER 1720–1813 | Jeanne Marie CRUEGHE 1743–1779 | Raymond VERMENOUZE 1732–1811 | Marie Rose VERMENOUZE 1789–1847 | Antoine Maurice LAVEISSIERE 1819–1891 | Noémie LAVEISSIERE 1847–1922 |
| ⌣ | ⌣ | ⌣ | ⌣ | ⌣ | ⌣ | ⌣ | ⌣ |
| Jean PELISSIER | Jeanne CROS | Jean CRUEGHE | Raymond VERMENOUZE | Marie CONTHE | Jean Pierre LAVEISSIERE | Caroline VERMENOUZE | Alphonse VERMENOUZE |
| Incomplete | Incomplete | Incomplete | sp | | | | |
| ▲x⟨ | ●⟩ | ●⟩ | | ○⟩ △ ○† △⟨x ●⟩ ○x ○x △† △† △⟨ ○ | ○■ △⟨ △⟨ △■ ○ ▲⟨x △† ○■ | ●⟩ ○x ○⟩ △⟨ | △ ▲x |

**Appendix 3.2**
**The Messac House: Crandelles**

| 1696 | 1726 | 1751 | 1783 | 1826 | 1854 | 1884 |
|---|---|---|---|---|---|---|
| Jeanne GELY 1673–1764 | Jean VERMENOUZE 1699–1748 | Pierre VERMENOUZE 1727–an XII | Jeanne Marie VERMENOUZE 1761–1837 | Jeanne Marie MAISONOBE 1796–1877 | Amédée MAISONOBE 1829–1894 | Marie Louise MAISONOBE 1862–1886 |
| Pierre VERMENOUZE | Jeanne Marie LESCURE | Marie CRUEGHE | François MAISONOBE | Jean Ambroise MAISONOBE | Justine LAVEISSIERE | Firmin MAGER |
| Incomplete | Incomplete | | | | | |

**Appendix 3.3**
**The Rigou House: Passefons, Crandelles**

| 1681 | 21 April 1711 | 12 July 1741 | 16 May 1752 | 14 July 1767 | 26 prai. An X | 27 Jan 1836 | 30 June 1873 |
|---|---|---|---|---|---|---|---|
| Antoine BURG 1660– | Jeanne BURG 1697–1747 | Marie BOUSSAC 1723–1774 | | Marguerite CRUEGHE 1753–1823 | Jeanne VERMENOUZE 1775–1863 | François VERMENOUZE 1805–1904 | Antoine VERMENOUZE 1840–1922 |
| Catherine LESPINAT | Antoine BOUSSAC | Antoine CRUEGHE | Pierre CRUEGHE | Géraud VERMENOUZE | Jean Baptiste VERMENOUZE | Jeanne. Marie LAVEISSIERE | Emilie CAUMEL |
| Incomplete ●x | ox Δx Δ ●x o o Δ | ox | ●) Δ ox o† | o† o† ●) o) o■ Δ⟨) Δ Δ† Δ⟨x Δ⟨ Δ⟨x o† Δ⟨x | ◄⟨x Δ⟨x Δ† Δ† | Δ⟨ o† o ◄⟨x Δ⟨x ox Δ⟨x o† | ●x |

64

**Appendix 3.4**
**The Sanhes House: Leyritz, Crandelles**

| 31 Jan 1696 | 26 Nov 1715 | 21 May 1744 | 21 June 1768 | 16 br. An XI | 5 Oct 1824 | 6 Nov 1844 | 5 June 1878 |
|---|---|---|---|---|---|---|---|
| Antoine SAINT CIRGUES 1665–1733 | Marguerite SAINT CIRGUES 1697–1770 | Antoine CRUEGHE 1717–an VII | Pierre CRUEGHE 1745–1816 | Jeanne CRUEGHE 1781–an XII | Marie Emilie LINTILHAC 1804–1841 | Marie Mélanie VERMENOUZE 1825–1891 | Anne Louise LAPARRA 1856–1950 |
| Marie LIMANHES | Pierre CRUEGHE | Marianne ROQUES | Marie VERNIOLES | Pierre LINTILHAC | Jean VERMENOUZE | Alexandre LAPARRA | Jean VERMENOUZE |

65

**Appendix 3.5**
**The Oustalniol House: L'Hôpital, Saint-Paul-des-Landes**

| 1685 | 26 June 1707 | 16 May 1736 | 10 July 1759 | 8 July 1783 | 5 August 1825 | 28 Sep 1862 | 20 Oct 1899 |
|---|---|---|---|---|---|---|---|
| Géraud LAPARRA | Isabelle LAPARRA | Jeanne DELZORS 1711–1756 | Marie COLIS 1739–1791 | Géraud JAMMES 1763– | Marguerite JAMMES 1800–1862 | François OUSTALNIOL 1834–1905 | Justine OUSTALNIOL 1871–1957 |
| Jeanne LINTILHAC | Pierre DELZORS | Géraud COLIS | Jean Antoine JAMMES | Delphine ROCHET | Barthélémy OUSTALNIOL | Marie PRUNET | Joseph VIDAL |

Appendix 3.6
The Montin-Bas House: La Ségalassière

| 1696 | 1730 | 1765 | 1799 | 1831 | 1875 | 1897 |
|---|---|---|---|---|---|---|
| Jean PICARD 1678–1743 | Pierre PICARD 1697–1744 | Toinette PICARD 1737–1782 | Catherine FOURCES 1772–1845 | Jean SERRES 1806–1883 | Baptiste SERRES 1837–1877 | Félicie SERRES 1876– |
| Marguerite MAS | Anne LAVIALLE | Guillaume FOURCES | Jean SERRES | Marguerite BARRIERE | Marguerite BRUNHES | Louis CLAMAGIRAND |
| Incomplete ▲ | △〈　○　●x　○　○　○x | △　△　△　●x　△†　△†　○　○† | ○x　△†　○†　△†　▲x　△†　△†　△〈x | △　○x　▲x　△x　△x　△x　○x | ● | ○†　● )　△　○x　△x　○x |

**Appendix 3.7**
**The Nozières House: Le Ribeyrès, Pers**

| 1700 | 1726 | 1756 | 1772 | 1804 | 1835 | 1863 | 1885 |
|---|---|---|---|---|---|---|---|
| Catherine MALRAS 1684–1724 | Jeanne MOULES 1700–1770 | Marie MONTINS 1726–1775 | Catherine GAZALS 1757–1823 | François FERES 1777–1848 | Jean FERES 1806–1880 | Marie FERES 1841–1894 | Pauline CARRIERE 1864–1911 |
| Pierre MOULES | Jean MONTINS | Jean GAZALS | Jean FERES | Anne DEVEZ | Catherine BADUEL | Bernard CARRIERE | François NOZIERES |
| ⌣ | | | | | | ⌣ | ⌣ |
| Incomplete | ●x | ●x | ○ | ▲⟨x | △⟨x | ●) | △⟨ |
| ●x | ○† | ○x | ρ | ○ | ●) | ○ | ○ |
| | △ | ρ⟨ | ρ⟨ | △⟨ | | △ | △⟨x |
| | ○ | | ▲x | △⟨ | | △ | △† |
| | ○ | | ○ | △⟨ | | ○) | ○† |
| | △ | | △ | △⟨x | | | ○⟨ |
| | △ | | ○x | △⟨ | | | △† |
| | | | | △⟨ | | | ●x |
| | | | | △⟨ | | | ○) |

## NOTES

I am grateful to Elisabeth Traissac, Pierre Vermenouze, Louis Nozières, Urbain Oustalniol, and Bernard Maury for their help in providing source material.

1. For a general discussion see Rose Duroux, *Les Auvergnats de Castille: Renaissance et mort d'une migration au XIXe siècle* (Clermont-Ferrand: Publications de la Faculté des Lettres et Sciences Humaines de l'Université Blaise-Pascal, 1992). For Béarn and the Baronnies see Antoinette Fauve-Chamoux, "Les frontières de l'autorégulation paysanne: Croissance et famille-souche," *Revue de la Bibliothèque nationale* 50 (1993): 38–47; Antoinette Fauve-Chamoux, "Les structures familiales au royaume des familles-souches: Esparros," *Annales Economies, Sociétés, Civilisations* XXXIX (1984): 514–28; and Antoinette Fauve-Chamoux, "Household Forms and Living Standards in Preindustrial France: From Models to Realities," *Journal of Family History* 18 (1993): 135–56. See also Georges Augustins and Rolande Bonnain, *Les Baronnies des Pyrénées, vol. 1: Maisons, mode de vie, société* (Paris: Ed. de l'Ecole des Hautes Etudes en Sciences Sociales, 1982) and Georges Augustins, Rolande. Bonnain, Yves Péron, and Gilles Sautter, *Les Baronnies des Pyrénées, vol. 2: Maisons, espace, famille* (Paris: Ed. de l'Ecole des Hautes Etudes en Sciences Sociales, 1986). On the Basque country see Marie-Pierre Arrizabalaga, "The Stem Family in the French Basque Country: Sare in the Nineteenth Century," *Journal of Family History* 22 (1997): 50–69 and Marie-Pierre Arrizabalaga, "Female Primogeniture in the French Basque Country," in *The Logic of Female Succession: Rethinking Patriarchy and Patrilineality in Global and Historical Perspective*, International Research Symposium Proceeding, No. 19 (Kyoto: International Research Center for Japanese Studies, 2003).

2. On the geography of the stem family in France, see Jean Yver, *Essai de géographie coutumière: Egalité entre héritiers et exclusion des enfants dotés* (Paris: Sirey, 1966); Jacques Poumarède, *Les Successions dans le Sud-Ouest de la France au Moyen Age* (Paris: Presses Universitaires de France, 1972); Anne Zink, *L'héritier de la maison: Géographie coutumière du Sud-Ouest de la France sous l'Ancien Régime* (Paris: Ecole des Hautes Etudes en Sciences Sociales, 1993); Bernard Derouet, "Pratiques successorales et rapport à la terre: Les sociétés paysannes d'Ancien Régime," *Annales Economies, Sociétés, Civilisations* XLIV (1989): 173–206; and Pierre Lamaison, "La diversité des modes de transmission: une géographie tenace," *Etudes Rurales* 110–12 (1988): 119–75.

3. The inland territory of France known as the Massif Central is divided into provinces, one of which is the Auvergne, consisting of two distinct parts, the High and Low Auvergne. With the French Revolution, the High Auvergne became a *département* called Cantal.

4. Rose Duroux, *Les Auvergnats de Castille: Renaissance et mort d'une migration au XIXe siècle* (Clermont-Ferrand: Publications de la Faculté des Lettres et Sciences Humaines de l'Université Blaise-Pascal, 1992), chapter 5.

5. The analysis is based on 1,327 notary acts signed by Auvergnats (immigrants from Auvergne or Cantal) in the French Consulate in Madrid, AMAE, Paris (1819–1907). The documents include 961 proxies, 119 obligations, 40 inheritance donations and sales, 33 identity certificates, 30 marriage agreements, and 4 mutual donations. Proxies concern a variety of acts and in some cases include inheritance donations and sales.

6. Pierre Lamaison, "La diversité des modes de transmission: une géographie tenace," *Etudes Rurales* 110–12 (1988): 136; Guillaume-Michel Chabrol, *Coutumes générales et locales de la province d'Auvergne,* vol. I and II (Riom: Dégouttes, 1784) vol. IX; and Abel Poitrineau, "Institutions et pratiques successorales en Auvergne et en Limousin sous l'Ancien Régime," *Etudes Rurales* 110–12 (1988): 31–43.

7. This is translated from the French: "Le patrimoine est considéré comme une entité qui doit se survivre identique à elle-même, où le paysan se perçoit, somme toute, comme servant un patrimoine dont il est dépositaire." See Diane Gervais, "La construction du consensus familial dans les successions inégalitaires du Lot au XIXe siècle," in *Transmettre, hériter, succéder: la reproduction familiale en milieu rural, France-Québec, XVIIIe–XXe siècles,* ed. Rolande Bonnain, Gérard Bouchard, and Joseph Goy (Lyon-Paris-Villeurbanne: Presses Universitaires de Lyon, 1992), 266.

8. Rose Duroux, "The Temporary Migration of Males and the Power of Females in a Stem-Family Society: the Case of Nineteenth-Century Auvergne," *History of the Family* 6 (2001): 33–49.

9. On this argument, see Lamaison, "La diversité des modes de transmission," 143.

10. On the traditional customs of the Auvergne, see Chabrol, *Coutumes générales,* vol. IX. The inheritance customs described by Chabrol favored the firstborn son.

11. For the Basque country see Marie-Pierre Arrizabalaga, "The stem family in the French Basque Country" and Arrizabalaga, "Female primogeniture in the French Basque Country." For the Pyrénées, Antoinette Fauve-Chamoux found only 20 percent of cases of property transmission through the female line, compared with the Soule valley where, in some cases, the figure was 40 percent. See Fauve-Chamoux, "Les frontières de l'auto-régulation paysanne," 41. In the Alpes de Haute-Provence this female inheritance was unknown. No father in Provence allowed a son-in-law to enter the family house when he had a firstborn or *cadet* son. See Alain Collomp, *La Maison du père: Famille et village en Haute-Provence aux XVIIe et XVIIIe siècles* (Paris: Presses Universitaires de France, 1983).

12. The term *original* is translated directly from the French as it appears in the family's documents.

13. This average is based on the study of 43 complete households, comprising 234 adults.

14. It is likely that most of them probably married an heir and moved into a propertied household, although the data do not allow this to be verified.

15. Gérard Bouchard, John A. Dickinson, and Joseph Goy, eds., *Les exclus de la terre en France et au Québec, XVIIe–XXe siècles: La reproduction familiale dans la différence* (Sillery: Septentrion, 1998) and Pierre Bourdieu, "Célibat et condition paysanne," *Etudes Rurales* 5–6 (1962): 32–135.

16. This is translated from the original French: "Si vous voulés avoir la bonté de me faire passer une some de 200 livres ou du moin 150 sur mes drois légitimaires je vous en sentiré bon gré [. . .]; cy je népas quéque secour de vous dans la situation ou je me truve je serois forcé avendre mais drois légitimaires a un quéqun pour ce quy me voudron donér et je ne voudrois pas vous faire cet outrage." This letter was found among the papers that belonged to Elisabeth Traissac, part of the Malbert household in Saint-Santin-Cantalès. This correspondence is unusual in

view of the fact that families regularly lost contact with *cadets* who had settled in Spain.

17. 4,000 francs was required in order to own a share in Chinchón Company.

18. The bakery known as the Tahona was located at number 6 Horno de la Mata street and was rented to two emigrants from Cantal, Pierre Valadou and Jean Causse. The information is provided in the notary acts of 1873, 1887, and various others from the Archives of the French Consulate in Madrid, AMAE, Paris.

# CHAPTER 4

# Headship Succession and Retirement in South Bohemia, 1640–1840

*Hermann Zeitlhofer*

## INTRODUCTION

This chapter deals with patterns of headship succession and retirement arrangements in households in the rural community of Kapličky in South Bohemia from the mid-seventeenth to the mid-nineteenth centuries. It is particularly concerned with the ways in which headship succession and retirement formed part of a strategy of family welfare provision. Accordingly, the chapter analyzes how the system of transmitting land and houses worked as a factor in the exchange of property rights and social status. It also considers the ways in which such systems of transmission enabled the redistribution of wealth among family members. Historical discussions of the transmission of headship in central Europe have been rare, although general consideration of inheritance and intergenerational wealth transfers have been more common. Notably, preindustrial societies of continental Europe have been described as familistic societies, where houses and land were handed down from one generation to another within the family. This meant that real estate was almost exclusively acquired through inheritance and was not accumulated on the market.[1] Different forms of real estate transmission are usually equated with different modes of inheritance. The assumed dichotomy between partible and impartible inheritance is considered to be particularly important in this context. These two systems of inheritance are seen as giving rise to particular demographic, social, and economic conditions. It was assumed, for instance, that in areas where the impartible system predominated, there was a marked social polarization because one child always received the majority of the devolved family wealth. Furthermore, it has been suggested that such a system of property transmission tended to retard population growth by increasing the mean age of first marriage—presumptive heirs had to postpone their marriages until the time of transmission. It is also argued that impartible inheritance encouraged the permanent emigration of those children who had no prospect of inheriting land. In contrast, partible inheritance regions have been regarded as places where strong population increase was likely. The equal portioning of wealth enabled more children to marry and reproduce. However, it is also often posited that the strict division of land leads to economically unviable holdings, providing an important incentive for seasonal migration.[2]

In German-language research, impartible inheritance is, for the most part, equated with the so-called *Anerbenrecht*. This was a legal form essentially codified in the nineteenth century. However, all forms of handing down the land undivided throughout the early modern period are also called *Anerbenrecht*.[3] The term denotes a legally established preference for one child compared with his or her siblings. The preferred heir would inherit the family house and all the land. Usually the choice of the heir (*Anerbe*) was already determined by the birth rank of a child.[4] It is assumed that the siblings of the heir would either be disinherited or receive only small gifts of money, usually at marriage. Many authors emphasize that because of their lesser means, siblings' social status would decline and they were more likely to become part of the rural poor.[5] Some believe that there was an "iron chain between inheritance and reproduction" in the early modern period, as siblings who did not acquire land through inheritance had to remain in permanent celibacy.[6]

In fact, to apply the term *Anerbenrecht* to the early modern period is often an anachronism, because in many regions this legal norm was only implemented in the nineteenth or even the twentieth century.[7] In numerous areas of central Europe, even in the eighteenth century, there was, in fact, no formal law of inheritance. Instead, the practice of property transmission was determined by local norms and customs. These very often did not intend for one child to be given preferential treatment. Moreover, some empirical studies have shown that partible and impartible systems could have quite similar social and demographic consequences. Cole and Wolf, for example, who studied two neighboring villages in northern Italy, one with a partible and one with an impartible inheritance system, found that marriage patterns and the size of holdings were similar in both communities. In these places, environmental constraints made it imperative to avoid the division of the estate in order to retain holdings of viable size.[8] Other recent studies have shown the importance of examining wider individual and family strategies of property transmission and succession rather than focusing solely on the outcomes of inheritance. Peasants were not captives of the law, and legal rules of property transfer were often no more than an object for discussion.[9]

In many regions of Europe with impartible transmission systems, headship succession frequently took place *inter vivos*, combined with a retirement contract for the former proprietors.[10] Contractual retirement was closely tied to the transmission process because former proprietors still retained certain rights, such as lifelong lodging on the holding. Retirement arrangements settled the question of who would have continued access to the resources of the house, and to what extent. Only those who owned a house were able to conclude a retirement contract. The main purpose and function of the retirement institution in premodern rural societies is usually seen as old-age support for the former proprietors. These former peasants are regarded as one of a small group of people who in preindustrial societies enjoyed a period of work-free independence in the later stages of their life. Because this involved a heavy financial burden, it was thought that only wealthy farm households could afford such arrangements.[11] Several studies of rural Austrian parishes from the seventeenth to the nineteenth century suggested that these retirement arrangements, in fact, rarely happened.[12] They did not appear to be very common prior to the so-called agrarian revolution at the start of the nineteenth century.[13]

This chapter will discuss the extent to which this system of retirement operated in South Bohemia. Like other eastern-central European countries, Bohemia was characterized from the late sixteenth century onward, and especially after the Thirty Years' War, by an agrarian system often described as "manorial lordship," "feudal seigneurie," or "second serfdom." In the early modern period the country was divided into territorially compact estates, most of which consisted of a few dozen villages and usually comprised between 1,000 and 10,000 inhabitants. The landlords demanded that their serfs provide a weekly corvée or service, known as the *robot*. Under this system landlords also restricted the mobility and legal rights of their serfs.[14] The predominant assumption was that in territories with second serfdom, landlords controlled the transmission of property and could arbitrarily dismiss peasant landholders or move them from one farmstead to another. It was also assumed that on reaching retirement they could force peasants to hand over their farmsteads.[15] In this context it was argued that feudal landlords who wished to ensure that the farm remained in capable hands forced widowed owners, especially women, to either quickly remarry or sell the farmstead.[16] Using evidence from South Bohemia it is useful to question these assumptions.

## THE PARISH OF KAPLIČKY

The small Bohemian parish of Kaplička belonged to the estate of the Cistercian monastery of Vyšší Brod and was located in a hilly and richly

**Figure 4.1**
**Map of Bohemia**

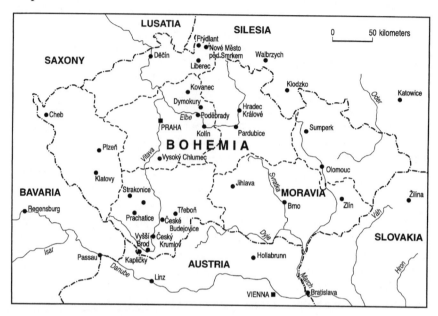

wooded region to the south, close to the Austrian border (Figure 4.1). The regional economy was based on a range of activities, with cattle breeding more important than grain growing. Different forms of woodworking such as shingle making, flax-processing, and spinning provided extra income for nearly every house in the parish.[17] At the start of the eighteenth century there were about 800 inhabitants rising to around 1,300 in 1860, who lived in 16 small villages. As elsewhere in Bohemia, the land was divided into demesne and serf land, with the landlords being supra-owners (*dominium directum*) of the peasants' landed property (*dominium utile*). The peasant holding comprised an indivisible unity of rights to a house, land, and use of the commons. This unity stemmed from the landlords' interest in maintaining the viability of peasant farmsteads as a means of providing manorial income. Whereas arable land was generally owned by individuals, most of the pastures belonged to the village. From the late sixteenth century these peasant holdings were freely inheritable and could be sold.[18] Despite the deterioration in the social and judicial status of peasants during the so-called second serfdom, strong tenancy rights (*emphyteuse*) survived in Bohemia.[19] This was quite different from many other regions of eastern Europe where second serfdom went hand in hand with the spread of various forms of insecure tenancy rights and where property law remained largely uncodified.[20]

Between the mid-seventeenth and the mid-nineteenth century the social structure of the parish of Kapličky underwent a remarkable change: in 1651 there were 70 families that owned a house or land together with 33 landless married couples who were lodgers.[21] The number of households increased considerably to 119 by 1840, growing particularly rapidly between 1680 and 1710 and during the 1780s. These new households were established either on demesne, communal, or peasant land but, in view of the strict indivisibility of peasant holdings, were virtually landless.[22] This is why the number of families owning no real estate remained high: in 1783, 43 out of a total of 142 families were landless lodgers.[23] While the number of landless households increased, the number of farmsteads of sufficient size remained stable. The tax roll of 1654 shows that the property sizes of 62 "landed" houses ranged from 2 to 10 hectares of arable land, while 5 "land-poor" holdings had less than 1 hectare.[24] The number of these landed houses remained constant at least until the early nineteenth century.[25]

This research is mainly based on nominal record linkage for the parish of Kapličky, using evidence gathered from land registers listing the transfers of land and houses from the late sixteenth century onward.[26] For the period from 1637 to 1848 they allow the reconstruction of a complete series of all property owners for each house in the parish. This information was linked with a family reconstitution, compiled in the nineteenth century by the former landlords, the Cistercian monks of Vyšší Brod.[27] The family reconstitution comprises all couples married from the early 1640s onward. Usually there was a link to the families of origin of both partners, and although sometimes details are missing for the start or end of the marriage, there is at least some information on the kin relations of all house owners born in the parish.[28] Additional sources, such as tax rolls and a census list, were also used. Finally, the data were linked with retirement contracts for the period between 1699 and 1738, the period for which the contracts themselves have been preserved.[29]

## THE PROPERTY TRANSMISSION SYSTEM IN SOUTH BOHEMIA

In the process of property transfer in Kapličky, the guiding principle was the strict indivisibility of peasant farmland.[30] Although such a system could in theory be termed impartible inheritance, in Kapličky, as in many regions of Bohemia, property transfer usually involved the sale and purchase of land.[31] The purchase was usually made by installments over several years, regardless of whether the purchaser was a stranger or a member of the family. Those heirs who did not inherit land received an equal share of the purchase price. For example, in 1696 Mathias Kern bought the family house from his widowed mother for 70 guilders. Because he had three siblings—Hans, Rosina, and Margareth—the purchase price was divided into fifths so that every member of the family, including his mother, received 14 guilders. Mathias's sisters received their share immediately; his brother Hans received his share in installments in 1701 and 1702; and his mother was paid her share in 1704.[32]

Despite the indivisibility of land per se, payments in lieu of ownership meant that in practice, property transmission in South Bohemia was relatively egalitarian. This situation continued unchanged from the late sixteenth to the early nineteenth century. Through the medium of the land market, an impartible system of inheritance was in theory made partible in a way that provided for the future well-being of all family members. However, this could be called egalitarian only if the purchase price paid to siblings represented the "real" market value of the property, a difficult issue to address.[33] Nor was this system of property transmission unique. In other parts of central Europe, impartibility meant nothing more than the fact that the house and the farmland formed an indivisible economic unit. Although only one successor might have taken over the farm, the other siblings were compensated with varying amounts of cash.[34]

Strictly speaking, therefore, headship succession should not be called *Anerbenrecht* because no child was preferred to the others. As studies of headship succession have shown, the successor did not necessarily have to be a biological child of the former proprietor. Quite frequently, for example, stepsons, foster children, or non-kin succeeded as household head.[35] Indeed, headship succession should not even be regarded as a form of inheritance. According to Jack Goody, the transmission of farmstead headships represents a transfer of an office and analytically can be separated from other forms of property devolution.[36] In Kapličky this distinction meant, for example, that none of the children automatically had claims on the house and land itself but had a right to a share of the value. This is a key issue to consider when distinguishing inheritance from headship succession.

## PATTERNS OF HEADSHIP SUCCESSION IN KAPLIČKY

In Kapličky, as Table 4.1 shows, headship succession was never restricted to members of the nuclear family alone. The successor could be a child of the former owner, another relative by blood or affinity, or a non-kin without any previous connection to the farmstead. However, during the early modern period there were considerable changes to the pattern of succession, especially during the early eighteenth century. For this reason Table 4.1 is divided into two periods: from 1651 to 1720 and from 1721 to 1840.

In the earlier period the mean duration of possession was relatively

**Table 4.1**
**Headship Successors in Kapličky, 1651–1840**

| New owner | Transfers of landed houses | | | | Transfers of land-poor houses | | | |
|---|---|---|---|---|---|---|---|---|
| | 1651–1720 | | 1721–1840 | | 1651–1750 | | 1721–1840 | |
| | n | % | n | % | n | % | n | % |
| Son | 67 | 36.4 | 162 | 64.5 | 15 | 23.8 | 95 | 54.0 |
| Son-in-law | 23 | 12.5 | 17 | 6.8 | 12 | 19.0 | 21 | 11.9 |
| Widow 2nd marr. | 24 | 13.0 | 23 | 9.2 | 11 | 17.5 | 18 | 10.2 |
| Stepson | 0 | 0.0 | 14 | 5.6 | 0 | 0.0 | 5 | 2.8 |
| Other kin | 14 | 7.6 | 10 | 4.0 | 4 | 6.4 | 8 | 4.7 |
| Unrelated* | 56 | 30.4 | 25 | 10.0 | 20 | 31.7 | 29 | 16.5 |
| Total | 184 | 100.0 | 251 | 100.0 | 63 | 100.0 | 176 | 100.0 |

\* or unknown relationship

Sources: SOA Třeboň, Sbírka jihočeskych matrik, Farní úřad Kapličky č. 9; fond C Vyšší Brod, Pozemková kniha č. 453, č. 465, č. 475, č. 479 and č. 480.

short: in half the cases less than 20 years, and in a quarter, less than 10 years. After 1720 the period of headship was longer than 30 years in around half the cases. Between 1651 and 1720, around half of all purchase contracts occurred between non-kin or distant relatives, suggesting that the land-family bond was weak. Children became household heads in less than 40 percent of cases, indicating that the land market was not dominated by kinship networks. During the second half of the seventeenth century, the rise of a more active land market meant that there was greater mobility of house ownership, and it was not uncommon even for young people to become heads of households.[37] According to a census in 1651 of the villages surrounding Vyšší Brod, more than a third of males in the 20–24 age group were household heads.[38] In the late eighteenth century, however, the market was more restricted, and hardly any landless lodgers or people from outside the parish bought houses or farmsteads.[39]

Another aspect of this first period from 1651 to 1720 was that sales to non-kin occurred frequently, even when children of the former householders were alive. In several cases sons-in-law or more distant relatives were preferred to sons as successors. In other instances widows remarried before their children reached legal adulthood (25 years), and as a consequence such children lost their right to remain in the house, though not their share of the inheritance.

From the end of the seventeenth century intrafamilial property transfers increased. Transfers from father to son became the dominant pattern, and between 1800 and 1840 this was the case in three out of four transmissions.

This pattern was true not only for the wealthier peasant farmsteads but also for land-poor houses. In Kapličky the high level of intrafamilial transfers among land-poor houses can be explained by the fact that many newly built houses were not entirely landless but came with rights to lease land.[40] They often included at least one meadow and a cow, which the new owners could hand down to their successors. However, despite the growing strength of the land-family bond, headship succession never became an entirely intrafamilial affair.[41] Other forms of transmission always remained possible.

Given the complexities of this system of transmission, assumptions about familistic European societies with immobile peasants managing "an ancestral estate that must . . . be handed down intact to descendants" cannot be applied to every period and for all regions of early modern central Europe.[42] In Kapličky the importance of family continuity occurred later than elsewhere. The second half of the seventeenth century is usually presumed to be an exceptional period because of the impact of the Thirty Years' War. However, the consequences of the war on the land market were quite modest. Compared with other regions of Bohemia, in the south of the country relatively few farms were destroyed.[43] The trend toward family continuity of ownership suggests that serfs were free to handle the succession of property without manorial interference, a result of their strong tenant rights. Landlords' roles in the region were limited to the formal supervision of headship transfer, and in only 5 out of more than 700 contracts is there any evidence of their intervention.[44]

## GENDER ASPECTS OF PROPERTY TRANSMISSION

In Bohemia female property rights followed the central and western European pattern rather than that of eastern Europe, where land was transferred on the basis of agnatic kinship ties alone.[45] After the death of her husband, it was possible for a widow to run the farmstead on her own. There is no evidence to show that landlords exerted pressure to force such women to hand over the farm or remarry immediately. But even if widows ran the farm for several years, they were by no means automatically recorded in the land register as the formal owner. For this reason it is often only through family reconstitution rather than from legal records that it can be shown that widows ran the farmstead after their husband's death. It was also possible for farmsteads to be transmitted to daughters. However, in such instances the son-in-law would have been recorded in the land registers as the new head because only widowed women were considered legally competent.[46] In Bohemia this changed in 1791, when reform of the law enabled women to own real estate.[47] From the early nineteenth century, this change is reflected in the Kapličky land registers, where in many cases both partners were recorded as owners of the property.

Despite various legal changes over the period under consideration, sons were preferred to daughters as successors to their parents. Table 4.1 indicates that this preference became more marked over time, suggesting that custom and ideology, rather than the law, increasingly marginalized women as successors.[48] However, male succession was not always followed. Sometimes the property was transferred to a daughter and son-in-law even when she had one or more brothers. Exceptions notwithstanding, most of these cases can be explained by the fact that the daughter was old enough to marry, whereas her brothers were far too young to run the farm.

Unlike in other parts of central Europe, widows in this region had the right to remarry and to hand over the farm to their second husband.[49] In line with the growing emphasis on family continuity, this pattern began to change. At the beginning of the eighteenth century a new status of "interim proprietor" appeared, whereby headship succession by second husbands of remarrying widows was confined to a limited period of time, usually between 15 and 18 years. This situation was most common where children of the first marriage were too young to take over the farm. On their coming of age the farm had to be transferred to the child in question, in return for which the second husband was guaranteed support for the period of his retirement. For this reason from the early eighteenth century we find stepsons as headship successors. In the seventeenth century there were no such cases because after a widow's remarriage, her children from the previous relationship usually lost their claims to succession.

As a whole, during the eighteenth century it was more likely for a widow to retire after the death of her spouse than to run a farmstead independently or to remarry, whereas the opposite was true for men.[50] Prior to 1800, headship successions through remarriages of widows amounted to about 10 to 13 percent of all successions, but declined thereafter to just over 4 percent. Between 1721 and 1738, for example, 18 widows formally retired whereas very few remarried.[51]

Gender was therefore one of the crucial criteria of choosing a successor, but it was not necessarily an important factor in understanding how wealth from peasant farmsteads was redistributed within the family. As well as their equal share of the purchase price, daughters sometimes received additional gifts such as clothes, flax, or a cow, often as a marriage portion. In 1769, for example, when Johannes Lackinger bought the peasant farmstead from his widowed mother-in-law, it was noted that Maria, his sister-in-law, should receive a calf by the time of her marriage in addition to her portion of the purchase price of 143 guilders.[52] The principles of the transmission of real property in this region—via purchase and sale and through an equal division of claims between both male and female siblings—made it comparatively easy for those children who were not headship successors to establish their own families and households. Many

**Table 4.2**
**Proportion of the 45–49 Age Group Who Were Married in Estate and Parish of Vyšší Brod**

| | | Men | | | Women | | |
|---|---|---|---|---|---|---|---|
| | | Married | Single or widowed | Total | Married | Single or widowed | Total |
| Location | Year | % | % | n | % | % | n |
| Estate | 1651 | 90.0 | 10.0 | 40 | 60.0 | 40.0 | 20 |
| Parish | 1798 | 95.2 | 4.8 | 21 | 70.0 | 40.0 | 30 |

Note: In some cases the sources do not clearly distinguish between single and widowed people. The figures for 1651 include Kapličky and two other parishes in the Vyšší Brod estate. The data for 1798 refer to the parish of Vyšší Brod; figures for Kapličky were not available.

Sources: Státní ústřední archiv Praha, SM, R 109/45, Bech. 5; Archiv Klaštera Vyšší Brod, Knihá č. 225.

were able to marry the successors of other houses. The share they received ensured their economic independence, even if they were forced to become lifelong lodgers. Woodworking and various forms of domestic production ensured that there were plenty of economic opportunities for landless people. As a result, marriage was a possibility for almost everybody, as is indicated by the high proportions of ever-married people in the several parishes of the estate of Vyšší Brod, shown in Table 4.2, although the age of marriage for men was relatively high.[53]

## THE INSTITUTION OF RETIREMENT

In this region most intergenerational transfers of property took place *inter vivos*. Table 4.3 shows that at the beginning of the eighteenth century, retirement contracts for former proprietors were already widespread. Moreover, such contracts were not, as some have argued, confined to wealthy landowning houses but occurred in all social strata.[54] Between 1699 and 1738 such contracts characterized a majority of retirement arrangements for landholding households and at least half of those for land-poor houses. It can be assumed from recent studies that this was also the case elsewhere in Bohemia.[55] In Bohemia, however, the *Ausgedinge* (as the institution of retirement was called in many parts of German-speaking central Europe) was, in the seventeenth and eighteenth centuries, more frequent than in other parts of central Europe.[56] In Kapličky retirement contracts already

Table 4.3
Retirement and Headship Succession in Landed and Land-Poor Houses,
Kapličky 1699–1738

| Successor | Transfer of landed houses | | | | | Transfer of land-poor houses | | | | |
|---|---|---|---|---|---|---|---|---|---|---|
| | Retired | | Nonretired | | Total | Retired | | Nonretired | | Total |
| | n | % | n | % | % | n | % | n | % | % |
| Son | 28 | 53.9 | 8 | 44.4 | 51.4 | 16 | 64.0 | 7 | 33.3 | 47.8 |
| Son-in-law | 7 | 13.5 | 1 | 5.5 | 11.4 | 4 | 16.0 | 5 | 23.8 | 19.6 |
| Stepson | 2 | 3.9 | 1 | 5.5 | 4.3 | 0 | 0.0 | 0 | 0.0 | 0.0 |
| Brother | 0 | 0.0 | 1 | 5.5 | 1.4 | 1 | 4.0 | 0 | 0.0 | 2.2 |
| Other kin | 6 | 11.5 | 1 | 5.5 | 10.0 | 2 | 8.0 | 1 | 4.8 | 6.5 |
| Nonrelative* | 9 | 17.3 | 6 | 33.3 | 21.4 | 2 | 8.0 | 8 | 42.1 | 23.9 |
| Total | 52 | 100.0 | 18 | 100.0 | 100.0 | 25 | 100.0 | 21 | 100.0 | 100.0 |

* or unknown relationship

Note: (N = 116)

Source: SOA Třeboň, Sbírka jihočeskych matrik, Farní úřad Kapličky č. 9; fond C
Vyšší Brod, Pozemkové knihy č. 453, č. 465, č. 475, č. 565.

occurred in the sixteenth and seventeenth centuries, but their number
apparently increased from the early eighteenth century, particularly among
the lower classes.[57] For the period from 1699 to 1720 there was an average
of 1.5 contracts per year, while from 1721 to 1738 the average was 2.4.
What also increased in frequency was retirement for both spouses. In
about half of all cases shown in Table 4.3, both partners were involved in
retirement. The occurrence of numerous retirement contracts among the
land-poor is remarkable.[58]

But there were important differences between the social groups. Landowning peasants usually retired as a couple and afterward often lived in
a separate house, still practicing small-scale agriculture. These wealthier
retired peasants often kept one or two meadows, perhaps a field, one or
two cows, and sometimes sheep or a few chickens. Thus, some of the
retired peasant couples owned more livestock than did cottagers. It is also
noteworthy that most pieces of land retained by retirees were not part of
the household's inalienable property but were sections of land leased from
the landlord.

Former cottagers, on the other hand, often retired after their spouse's
death and then lived in the house together with the next generation, either
in a separate room or merely in a corner of a room specially assigned to
them. In this class the contracts did not necessarily guarantee full support,
and in a few cases only the right to live in the house was agreed. Some-

times it was noted that to receive benefits, the retirees had to give some-thing in return, usually money.[59] For example, in 1713 Thomas Leitgöb, an owner of a very small holding and over 70 years old at the time, handed control to his 41-year-old daughter and her husband. According to the retirement contract, his claims to further support were outlined in one sentence, "to stay in the house for free during his life-time and have the care of the new owner."[60] The fact that the care the new owner should provide was left unspecified suggests that Thomas's status within the household was weak.

In general, the benefits agreed in the contracts were usually adapted to the economic potential of the household so that the viability of holdings was not endangered by the benefits granted to the retirees. This meant that many retirees did not receive sufficient maintenance, and when this occurred, domestic production, such as flax processing and woodworking, was an important additional source of income. In more than 80 percent of all retirement contracts former proprietors reserved the right to grow flax on the land handed over to their successors. In this context, most contracts mentioned a quantity of two Bohemian *Viertel* (about 0.143 hec-tare), which appears relatively large compared with the 0.57 hectare listed in the tax register of 1713 as the maximum amount of land cultivated by a peasant farmstead in this region.[61] Spinning provided retirees with some additional income, which meant that they did not have to rely on retire-ment benefits alone, and this extra cash seems to be one reason why re-tirement agreements were feasible even for such small holdings.

There were differences between the sexes, too. Widows frequently changed to the *Ausgedinge* shortly after their husband's death.[62] For landed proprietors, the economic well-being of the farm demanded a quick re-placement for the spouse who had died.[63] Regardless of age and fitness for work, therefore, both male and female widowed owners either had to remarry quickly or retire to the *Ausgedinge*. In some cases there would probably have been adult children pressing their claim to take over the holding, and in these circumstances it was often the case that widows, unlike widowers, apparently retired through their own free will, choos-ing this rather than a hasty remarriage. By contrast, widowers were more likely to remarry as a way of maintaining their status as head of household.[64] Widows were also more able to remain economically semi-independent, provided that they could still practice some small-scale farming or could call on other sources of income such as flax processing. In this situation, a widow's retirement did not necessarily mean that she became completely dependent on the new holder. Following the death of her husband, the 49-year-old widow Agnes Lang in the village of Hodoň did not remarry but in 1728 sold the small holding to her son. She was allowed to keep for herself two cows, to cultivate cabbages in the house garden, and to grow linseed on an area comprising two Bohemian *Viertel*.

Her son was required to provide hay for her cows taken not from any but from a specific meadow.[65] Such conditions suggest that when their husband died, widows were quite capable of exerting some power over their future in the household.

As suggested earlier, most of the retirees in Kapličky did not retire in the strict sense of the word but were still engaged in productive activities even after they had handed over the farm. Retiring as household head, therefore, was by no means the same as ceasing work. In some instances, individuals handed over control at a relatively young age, which suggests that retirement was welcome as an alternative to the status of being a house owner and a means of escaping the various obligations connected to the possession of a farmstead. For example, landed peasants had to provide the landlord with a worker and draught cattle for three or more days per week, whereas the *robot* duties for those without land, including retirees, usually amounted to no more than 16 days per year. Also, retirement could have been used as a provisional solution before changing to other forms of existence.[66] The ages at which people retired, shown in Table 4.4, seem to confirm this. Although it was impossible to discover the exact dates of birth for about 42 percent of retirees in Kapličky, it can be noted that 14 out of 38 women and 6 out of 29 men for whom such evidence exists were under 50 years old when they retired.[67] The youngest male retiree was only 33, and there were 2 couples in which both partners were still aged under 40. Elsewhere in central Europe in the nineteenth century, other studies have shown that retirement took place relatively early, the most common age bracket seeming to have been 50–65 years old.[68] In Kapličky older retirees, many of whom were already in their

**Table 4.4**
**Age of Retirement, Kapličky 1699-1738**

| Age group | Widowers | Widows | Married men | Married women |
|---|---|---|---|---|
| 30–39 | 0 | 1 | 4 | 3 |
| 40–49 | 0 | 4 | 2 | 6 |
| 50–59 | 0 | 4 | 7 | 8 |
| 60–69 | 3 | 5 | 7 | 5 |
| 70+ | 3 | 2 | 3 | 0 |
| Unknown | 6 | 10 | 16 | 17 |
| Total | 12 | 26 | 39 | 39 |

Sources: SOA Třeboň, Sbírka jihočeskych matrik, Farní úřad Kapličky č. 9; fond C Vyšší Brod, Pozemková kniha č. 565.

sixties or seventies, with the oldest being 76 years old, tended to come from land-poor houses.

In addition to retirement, the institution of *Ausgedinge* had other functions over and above support in old age. It was restricted solely to the maintenance of former proprietors but was also open to other people. For example, sometimes contracts included specific benefits for retirees' children. In six of the contracts examined there were clauses that allowed underage children to remain in the house. In two, this right was limited to the period until they married, and in the remainder, children of the former proprietors were granted unlimited right to stay. These individual cases suggest that the clauses were inserted to provide for children who had no expectations of marrying, either because they were handicapped or—as can be shown through the family reconstitution—because they were already comparatively old but for some reason were still single.[69] In 1726, the retirement contract for Paul Schwendtner and his wife concluded with the clause, "N.B. the orphan Helena, because of her ill sense of hearing, has a permanent right of residence in the house, but if she marries, the proprietor owes her nothing."[70] However, this did not necessarily imply that the person who took over the farm was liable to shoulder the financial burden without recompense because he was entitled to receive a portion of the purchase price that was due to Helena when her parents eventually died.

Establishing an *Ausgedinge* was much more common with one's own children than with strangers, and such agreements took place in nearly 80 percent of cases when the successor was the son of the retiring peasant. In this region *Ausgedinge* was clearly a claim on the farmstead, and not on a certain person or family, and for this reason there were numerous instances of retirement contracts being made between non-kin. This situation becomes perfectly clear in cases where the new proprietor died before the retiree, when the obligations contained in the contract were passed on to the next owner along with the property. In one case a retiree even lived long enough to know his third successor. Thus, the *Ausgedinge* must not be seen as an exclusively intrafamilial institution. For this reason the concept of the stem family does not seem appropriate for households consisting of the owner's family and a co-resident, though not necessarily related, retired couple.[71]

Passing into retirement may have been in the peasants' interest for various reasons, one of which was the preservation of property for one's own offspring. As has already been mentioned, however, in early modern central Europe this was not true of all regions. To achieve the goal of preserving family continuity, the transfer had to be planned carefully, and what was crucial was to choose the right moment. There were numerous examples where waiting too long involved having to accept an undesirable successor, for instance, when children were already married and living elsewhere and others were still too young to take on responsibilities. Death of the proprietor required a quick solution to the problem of finding a successor whereas *inter vivos* transfer of property allowed more active control on the part of the head and provided more opportunities to plan succession within the family.[72]

What happened to former proprietors who did not receive retirement benefits? This question is hard to answer because some sold their houses to live elsewhere, perhaps as owners of a house and land. In a few cases, however, nominative record linkage has shown that they became lodgers in other households, partly in the rooms or houses usually reserved for retirees, but with no right to stay permanently and no claims on support by the owner of the house. Such a situation was highly insecure, and when these people became incapable of work, they could all too easily decline to the status of *Einleger*, which meant that they would be passed among farmsteads, receiving board and lodging for short periods of time from each household in turn.[73]

## CONCLUSIONS

In many regions of central Europe retirement meant stepping down from the status of household head to that of a person whose co-residence in the house was secured by contract.[74] Despite this potential decline in status, however, the institution of *Ausgedinge* served several functions. It was an important premodern social institution that could be used to make provision for old age, disability, or the sudden death of a spouse or of the parents. It was open not only to the former house owners themselves but also to additional individuals. It was the household and not necessarily the family that provided the means for support, although it is important to realize that in many cases the contractual agreements of retirement provided only partial support and did not automatically mean protection against impoverishment.[75]

Nor was the system immune to change, and in South Bohemia *Ausgedinge* underwent some interrelated alterations, especially in the early eighteenth century. Transfers from father to son became more common; succession by interim proprietors was invented; retirement arrangements became more important; and *inter vivos* transfer became more frequent. As the land-family bond became stronger, the number of *Ausgedinge* arrangements increased. This did not automatically mean that kinship relations became more significant but merely that real estate was more often transmitted within the family. By selling houses and farmsteads only to children, social endogamy was promoted, and the market for land was replaced by one dominated by intrafamilial transfers. This change effectively transformed the status of lodgers into a lifelong social position. While in the seventeenth century it was possible for the son of an owner of a landed house to marry as a lodger and buy a farmstead later on, in the course of the eighteenth century this possibility largely disappeared. The son' s succession and the parents' retirement became closely related elements in the system of property transmission. The preference of sons to daughters as headship successors became more marked, and therefore these changes had a significant impact on the fortunes of women.

By contrast with rural regions, retirement contracts in central European cities were relatively rare. This difference has usually been explained in relation to the lack of communal institutions in urban areas to enforce contracts and with the lack of cash in rural societies. But the analysis of real estate transmissions in Kapličky has demonstrated the importance of cash transactions among family members and between the generations. The maintenance of aged individuals in many rural areas was in the first place provided by the household and not by the community. In the country-side it was easier to provide someone with a place to live, food, or even small parcels of land, whereas in cities space was precious and food had to be purchased, making the need for financial support more pressing.[76] The same was true, of course, for those rural households that were entirely landless, for whom communal support was of more importance.

In other rural regions, old-age support was similar to the South Bohe-mian practice, even if it was not regulated by retirement contract. Where postmortem transfer was common, it was possible for heads of household to enjoy a work-free period in their latter years. With partible transmission systems, succession was a matter of step-by-step transfer of landed prop-erty, tools, goods, and social status. The former proprietors expected their children to support them in old age, and therefore they were careful to retain some property prior to their death. In some cases, for example, they donated land but not the tools to work it. In such situations, households were forced to cooperate in order to maintain elderly parents and other relatives.[77]

As shown by other authors, broad regional categorizations of European inheritance practices that dichotomize partible and impartible systems can be misleading.[78] In some parts of France, for example, as Gérard Béaur has shown elsewhere in this book, there was a wide range of intermediate forms of inheritance ranging between egalitarian and nonegalitarian sys-tems of property transmission.[79] By exploring headship succession, this chapter has argued that we need to incorporate other ways over and be-yond role of inheritance by which property was transferred between in-dividuals and generations. In this manner, *inter vivos* transfer connected with retirement contracts can be interpreted as a form of successive trans-mission of property. For the eighteenth century, in South Bohemia con-tractual retirement appears to have been more common than in many other parts of Europe. It can be argued that this regional practice stood midway between the two poles of partible and impartible systems. Viewed in this way, the system of property transmission in Kapličky consisted of both egalitarian and nonegalitarian elements at the same time. The impartibility of landholding was enforced by powerful landlords who supervised property transfers and retirement agreements but rarely interfered with the arrangements once they had been agreed. They neither furthered the transfer of holdings by remarriage of the widow nor forced an *inter vivos* transfer when a proprietor reached a certain age. At the same time, however, the strict rule of indivisibility of land and farmstead, and thus unigeniture, coincided with the apportioning of the purchase price in equal portions for all family members. In South Bohemia this led to a more egalitarian distribution of wealth among all siblings. Therefore, to understand fully how individuals, families, and households provided for themselves, it is necessary to broaden our analysis of the provision of welfare to incorporate a range of institutional arrangements, of which *Ausgedinge* is but one, that regulated the flow of property not only at the end but also during the lifetime of its owner.

## NOTES

The results presented in this chapter are based in part on the international research project "Social structures in Bohemia from the sixteenth to the nineteenth centuries" (Universities of Vienna, Prague, and Cambridge). I would like to thank all the members of the project for helpful comments and the Volkswagen Foundation (Hannover, Germany) for funding the research.

1. Alan Macfarlane, *The Origins of English Individualism: The Family, Property and Social Transition* (Oxford: Oxford University Press, 1978) and Roger Schofield, "Family Structure, Demographic Behaviour, and Economic Growth," in *Famine, Disease and the Social Order in Early Modern Society,* ed. John Walter and Roger Schofield (Cambridge: Cambridge University Press, 1989), 279–304.

2. H. John Habakkuk, "Family Structure and Economic Change in Nineteenth-Century Europe," *Journal of Economic History* 15 (1955): 1–12; Lutz Berkner, "Inheritance, Land Tenure and Peasant Family Structure: A German Regional Comparison," in *Family and Inheritance: Rural Society in Western Europe 1200–1800,* ed. Jack Goody, Joan Thirsk, and Edward P. Thompson (Cambridge: Cambridge University Press, 1976), 71–95; Lutz Berkner and Franklin Mendels, "Inheritance Systems, Family Structure and Demographic Patterns in Western Europe, 1700–1900," in *Historical Studies of Changing Fertility,* ed. Charles Tilly (Princeton, N.J.: Princeton University Press, 1978), 209, 213, 223; and Christian Pfister, *Bevölkerungsgeschichte und Historische Demographie, 1500–1800* (München: Oldenbourg, 1994). For a revisionist interpretation of the relationship between different kinds of inheritance systems and patterns of social and economic development within the context of France, see the chapter by Gérard Béaur in this volume. For a recent study of the connections between transmission systems and migration, see Simone Wegge, "To Part or Not to Part: Emigration and Inheritance Institutions in Nineteenth-Century Hesse-Cassel," *Explorations in Economic History* 36 (1999): 30–55; see also the chapter by Rose Duroux in this volume.

3. Erhard Bürger, "Bäuerliche Liegenschaftsübertragung und Vererbung im Gebiete der Tschechoslowakei," in *Die Vererbung des ländlichen Grundbesitzes in der Nachkriegszeit*, vol. 2, ed. Max Sering and Constantin von Dietze (München/ Leipzig: Dunker, 1930), 109–58; Dietmar Sauermann, "Hofidee und bäuerliche Familienverträge in Westfalen," *Rheinisch-westfälische Zeitschrift für Volkskunde 17* (1970): 58–78; Walter Rödel, "Die demographische Entwicklung in Deutschland 1770–1820," in *Deutschland und Frankreich im Zeitalter der Französischen Revolution*, ed. Helmut Berding, Etienne Francois, and Hans-Peter Ullmann (Frankfurt a. M.: Suhrkamp, 1989), 32; and Pfister, *Bevölkerungsgeschichte und Historische Demographie*, 27, 56.

4. Jürgen Schlumbohm, *Lebensläufe, Familien, Höfe: Die Bauern und Heuerleute des Osnabrückischen Kirchspiels Belm in proto-industrieller Zeit, 1650–1860* (Göttingen: Vandenhoeck and Ruprecht, 1994), 379–81 and Josef Mooser, *Ländliche Klassengesellschaft 1770–1848: Bauern und Unterschichten, Landwirtschaft und Gewerbe im östlichen Westfalen* (Göttingen: Vandenhoek and Ruprecht, 1984).

5. Mooser, *Ländliche Klassengesellschaft*, 195, 198.

6. Charles Tilly and Richard Tilly, "Agenda for European Economic History in the 1970s," *Journal of Economic History* 31 (1971): 184–98. Within German-language demographic and social historical research this position has a long tradition reaching back to the beginning of the twentieth century. Its prominence is due to the influence of the "standard" work on population science in Germany: Gerhard Mackenroth, *Bevölkerungslehre: Theorie, Soziologie und Statistik der Bevölkerung* (Berlin: Springer, 1953).

7. In many parts of present-day Austria, for example, the *Anerbenrecht* was implemented in 1938 after the German occupation. See Helmuth Feigl, "Bäuerliches Erbrecht und Erbgewohnheiten in Niederösterreich," *Jahrbuch für Landeskunde von Niederösterreich* 37 (1967): 177–78.

8. John Cole and Eric Wolf, *The Hidden Frontier: Ecology and Ethnicity in an Alpine Valley* (New York: Academic Press, 1974) and Pier P. Viazzo, *Upland Communities: Environment, Population and Social Structure in the Alps since the Sixteenth Century* (Cambridge: Cambridge University Press, 1989), 93–99, 258–85.

9. Hans Medick and David W. Sabean, eds., *Interest and Emotion: Essays on the Study of Family and Kinship* (Cambridge: Cambridge University Press, 1984); David W. Sabean, *Property, Production and Family in Neckarhausen, 1700–1870* (Cambridge: Cambridge University Press, 1990); Giovanni Levi, *Das immaterielle Erbe: Eine bäuerliche Welt an der Schwelle zur Moderne* (Berlin: Wagenbach, 1986); and Schlumbohm, *Lebensläufe, Familien, Höfe*. For an overview of theories of inheritance and succession see Henk de Haan, *In the Shadow of the Tree: Kinship, Property and Inheritance Among Farm Families* (Amsterdam: Het Spinhuis, 1994).

10. Retirement contracts seem to have been widespread in northern and central Europe. See Lutz Berkner, "The Stem Family and the Development Cycle of the Peasant Household: An Eighteenth-Century Austrian Example," *American Historical Review* 77 (1972): 398–418; David Gaunt, "The Property and Kin Relationships of Retired Farmers in Northern and Central Europe," in *Family Forms in Historic Europe*, ed. Richard Wall, Jean Robin, and Peter Laslett (Cambridge: Cambridge University Press, 1983), 249–79; Jack Goody, "Erbschaft, Eigentum und Frauen: Einige vergleichende Betrachtungen," in *Historische Familienforschung*, ed. Michael Mitterauer and Reinhard Sieder (Frankfurt a.M.: Suhrkamp, 1982), 88–

122; Cyril Horáček, "Das Ausgedinge: Eine Agrarpolitische Studie mit besonderer Berücksichtigung der Böhmischen Länder," *Wiener Staatswissenschaftliche Studien* 5 (1904): 1–96; Michal Kopczyński, "Old Age Gives No Joy? Old People in the Kujawy Countryside at the End of the Eighteenth Century," *Acta Poloniae Historica* 78 (1998): 81–101; and Beatrice Moring, "Family Strategies, Inheritance Systems and the Care of the Elderly in Historical Perspective—Eastern and Western Finland," *Historical Social Research* 23 (1998): 67–82.

11. Michael Mitterauer and Reinhard Sieder, *Vom Patriarchat zur Partnerschaft: Zum Strukturwandel der Familie* (München: C. H. Beck, 1977) and Michael Mitterauer, "Problemfelder einer Sozialgeschichte des Alters," in *Der alte Mensch in der Geschichte*, ed. Helmut Konrad (Wien: Verlag für Gesellschaftskritik, 1982), 22.

12. Thomas Held, "Rural Retirement Arrangements in Seventeenth-Century to Nineteenth-Century Austria: A Cross-Community Analysis," *Journal of Family History* 7 (1982): 227–54 and Josef Ehmer, "The 'Life Stairs': Aging, Generational Relations, and Small Commodity Production in Central Europe," in *Aging and Generational Relations over the Life Course*, ed. Tamara Hareven (Berlin: Walter de Gruyter and Co., 1996), 53–74.

13. In Austria the increase in the number of retirement contracts during the nineteenth century led to a decrease in property transfers as a result of the remarriage of widows. See Held, "Rural Retirement Arrangements"; Michael Mitterauer, *Grundtypen alteuropäischer Sozialformen: Haus und Gemeinde in vorindustriellen Gesellschaften* (Stuttgart: Bad Cannstatt, 1979); and Michael Mitterauer, "Formen ländlicher Familienwirtschaft im österreichischen Raum: Historische Ökotypen und familiale Arbeitsteilung im österreichischen Raum," in *Familienstruktur und Arbeitsorganisation in ländlichen Gesellschaften*, ed. Josef Ehmer and Michael Mitterauer (Wien: Böhlau, 1986), 185–323. For similar developments in Finland during the nineteenth century see Moring, "Family Strategies," 79.

14. Robert A. Kann and David Zděnek, *The Peoples of the Eastern Habsburg Lands, 1526–1918* (Seattle: University of Washington Press, 1984), 23–29 and Miroslav Hroch and Josef Petraň, *Das 17. Jahrhundert: Krise der feudalen Gesellschaft?* (Hamburg: Hoffmann und Campe, 1981). For a more recent overview see Eduard Maur, *Gutsherrschaft und "zweite Leibeigenschaft" in Böhmen: Studien zur Wirtschafts-, Sozial- und Bevölkerungsgeschichte (14.–18. Jahrhundert)* (Wien: Oldenbourg, 2001); Markus Cerman, "Gutsherrschaft vor dem 'Weißen Berg': Zur Verschärfung der Erbuntertänigkeit in Nordböhmen 1380 bis 1620," in *Gutsherrschaftsgesellschaften im europäischen Vergleich*, ed. Jan Peters (Berlin: Akademie-Verlag, 1997), 91–111; and Markus Cerman and Hermann Zeitlhofer, eds., *Soziale Strukturen in Böhmen: Ein regionaler Vergleich von Wirtschaft und Gesellschaft in Gutsherrschaften, 16.–19. Jahrhundert* (Wien: Oldenbourg, 2002).

15. Gaunt, "The Property and Kin Relationships," 264.

16. Maur, *Gutsherrschaft und "zweite Leibeigenschaft,"* 117–18 and Mitterauer and Sieder, *Vom Patriarchat zur Partnerschaft*, 144. For a recent study of North Bohemia that supports this argument, see Sheilagh Ogilvie and Jeremy Edwards, "Women and 'Second Serfdom': Evidence from Early Modern Bohemia," *Journal of Economic History* 60 (2000): 961–94.

17. For more details see Zeitlhofer, "Besitztransfer und sozialer Wandel in einer ländlichen Gesellschaft der Frühen Neuzeit: Das Beispiel der südböhmischen Pfarre Kaplicky, 1640–1840." Ph.D. diss., University of Vienna, 2001.

18. This means that in many parts of Bohemia the tenancy rights of the serfs throughout the early modern period were better than in other parts of Europe. See, for example, the excellent discussion of the meaning of different peasant tenancy rights in the Bavarian region with both *emphyteuse* and the weaker *freistift*, in Rainer Beck, *Unterfinning: Ländliche Welt vor Anbruch der Moderne* (München: C. H. Beck, 1993), 391–412.

19. See the various regional case studies of property transmission in Cerman and Zeitlhofer, *Soziale Strukturen*. More generally, see Vladimír Procházka, *Česká poddanská nemovitost v pozemkových knihách 16. a 17. století* (Praha: ČSAV, 1963) and Eduard Maur, "Das bäuerliche Erbrecht und die Erbschaftspraxis in Böhmen im 16. bis 18. Jahrhundert," *Historická demografie* 20 (1996), 93–118.

20. For a study of property transmission under such conditions see Charles Wetherell and Andrejs Plakans, "Intergenerational Transfers of Headships over the Life Course in an Eastern European Peasant Community, 1782–1850," *The History of the Family* 3 (1998): 333–49.

21. Státní ústřední archiv Praha, SM, R 109/45, Bech. 5.

22. For more details see Hermann Zeitlhofer, "Besitztransfer und sozialer Wandel."

23. Archiv Klaštera Vyšší Brod, Kart. č. 219. Information about one village is missing in this list.

24. Státní ústřední archiv Praha, BR 2, fol. 822–828. Other houses were not mentioned in this source.

25. In all tax rolls (1654, 1682, 1713) these 62 peasant farmsteads were the only ones to have cattle, while the total number of houses increased from 67 in 1654 to 101 in 1713. Ownership of cattle is an important qualitative indicator of property size. Using their own cattle enabled peasants to till their land independently. This indicator is used instead of information on property size because over time the measurements for the latter changed. In early modern Bohemia the landlords also used the ownership of cattle as a social distinction: farms with cattle were obliged to pay higher *robot* duties than other houses. See: Státní ústřední archiv Praha, BR 2 (1654); BR 30 (1682); TK 684, fol. 43–67, 232, 234 (1713).

26. Státní oblastní archiv (further cited as SOA) Třeboň, fond C Vyšší Brod, Pozemkové knihy č. 453, č. 465, č. 475, č. 479, and č. 480.

27. SOA Třeboň, Sbírka jihočeskych matrik, Farní úřad Kapličky č. 9. For a survey of the family reconstitutions compiled by the monks of Vyšší Brod, see Jiřina Psíková, "Rodové katastry uložené ve Státním oblastním archivu v Třeboni," *Historická demografie* 8 (1983): 75–80. The retirement contracts are listed in a separate book: SOA Třeboň, fond C Vyšší Brod, Pozemková kniha č. 565 (kniha výmenkářská, hereafter cited as KV).

28. Because the family reconstitution starts only 10 years before the period of analysis here, the reconstruction of kin relations for the first decade is not of the same quality as for later periods. However, this has no influence on the proportions of "close" relationships between buyer and seller because relations such as "son," "son-in law," and "widow remarriages" can also be established from the land registers.

29. Prior to 1699 retirement contracts are listed in the land registers. It is possible that a small number were concluded without being recorded in the registers. In some cases, after 1738, the land registers contain references to already existing

retirements. Unfortunately, they do not provide detailed information on these contracts.

30. According to the land registers, between 1640 and 1840 there was only one exception to this rule: in the 1830s, a heavily indebted farmstead was divided into three new units.

31. This was the case in most parts of premodern Bohemia. See Maur, "Das bäuerliche Erbrecht."

32. SOA Třeboň, fond C Vyšší Brod, Pozemková kniha č. 453, fol. 340.

33. This question also arises in partible inheritance regions that had a similar system of apportioning the purchase price of property to relatives. See Sabean, *Property, Production and Family;* Martine Segalen, "'Sein Teil haben': Geschwister-beziehungen in einem egalitären Vererbungssystem," in *Emotionen und materielle Interessen: Sozialanthropologische und historische Beiträge zur Familienforschung,* ed. Hans Medick and David W. Sabean (Göttingen: Vandenhoeck und Ruprecht, 1984), 181–98.

34. See Josef Ehmer, "House and the Stem Family in Austria," in *House and the Stem Family in Eurasian Perspective: Proceedings of the 12th International Economic History Congress,* ed. Antoinette Fauve-Chamoux and Emiko Ochiai (Kyoto, 1998), 61 and Feigl, "Bäuerliches Erbrecht."

35. Reinhard Sieder and Michael Mitterauer, "The Reconstruction of the Family Life Course: Theoretical Problems and Empirical Results," in Wall, Robin, and Laslett, *Family Forms in Historic Europe,* 309–45.

36. See Jack Goody, "Strategies of Heirship," *Comparative Studies in Society and History* 15 (1973): 3–20; Wetherell and Plakans, "Intergenerational Transfers of Headships," 334; and Haan, *In the Shadow of the Tree,* 154.

37. Between 1640 and 1720, 19 out of a total of 247 house owners (more than 7 percent) moved from one holding to another within the parish; between 1721 and 1840 only 6 moved.

38. Josef Grulich and Hermann Zeitlhofer, "Lebensformen und soziale Muster in Südböhmen im 16. und 17. Jahrhundert," *Jihočeský sborník historický* 66/67 (1997/98): 46. On using headship rates as an important social indicator of different historical societies see Richard Wall, "Introduction," in Wall, Robin, and Laslett, *Family Forms in Historic Europe,* 1–63.

39. Similar evidence for Bavaria can be found in Rudolf Schlögl, *Bauern, Krieg und Staat: Ober bayerische Bauernwirtschaft und frühmoderner Staat im 17. Jahrhundert* (Göttingen: Vandenhoeck and Ruprecht, 1988), 102–4.

40. See, for example, Sieder and Mitterauer, "The Reconstruction of the Family Life," 312. In many southern Bohemian regions it was quite common for house-holds to lease cleared forest land.

41. For the debate on the land-family bond in early modern England, see Zvi Razi, "The Myth of the Immutable English Family," *Past and Present* 140 (1993): 3–44 and Govind Sreenivasan, "The Land-Family Bond at Earls Colne (Essex) 1550–1650," *Past and Present* 131 (1991): 3–37.

42. Macfarlane, *Origins of English Individualism,* 23.

43. For discussion of the impact of the Thirty Years' War on the population in other regions of Bohemia, see Markus Cerman, "Bohemia after the Thirty Years' War: Some Theses on Population Structure, Marriage and Family," *Journal of Family History* 19 (1994): 149–75.

44. An example can be found in a purchase contract of 1649, which, although naming the new proprietor, reveals that the monks refused to ratify him and installed somebody else instead *pro interim:* SOA Třeboň, fond C Vyšší Brod, Pozemková kniha č. 453, fol. 163.

45. Karl Kaser, *Macht und Erbe: Männerherrschaft, Besitz und Familie im östlichen Europa (1500–1900)* (Wien: Böhlau, 2000).

46. All other women were under the supervision of a guardian; for a married woman, this was usually her husband.

47. For an analysis of the impact of these legal changes on the rural property transmission system of another Bohemian region, see Alice Velková, "Eingriffe des Staates in die Beziehung zwischen der Obrigkeit und den Untertanen und ihre Wirkung auf die Dorffamilie an der Wende des 18. zum 19. Jahrhundert," in *Untertanen, Herrschaft und Staat in Böhmen und im 'Alten Reich,'* ed. Markus Cerman and Robert Luft (München: Oldenbourg, 2004).

48. A similar trend has been observed in southwest Germany in the late eighteenth century. See Michaela Hohkamp, "Wer will erben?" in *Gutsherrschaft als soziales Modell,* ed. Jan Peters (München: Oldenbourg, 1995), 339.

49. For example, in many Alpine regions of Austria a widow had no such right. See Michael Mitterauer, "Formen ländlicher Familienwirtschaft," 314.

50. For similar evidence see Schlumbohm, *Lebensläufe, Familien, Höfe,* 257 and Gertrude Ostrawsky, "Die Zusammensetzung der Hausgemeinschaften in der Pfarre Maria Langegg im Dunkelsteinerwald, 1788–1875" (Ph.D. diss., University of Vienna, 1979), 220.

51. Zeitlhofer, "Besitztransfer und sozialer Wandel," 204.

52. SOA Třeboň, fond C Vyšší Brod, Pozemková kniha č. 465, fol. 19.

53. The average age of marriage for males was about 30 years. See the compilation of data on marriage ages in premodern Europe in Michael Flinn, *The European Demographic System, 1500–1820* (Brighton: Harvester, 1981). On marriage ages in Bohemia see Markus Cerman, "Central Europe and the European Marriage Pattern: Marriage Patterns and Family Structure in Central Europe, 16th–19th centuries," in *Family History Revisited: Comparative Perspectives,* ed. Richard Wall, Tamara K. Hareven, and Josef Ehmer (Newark: University of Delaware Press, 2001), 282–307.

54. Mitterauer, "Problemfelder einer Sozialgeschichte des Alters" and Mitterauer and Sieder, *Vom Patriarchat zur Partnerschaft.*

55. Alice Klášterská, "Forma sociálního zabezpečení na vesnici v 18. a v první polovine 19. století," *Historická demografie* 21 (1997): 95–132 and Dana Štefanová, "Die Erbschaftspraxis, das Ausgedinge und das Phänomen der 'zweiten Leibeigenschaft' in den nordböhmischen Dörfern der Herrschaft Frydlant," in *Wiener Wege der Sozialgeschichte,* ed. Erich Landsteiner, Franz X. Eder, and Peter Feldbauer (Wien: Böhlau, 1997), 225–41. Dana Štefanová and Hermann Zeitlhofer, "Alter und Generationenbeziehungen in Böhmen. Zum Ausgedinge in nord- und südböhmischen Dörfern 1650–1750," in *Das Alter im Spiel der Generationen: Historische und sozialwissenschaftliche Beiträge,* ed. Josef Ehmer and Peter Gutschner (Wien: Böhlau, 2000), 231–58.

56. Ehmer, "House and the Stem Family in Austria," 69. Held, "Rural Retirement." Schlumbohm, *Lebensläufe, Familien, Höfe,* 257.

57. Among the few retirement contracts from the seventeenth century, there was none from the lower classes.

58. *Ausgedinge* is usually thought to have been limited to wealthier peasant farmsteads. However, in other regions it also occurred among lower social classes. Around 1800, for example, it was widespread among the ribbon weavers of Lusatia. See Bernd Schöne, *Kultur und Lebensweise Lausitzer Bandweber 1750–1850* (Berlin: Akademie-Verlag, 1977).

59. SOA Třeboň, fond C Vyšší Brod, KV, fol. 368.

60. SOA Třeboň, fond C Vyšší Brod, KV, fol. 78. Typically retirement contracts in land-poor households were far less detailed than those of landed peasant farmsteads.

61. Státní ústřední archiv Praha, TK Spisy 619, fol. 65.

62. This pattern can also be shown for several Austrian regions. See Ostrawsky, "Die Zusammensetzung," 220.

63. Michael Mitterauer, *Familie und Arbeitsteilung: Historischvergleichende Studien* (Wien: Böhlau, 1992), 171–72.

64. In this region, couples who retired together had the right to remarry after the death of their spouse. Whereas seven retired men did so, there was no record of retired women ever having married again.

65. SOA Třeboň, fond C Vyšší Brod, KV, fol. 368.

66. In seventeenth-century north Bohemian villages, retirement was often of relatively short duration (in many cases less than five years) and thus was not necessarily connected to old-age support. See Štefanová and Zeitlhofer, "Alter und Generationenbeziehungen in Böhmen."

67. There are two explanations for the high proportion of missing information on ages. First, some of those who retired at the beginning of the eighteenth century were born before the church registers commenced (in 1642). Second, during the second half of the seventeenth century, regional mobility was comparatively high.

68. Ehmer, "The 'Life Stairs,'" 63.

69. SOA Třeboň, fond C Vyšší Brod, KV, fol. 10 "Leibsdefect."

70. The German original: "NB wais Helena soll wegen ihres üblen gehörs das stete verbleiben beim Haus haben, wenn sie sich aber verheiratet, ist ihr der stifter nichts schuldig." SOA Třeboň, fond C Vyšší Brod, Pozemková kniha č. 465, fol. 20.

71. Ehmer, "House and the Stem Family in Austria," 316.

72. Ehmer, "The 'Life Stairs,'" 61.

73. Josef Ehmer, *Sozialgeschichte des Alters* (Frankfurt a M.: Suhrkamp, 1990), 36. In South Bohemia the *Einleger*-system was not unknown, but it seems to have been much more common in regions with a high proportion of never-married population. For example, in an Austrian district, roughly 70 kilometers south of Kapličky, in 1921 about 1.5 percent of people older than 60 years lived as *Einleger*. See Norbert Ortmayr, "Oarbeits, sunst kemts ins Quartier': Alter und Armut am Land im frühen 20. Jahrhundert," in '. . . und i sitz' jetzt allein': Geschichte mit und von alten Menschen, ed. Helmut Konrad and Michael Mitterauer (Wien: Böhlau, 1987), 87.

74. Andrejs Plakans, "Retirement, Inheritance, and Generational Relations: Life-Course Analysis in Historic Eastern Europe," in *Aging and Generational Relations over the Life Course*, ed. Tamara Hareven (Berlin/New York: Walter de Gruyter and Co., 1996), 147.

75. This is shown, for example, by the south Bohemian poor registers of the late eighteenth century, where a considerable number of retirees are to be found. See Margarethe Buquoy, "Die Armen auf dem Lande im späten 18. und frühen 19. Jahrhundert," *Bohemia* 26 (1985): 37–78.

76. Ehmer, *Sozialgeschichte des Alters,* 37–38.

77. Sabean, *Property, Production and Family,* 247–99.

78. There are examples of German-speaking regions with a strict egalitarian system in principle but, in practice, a tendency toward an impartible transmission of land. See John Theibault, *German Villages in Crisis: Rural Life in Hesse-Kassel and the Thirty Years' War* (Atlantic Highlands, N.J.: Humanities Press, 1995), p. 94; Albert Tanner, *Spulen—Weben—Sticken: Die Industrialisierung in Appenzell-Ausserrhoden* (Zürich: Junis Druck, 1982), 10; and G. Schmid, "Hofgröße—Familiengröße—Vererbungsgewohnheiten. Eine Fallstudie über fünf Familien," in *Historische Demographie als Sozialgeschichte,* vol. 2, ed. Arthur Imhof (Darmstadt: Hessische Historische Kommission, 1975), 697. For the general argument see also Jürgen Schlumbohm, "The Land-Family Bond in Peasant Practice and in Middle-Class Ideology: Evidence from the North-West German Parish of Belm, 1650–1860," *Central European History* 27 (1994): 463.

79. Martine Segalen, *Die Familie: Geschichte, Soziologie, Anthropologie* (Frankfurt a M.: Campus, 1990), 98–101.

# CHAPTER 5

# Close Relatives and Useful Relatives: Welfare, Inheritance, and the Use of Kinship in an Alpine Dynasty, 1650–1800

*Sandro Guzzi-Heeb*

> Monsieur Grandet, que la providence voulut sans doute consoler de sa dis-grâce administrative, hérita successivement pendant cette année de madame de la Gaudinière, née La Bertellière, mère de madame Grandet; puis du vieux monsieur La Bertellière, père de la défunte, et encore de madame Gentillet, grand-mère du côté maternel: trois successions dont l'importance ne fût connue de personne ... Monsieur Grandet obtint alors le nouveau titre de noblesse que notre manie d'égalité n'effacera jamais, il devint le plus imposé de l'arrondissement.
>
> —Honoré de Balzac, *Eugénie Grandet*

## INTRODUCTION: SOME METHODOLOGICAL ISSUES

In recent years historians have emphasized the need to expand research on the family beyond the restrictive boundaries of the single household in order to include more complex and hidden forms of relationships and cooperation between relatives. One of the first to argue for such a broader perspective was Giovanni Levi, who demonstrated the enormous poten-tial of this methodological approach for understanding family and society in the *ancien régime* using cases from Liguria and Piemonte.[1] Since then, several studies have appeared on the topic, although a common set of historical models of the relationships between family and relatives has yet to be found.

Addressing such issues raises significant conceptual and methodolog-ical problems. In an important work David Sabean has shown how rela-tives can comprise a privileged, though flexible, network of contacts and source of cooperation within kinship groups.[2] Yet how exactly does this network function and cooperation take place, and how can the priority ascribed to relatives as opposed to other members of the community be explained? The problem of establishing a precise definition of kin and non-kin is unclear. In small communities of between about 600 and 800 inhabitants, such as those considered in this chapter, each individual is surrounded by a substantial group of agnate and cognate relatives. In such communities, who are those relatives that play an essential role in the family? In one of the most significant recent studies that addresses this question, Barry Raye has analyzed relationships in small communities in Kent, England, showing the importance of cooperation among different family groups.[3] However, the problem is to evaluate the relevance of the social relationships and to distinguish between cooperation based wholly on kinship and the broader range of contacts and interactions of a single individual or family unit.

One way of approaching these wider familial relationships is to explore their quantitative significance in terms of financial flows or frequency of contact. However, such efforts are hindered by the high variation and flexibility of individual and family relationships.[4] If this approach is applied to an Alpine society, as discussed in this chapter, it can result in misleading conclusions. Instead, the approach adopted here argues that in order to reach a precise and differentiated conceptualization of intra-familial relationships, it is necessary to start with individual cases and try to map the most important patterns of interaction between family and relatives. In this context, inheritance and other forms of assistance are excellent ways in which to explore such structures of interaction. Assistance here is understood not in the narrow meaning of being socially restricted to the poor and old, but rather in the broader sense of supporting relationships that were activated in critical life situations. Considered in this way, families can be seen in a dynamic sense, taking into account changes across the life cycle, registering the crises, breakups, and inevitable conflicts that occurred and the ways in which such difficulties were confronted.

The key concept on which this research is based is "interdependence." This concept, informed by psychological approaches to the study of societies, suggests that while some behavior can be termed "individualist," it is often set within a broader framework of relationships that bind individuals, consciously or otherwise, together and renders them interdependent.[5] In particular, individuals and family relatives interact according to a set of culturally accepted interdependent links that establish an objective relationship between any given individual and the rest of the kinship group. A consideration of such interdependencies focuses attention away from the co-residing nuclear family, about which demographic historians have written so much, and toward a broader and more dynamic set of kinship relationships.[6] What follows is an attempt to examine these interdependencies in the context of inheritance, succession, and assistance.

This research focuses on a microhistorical study of two related families in the Vallesan Alps in Switzerland: the de Rivaz of St Gingolph and the de Nucé of Vouvry, on the border between Valais and Savoy. In the late sixteenth century, the de Rivaz family were small landowners and animal breeders and by the eighteenth century had become relatively wealthy, as had the de Nucé family. Their story provides an opportunity to explore the welfare strategies of different social classes, taking into account changes in social status from the start of the eighteenth century and in particular the consequences this had for the organization of the kinship group.

The communities of St Gingolph and Vouvry consisted of several small villages about 10 kilometers apart. In about 1800 they each contained between 700 and 800 inhabitants. Both communities were situated in the Alpine foothills and were characterized by mixed agriculture and cattle breeding and based on a pattern of small land ownership typical of the Swiss Alps. The mountains themselves formed an important hinterland for economic activities: high meadows and alps were essential resources for the maintenance of livestock. But there were also clear differences between the two communities: Vouvry lay on the western plain of the river Rhône, while St Gingolph was situated on the southern bank of Lake Geneva. Fishing, boat building, and a limited amount of commerce were important additional activities.

## WELFARE AND ASSISTANCE IN ALPINE COMMUNITIES

In his will issued in 1750, Etienne de Rivaz, a wealthy man from St Gingolph, instructed his heirs to "dress six poor people from head to feet" and, following local custom, ordered them to provide general charity to those in need.[7] These instructions were common among the wealthy. Indeed, until the latter half of the nineteenth century support for the poor was mainly left to the individual initiatives of these and other groups. There was nothing like the institutional support provided by the English poor law. Even when parishes and confraternities provided assistance, and there were various forms of spontaneous support in Alpine communities such as providing food to the poor and old, they were sporadic. Only from the 1800s did the Vallesan state introduce legislative measures to assist the poor, although these were largely ineffectual for the first half of the century.[8]

In the absence of institutional provision of welfare until the middle of the nineteenth century, family and relatives were the main sources of assistance to the poor, the elderly, the ill, and others in general need. However, in the specific context of the Alps, the provision of welfare was based on a totally different logic compared with modern conceptions of assistance. In particular, cultural traditions emphasized not the redistribution of resources *ex post*, but rather preventive efforts to guarantee a stable balance between scarce resources and the demands arising from population growth. In this way, social and economic life functioned in a context that can best be described in terms similar to those used by George Foster in relation to the "image of limited good."[9] In Alpine societies, strong local corporations managed and assigned essential resources to different groups and families, or more precisely to the households. Economic life in its entirety underwent scrupulous control in an effort to ensure stability through the distribution of scarce goods among a limited number of people who had rights of access. Such controls also included the surveillance of markets, trade, and prices—a practice that elsewhere has been interpreted in terms of a "moral economy."[10]

The fundamental problem for such communities, as well as families, was how to maintain the balance between individuals on the one hand and scarce resources on the other, and in this sense we can talk about a "Malthusian" society.[11] However, this should not be interpreted in any deterministic sense because scarcity generated a variety of responses. Rather, the crucial question is how scarcity of resources influences the behavior of kinship groups in different social strata, ranging from the elite to the poor.

In the case of single families the essential point of welfare systems was not the redistribution of resources toward the end of the life cycle, but rather their control and distribution beforehand. This factor reverses the usual conception of preindustrial welfare systems: the fundamental problem for this kind of society was not the support of the old, but rather assistance to the young to enable them to achieve an independent position as an adult. In general the elderly did not need economic support because they managed their own property. When they required assistance in case of illness or infirmity, they could normally turn to their potential heirs while preserving their control over property, often until death. The main problem lay not with them but with the young: in the context of consistently scarce resources, parents were expected to provide support for all their children or dependent relatives. The strategies by which heads of families made such provision was strongly influenced by the Malthusian concept of a limited number of available posts, and it was the fundamental task of any respectable parents to provide the opportunity for their children to earn their own living—*placer les enfants*—through the provision of a business, career, rent, or a combination of these.[12]

The context of resource scarcity is therefore fundamental for understanding family behavior. The scarcity of posts *in loco* and the fierce competition to acquire them required that families organize themselves in an interdependent and hierarchical system in order to control the available resources and pass them to future generations. Nor was this problem of scarcity confined to the poorer sections of society. It also existed for elite families, for whom scarcity was a relative concept concerned more with the distribution of power in the form of political posts than with absolute need. Some members of the elite inevitably had to accept subordinate positions in the hierarchy of power while others fared much better. In practice, however, the different phases of the family life cycle and other unforeseen events encouraged flexibility and continuous reformulation of the kinship group. As a consequence, continuity was in reality achieved only by cooperation between the various family unities linked by broader kinship relationships.

## PATTERNS OF INHERITANCE

In the Alpine communities under discussion here, patterns of inheritance played a significant role in the way that families were organized and kinship relations structured. As already mentioned, the older generation normally maintained control over its property until at least the male household head died. The role played by his wife was more complex due to the fact that it depended on the possessions she owned personally and on the way usufruct was regulated after her husband's death. Rules over the gradual withdrawal by parents from the ownership of property often concerned widows, who sometimes renounced some of their rights in favor of their children. However, even when sons and daughters married there was no clear-cut legal distinction between the parents' property and that of the new household. In cases where the groom's father was still alive at the time of marriage, it was common that he received the dowry and also guaranteed for its potential restitution. As a consequence, the property belonging to the new couple remained integrated in the parents' estate. In the eighteenth century it was not uncommon that male children preserved the unity of the estate even after their parents' death, sometimes until the youngest sibling married and, in certain cases, for their entire lives. Therefore, in Valais marriage did not necessarily result in the formation of a new economic unit, but rather the extension of an existing household. In those rare cases in which parents lived long after their children's marriage, close cooperation with the descendant group was necessary.

Although the norms that regulated inheritance practices were important, they were also a flexible instrument that could be adapted to various situations, and for that reason their social impact should not be overestimated. For example, in *ancien régime* Valais, as in most of the Swiss Alps, the equal partitioning of family estate among sons and daughters was common. According to the statutes of 1571, in the case of death *ab intestato* the estate was divided into equal parts among male and female children. If there were no offspring the equivalent shares were passed to the grandparents, or brothers and sisters. However, not only did the norms differ from one district to another, and at times from one village to the other, they could even change from one family to another, depending on specific traditions and the interests of those involved. Statutes gave parents the chance to exclude their daughters from the inheritance by providing a dowry for them at the time of their marriage. However, while this practice was common, it was not always followed either by the elite or the lower class. There were also intermediate forms of inheritance, such as where parents established prerogatives for certain children, often males. In some circumstances special benefits were given to individuals from whom the testator had received some favor, or hoped to receive one in the future. Such practices, however, could vary within as well as between generations. For example, when Marie-Caterine de Nucé married Charles-Emmanuel de Rivaz in 1776, her mother annulled previous conditions stemming from an inheritance settlement that had favored her sons and compensated her daughters, to benefit the newly wed wife.[13]

If in theory partition of property followed customary norms, in practice different strategies prevailed. Even after inheritance had occurred further settlement of property within the kinship group could take place. To keep real estate intact and preserve rights of use to family property in the hands of a single household head, it was not uncommon for other siblings to move into new accommodation in return for some form of compensation, usually in cash. Complexities arose over the distribution of goods with a symbolic as opposed to a merely economic value, such as the family home, a social position, influence, and in some cases, also political power. As we shall see, political roles also shifted within the family or, more often, within a specific kinship group.

Such practices, it is argued, ensured that at each generation the family hierarchy was reorganized so that continuity and optimal exploitation of the available resources could occur. This Malthusian organization is clearest amongst elite families, particularly in relation to the inheritance of intangible property, such as power, influence, and family status. This pattern can be illustrated by the de Rivaz family in the eighteenth century, shown in Figure 5.1. The strategy for succession planned by the head of the family, Etienne de Rivaz (1675–1753), *châtelain* of St Gingolph, can best be understood as an attempt to create a political lineage, based on continuity of the male line, excluding female relatives through a compensatory system of dowry payments.[14] Succession was therefore built around the future head of family, in this instance the eldest son, Pierre-Joseph, who inherited his father's offices.[15] This patriarchal system also affected the status of wives: if a husband became head of family and inherited political positions, his wife would also become more prominent in the female hierarchy. The aim of this strategy was therefore to create a unified family

**Figure 5.1**
**Actual Strategy of the de Rivaz Family, Second Generation (1740–1750)**

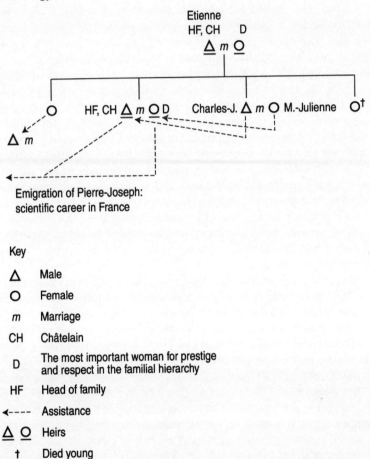

Emigration of Pierre-Joseph:
scientific career in France

Key

| | |
|---|---|
| △ | Male |
| ○ | Female |
| *m* | Marriage |
| CH | Châtelain |
| D | The most important woman for prestige and respect in the familial hierarchy |
| HF | Head of family |
| ◄---- | Assistance |
| △ ○ | Heirs |
| † | Died young |

team that, despite internal differences and conflicts, could work toward a common goal, namely the well-being, influence, and, in some cases, fame of the family lineage.[16]

The strategic ambitions of families like the de Rivaz could be disrupted by events such as premature death, disease, economic misadventure, or individual choice. A good illustration is provided by Pierre-Joseph de Rivaz's decision to move away from the village and become a scientist, thereby permanently changing the internal balance of the family. This decision led to his replacement as political representative and head of the family by his brother Charles-Joseph. At the same time, his wife's role as female head of the family was taken by Charles-Joseph's wife, Marie-

Julienne de Nucé, who, as a result, was able to play a decisive role within the family and the village, especially after her husband died.

What this example illustrates is how each individual's life trajectory was intrinsically dependent on the actions of others. Such interdependency was true of brothers and sisters no less than husbands and wives. Siblings could be substituted for one another in the system of family succession, as the example of Pierre-Joseph and Charles-Joseph illustrates. In cases of death they could also inherit from one another. A more fundamental interdependence existed between husbands and wives because widows replaced their dead partners in the family hierarchy and often assumed their economic responsibilities. Other events could have consequences for the group as a whole. For example, the death of a daughter increased the availability or size of a dowry for her sisters and accordingly improved their matrimonial chances. This was particularly true where the firstborn son or daughter died leaving younger siblings to assume a more significant position in the family hierarchy. Similar interdependencies could also occur among more distant relatives: where testators did not have sons, they often nominated nephews, cousins, brothers, sisters-in-law, or other kin as universal heirs.

In fact, in preindustrial societies a relatively large portion of the population did not have direct heirs: single people, couples without children, and those whose children died prematurely fell into this category.[17] Under these circumstances inheritance and succession occurred in different ways and incorporated a wider circle of kin. For this reason, parents' inheritance choices were not the only factor to define a man's or woman's status. For example, Etienne de Rivaz's wife, Anne Marie Cayen, received a dowry from her parents of 4,500 Savoy florins between 1702 and 1707. Between 1685 and 1716, she also inherited a similar amount of money and some personal property from her grandmother, aunt, a brother, and two sisters. Her social and economic status was therefore defined not only by her parents, but also by the events that occurred in the wider kinship group.

These points are illustrated in Figure 5.2, which charts how replacements in the second-generation Rivaz family had lasting effects on subsequent generations. The decisive point is the systemic consequence of Pierre-Joseph de Rivaz's decision to emigrate. By doing so he effectively consigned his descendants to positions of relative poverty and, ultimately, extinction. Such systemic consequences were not uncommon among the Alpine families considered later. By contrast, Charles-Joseph's descendants, and especially the only son to survive, Charles-Emmanuel, were able to take advantage of the situation that occurred after Pierre-Joseph's departure. Once they had gained positions of authority within the family, which otherwise would have gone to Pierre-Joseph's children, they were able to transfer them to subsequent generations. As the closest collateral line, Charles-Emmanuel's lineage also benefited from inheritance of Pierre-

**Figure 5.2**
**The Consequences of Interdependence for the Third Generation of the de Rivaz Family, c. 1740–1770**

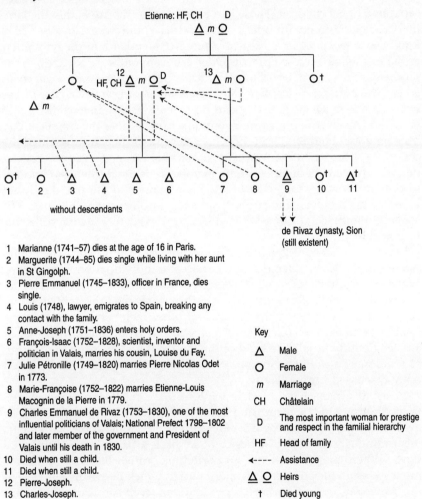

1  Marianne (1741–57) dies at the age of 16 in Paris.
2  Marguerite (1744–85) dies single while living with her aunt in St Gingolph.
3  Pierre Emmanuel (1745–1833), officer in France, dies single.
4  Louis (1748), lawyer, emigrates to Spain, breaking any contact with the family.
5  Anne-Joseph (1751–1836) enters holy orders.
6  François-Isaac (1752–1828), scientist, inventor and politician in Valais, marries his cousin, Louise du Fay.
7  Julie Pétronille (1749–1820) marries Pierre Nicolas Odet in 1773.
8  Marie-Françoise (1752–1822) marries Etienne-Louis Macognin de la Pierre in 1779.
9  Charles Emmanuel de Rivaz (1753–1830), one of the most influential politicians of Valais; National Prefect 1798–1802 and later member of the government and President of Valais until his death in 1830.
10  Died when still a child.
11  Died when still a child.
12  Pierre-Joseph.
13  Charles-Joseph.

Key

△   Male
○   Female
m   Marriage
CH  Châtelain
D   The most important woman for prestige and respect in the familial hierarchy
HF  Head of family
◄----  Assistance
△ ○  Heirs
†   Died young

Joseph's property. What this example of the de Rivaz family shows is how family interdependence helped determine individual destinies.[18]

## WIDER LINKAGES

The circle of hereditary connections described earlier was also a privileged arena for relationships that could be used to provide mutual assistance. For example, the systemic interdependence between Pierre-Joseph de Rivaz and his brother Charles-Joseph was underlined by the fact that the latter provided help to the former in difficult moments: not only did he look after his business, he also lent him money and sheltered and educated two of his children. Those in a position of authority within the family bore responsibility for others and in return could expect loyalty. *"Tu es le pilier et le seul pilier de la maison,"* (You are the pillar and the only pillar of the household) wrote François Odet, a cousin of the de Rivazes, to the brother Charles in 1803, adding, *"Si je pouvais faire quelque chose, commande; je suis à tes ordres; tu es notre capitaine, mais fais attention que c'est sur toi que roule toute la responsabilité"* (If I can do something, command it; I am at your service; you are our captain, but take care because the responsibility rests on your shoulders).[19] In this way the head of the family decided the collective strategy, but he was also responsible for the assistance, protection, and placement of other family members. Generally, he was expected to provide dowries for his sisters if his parents had already died, find work for his brothers, and support spinsters or other needy relatives. His economic and social power was therefore linked to a wider collective responsibility.

What this system of kinship interdependency means is that the family estate cannot be considered solely in terms of individual property rights. The concrete practices of kinship groups and families, the respective responsibilities and collective rights over the estate, and the interdependencies between the head of the family and other members, meant that the estate resembled the collective property of the group more than that of any single individual. The head of the family, therefore, exercised a form of temporary administration subject to the collective rights of others, a point discussed further below.

Many historians have tried to explore these relations among single-family households by measuring financial flows among relatives.[20] However, the example considered here shows how this approach can be misleading since such assistance can take place without explicit financial flows. When Etienne de Rivaz supported his brother Bernard's children, money was deducted from the inheritance to which they were entitled. In the same way, when Charles-Joseph de Rivaz received his brother's children in his house, the related expenses were deducted from Pierre-Joseph's inheritance, which still had to be divided. Assistance, therefore, followed patterns of economic interdependence: whenever those who received such help had something to inherit, assistance took the form of credit on their portion of the inheritance. However, services such as sheltering children in one's home or providing for their education cannot be quantified exactly. The provision of a service or favor created an obligation, a relational debt, which was not quantifiable in financial terms but could be repaid within a complex and flexible network of reciprocity. In this case, the debt owed to Etienne de Rivaz for the care of his niece was partly repaid by the work performed by her husband on Etienne's land.[21] In order to understand the true nature of mutual assistance, it is therefore necessary to incorporate nonmonetary as well as monetary transactions.

The logic of interdependence as a typically "limited good," that is, one limited both in an absolute sense as well as in relation to a specific group of kin who stood to benefit, is also fundamental to an understanding of the extent of family solidarity and mutual assistance as well as the structural potential for conflict within the family. As previously noted, after Pierre-Joseph's failure, two of his children, Marguerite and Pierre-Emmanuel, were sheltered and raised by their uncle, Charles-Joseph. Since the uncle and aunt had, in a sense, adopted the children, it could have been expected that they would have paid for their education and dowry. In addition, the fact that Charles-Joseph and his wife Marie-Julienne had only one male child meant that in the not improbable case of his death, Pierre-Emmanuel could have maintained the family name and property, with obvious advantages in relation to dynastic succession. However, to pay for Pierre-Emmanuel's education and to support his career would have been counterproductive because in a context of limited resources it would have disadvantaged their own children, and especially the heir Charles-Emmanuel. As a consequence, Pierre-Emmanuel himself was forced to abandon his desire to study at university and, against his will, work as an official in France, where he died in 1833, never having been married. His sister, Marguerite, who according to her brother was a "victim of a spinsterhood to which she had been condemned by the lack of property," died in 1775.

In this context of dynastic relations and succession, Pierre-Emmanuel's position was particularly problematic. On the one hand, he was the potential successor. On the other, he was also a dangerous potential rival. In the 1760s his aunt, Marie-Julienne, wife of Charles-Joseph, actively plotted to exclude him from the office of *châtelain* and remove him from the village in order to preserve the position and family supremacy for her own son Charles-Emmanuel.[22] In this case, competition within the family group determined the fundamental limits to collective solidarity. It also shows how Marie-Julienne's dominant position within the kinship group provided her with a degree of political autonomy. Despite the interests of her husband's family, she later supported a stranger in the office of *châtelain* instead of her own nephews.[23]

The case of the de Rivaz family, as described previously, illustrates how inheritance was in fact part of a wider set of relationships influenced by the interdependence and cooperation that extended beyond the immediate circle of Etienne's descendants to include a larger group of relatives. Indeed, the times of crisis when assistance was needed were often those in which vertical inheritance of property was no longer possible. In common cases of early death of heirs, for example, when inheritance was distributed in collateral ways, interdependence was automatically extended to a larger group. Generally it was in those cases that the connection between inheritance and assistance became explicit. For example, in his will of 1718 François de Rivaz appointed as heirs his sister's children, specifying that this bequest was done *"in spem et considerationem benefi- ciorum et assistentiarum quas sperat habere in futurum a dictis nepotibus"* (in the hope and consideration of benefits and acts of assistance which he or she hopes to have in the future from the said nephews or nieces).[24] For this reason, research on the relationships between the provision of welfare and the family needs to take account of other members of the *ménage*, or household.[25]

Laws and customs in eighteenth-century Valais provided relatives with a set of opportunities with which to influence individual destinies. For instance, where the parent died intestate, the law dictated that the appointment of tutors and advisers for orphans should be determined by a council consisting of unspecified relatives. This procedure was outlined in Charles-Joseph de Rivaz's will in case of the death of his wife, Marie-Julienne. Relatives could also become involved in economic matters, as happened elsewhere in Europe, through the laws of preemption. In Valais this is most particularly associated with the so-called *droit de tente*: relatives had a right of preemption in the sale of real estate that in practice meant they were able to exercise some control over an individual's property.

Even more important was their capacity to exercise some control over marriage, especially in the wedding contracts of the middle and upper classes. In some cases, close relatives and collateral kin could be involved, as happened in the case of the powerful de Riedmatten family.[26] This is often ignored by those researching inheritance, given that generally it was not the will but the marriage contract that set the basis of the succession strategy within the family. In marriage contracts, in fact, there were often binding agreements concerning future inheritance, and for that reason they were not infrequently influenced by the approval of those relatives who had a real or potential interest in the family property. What did this involvement mean? It attempted to ensure that the interests of relatives with a stake in the inheritance were not compromised. Collateral consent also had the practical aim of avoiding potentially expensive lawsuits in the future, examples of which abound in the Vallesan documentation.[27] As a result, when we consider questions of assistance, cooperation, and interdependence within a wider family context, we necessarily confront a situation that involves the extensive kin relationships within which families operated.

These wider relationships are illustrated in Figure 5.3, which outlines some of the crucial interrelations in the de Rivaz family considered earlier. This figure shows the successions and various kinds of help that were of crucial importance for the de Rivaz family between 1710 and 1770. These

Figure 5.3
The Primary Kinship of the de Rivaz Family: Relationships of Assistance, Replacement, and Succession That Were External to the Nuclear Family

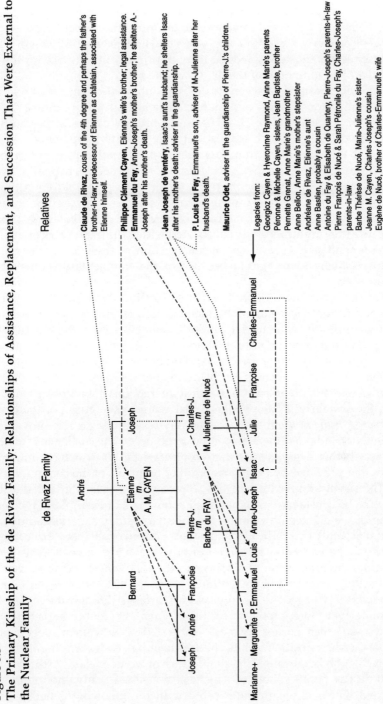

reflected the needs of the group, such as the care of minors or assistance for the needy. They could include, for example, the transfer between relatives of property, a position, a job, or a house. The group shown in Figure 5.3 represents those people who were of primary importance for the survival and continuation of the de Rivaz lineage.

The relationships between this closely interdependent set of relatives, set within a much larger and more diffuse kinship group, can be defined as *primary kinship relationships*. These relationships can be further strengthened by other links, such as those between parents, godparents, and godsons, or those resulting from guardianships and other forms of practical cooperation. Joseph de Rivaz, for example, succeeded his nephew Charles-Joseph as *châtelain* and also the tutor of Pierre-Joseph's children. Although these primary kinship relationships are not necessarily based on the most intense day-to-day social interactions, they are nevertheless significant because they are structurally constituted within the framework of dynastic interdependence. Clearly any reconstruction of these kinds of relationships is likely to be partial because of the fragmentary nature of the sources.[28]

On the other hand, the full extent of kinship interdependence extends beyond formal moments of interaction, such as inheritance or marriage. For example, if we consider family account books, a thick network of everyday interactions becomes evident: small loans, exchanges of products, provision of minor services, and other forms of immediate help. This second set of relationships can be defined as *everyday kinship relationships* and were made up of intense practical interactions not necessarily involving the systemic interdependence that would have arisen in the case of *primary kinship relationships*. Yet everyday assistance was also provided by neighbors and other members of the community. The challenge is to determine whether everyday assistance provided by kin was more important than that provided by neighbors or other members of the community.[29]

The second implication of this approach is that kinship relationships need to be considered as dynamic phenomena. For example, at the beginning of the eighteenth century, the de Rivaz family experienced upward social mobility that radically changed its pattern of alliances. Once Etienne de Rivaz had attained a position of power, having succeeded his cousin Claude, the orientation of alliances in the following generation changed radically.[30] Etienne and his children were the first ones to get married outside the village. Access to powerful families through the female line became ever more important for the de Rivaz's ascent to higher political office. As other studies have also shown, despite women's legal subordination, their position as links in the kinship network was highly significant.[31] A good example of the significance of women relates to the de Nucé and du Fay families, both of which became strategically important in the second half of the eighteenth century. In the following generation this importance was emphasized through the marriages of Charles-Emmanuel de Rivaz to Marie-Caterine de Nucé and Isaac de Rivaz to Louise du Fay. The two women were cousins through their mothers. The conclusion that can be reached is that social mobility and economic interests can shape the pattern of kinship alliances over long periods of time, and for that reason we need to move beyond a structural analysis of kinship toward an approach that stresses its more dynamic and fluid nature.[32]

## THE TRANSMISSION OF SOCIAL CAPITAL

Inheritance is important, not only in terms of property transfer, but also in relation to the transmission of political, economic, and social power. An example of the transmission of social power through inheritance is provided by the de Nucé family (Figure 5.4). This shows the transmission of positions within the family of Marie-Julienne de Nucé, the wife of Charles-Joseph de Rivaz, in Vouvry. In the period from 1630 to 1680, the most important positions were transmitted within a single family, the deputy head of which was Petermand de Nucé. This strategy was extended later to men that married women of the de Nucé dynasty such as Antoine Girod, Joseph Pignat, and Jean Pot.

The practice of replacing the positions from within the de Nucé clan affected a relatively large group of kin. This pattern of succession assumes a different configuration if we consider not only the transmission of offices but also wider forms of cooperation that include financial support as well as the provision of services. In the context of Malthusian scarcity, assistance in the form of help in difficult times, protection, or political and social support was crucial. These wider forms of cooperation can be illustrated by the connections that were decisive in the social and political ascent of Charles-Emmanuel de Rivaz in the first part of his public career between 1778 and 1798 (Figure 5.5). His mother's powerful relatives, notably Pierre-Louis du Fay and Joseph de Ventéry, promoted the administrative career of Charles-Emmanuel in the district of Monthey. His brother-in-law, the Comte de Paradés, was a central figure in a risky investment in French territory overseas, in which various members of the de Rivaz and de Nucé families participated. In 1784, Charles-Emmanuel was on the point of emigrating to Santo Domingo, where he would have become the overseer of his brother-in-law's land. However, the venture was interrupted by the Comte's death, and the scheme never materialized. Nevertheless, it demonstrated how kinship could function as a means by which opportunities, jobs, and investments could be transferred to members of the group.

In this case the links among relatives are different from those previously identified and involve those persons in the network who were in a strategic position to influence others. Without the assistance of such relatives,

**Figure 5.4**
**Transmission of Offices in the de Nucé Family, Vouvry, 1600–1760**

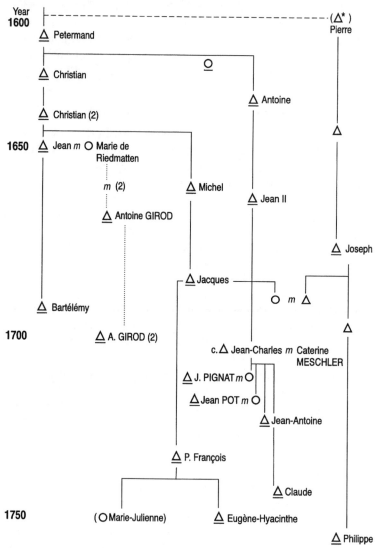

Key
△  Male
O  Female
m  Marriage
△̲  Châtelain

\*  Lateral branch decending from Pierre de Nucé in the male line, brother of Petermand's great-grandfather.

Figure 5.5
**Strategic Kinship: The Example of Charles-Emmanuel de Rivaz, 1778–1798**

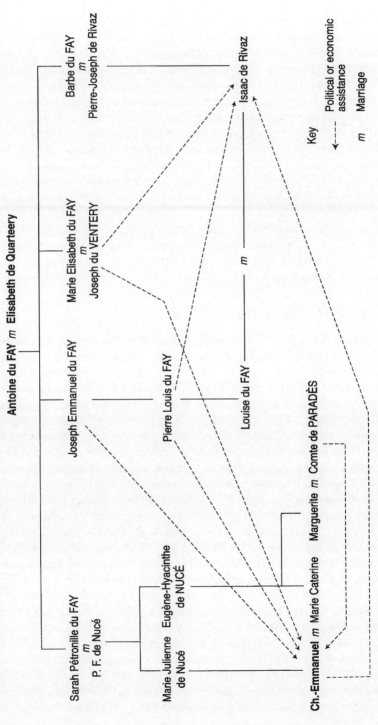

Charles-Emmanuel's career would not have been possible, and in this sense, we can define such kin as *strategic relatives*. Sometimes these relationships were strengthened by godparent and guardianship ties. The resulting situation was that individuals were placed in a dense and complex web of interdependent linkages, incorporating primary, everyday, and strategic relationships. However, the activation of these strategic relationships was by no means automatic and often depended upon other forms of mutually reinforcing social interaction. For example, before Etienne de Rivaz "inherited" the office of *châtelain* from his cousin Claude, they had been partners in a company that provided postal services in the St Gingolph area. In a similar way, Charles-Emmanuel de Rivaz was joint owner of some land in Vouvry with his relative, Joseph-Emmanuel du Fay, prior to succeeding him as head of the district of Monthey (Figure 5.5).[33] The implications of unraveling these sets of linkages are that the activation of strategic relationships did not depend solely on existing genealogical links, but also on the active policy and strategic objectives of the family at critical points in its life cycle.

## THE ROLE OF WOMEN

Rather than playing a passive role, women were actively involved in the functioning of kinship networks and corresponding flows of economic, social, and political capital.[34] For example, at points of discontinuity or cessation of the patriarchal line in the de Nucé family, the transmission of power was governed by women through personal alliances and relationships (Figure 5.4). After Jean de Nucé's death, his wife, Marie de Riedmatten, married Antoine Girod, who then became the political head of the de Nucé family and was twice made *châtelain* of Vouvry. However, this succession did not happen without opposition from others in the de Nucé family. For example, on several occasions Marie de Riedmatten questioned the legality of her brother-in-law Michel's inheritance, and later her son contested the conduct of his stepfather's handling of family affairs. A similar situation arose with Caterine Meschler, wife and then widow of Jean-Charles de Nucé (Figure 5.4). The transmission of power in both these cases clearly passed through the woman, who acted in part against the interests of other members of the kinship group. These examples focus attention on how the status of women could change substantially depending on the standing of the family, relationships with kin, the death of a husband, and the supply of potential successors.

What this evidence shows is how family strategies were fluid in the context of changing circumstances, providing opportunities for women to exert their influence. As discussed earlier, Marie Julienne de Nucé used her not inconsiderable influence to exclude her husband's nephews from political power when they threatened her own son's interests. Similarly, during her long period as a widow between 1759 and 1791 she behaved in a very different way to her husband, Charles-Joseph de Rivaz. During his lifetime, and to his daughters' disadvantage, Charles followed an agnatic dynastic strategy by appointing his nephew, Pierre-Emmanuel, as his universal heir and replacement. In contrast, once she became a widow, Marie-Julienne favored the opposite strategy, marginalizing Pierre-Emmanuel and his father Pierre-Joseph while promoting her own children's interests, even to the extent of supporting nonfamily members in the office *châtelain*. Using the words of an emigrant to the region in the eighteenth century, this structural conflict between male and female interests within the family can best be summarized as "women point to women and don't think about men."[35]

The broad conclusion that can be reached regarding the status of women is that their role should be interpreted in a more dynamic way and understood in the context of the network of relationships within which they operated. In general, apart from legal discrimination, women's social and familial status were not determined in any mechanistic way but rather depended, as did men's, on life cycle, events related to inheritance, and their position in kinship and wider social networks. For example, a significant proportion of married women become head of the family after their husband's death and in doing so acquired considerable power in directing the path of inheritance. In this role women had real power, not only over the care of children but also in relation to the politics of the family and its economic fortunes. By contrast, those children whose parents lived to an old age, *cadets*, or the poor were likely to have remained single and in a subordinate position throughout their lives. This was the fate of Pierre-Emmanuel de Rivaz and in part of his brothers. While legal constraints might have circumscribed the formal limits of women's freedom to act, in practice family relationships were acted out in a dynamic and highly variable context.

## CONCLUSION

Welfare in eighteenth-century Alpine societies was based on a system of control and allocation of scarce resources, including political positions. In this logic communities played an important role, but within them the family was paramount. Interdependence in relation to inheritance and mutual assistance promoted the internal cohesion of these family groups. In a context of high mortality and economic uncertainty, however, the family nucleus was too restricted and therefore too precarious to guarantee continuity. As a consequence, economic stability was entrusted to a wider network of relatives that was activated at specific points in the family life cycle. Requests made to this wider network in terms of solidarity and assistance could vary in kind and incorporate different subgroups.

Using the terminology already discussed, *primary kinship relationships* were accompanied by *strategic kinship relationships* and *everyday kinship relationships*.

However we consider these issues, the systemic interdependence of the family group is of fundamental importance, resulting in an organic collective within which each individual is intimately bound to others. This systemic approach has important consequences for understanding the social dynamics of preindustrial societies. In such societies, dynastic relationships and familial cooperation were important in the organization of power over property and political authority.[36] When individuals acted in their own interests as opposed to those of the wider kinship group, they were always likely to face conflict. Community claims over property, as well as those of family and relatives, therefore require us to question the primacy of modern bourgeois conceptions of possessive individualism. In this sense, we need to take account of the collective nature of the family patrimony over which the household head had temporary rights of usufruct rather than outright ownership.[37] By identifying the significance of usufruct in relationship to family property it is also possible to question the relative power of men and women over resources.[38]

This detailed study of two elite families in Valais, while in some ways unique, points to general issues common in other Alpine communities and social classes. Although families without property faced different pressures, even among these groups recent studies show that cooperation among relatives was important.[39] The peripheral situation of Valais, the existence of powerful corporate autonomies, the absence of urban centers, lack of industry, and the low incidence of waged work coupled with economic stagnation and slow demographic growth ensured that Malthusian scarcity remained endemic. In those parts of Switzerland that were more commercialized family groups were less cohesive. However, work on other rural societies in different countries during the *ancien régime* suggests similar patterns of family interdependency prevailed.[40]

## NOTES

The research on which this chapter is based has been supported by the Swiss National Science Foundation, and the full findings will be published shortly. My thanks go to Giovanni Levi and the editors for their helpful suggestions and critical comments. Naturally, any errors remain my responsibility.

1. Giovanni Levi, *L'eredità immateriale: Carriera di un esorcista nel Piemonte del Seicento* (Turin: Einaudi, 1985; English edition: *Inhering Power: The Story of an Exorcist*, Chicago: University of Chicago Press, 1988) and Gérard Delille, *Famille et propriété dans le Royaume de Naples, XVIe–XIXe siècle* (Paris and Rome: Ecole française de Rome, 1985).

2. David W. Sabean, *Kinship in Neckarhausen, 1700–1870* (Cambridge: Cambridge University Press, 1998).

3. Barry Reay, "Kinship and the Neighbourhood in Nineteenth-Century Rural England: The Myth of the Autonomous Nuclear Family," *Journal of Family History* 21 (1996): 87–104.

4. For the theoretical debate on the problems related to social variability, see especially Frederik Barth, *Balinese Worlds* (Chicago: University of Chicago Press, 1993). Examples of superficial and misleading use of quantitative data are common. See, for instance, Alfred Perrenoud, "The Coexistence of Generations and the Availability of Kin in a Rural Community at the Beginning of the Nineteenth Century," *The History of the Family* 3 (1998): 1–15.

5. Michael Mitterauer, "Sozialgeschichte der Familie als landeskundlicher Forschungsgegenstand: Anwendungsmöglichkeiten historischer Personenstandlisten," in *Historisch-anthropologische Familienforschung: Fragestellungen und Zugangsweisen* (Wien: Böhlau, 1990) and Michael Mitterauer and Reinhard Sieder, "The Reconstruction of the Family Life Course: Theoretical Problems and Empirical Results," in *Family Forms in Historic Europe,* ed. Richard Wall, Jean Robin, and Peter Laslett, (Cambridge: Cambridge University Press, 1983), 309–45. For a psychological perspective, see the classic work by Ivan Boszormenyi-Nagy and Geraldine M. Spark, *Invisible Loyalties* (New York: Harper and Row, 1973). See also Bert Hellinger, *Ordnungen der Liebe: Ein Kurs-Buch mit B.H. Zweite überarbeitete und ergänzte Auflage* (Heidelberg: Carl Auer Systeme, 1995) and Bert Hellinger and Hunter Beaumont, *Touching Love* (Heidelberg: Cael Auer Systeme, 1999).

6. The Cambridge school of historical demography is perhaps the best known of this genre. The classic works are Peter Laslett and Richard Wall, eds., *Household and Family in Past Time* (Cambridge: Cambridge University Press, 1972); and Richard Wall, Jean Robin, and Peter Laslett, eds., *Family Forms in Historic Europe* (Cambridge: Cambridge University Press, 1983). For the Alpine region see Robert M. Netting, *Balancing on an Alp: Ecological Change and Continuity in a Swiss Mountain Community* (Cambridge: Cambridge University Press, 1981) and Pier Paolo Viazzo, *Upland Communities: Environment, Population and Social Structure in the Alps since the Sixteenth Century* (Cambridge: Cambridge University Press, 1989).

7. Archives d'Etat du Valais (AEVS), Sion, *fonds de Rivaz* 14, 2, 2. Unless otherwise stated, documentation on this family comes from this section (hereafter *Rz*).

8. Daniel Salamin, *Pauvreté et assistance en Valais au XIXe siècle: Le cas de la communauté de Bagnes* (Mémoire: Université de Genève, 1976); Marcelle Mayor-Gay, "L'assistance publique en Valais de 1800 à nos jours" (Travail de diplome, University of Lausanne, 1978); and Dyonis Imesch, "Beiträge zur Geschichte und Statistik der Pfarrgemeinde Naters," *Zeitschrift für schweizerische Statistik* 44 (1908): 369–414.

9. George Foster, "Peasant Societies and the Image of Limited Good," *American Anthropologist* 67 (1965): 293–315.

10. Edward P. Thompson, "The Moral Economy of the English Crowd in the Eighteenth Century," *Past and Present* 50 (1971): 78–98 and Edward P. Thompson, "The Moral Economy Reviewed," in *Customs in Common* (Harmondsworth: Penguin, 1993), 259–351.

11. The concept of a "Malthusian" society is based on the work of George Foster. See Foster, "Peasant Societies." However, it is used here in a looser way that takes account of social and economic changes over time. On the influence of the "Malthusian" logic on Alpine societies see Sandro Guzzi, "Antonomies locales et sys-

tèmes politiques alpins: La Suisse italienne au XVIIe et XVIIIe siècles," in *La découverte des Alpes*, ed. Jean-François Bergier and Sandro Guzzi (Basel: Schwabe and Company, 1992), 229–55. On Valais, see Netting, *Balancing on an Alp*. More recently, see Anne-Lise Head-König, "Malthus dans les Alpes: La diversité de régulation démographique dans l'arc alpin du XVIe au début du XXe siècle," in *Quand la montagne aussi a une histoire: Mélanges offerts à Jean-François Bergier*, ed. Martin Körner and François Walter (Bern: Haupt, 1996), 361–70.

12. See, for instance, a letter in AEVS, *Fonds de Nucé* (hereafter *Nc*), P 240. The concept of *place* is similar to the term *niche* ("Stelle" in German) used by Peter Laslett and others from the Cambridge Group for the History of Population and Social Structure as a way of understanding strategies of family reproduction. See Peter Laslett, "Familie und Industrialisierung: Eine starke Theorie," in *Sozialgeschichte der Familie in der Neuzeit Europas*, ed. Werner Conze (Stuttgart: Klett-Cotta 1976), 13–31.

13. *Nc*, P 426.

14. The *châtelain* (castellan) was the principal representative of the state in the village and at the same time was the representative of the feudal lord. It was the most important office in the village.

15. Once they reached maturity, the firstborn children of officials were co-opted into economic activities and started to represent their father in external contacts. Etienne de Rivaz included in his will a special bequest to the firstborn grandson, Pierre-Emmanuel: *Rz*, 14, 2, 2 (1750).

16. The concept of "team games" introduced by Renata Ago is an eloquent metaphor for the interdependence of the family group. Renata Ago, "Giochi di squadra: Uomini e donne nelle famiglie nobili del XVII secolo," in *Signori, patrizi, cavalieri in Italia centro-meridionale nell'età moderna*, ed. Maria Antonietta Visceglia (Roma: Laterza, 1992), 256–64.

17. The high percentage of single people in preindustrial societies is also discussed in Wall, Robin, and Laslett, *Family Forms*. See also John Hajnal, "Two Kinds of Pre-Industrial Family Formation Systems," in Wall, Robin, and Laslett, *Family Forms*, 65–104. However, in the boroughs of Vouvry and St Gingolph the percentage of single people was low. In the inventory of St Gingolph of 1783, single people over the age of 30 comprised just 3 percent of the resident population. In other Vallesan boroughs, the situation was very different; for the case of Törbel see Netting, *Balancing on an Alp*, 76.

18. Sabean, *Kinship in Neckarhausen*, 11. For a practical analysis of the functioning of this model see Netting, *Balancing on an Alp*.

19. Cited in Pierre Alain Putallaz, *Eugénie de Troistorrents et Charles d'Odet: Etude sur leur corréspondance inédite (1812–17)*, vol. 1 (Lausanne: Payot, 1985), 45, my emphasis.

20. See in particular Richard Wall, "Introduction," in Wall, Robin, and Laslett, *Family Forms*, 1–63.

21. *Rz*, 14, 7, 1.

22. Henri Michelet, "A St Gingolph chez Marie-Julienne de Rivaz (1725–1791): Une famille d'autrefois," *Vallesia* 33 (1978): 443–66.

23. On the interesting figure of Marie-Julienne and her feminine strategies of power see Sandro Guzzi-Heeb, "Marie-Julienne de Nucé, die Politik und die Re-

ligion: Elemente einer weiblichen Machtstrategie," *Traverse: Zeitschrift für Geschichte* 3 (2001): 132–40.

24. Private archive of André François de Rivaz (Drivaz), Monthey, number 64 (1718).

25. On the possible meanings of *ménage* (household) in the context of kinship relationships see Euthymios Papataxiachis, "La valeur du ménage: Classes sociales, stratégies matrimoniales et lois ecclésiastiques à Lesbos au XIXe siècle," in *Espaces et familles dans l'Europe du Sud à l'âge moderne*, ed. Stuart Woolf (Paris: Edition Maison des Sciences de l'Homme, 1993), 109–41.

26. See, for example, AEVS, *fonds Léon de Riedmatten*, 9 (1664). Sometimes the contracts contained the phrase *aprés consentement des parents respectifs* (after the consent of the respective parents). See the contracts of the de Rivaz family in *Rz* 14. Clauses indicating the consent of relatives were also found in various popular marriage contracts. In such documents the relatives also often appeared before the court. See, for example, *Nc*, M 7 (19.7.1716).

27. This aim was made explicit in some marriage contracts. See, for example, AEVS, *Nc*, P 138 a (1662).

28. The analysis here is based on a variety of sources, including wills, marriage contracts, economic documents, and correspondence of the de Rivaz family.

29. Analysis of transactions undertaken by the de Rivaz family from 1650 show that relatives had a privileged position, especially in relation to the care, acquisition, and sale of land. A larger and more systematic analysis of similar transactions is currently in progress for the community of Vouvry.

30. Claude was probably a cousin in the fourth grade and brother-in-law of his father through his second wife. However, the precise relationship mentioned in the father's will is ambiguous because of the frequent homonymy: *Rz*, 23, 2 (1712).

31. Sabean, *Kinship in Neckarhausen*, 490 and passim; Netting, *Balancing on an Alp*, 194.

32. Pierre Bourdieu, "La parenté comme représentation et comme volonté," in *Esquisse d'une théorie de la pratique, précédée de trois études d'ethnologie cabyle* (Paris: Seuil, 2000).

33. AEVS, *Archives de la commune de Vouvry*, R 17 (land register, eighteenth century).

34. This contrasts with depictions of women in other studies of kinship networks. See, for example, Raul Merzario, *Adamocrazia: Famiglie di emigranti in una regione alpina (Svizzera italiana, XVIII secolo)* (Bologna: Il Mulino, 2000). This interpretation is partly explained by the scarcity of sources on women's roles.

35. Merzario, *Adamocrazia*, 24; Wall, "Introduction," 11.

36. Giovanni Levi, "Famiglie contadine nella Liguria del Settecento," in *Centro e periferia di uno stato assoluto: Tre saggi su Piemonte e Liguria in età moderna*, ed. Giovanni Levi (Torino: Rosemberg and Sellier, 1985), 71–149 and Osvaldo Raggio, "Parentèles et espaces politiques en Ligurie à l'époque moderne," in Woolf, *Espaces et familles*, 143–63.

37. Paolo Grossi, *Un altro modo di possedere: L'emersione di alternative di proprietà alla coscienza giuridica post-unitaria* (Milano: Giuffré, 1977) and Paolo Grossi, *Il dominio e le cose: Percezioni medievali e moderne dei diritti reali* (Milano: Giuffré, 1992). See also Chris Hann, ed., *Property Relations: Renewing the Anthropological Tradition* (Cambridge: Cambridge University Press, 1998). On the origin of the concept of

property and kinship rights in Valais, see Gottfried Partch, *Das Mitwirkungsrecht der Familiengemeinschaft im älteren Walliser Recht (Laudatio parentum et hospicium)* (Genève: Librairie Droz, 1955).

38. See Giulia Calvi and Isabelle Chabot, eds., *Le ricchezze delle donne: Diritti patrimoniali e poteri famigliari in Italia (XIII–XIX secolo)* (Torino: Rosemberg and Sellier, 1998). On family limitations of male property see Sandra Cavallo, "Proprietà o possesso? Composizione e controllo dei beni delle donne a Torino (1650–1710)," in Calvi and Chabot, *Le ricchezze delle donne,* 205.

39. Jürgen Schlumbohm, "Micro-History and the Macro-Models of the European Demographic System in Pre-Industrial Time: Life-Course Patterns in the Parish of Belm (Northwest Germany), Seventeenth to the Nineteenth Centuries," *The History of the Family* 1 (1996): 81–95 and Reay, "Kinship and the Neighbourhood."

40. See Sabean, *Kinship in Neckarhausen;* Levi, "Famiglie contadine"; Mitterauer, "Sozialgeschichte der Familie"; Martine Segalen, *Fifteen Generations of Bretons: Kinship and Society in Lower Brittany 1720–1980* (Cambridge: Cambridge University Press, 1981); and Franco Ramella, *Terra e telai. Sistemi di parentela e manifattura nel Biellese dell'Ottocento* (Turin: Einaudi, 1984). On the Alpine elite see, in particular, Urs Kälin, *Die Urner Magistratenfamilien: Herrschaft, ökonomische Lage und Lebensstil einer ländlichen Oberschicht 1700–1850* (Zürich: Chronos, 1991). On the Italian elite see Ago, "Giochi di squadra."

## CHAPTER 6

# Wealth, Gender, and Inheritance Among the U.S. Elite: The Rockefellers and Binghams

*Marsha Shapiro Rose*

## INTRODUCTION

In the context of inheritance, affective perceptions of gender are arguably as important as, if not more important than, the legal requirements that structure the formal transfer of property and wealth between the generations. This chapter explores this issue in the context of intergenerational property transfers among the American upper class in the twentieth century. Specifically, it examines the transfer of resources between generations within two elite American families, the Rockefellers and Binghams. Among the Rockefellers, the youngest child and only son received the bulk of his family's cultural, social, and economic capital. While the distribution of capital among the Binghams was apparently more partible in the sense that daughters and sons received similar educational advantages, the family business and its accompanying capital nevertheless passed to the sons. Thus, while overall the distribution of family wealth among the Binghams was more equally divided than that of the Rockefellers, a veil of male primogeniture in fact shrouded both families.

Such gender inequalities permeated the allocation of cultural, social, and economic capital, both *inter vivos* and testate. However, the movement of these various forms of capital across generations not only perpetuates class solidarity and social reproduction, it also preserves family continuity. Children may attend a parent's alma mater, join the same elite country club, or receive a sentimental book, the family's summer home, the family's business, or the most liquid of all capital, money. In each instance, the children receive unearned benefits by virtue of their birthright in ways that provide insights into the reproduction of elite family structures. By examining inheritance strategies within upper-class families, we can gain valuable insights into the relationships between family provision, gender ideology, and social reproduction. The ways in which parents transmit the symbolic aspects of their class status along with the business and cultural connections in order to ensure class impermeability and endogamy is a theme of particular interest.

Paradoxically, perhaps, the connection between love and money within families is most evident in the intergenerational transfer of property—who gets what, and when do they get it? Some children receive large sums of money from their parents during their lifetime, others receive generous bequests at death, while certain children receive substantial *inter vivos* and testamentary gifts. Parents can, and often do, use monetary rewards to illustrate their pleasure with their children's behavior. Thus it is often the case that the movement of money from one generation to another is inflected with normative understandings of familial relationships and structures as well as more rational legal and economic considerations.

However, the emotional side of life focused within the family has traditionally been viewed as relatively immune to calculative discussions about money. For this reason, inheritance and *inter vivos* gifts are potential sources of conflict among family members. When affection is counted in monetary terms as if it were a ledger sheet, social relationships within families are likely to be disrupted. Ironically, while money continues to provide the leading characterization of the American upper class, there is often a disdain among the elite to discuss its very existence. As Joanie Bronfman, daughter of Edgar Bronfman, founder of the Seagrams conglomerate, claimed, there is an "upper class norm that one doesn't talk about money."[1]

In *Wealth Addiction*, Philip Slater characterized the meaning of money in three ways: First, it has a symbolic quality, by which he meant "that it has value only as long as we collectively believe that it does. Second, money provides an accepted tool of measurement, enabling groups to eliminate subjective and qualitative descriptions and instead direct attention to quantifiable distinctions. Finally, money is the means to achieve what we believe are necessary or desirable ends.[2] According to Slater, "people need money to spend on things that we have spent billions persuading ourselves we need."[3] For some scholars, the idealized myth of family relationships as separate from monetary considerations is difficult to sustain. It is argued that familial interactions are based on the same reciprocity that permeates other types of social relationships. So, for example, within the family, money is not infrequently used as a means to gauge affection and preference. In the context of mixing love and money, Marcia Millman, for example, has debunked the mysticism of the family by maintaining that "there is probably more counting in families than in any other close circle."[4] In agreeing with Georg Simmel's assessment of the corrupting influence of money on relationships, she argues that this belief in its nefarious influence often makes discussions of money within the family difficult: "dealing with family money is embarrassing and awkward because money challenges our romanticized views of the family, and talking about it exposes family grudges and envies, as well as the almost-universal feeling that one was not loved enough or given enough attention."[5]

The movement of money across generations, therefore, is not a random process. Sometimes bequests are driven by concern for family welfare; in other instances, parents will use inheritance to manipulate their children's behaviors.[6] This chapter will explore the place of gender in determining the passage of resources and argues that in the context of twentieth-century America, most intergenerational transfers do not distinguish by gender.[7] However, it will also demonstrate that in those cases where gender does play a role, sons are usually advantaged over their sisters.[8]

In the partible distribution of inheritance, male preference is subtle. While assets may be divided equally, the nature of the transfer varies by gender. According to historian Gerda Lerner, "we can best express the complexity of gendered class positions by comparing each woman with her brother and considering how the sister's and brother's lives and opportunities would differ."[9] In this respect, sons, more often than daughters, receive their inheritances outright. For female heirs, estates are held in trusts controlled by their husbands, brothers, sons, or advisors.[10] The daughters, wives, and sisters of wealthy men rarely inherit leadership positions in the family's corporations. As Kate Mulholland suggests, "daughters are simply not encouraged, nor expected to see themselves as heirs or as leaders in the business."[11] Pierre Bourdieu addressed the often unspoken subordination of women in his essay on *Masculine Domination*. He argues that "the strength of the masculine order is seen in the fact that it dispenses with justification: the androcentric vision imposes itself as neutral and has no need to spell itself out in discourses aimed at legitimating it. The social order functions as an immense symbolic machine tending to ratify the masculine domination on which it is founded."[12] Thus, it is the case that female heirs reinforce traditional gender stereotypes and occupy supportive roles within the upper class.[13] As will be shown, for those women of wealth who question patriarchal hegemony, the costs can be high.

## THE ELITE CLASS

Possession of cultural and social, as well as economic capital is of particular significance to members of the upper class.[14] According to Lerner, "the resources that distinguish a rich man from a poor one are tangible.

They may be elaborated culturally and defined in various ways, but they are quantifiable and real."[15] The possession of certain types of social and cultural capital sets the upper class apart and gives the group its defining characteristics and cohesiveness. Using rites of passage such as debutante balls, philanthropic activities, and other social events, the upper class maintains class cohesion and exercises a veto over newcomers. In a similar vein, often housed in private, elite, remote areas, children of wealthy families have limited contact with those of other social ranks. The formal rituals of the upper class such as charity balls, weddings, and membership in social clubs act to certify a person's social standing and reinforce the social reproduction of the group. Similarly, the "norm of exclusivity" serves to perpetuate the restricted membership of the upper class.[16] The ability to restrict entry into elite society is "status power par excellence."[17] In turn, the connected issues of privacy, exclusivity, and endogamy ensure the perpetuation of this elite group.

The privacy, exclusivity, and endogamy of the U.S. upper class are visible through the education of their children. According to the legal historian John Langbein, the provision of an elite education for the children of upper-class families is "very American."[18] Such an education is seen to provide the child with an opportunity to succeed in life in his or her own right rather than to rely upon family wealth. However, prestigious schools also serve another important function because they further the separation of the different social classes. For some, elite schools and universities are "an essential element in the calculus of preserving [upper class] privilege."[19] As sociologists Peter W. Cookson, Jr., and Carolyn Hodges Persell argue, "to be accepted into a private school is to be accepted into a social club . . . a status group that is defined as a group of people who feel a sense of social similarity."[20] Pierre Bourdieu asserts that the educational system has overshadowed the family in the development of social capital. Alumni of elite schools, according to Bourdieu, owe their influence "to the magnitude of the social capital held by its members, precisely because of their small number and hence their scarcity, and because of the solidarity which unites them and enables them to pool symbolically and often practically the capital which they possess individually."[21]

Aside from privacy and exclusivity, the upper class is also notable for its moral self-righteousness. A persistent American belief is that "wealth is nature's reward for special cleverness, industry, or talent."[22] Along with these abilities, some Americans assume a high moral position for the wealthy and a lower one for the poor. The upper class has internalized this moral elitism along with the freedom, power, and responsibilities that accompany wealth.[23] Such beliefs in the moral and economic superiority of the wealthy, however, contradict the American mythology of equality of opportunity. This paradox of wealth is most apparent among the heirs to fortunes. While the originators of wealth often embody ideals of self-reliance, hard work, and success, their children enter the realm of the wealthy only through an accident of birth.[24] However, among the elite the intergenerational transfer of resources is instrumental in perpetuating the family dynasty. The questions of who gets what and when they get it carry more than rhetorical or academic interest. With the family as the central agent, the passing of economic, social, and cultural capital from parents to future generations is central to the social reproduction of elite status, not to mention the family name, business, and money.[25]

Two further questions that arise in relation to the transfer of resources within elite families are the extent to which it deviates from the middle-class norm of partible estate division and the way in which gender issues influence the nature of that transfer. Under American law, unequal division of resources is a purposive action and requires the donor to make a will, which usually necessitates an attorney and accompanying legal costs. Hence, there is a tendency in the middle class toward equality and a "relative inequality aversion" among parents.[26] However, among upper-class families the consequences of partibility can destroy a family dynasty. According to one view, "in order to keep their influence on the organizations they already control, heads of dynasties appoint specific heirs to the most significant boards on which they sit."[27] In her analysis of the Rockefellers and Kennedys, Suzanne Keller concluded there was no pretense of partibility and that the division of resources was predicated along gender lines. "In each family, moreover, a patriarchal constellation exerted differential pressures on the men and the women. The sharply sex-segregated worlds with the men destined for featured and the women for supportive roles, created great, if largely unacknowledged costs for both families."[28]

The remainder of this chapter explores the implications of this gendered transfer of resources for two women from elite families, Edith Rockefeller McCormick and Sallie Bingham. The Rockefeller family is synonymous with wealth: John D. Rockefeller created the largest oil production and distribution company in the world. Even after the U.S. Supreme Court mandated the breakup of Standard Oil in 1911, Rockefeller remained one of the richest men in the world. The Bingham family was not nearly as wealthy as the Rockefellers, but it nevertheless dominated the successful Kentucky media outlets from 1917 until 1986, when Bingham Enterprises sold its newspapers and television and radio stations.[29]

## WOMEN AND INHERITANCE: A ROCKEFELLER AND A BINGHAM

Edith Rockefeller was born in 1872 and was the third surviving child of oil tycoon John D. Rockefeller and his wife, Laura Spelman (see Figure 6.1).[30] In 1895, she married Harold Fowler McCormick, heir to the International Harvester Company fortune, following which she assumed the

**Figure 6.1**
**The Rockefeller Family**

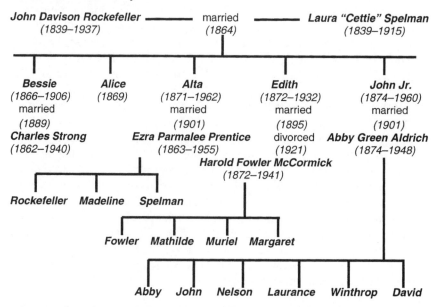

unofficial leadership of Chicago's social elite.[31] While her divorce, failed businesses, and perceived flamboyance were anathema to the Rockefeller men, it was Edith's public defiance of her father, coupled with her unwillingness to follow, or for that matter seek, her father's advice that led to her ostracization within the Rockefeller family.

Edith Rockefeller McCormick was different from her siblings: she was public and ostentatious, and she often violated the family's strict Baptist beliefs.[32] In 1913, against her father's advice, Edith, Harold, and their children moved to Switzerland to study with Carl Jung. The family remained in Europe throughout World War I and returned to Chicago in 1921, when Edith and Harold underwent a scandalous divorce—both had taken up with different partners. Edith's business and philanthropic ventures were an additional embarrassment to her family. At least twice she invested large sums of money into businesses that were short lived. She borrowed money to sustain the Chicago Opera Company and also gave land to house the Chicago Brookfield Zoo. Neither action was approved by her father, John D. Rockefeller, Sr.

Gender distinctions are most apparent when comparing the resources and opportunities available to Edith Rockefeller and her younger brother, John D. Rockefeller, Jr. On July 3, 1917, John D. Rockefeller, Sr., established a trust for his two surviving daughters, Alta and Edith. In establishing

the trusts, he followed a long-standing tradition of denying women control and information about their financial position. The trustees included
their brother, John D. Rockefeller, Jr.; Alta's husband, Ezra Parmalee Prentice; Edith's husband, Harold F. McCormick; and John D. Rockefeller, Sr.'s
personal attorney, Starr J. Murphy. Neither Alta nor Edith had any direct
say in how to manage their trusts.[33]

Throughout her life, Edith's financial records were scrutinized by her
father and younger brother, John D. Rockefeller, Jr. While Edith no doubt
resented this intrusion, she nevertheless continued to accept her father's
largesse. During her lifetime, the *inter vivos* transfer from father to daughter was nothing short of remarkable, and it made her one of the wealthiest
women in the world.[34] However, whatever money Edith received, it was
nowhere near the amount transferred from father to son. John D. Rockefeller, Sr., transferred *inter vivos* nearly half his assets, about $450 million,
to his youngest child and only son.[35] Rockefeller biographers John Harr
and Peter Johnson justify the unequal distribution of assets this way:

Latter-day feminists may chafe at this concentration on the son to the neglect of
the daughters, but the historical context is sufficient explanation. The Rockefellers
were not alone in thinking dynastically only of the male line.... Alta [Edith's
older sister] and Edith were not good at figures or managing affairs, and Junior
[John D. Rockefeller, Jr.] took care of their holdings from an early age.[36]

However, it is clear that neither Alta nor Edith was ever considered as
a viable heir.[37] True, Rockefeller followed a long-standing tradition of preparing sons, rather than daughters, for positions of leadership and being
guardians of wealth. Nevertheless, in the case of the first Rockefeller generation, the father groomed his son from an early age to assume the mantle
of responsibility. When John D. Rockefeller, Jr., was only 13 years old, his
father wrote to him discussing business affairs. Alta and Edith were in
their thirties before there was any correspondence between them and their
father about financial matters. Much to Edith's chagrin, at no time did her
father tell his daughter about his own business affairs. During the final
10 years of her life, prior to her death in 1932, Edith struggled for money
to continue financing her lifestyle and philanthropic ventures, and she
was forced to sell many of her stocks and her jewelry in order to meet
expenses. While her father and brother regretted Edith's situation, neither
rescued her from her financial downfall.[38]

In 1937, five years after Edith's death, Sarah Montague Bingham (Sallie)
was born to Kentucky media magnate Barry Bingham, Sr., and Mary
Clifford Caperton.[39] After attending private preparatory schools, Sallie
graduated from Radcliffe College at a time when the feminist movement,
influenced by Betty Friedan's book *The Feminine Mystique* was gathering
pace.[40] For Sallie, phenomenal wealth, feminism, and the women's move-

**Figure 6.2**
**The Bingham Family**

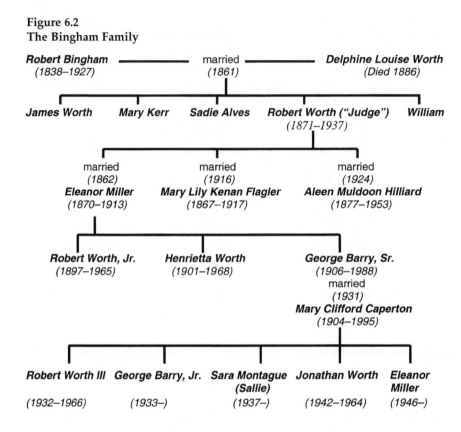

ment ran parallel, and while her three marriages and subsequent divorces were distasteful to her parents, it was her independence, tenacity, and public assertiveness that drove a wedge between herself and her family.

The saga of the Bingham family is one of intrigue and the usurpation of the women's status and economic capital for the benefit of the men.[41] Robert Worth Bingham—popularly known as the "Judge"—Sallie Bingham's grandfather, brought the family from local recognition to national status. The "Judge" married three times, being widowed twice (see Figure 6.2). His first wife and mother to his three children, Eleanor Miller, was a wealthy heiress. Following her death in a car accident, Robert Worth Bingham married Mary Lily Kenan Flagler, heiress to the $90 million estate of Henry Flagler, railroad entrepreneur and former partner of John D. Rockefeller, Sr.[42] The "Judge" used the $5 million he inherited following her death in 1917 to purchase the Louisville *Courier-Journal*, the future Pulitzer-prize-winning Kentucky newspaper and flagship of Bingham Enterprises. In 1933, he reached the pinnacle of his political success when President Franklin Roosevelt appointed him as ambassador to the United Kingdom.

In 1930, Bingham passed control of his media empire to his youngest son, George Barry (Barry, Sr.), Sallie's father. Had Barry, Sr., not agreed to assume the helm of the family company, his father threatened to sell it to outsiders. Neither of Barry's older siblings, both of whom had suffered from bouts of alcoholism, was considered a viable leader. Moreover, Barry's brother was described as a "playboy" and dilettante. His sister, Henrietta, flaunted her lesbianism and sought refuge among the Blooms-bury writers in London. After 33 years at the helm of an expanded Bingham Enterprises, Barry, Sr., prepared to pass the business to the next generation. Two of his sons, Robert and Jonathan, had died prematurely in separate freakish accidents. Initially, Sallie showed little interest in the business and was actively pursuing a writing career, while her younger sister, Eleanor, was caught up in the social movements of the 1960s. Hence, in 1966, shortly after his older son's funeral, he appointed his son and namesake, Barry, Jr., as the heir apparent.

Sallie Bingham often lamented the privileges given to her brothers and denied to her and her younger sister.[43] Deeply influenced by the feminist movement that had emerged in the 1960s and 1970s, when she returned to Louisville in 1977 after a 20-year absence, two failed marriages, and a waning writing career, her distrust and resentment of Barry, Jr., resurfaced. In 1975, Barry, Sr., appointed his daughters, Sallie and Eleanor, and Barry, Jr.'s wife, Edith, to various company boards. However, their appointments were titular. The male Binghams expected their women to attend meetings and do as Barry, Jr.'s wife did—"needlepoint during board meetings."[44]

The demise of the Bingham empire began in the mid-1970s. As the fortunes and reputation of the Louisville *Courier-Journal* began to slip, the Bingham women started to question male hegemony and management practices. After all, the dividends from Bingham Enterprises provided Sallie and Eleanor with an annual income of around $300,000. Frustrated by her inability to exert influence at the newspaper, coupled with what she believed was her brother's ineptitude, Sallie decided to sell her interests in the family company. When she refused a buyout at the price her brother offered, she was ostracized and portrayed as "the black sheep" of the family who prompted the sale of Bingham Enterprises and the breakup of a family empire.[45] Reaffirming her feminist beliefs, Sallie took part of her assets from the sale and founded the Kentucky Foundation for Women in 1986. She currently lives in New Mexico and has never been fully reconciled with her brother.

Edith Rockefeller McCormick and Sallie Bingham lived two generations apart, and the differences between them are glaring. Edith lived most of her life before women could vote; Sallie spent her twenties and thirties in the midst of the women's movement. Edith's education was limited, attending the Rye Female Seminary while her brother graduated from Brown University; Sallie's education was on par with her brothers'. Edith was never given a voice in the Rockefeller corporations or philanthropies; Sallie briefly sat on the board of Bingham Enterprises and worked for a time at the newspaper. Yet they shared an important family dynamic: in the Rockefeller and Bingham dynasties, male prerogatives were maintained. Both Edith and Sallie questioned their family patriarchs, and both were ostracized as a result. In each case, the disputes that ultimately divided the families focused on Edith's and Sallie's independence regarding the management of their share of the family fortune.

## LOVE AND MONEY: DECIDING WHO GETS WHAT AND WHEN THEY GET IT

As a purposive and instrumental action, the selection of heirs provides an insight into family dynamics. On the one hand, transferring cultural, social, and economic capital to children ensures social reproduction and fulfills the dynastic needs of the family.[46] Indeed, according to Slater, it also provides parents with a justification for accumulating wealth: "many wealth addicts claim that the reason they are so agitated and driven in their personal lives is that they want security for their children."[47] On the other hand, the selection of heirs allows testators to exert control over their progeny: "to be able to designate one or more individuals upon whom you will bestow a lifetime income sufficient to cover all creature comforts, without any personal effort on the part of the recipient, is power."[48]

Remi Clignet identified three strategies in the selection of heirs: efficiency, reciprocity, and ascriptive justice. In the pursuit of efficiency, Clignet argues that testators minimize external claims to their estates, such as those of the government. More importantly, the intergenerational transfer of capital is most efficient if it facilitates the family unit. From an economic point of view, Paul Menchik maintains that it is the preservation of family continuity that leads most often to the equal division of family property:

The only reason for equal division which to me seems even semi-plausible is one based upon non-pecuniary transaction costs. Only equality dispels the notion of favoritism among the children, a notion that may reduce the trust and cohesion found among siblings. Economists may liken this familial trust to a public good that can be dissipated by the suspicion of preferential concern. Parents recognize the benefits of intrafamily trust and cohesion, realize that unequal division may endanger its existence, and as a consequence strict neutrality in bequest behavior becomes a firmly ingrained practice.[49]

However, what this view fails to appreciate is that in relation to dynastic families, gender considerations are significant in structuring the way that the selection of heirs takes place. In the Rockefeller and Bingham families, males were clearly preferred in relation to the family businesses and charities. In both families, moreover, the transfer from father to son occurred *inter vivos*. Their daughters either received trust income (Rockefeller) or shared in the business profits (Bingham). It is the case, however, that both fathers believed that transferring family property to the sons was an efficient distribution of resources. Rockefeller did not believe his daughters competent to successfully direct the family interests, and Bingham found his daughters initially uninterested in the family business.

Clignet's second strategy in the selection of heirs is reciprocity, by which parents reward children who have met their expectations in one way or another. By the same token, parents can choose to disinherit, or at least withhold resources, from those children who for one reason or another fail to act in an acceptable way. For Alvin Gouldner, this "norm of reciprocity" was a fundamental building block that provided the cement for a whole range of social relationships.[50] However, this aspect of reciprocity has often been ignored when it comes to discussing the nature of inheritance or the distribution of resources within families. In this context, Millman suggests that part of the interest in reciprocity stems from the premise that parents should love each of their children equally. In reality, parents have preferences, and children are usually aware of who the favored one is in the family. Thus, "however much parents talk about treating their children equally, those who don't 'give back' to their parents" are in jeopardy of losing the family money.[51]

To their fathers, both Edith Rockefeller McCormick and Sallie Bingham defied the norm of reciprocity and were dealt with accordingly when it came to the transfer of resources across generations. Edith resisted her father's and brother's advice throughout her life and brought consternation and even embarrassment to her father and other family members.[52] Her independence proved costly. In 1923 she sold stocks in order to cover her house payments. By 1931 she was so desperate for cash that she asked her father for a gift of her houses; sought $1 million from her brother; sold her jewelry; and announced to her family that without additional money, "I shall have to declare myself bankrupt." In each instance, as "hard" as it was, and as much they "regretted" it, both her father and brother declined Edith's requests.[53] The reciprocity that was present between father and son clearly did not transfer to father and daughter.

Similarly, Sallie Bingham's parents were furious with her behavior surrounding Bingham Enterprises, unhappy about the way she treated her children, and angry over her obstinacy regarding other family members. To Barry Bingham, Sr., Sallie had not reciprocated his generosity. In 1983, Barry, Sr., asked all the family women to leave the board in order to allow Barry, Jr., to run Bingham Enterprises as he thought best. Each accepted Barry, Sr.'s request except Sallie, who refused to resign. She was eventually voted off the board, but Barry, Sr., never forgave her unwillingness to leave gracefully, and he and his daughter rarely spoke again.

Sallie's perceived violation of the Bingham family privacy and her disruption of the family legacy resulted in grave consequences. For example, Barry, Sr.'s will provided that should his wife predecease him, his son and younger daughter "would have received their shares outright. But Sallie Bingham Peters' share would have gone to a trust for her children."[54] For her father's funeral procession, Sallie's mother, brother, and sister rode in "Car 1" while Sallie was relegated to "Car 2."[55] Her mother's resentment toward Sallie ran deep, and, following her mother's death in 1995, Sallie was the only family member excluded from receiving anything from her mother's estate, which was valued at about $11.7 million.[56]

A third strategy for selecting heirs focuses on the distribution of estates equally among members of a similar group. Ascriptive equality does not, however, mandate that each child should receive an equal sum. Rather, testators may choose to compensate the less-successful child in order to level the standard of living for their children. Menchik and Jianakoplos argue that parents use *inter vivos* transfers to encourage the development of the most qualified children and testator bequests to equalize their children's statuses.[57] Nigel Tomes is most succinct in his assessment of ascriptive equality. Parents, most of whom he contends are averse to inequality, have two alternatives: they can compensate the less-able child by providing him or her with a larger share of the inheritance, thus equalizing the total wealth of their children, or they can give equally to all children, thus actually increasing sibling inequality. A third alternative is for those parents who are not averse to inequality to favor the more capable child. In this case, as Tomes suggests, "other things being equal, the greater the inequality in siblings' incomes, the lower the probability that heirs will inherit equally."[58]

In relation to gender, the issue raised by ascriptive justice is that because lifetime earnings tend to be greater for men than women, if testators distributed their assets under the guise of ascriptive equality, then they would be more likely to favor their daughters than their sons. In this respect, the intergenerational transfer of wealth would tend to comprise a more significant determinant of women's status than men's. Moreover, this would arguably have been even more important for women from elite families, whose wealth tends to be derived primarily either from inheritance or their husband's position.[59] When it came to it, however, neither John D. Rockefeller, Sr., nor Barry Bingham, Sr., adhered to a strategy of ascriptive equality when distributing the family's wealth. Rather, because they disapproved of their respective daughter's behavior, they not only failed to apportion them equal amounts but also ensured that they would never hold the same status as their sons, and in this respect the pattern of bequesting more closely resembled Clignet's pattern of reciprocity.

While Clignet and others have focused on the intergenerational transfer of money, it is equally, if not more, important to include the movement of cultural capital *inter vivos*.[60] In doing so, we enter the realms of qualitative differences in the types of provision made for the women. Unlike economic capital, cultural capital cannot be lost, placed in trust, or taken away once given. The *inter vivos* transfer of cultural capital is most clearly manifested in the educational opportunities available to the children of wealthy parents. In this respect, the opportunities provided by John D. Rockefeller, Sr., for his son far exceeded those for his daughter. From an early stage, he groomed his son to take on the business: when Rockefeller, Jr., was 13, his father wrote to him describing various business transactions and told him, "you are monarch of all you survey."[61] To his daughter, Rockefeller, Sr., wrote about her health, children, and errant ways. While Edith's formal education ended at Rye Female Seminary, John D. Rockefeller, Jr., became the first of his family to graduate from college when he received his degree from Brown University, one of the elite Ivy League schools. Then, at age 23, he began working at his father's company, Standard Oil. In 1907, when Junior was 33, Senior placed him in charge of distributing assets to his sisters.[62]

The provision of cultural capital in the form of educational opportunities was more equal in the Bingham's house than it was in the Rockefeller's. Sallie Bingham, for example, received an education comparable to that of her brothers. They attended Harvard University, while she finished at Radcliffe, the women's college associated with Harvard. However, what she did not receive was the grooming for corporate leadership, her parents instead encouraging her writing career. Not equipping Sallie with the skills necessary to manage Bingham Enterprises proved problematic. When she wanted to take a more active role in the family business and demanded a voice in business affairs, the prevailing view was that she was ill prepared to do so.

## CONCLUSION

Among upper-class Americans, the family is the nexus through which dynasties are perpetuated and gender roles reinforced. The movement of cultural, social, and economic capital from one generation to the next is the vehicle for the social reproduction of class and gender. As has been shown, for women, dynastic transfers are often confined to the home, rather than the family business. Sallie Bingham lamented the separate spheres of inheritance that befell the Bingham men and women. In June 1986, *Ms.*, a feminist magazine founded by Gloria Steinem, published a group of articles decrying the distinctions of gender, regardless of class. Sallie authored one of the pieces, entitled "The Truth about Growing Up Rich," in which she wrote:

for no matter how well paid we are for our compliance, in the end, we do not inherit equally. Most rich families work on the English system and favor male heirs.... When the will is read, the women inherit houses, furniture, and jewels; the men inherit cash, stocks, and securities.... We learn to accept, to be grateful for what we are given.... We are dependent, after all, on the fickle goodwill of those who will never proclaim us their heirs.[63]

Sallie was determined not to continue what she perceived as the patriarchal hegemony. In 1986, she purchased a large plot of land in rural Kentucky, which, she stated, "will not be inherited by my sons," but rather would remain open and uncultivated. In doing so she recognized that "the patriarchy itself is dead set against my decision. The right of sons to inherit is fundamental to capitalism, and to the more secretive continuation of a ruling class."[64]

Edith Rockefeller McCormick also voiced her displeasure at perceived gender inequities, albeit in a less-public forum. Following their mother's death, she wrote to her brother expressing disappointment that she was excluded from decision making regarding her mother's estate. Edith beseeched her father to be allowed to participate in the family philanthropies in the same manner that he encouraged her brother. Frustrated with her father's rejection and envious of her brother's activities, in 1918 she wrote, "Dear Father, I sometimes wish that you could forget that I am a woman, so that you might give to me some of the advantages which John has in administrating."[65]

The larger question that this work raises is whether the intergenerational transfer of resources is directed by the relative rationality of efficiency, reciprocity, ascriptive justice, or the more prejudicial criteria of gender. Sallie Bingham and Edith Rockefeller McCormick maintained that their secondary status within the family emanated from their gender, rather than from their personal inadequacies. Among the Rockefellers, and to a lesser extent the Binghams, decisions dealing with the allocation of cultural, social, and most significantly, economic capital were made by family patriarchs as a way of perpetuating male hegemony.

Of course, the two families operated under different cultural conditions, arising from ideological changes relating to gender roles more generally, and the different experiences of both women can be explained in part by these historical changes. The pattern of primogeniture seen in the Rockefeller bequests is reminiscent of the English aristocracy, while for the Binghams inheritance was more partible in the sense that Sallie and her sister received in theory an equal share of the estate with their brother. Nevertheless, this veneer of partibility masked the fact that the culture of primogeniture remained intact. Sallie knew little of her trust, she was not consulted about its investments, and when she tried to exert some influence over the family businesses, she met with strong resistance.

Critical to an understanding of the differences between the Rockefellers and the Binghams is the historical context within which each family acted. Inequality of inheritance would have been less problematic for the cohesion of the Rockefellers, for whom gender inequality was an underlying assumption. However, by the late twentieth century, ideas of separate spheres had all but disappeared, and gender equity dominated familial and commercial discourse. Thus, for the Binghams, impartibility was disastrous and helped only to disrupt the family enterprise.

Together, the picture that emerges from these studies is one of women who held vast fortunes and yet were often constrained by gender. Such status inconsistencies for wealthy women may seem at odds with their social position, and individuals such as Edith Rockefeller McCormick and Sallie Bingham were not victims, nor should they appear as objects of sympathy. Indeed, these women were active agents in shaping their own domestic situations. But gender also conditioned their every action and was embedded in the arrangement of their households and in the many institutions they created outside the home. For most wealthy women, including McCormick and Bingham, the money that made them rich came from the men in their lives: their fathers, husbands, and brothers. In studying upper-class families, therefore, no less than those lower on the social hierarchy, we can learn about the tenacity of gender prescriptions and the strategies men and women employed to facilitate social reproduction.

## NOTES

1. Joanie Bronfman, "The Experience of Inherited Wealth: A Social-Psychological Perspective" (Ph.D. diss., Brandeis University, 1987), 262.

2. Philip Slater, *Wealth Addiction* (New York: E. P. Dutton, 1980), 4.

3. Ibid., 12.

4. Marcia Millman, *Warm Hearts and Cold Cash: The Intimate Dynamics of Families and Money* (New York: Free Press, 1991), 8.

5. Millman, *Warm Hearts and Cold Cash,* 14. See also Jeffrey P. Rosenfeld, "The Heir and the Spare: Evasiveness, Role-Complexity and Patterns of Inheritance," in *Social Roles and Social Institutions: Essays in Honor of Rose Laub Coser,* ed. Judith R. Blau and Norman Goodman (Boulder, Colo.: Westview Press, 1991), 78–81. For a discussion of the corrupting influence of money on social relationships, see also Georg Simmel, *The Philosophy of Money* (London: Routledge, 1990, first edition 1907), 128–29.

6. Paul L. Menchik and Nancy J. Jianakoplos, "Economics of Inheritance," in *Inheritance and Wealth in America,* ed. Robert K. Miller, Jr., and Stephen J. McNamee (New York: Plenum Press, 1998), 54 and Herbert Inhaber and Sidney Carroll, *How Rich is Too Rich?: Income and Wealth in America* (New York: Praeger, 1992), 72.

7. Paul L. Menchik, "Unequal Estate Division: Is It Altruism, Reverse Bequest, or Simply Noise?" in *Modeling the Accumulation and Distribution of Wealth,* ed. Denis Kessler and André Masson, (New York: Oxford University Press, 1988), 109; Paul

L. Menchik, "Primogeniture, Equal Sharing, and the U.S. Distribution of Wealth," *The Quarterly Journal of Economics* 94 (1980): 314–15; Nigel Tomes, "Inheritance and Inequality within the Family: Equal Division among Unequals, or Do the Poor Get More?" in Kessler and Masson, *Modeling the Accumulation and Distribution of Wealth*, 102; Marlene S. Stum, "'I Just Want to be Fair': Interpersonal Justice in Intergenerational Transfers of Non-Titled Property," *Family Relations* 48 (1999): 160; and Inhaber and Carroll, *How Rich Is Too Rich?*, 74.

8. Stephen John Gross, "Handing Down the Farm: Values, Strategies, and Outcomes in Inheritance Practices among Rural German Americans," *Journal of Family History* 21 (1996): 203 and Menchik, "Primogeniture, Equal Sharing, and the U.S. Distribution of Wealth," 314. Menchik concludes that "when a larger, more partible business is bequeathed, the stock in the business is bequeathed equally by sex. Among the smaller, less partible businesses, where the child would probably have to be the owner-operator, preference for the male child is the rule. This behavior suggests unequal inheritance of *occupation*, while inheritance of *wealth* is equal between the sexes" (313–14). See also Sarah Blaffer Hrdy and Debra S. Judge, "Darwin and the Puzzle of Primogeniture," *Human Nature* 4 (1993): 4–5, 27, 32–33. Preference for sons over daughters could also be found among new immigrants to the United States. See Remi P. Clignet, "Ethnicity and Inheritance," in Miller and McNamee, *Inheritance and Wealth in America*, 127, 130. In an earlier article, Clignet maintains that "the selection of heirs along gender lines seems to be universal" and that "wealthy individuals are said to favor their sons because the latter are more likely than their sisters to marry, have children, and carry forward the identity of the family." See Remi Clignet, "Efficiency, Reciprocity, and Ascriptive Equality: The Three Major Strategies Governing the Selection of Heirs in America," *Social Science Quarterly* 76 (1995): 279. For the opposite scenario see Debra S. Judge, "American Legacies and the Variable Life Histories of Women and Men," *Human Nature* 6 (1995): 304–9.

9. Gerda Lerner, *Why History Matters: Life and Thought* (New York: Oxford University Press, 1997), 172.

10. Kate Mulholland, "Gender Power and Property Relations Within Entrepreneurial Wealthy Families," *Gender, Work and Organization* 3 (1996): 83; Teresa Odendahl, *Charity Begins at Home: Generosity and Self-Interest Among the Philanthropic Elite* (New York: Basic Books, 1990), 122; Susan Ostrander, *Women of the Upper Class* (Philadelphia, Penn.: Temple University Press, 1984), 59, 65; and Ann R. Tickamyer, "Wealth and Power: A Comparison of Men and Women in the Property Elite," *Social Forces* 60 (1981): 466.

11. Mulholland, "Gender Power and Property Relations": 95. See also Michael Patrick Allen, *The Founding Fortunes: A New Anatomy of the Super-Rich Families in America* (New York: Truman Talley, 1987), 35 and Phyllis Chesler and Emily Jane Goodman, *Women, Money and Power* (New York: William Morrow, 1976), 18–19.

12. Pierre Bourdieu, *Masculine Domination* (Stanford, CA: Stanford University Press, 2001), 9.

13. Bourdieu, *Masculine Domination*, 97–101; Chesler and Goodman, *Women, Money and Power*, 63; G. William Domhoff, *The Higher Circles: the Governing Class in America* (New York: Random House, 1970), 34–36; Suzanne Keller, "The American Upper-Class Family: Precarious Claims on the Future," *Journal of Comparative Family Studies* 22 (1991): 178; Teresa Odendahl, "Women's Power, Nonprofits, and

the Future," in *Gender and the Professionalization of Philanthropy: Essays on Philanthropy*, No. 19, ed. Teresa Odendahl and Marilyn Fischer (Indianapolis, Ind.: Indiana University Center on Philanthropy, 1996), 2, 7–8; Ostrander, *Women of the Upper Class*, 39; and Mulholland, "Gender, Power, and Property Relations," 96.

14. This research draws on the class analysis of Pierre Bourdieu, who favors the concept of "social space," based on the allocation of economic, cultural, social, and symbolic capital. According to Bourdieu there are variations in the quantity of types of capital each person possesses. See Pierre Bourdieu, "What Makes a Social Class? On the Theoretical and Practical Existence of Groups," *Berkeley Journal of Sociology: A Critical Review* 32 (1987): 4. The use of different compositions of types of capital is problematic in relation to the definition of social space, particularly with regard to what Bourdieu refers to as the "intermediate zones" (12). However, he argues that differentiation according to economic and cultural capital "produce[s] clear-cut differences between agents situated at extreme ends of the distributions" (12). In the context of this chapter the terms *elite* and *upper class* are used interchangeably because they represent those situated at "the extreme end of the distribution." For a discussion of the definition of elites in an anthropological context see George E. Marcus, "'Elite' as a Concept, Theory, and Research Tradition," in George E. Marcus, ed., *Elites: Ethnographic Issues* (Albuquerque, N. Mex.: University of New Mexico Press, 1983), 12.

15. Lerner, *Why History Matters*, 149.

16. Diana Kendall, *The Power of Good Deeds: Privileged Women and the Social Reproduction of the Upper Class* (Lanham, Md.: Rowan & Littlefield, 2002), 25, 113–42. For discussions about the exclusivity of the upper class see Bronfman, *The Experience of Inherited Wealth*, 79–83; Keller, "The American Upper-Class Family," 165; Stephen R. Higley, *Privilege, Power, and Place: The Geography of the American Upper Class* (Lanham, Md.: Roman and Littlefield, 1995), 26–27; Francie Ostrower, *Why the Wealthy Give: The Culture of Elite Philanthropy* (Princeton, N.J.: Princeton University Press, 1995), 9; Slater, *Wealth Addiction*, 142; Marcus, "'Elite' as a Concept," 11; and Ostrander, *Women of the Upper Class*, 97–115.

17. Keller, "The American Upper-Class Family," 165.

18. John H. Langbein, "The Twentieth-Century Revolution in Wealth Transmission," *Michigan Law Review* 84 (1988): 737.

19. Higley, *Privilege, Power and Place*, 19. See also Peter W. Cookson, Jr., and Caroline Hodges Persell, *Preparing for Power: America's Elite Boarding Schools* (New York: Basic Books, 1985), 15–19; Kendall, *The Power of Good Deeds*, 35, 81–85; Keller, "The American Upper-Class Family," 164; Allen, *The Founding Fortunes*, 25; and Ostrander, *Women of the Upper Class*, 81–85.

20. Cookson and Persell, *Preparing for Power*, 22.

21. Pierre Bourdieu and Luc Boltanski, "Formal Qualifications and Occupational Hierarchies: The Relationship between the Production System and the Reproduction System," in Edmund J. King, ed., *Reorganizing Education: Management and Participation for Change* (London: Sage, 1977), 67. For an understanding of the place of education in legitimating high culture see Paul DiMaggio and Michael Useem, "The Arts in Class Reproduction," in *Cultural and Economic Reproduction in Education: Essays on Class, Ideology and the State*, ed. Michael W. Apple (London: Routledge and Kegan Paul, 1982), 182. For a discussion of the relationship between social class and attendance at elite universities, see Robert Lerner, Althea K. Nagai,

and Stanley Rothman, *American Elites* (New Haven, Conn.: Yale University Press, 1996), 29–30.

22. Slater, *Wealth Addiction*, 19.

23. Ostrander, *Women of the Upper Class*, 26; Paul G. Schervish, "Introduction: The Wealthy and the World of Wealth," in *Gospels of Wealth: How the Rich Portray Their Lives*, ed. Paul G. Schervish, Platon E. Coutsoukis, and Ethan Lewis (Westport, Conn.: Praeger, 1994), 10–13; and Louise W. Knight, "Jane Addams's Views on the Responsibilities of Wealth," in Dwight F. Burlingame, ed., *The Responsibilities of Wealth* (Bloomington, Ind.: Indiana University Press, 1992), 118–25.

24. For a discussion of the disjuncture between inherited wealth and the ideology of equality of opportunity see, for example, Stephen J. McNamee and Robert K. Miller, Jr., "Estate Inheritance: A Sociological Lacuna," *Sociological Inquiry* 59 (1989): 7–29; Lerner, Nagai, and Stanley, *American Elites*; and Robert A. Rothman, *Inequality and Stratification: Class, Color, and Gender* (Englewood Cliffs, N.J.: Prentice Hall, 1993). Inheritance in the United States was a civil rather than a natural right. This designation allowed for legal intervention in estate distributions. For a history of U.S. inheritance and estate taxes see Ronald Chester, "Inheritance in American Legal Thought," in Miller and McNamee, *Inheritance and Wealth in America*, 23–43; Menchik and Jianakoplos, "Economics of Inheritance," 45–59; and Barry W. Johnson and Martha Britton Eller, "Federal Taxation of Inheritance and Wealth Transfers," in Miller and McNamee, *Inheritance and Wealth in America*, 61–90.

25. George E. Marcus, "The Fiduciary Role in American Family Dynasties and Their Institutional Legacy," in Marcus, *Elites*, 250.

26. Tomes, "Inheritance and Inequality within the Family," 102. See also Stum, "'I Just Want to be Fair,'" 160–61; and Millman, *Warm Hearts and Cold Cash*, 2.

27. Clignet, "Efficiency, Reciprocity, and Ascriptive Equality," 278.

28. Keller, "The American Upper-Class Family," 178.

29. The Louisville *Courier-Journal*, flagship of the Bingham family business, earned a national reputation for excellence.

30. For a more detailed analysis of inheritance among the Rockefellers see Marsha Shapiro Rose, "The Legacy of Wealth: Primogeniture Among the Rockefellers," *Journal of Family History* 27 (2002): 172–85.

31. Higley, *Privilege, Power, and Place*, 53.

32. Cleveland Amory, *Who Killed Society?* (New York: Harper and Brothers, 1960), 380; Ron Chernow, *Titan: The Life of John D. Rockefeller, Sr.* (New York: Random House, 1998), 414; Peter Collier and David Horowitz, *The Rockefellers: An American Dynasty* (New York: Holt, Rinehart and Winston, 1976), 73; Bernice Kert, *Abby Aldrich Rockefeller: The Woman in the Family* (New York: Random House, 1993), 94; Allan Nevins, *Study in Power: John D. Rockefeller, Industrialist and Philanthropist* (New York: Charles Scribner and Sons, 1953), 410; and John Tebbel, *The Inheritors: a Study of America's Great Fortunes and What Happened to Them* (New York: G. P. Putnam and Sons, 1962), 221.

33. The Rockefeller correspondence and other documents cited in this chapter are housed at the Rockefeller Archive Center in Tarrytown, New York. Trust, July 3, 1917, Rockefeller Family Archives (RFA) 2, John D. Rockefeller, Sr Series (JDR Sr Se), Box (B) 31, Folder (F) 239.

34. For examples of her father's and brother's control over her finances see Bertram Cutler to John D. Rockefeller, Sr., May 13, 1919, RFA 1, JDR Sr Se, B33,

F253; John D. Rockefeller, Sr. to John D. Rockefeller, Jr., January 5, 1920, RFA 2, JDR Sr Se, B33, F254; and Bertram Cutler to John D. Rockefeller, Sr., August 31, 1926, RFA 2, JDR Sr Se, B34, F260. Examples of Edith's resentment of her father's favoritism toward her brother are found in Edith Rockefeller McCormick to John D. Rockefeller, Jr., May 29, 1915, RFA 1, Spelman Family Series, B2, F14 and Edith Rockefeller McCormick to John D. Rockefeller, Sr., January 24, 1918, RFA 2, JDR Sr Se, B33, F252.

35. Allen, *The Founding Fortunes*, 100; Joseph W. Ernst, *"Dear Father"/"Dear Son": Correspondence between John D. Rockefeller and John D. Rockefeller, Jr.* (New York: Fordham University Press, 1994), 68; Keller, "The American Upper-Class Family," 166; and Joseph J. Thorndike, Jr., *The Very Rich: A History of Wealth* (New York: Bonanza, 1976), 93.

36. John Ensor Harr and Peter J. Johnson, *The Rockefeller Century* (New York: Charles Scribner and Sons, 1988), 118.

37. Rose, "The Legacy of Wealth," 178.

38. See correspondence between Edith Rockefeller McCormick, John D. Rockefeller, Sr., and John D. Rockefeller, Jr., June 16, 1923—December 29, 1931, RFA 2, JDR Sr Se, B33, F255 and B34, F262.

39. Some of the material in this section derives from Marsha Shapiro Rose, "Southern Feminism and Social Change: Sallie Bingham and the Kentucky Foundation for Women," in *The New Deal and Beyond: Social Welfare in the South Since 1930*, ed. Elna Green (Athens, Ga.: University of Georgia Press, 2003), 239–58.

40. Betty Friedan, *The Feminine Mystique* (New York: W. W. Norton, 1963).

41. A more complete history of the Bingham family can be found in the following: Sallie Bingham, *Passion and Prejudice: A Family Memoir* (New York: Applause Books, 1989); Marie Brenner, *House of Dreams: The Bingham Family of Louisville* (New York: Knopf, 1988); David Leon Chandler with Mary Voelz Chandler, *The Binghams of Louisville: The Dark History Behind One of the Country's Great Fortunes* (New York: Crown Publishers, 1987); William E. Ellis, *Robert Worth Bingham and the Southern Mystique: From the Old South to the New South and Beyond* (Kent, Ohio: The Kent State University Press, 1997); George E. Marcus with Peter Dobkin Hall, *Lives in Trust: The Fortunes of Dynastic Families in Late Twentieth-Century America* (Boulder, Colo.: Westview Press, 1992), 207–19; Susan E. Tifft and Alex S. Jones, *The Patriarch: The Rise and Fall of the Bingham Dynasty* (New York: Summit, 1991); and Joe Ward, "The Binghams: Twilight of a Tradition," *The Courier-Journal Magazine* (April 20, 1986): 16–38.

42. The mystery surrounding Mary Lily Kenan Flager's death has never been resolved, and suspicion remains about the "Judge's" role in the event. See Chandler and Chandler, *The Binghams of Louisville*, 8–12, 158–70; Brenner, *House of Dreams*, 72–80; and Tifft and Jones, *The Patriarch*, 69–75.

43. Sallie Bingham's papers are housed at the Rare Book, Manuscript, and Special Collections Library, Duke University, Durham, North Carolina. Michael Kirkhorn, "The Bingham Black Sheep," *Louisville Today* (1979): 36–41, Subject Files Series, Box (B) 2, Folder (F): Newspaper Clippings, 1952–1980, Sallie Bingham Papers (Bingham Papers); Alanna Nash, "The Woman Who Overturned an Empire," *Ms.* 14 (June, 1986): 44; Sallie Bingham, "The Truth About Growing Up Rich," *Ms.* 14 (June, 1986): 48; Sallie Bingham, "Biting the Hand: The Break-up of the Bingham Family Empire," *Radcliffe Quarterly* (June, 1986): 32; Sallie Bingham,

"Women and the Creative Process: A Widening Vision," speech delivered at Oberlin College (December 5, 1987), Speeches Series, B 1, F: 1987, Bingham Papers; Bingham, *Passion and Prejudice*, 433–34; Sallie Bingham, "The Garden of Eden," speech for a Conference on Women in Media (January 24, 1989), Speeches Series, B 1, F: 1989, Bingham Papers; Sallie Bingham, "Developing New Perspectives: Women Who Live Near Power," (undated) Writings Series, B 5, F: Developing New Perspectives: Women Who Live Near Power (undated), Bingham Papers.

44. Bingham, *Passion and Prejudice*, 399.

45. Kirkhorn, "The Bingham Black Sheep," 36–41; John Nielsen, "After a Woman Is Scorned, a Publishing Family Cashes Out," *Fortune* 115 (January 5, 1987): 93; Obituaries of Barry Bingham, Sr. (August 15–16, 1988), Subject Files Series, B 1, F: Barry Bingham, Sr.'s Death, 1988, Bingham Papers. In 1991, Alex S. Jones, co-author of *The Patriarch*, told a reporter for the *Lexington Herald-Leader* that "Sallie had her role, [in bringing down the empire] but it was only one of several leading roles. And at the end, Sallie was really not an important player." Cited in Kevin Nance, "Villainess image beginning to fade," *Lexington Herald-Leader* (April 14, 1991), K1, Subject Files Series, B 1, F: Articles about and interviews with Bingham, 1958–1997, Bingham Papers.

46. Allen, *The Founding Fortunes*, 10–11.

47. Slater, *Wealth Addiction*, 102.

48. Inhaber and Caroll, *How Rich is Too Rich?*, 72. See also Menchik and Jianakoplos, "Economics of Inheritance," 54; Rosenfeld, "The Heir and the Spare," 82; and Millman, *Warm Hearts and Cold Cash*, 5.

49. Menchik, "Unequal Estate Division," 113.

50. Alvin Gouldner, "The Norm of Reciprocity: A Preliminary Statement," *American Sociological Review* 25 (1960): 161–78.

51. Millman, *Warm Hearts and Cold Cash*, 19, 30–31 and Rosenfeld, "The Heir and the Spare," 80.

52. Judith Sealander, *Private Wealth and Public Life: Foundation Philanthropy and the Reshaping of American Social Policy from the Progressive Era to the New Deal* (Baltimore, Md.: Johns Hopkins University Press, 1997), 279, n. 12; Collier and Horowitz, The Rockefellers, 73.

53. Edith Rockefeller McCormick to John D. Rockefeller, Sr., June 16, 1923, RFA 2, JDR Sr Se, B33, F258; Edith Rockefeller McCormick to John D. Rockefeller, Sr., May 13, 1931, RFA 2, JDR Sr Se, B34, F262; John D. Rockefeller, Sr., to Edith Rockefeller McCormick, May 18, 1931, Ibid.; Edith Rockefeller McCormick to John D. Rockefeller, Jr., December 23, 1931, Ibid.; John D. Rockefeller, Jr., to Edith Rockefeller McCormick, December 24, 1931, Ibid.; John D. Rockefeller, Jr., to John D. Rockefeller, Sr., December 24, 1931, Ibid.; John D. Rockefeller, Sr., to John D. Rockefeller, Jr., December 29, 1931, Ibid.; John D. Rockefeller, Sr., to John D. Rockefeller, Jr., December 29, 1931, Ibid.

54. "Bingham, Norton wills to divide more than $110 million among heirs, charities," *Courier-Journal*, Louisville, Ky. (December 29, 1988) Subject Files Series, B 1, F: Barry Bingham, Sr.'s Death 1988, Bingham Papers.

55. "Transportation for Wednesday, 17 August," ibid.

56. "Philanthropist Bingham left out of will," Writings Series, B 5, F: Finding My Mothers, Second Draft, Bingham Papers.

57. Menchik and Jianakoplos, "Economics of Inheritance," 53–55.

58. Tomes, "Inheritance and Inequality within the Family," 102.

59. Ostrander, *Women of the Upper Class*, 65–67; Odendahl, *Charity Begins at Home*, 100–102; and Ostrower, *Why the Wealthy Give*, 69.

60. With few exceptions, scholars of inheritance focus on the movement of money from one generation to the next. For example, see Clignet, "Efficiency, Reciprocity, and Ascriptive Equality"; Menchik, "Unequal Estate Division"; McNamee and Miller, *Inheritance and Wealth in America*; Rosenfeld, "The Heir and the Spare"; Franco Modigliani, "The Role of Intergenerational Transfers and Life Cycle Saving in the Accumulation of Wealth," *Journal of Economic Perspectives* 2 (1988): 15–40; and Tomes, "Inheritance and Inequality within the Family."

61. John D. Rockefeller, Sr., to John D. Rockefeller, Jr., November 19, 1887; John D. Rockefeller, Sr., to John D. Rockefeller, Jr., November 28, 1887, in Ernst, *"Dear Father"/"Dear Son,"* 1–4.

62. John D. Rockefeller, Sr., to John D. Rockefeller, Jr., September 18, 1907, in Ibid., 28.

63. Bingham, "The Truth about Growing Up Rich," 50.

64. Sallie Bingham, "A Woman's Land," *The Amicus Journal* 12 (Fall, 1990): 38, Writings Series, B 20, F: "A Woman's Land," (undated), Bingham Papers.

65. Edith Rockefeller McCormick to John D. Rockefeller, Jr., May 29, 1915, RFA 2, JDR Sr Series, B32, F250. See also Edith Rockefeller McCormick to John D. Rockefeller, Sr., September 4, 1915, Ibid.; Edith Rockefeller McCormick to John D. Rockefeller, Sr., January 24, 1918, Rockefeller Family Archives 2, JDR Sr Series, Box 33, Folder 252.

# CHAPTER 7

# Family Networks and the Transmission of Assets: Managing the Property and Care of Orphans in Eighteenth-Century Amsterdam

*Anne E. C. McCants*

## INTRODUCTION

Providing for the sustained period of nurture required to bring a child to a productive adulthood is one of the most fundamental demands on human economic activity. If it were systematically neglected, or abandoned altogether, as just another superfluous expense on yet another consumer good—that is, if we collectively lost our taste for the company of children relative to our taste for consumer goods—the species would become extinct. Yet the children-as-consumer-goods model lives a tenacious life in the conceptual framework of neoclassical economics.[1] Despite the vocal protestations of the new feminist economics, most models of the productive capacity of the economy depend, either implicitly, or less often explicitly, on the availability of labor irrespective of the cost of raising children.[2] Even when the processes of human capital formation are evaluated formally, it is usually in the context of secondary education and job training, as if years of food, clothing, nursing, mental development, and socialization, to cite only the most obvious categories, could be provided at some trivial and nonmeasurable cost. However, people do not base their reproductive behavior simply on their preferences for children in comparison with other consumer goods. Indeed, if they did, parents would not need to make provisions for the care of their children following their death, and yet history is replete with the evidence of such provisioning arrangements.[3]

What this evidence consistently shows is that the provisioning of the young is an expensive proposition by virtually every conceivable measure. A full accounting would be too long to present here, but clearly the most significant elements would include the cost of maternal health; the opportunity cost of time allocated to caring for young children in particular, and therefore lost to market-based or home-based 'productive work'; the purchase and preparation cost of food, clothing, and other material needs to ensure survival; the cost of education and/or job training so that children become productive members of adult society; and the emotional and material costs of nurturing the sick and grieving for the dead. Although these measures do not submit themselves equally well to quantification, all have been the subject of historical research because of their consistent importance to all human communities. Indeed, in most societies and at most times, the expense of social reproduction has been so high that short of adult labor power being specifically allocated for current children's needs in fairly close ratios, it cannot be borne. This truism lies at the heart of the Malthusian understanding of the dismal connection between population and economy, and informs all neo-Malthusian historical analysis that has followed.[4] It also helps to explain the extensive moral literature about community responsibility for children bereft of parents before the time that they can fully support themselves.[5] Nor has this concern disappeared with economic prosperity. Even in the wealthy West, parents are constantly exhorted to make arrangements for the financial support (and more incidentally, the emotional care) of their children, in case the parents die prematurely. This concern does not stem from the statistical likelihood of parental death, but rather, it reflects the severity of the consequences for those few families to which it does happen.

How, then, did societies in the past, not nearly as wealthy as our own, manage this most pressing of human problems? This chapter attempts to answer this question in the context of the emerging urban and commercial society of the Dutch Republic in the early modern period. As a prototype for the development of early capitalist economies, the Dutch case is particularly interesting in light of the methodological concerns raised at the outset of this chapter about the basic assumptions of neoclassical models of economic behavior. The work discussed here focuses on the transmission of property and the arrangements for the care of minor children following their parents' death among the lower middling strata of the Amsterdam citizenry in the eighteenth century. In particular, it seeks to clarify the ambiguous and changing relationship between communal and familial responsibility for the care of parentless children during a period of tumultuous social and economic change. The research for this work is grounded in an analysis of a previously unexamined collection of household inventories drawn up by the regents of the Amsterdam Municipal Orphanage (Burgerweeshuis) as part of their effort to secure familial resources whenever available for the support of the orphans in their care. This source provides an unusual opportunity to examine household assets and liabilities and their dispersal following the death of both male and female decedents from social strata well below the propertied elites most commonly represented in research reliant on either probate inventories or wills, dependent as such documents were on the family's ability to pay for notarial services. Moreover, since the families documented in these records were all included because of their connection to the orphanage, they represent an obvious source for exploring the particular problem of the allocation of responsibility for the welfare of children between the family in question and the community at large.

When the Amsterdam Burgerweeshuis opened its doors to seven children sometime in the early 1520s, it became the first residential home for orphans in the city. Prior to that time, care of orphans had been handled on a case-by-case basis; unfortunate children either remained within an extended family network or were placed in the care of cloistered nuns. Even so, orphans were understood to be the special concern of the larger community. The earliest extant *privilegeboek* in Amsterdam, dating from around 1420, makes it clear that from the outset the city's corporate identity was inextricably bound up with the burden of relieving parentless children. It specified that "the Council of the city holds ultimate guardianship over orphans and widows."[6] Nonetheless, the municipal Orphan Chamber—established in the mid-fifteenth century to assist magistrates in the increasingly burdensome task of managing the property of an orphan population growing commensurately with the city itself—did not concern itself with the practical matters of daily existence. Moreover, it had contact primarily with the children of the economically stable classes, as they alone had property to be managed. The lower stratum of Amsterdam residents, including the children of all noncitizens, remained outside this civic welfare network entirely.

Of course, this group found the new Municipal Orphanage to be only slightly more open to them than the old system had been. The stipulation that children could enter the orphanage only if both their parents had been members of the city corporation for a minimum of seven years effectively excluded the lowest social group in the city, composed largely of immigrants. Large numbers of the next-lowest strata, consisting of unskilled wage workers, were ineligible as well. The children of *poorters* (as the town's burghers were called) were born with the rights and obligations of citizenship, but all others had to pay a fee for the privilege, the price of which increased substantially as Amsterdam became a more and more attractive destination for immigrants over the course of the seventeenth century.[7]

Perhaps ironically, the Amsterdam elite were also unlikely to use the services of this new institution. Because of the tight social networks that existed among members of the regent class and the highly successful families of commerce and industry, their orphaned children continued to be cared for in the more traditional way by kin.[8] Thus, it was mainly the children of what we might call the "middling sorts" (*de kleine burgerij*) who benefited from the generosity and vision of Haesje Claes, the orphanage's founder, and members of the town council who supported her proposal and ultimately supplemented her testamentary bequest with substantial financial resources.

It was not until 1613, when the city government established an additional system of outdoor relief for poor orphans and foundlings, that there was any formal civic provision for the children of the lowest social orders. This latter program was funded directly by the city via an assortment of indirect taxes and was administered by the *Aalmoezeniers*, a group of men appointed by the municipality to manage the civic branch of poor relief. When this care was finally institutionalized in 1664, the new orphanage became known as the *Aalmoezeniersweeshuis*. The founding of this institution was not, however, so much a response to the needs of orphaned children per se as it was an extension of the poor-relief system in general. Its creation was a response to the wider problem of urban poverty, of which abandoned children comprised a major part.

What was particularly innovative about both these orphanages was the development of a new institutional form for the application of a social policy that was itself more or less static in its aims. Indeed, it seems likely that even this innovation was largely forced by economic and demographic circumstances. Throughout the early modern period, whenever possible, small communities in the United Provinces maintained the practice of caring for orphans privately.[9] It is worth noting as well that not until the modern period were such civic orphanages common throughout northern Europe in general. The more typical expectation, especially among the middling classes, was that the family or kin group was the logical locus for the provision of welfare services to otherwise vulnerable dependants.[10] The activities of social reproduction were overwhelmingly located in the family, and not surprisingly, the moral imperative of most European societies dictated that there they should remain, even following the disruption of parental death. Yet the Dutch case offers a clear alternative to this wider European pattern, dominated as it was by an urban landscape increasingly dotted with orphanages that were, in addition to being homes for children, a source of civic pride and often housed in monumental buildings. Why, then, did Amsterdam and many other Dutch urban municipalities pursue an institutional mode of welfare provision (and in the case of the foundling hospital, charitable relief) and not something more traditional? More specifically, what were the connections between the impressive economic developments of the Dutch Golden Age and the changing strategies employed by families, and the community at large, to ensure that adequate resources were available to support the activities of social reproduction? Can we see in this movement a reflection of the response hypothesized by Karl Polanyi to the rapid development of market capitalism, namely the need to create new social institutions to "safeguard the welfare of the community?"[11] Or was it, in fact, a changing definition of adequacy that precipitated the emergence and eventual domination of the orphanage as the solution for parentless children in Dutch social policy? Finally, did the emergence of these civic institutions absolve the family from any or all financial responsibility for the care of its orphaned dependants; or, as a corollary, did such institutions pose a threat to the ability of families to maintain control over the transmission of family assets from one generation to the next?

The timing of the establishment of the Amsterdam Burgerweeshuis during a period of rapid economic growth and social change suggests strongly that the institution itself was a response to the needs of the many children who could no longer claim support from their extended family or neighbors and attests to the belief that it was not considered acceptable just to abandon such children, particularly those who enjoyed the status of citizenship.[12] This is not to say, however, that their extended familial relationships had ceased to exist, as the research presented here will amply attest. All of the extant evidence from the Burgerweeshuis suggests that the typical orphan was, in fact, part of a larger family network that took an active interest in the devolution of the property of deceased kin, even if the individual members did not actually take in their deceased kin's children. Evidence of these wider family networks is provided by the 221 probate inventories drawn up by the orphanage's bookkeeper recording the assets and debts of the parents of incoming orphans during the 1740s. Over 55 percent of these documents were signed by a family member only one step removed from the nuclear household, such as a grandparent, aunt, uncle, or older cousin. Another quarter was signed by a surviving stepparent, for whom there was no expectation that he or she should care for the children from the deceased spouse's earlier marriages. Even older, independently settled, full siblings were not required to take in their younger brothers and sisters at the death of their parents. Sibling relationships existed for another 11 percent of the inventoried cases. Indeed, only a paltry 6 percent of these 221 cases turned up orphans who lacked anyone other than neighbors or civic officials to vouchsafe their material possessions for them.[13] Clearly, even institutionalized orphans did not lack for extended families. Rather, they simply were not physically incorporated into the households of their kin following the loss of their parents.

Who, then, depended on the welfare services of the Burgerweeshuis? What contribution were they expected to make for the care of the children they left behind at death? What recourse did the larger family network have to preserve the financial assets of its deceased members over and against the claims of the care-granting institution? Finally, what impact did this form of institutionalized care and the bequeathing strategies it spawned have on the intergenerational distribution of wealth? Did it work to maintain the social position of families over time, or did it redistribute resources in such a way as to promote social mobility either upward or downward?

## THE EVIDENCE

To address these questions this paper draws on the extensive household documentation collected in the eighteenth century by the bookkeeper of the Burgerweeshuis and by the various notaries in its employment. When combined with marriage, baptism, and burial records, this evidence allows for the reconstruction of the household circumstances, be they material, financial, or demographic, of the families associated with the institution. The orphanage regents required that household inventories be drawn up for the estates of all citizen decedents leaving minor children to be cared for at municipal expense with a view to assessing the ability of those estates to contribute to the institutional costs of maintaining the orphans. Thus, even the estates of very poor deceased parents were evaluated, as long as they had been citizens of the city and their children were eligible for residence in the city orphanage. The regents also required that inventories be drawn up at the death of former orphans, regardless of whether they had ever married, as long as they did not have surviving children of their own. For unless a childless orphan had bought out the right to name his or her own heir (literally the *uitkoop*), the orphanage also had a legal claim to a share of the final estate. The fundamental operating principle here is entirely consistent with the larger argument outlined earlier. A surviving spouse, being an adult, was in theory capable of supporting him- or herself. Thus, any remaining assets at the death of the former orphan could be tapped to help defray expenses he or she had incurred possibly even long before as children. However, if the former orphan had children of his or her own, there was little point in jeopardizing their care in the present to pay back the old debt of their parent.

Given this set of operating principles, the collection of inventories represents an unusually broad spectrum of the citizen working poor and middling shopkeepers of the city, both male and female. The collection also provides a remarkably comprehensive source of detailed information on the households that came into contact with the orphanage.[14] The regents required a complete accounting of family members, usually including the names and ages of all living children, even those grown and married or those being sent to other orphanages in the city. Where applicable the presence of stepparents was noted as well. The orphanage was, after all, in the business of taking in the qualified minor children of the decedents, and because full orphanhood was a requirement for admission, the distinction between biological parents and stepparents was an especially critical one. Moreover, because all family members, including those resulting from a second or later marriage, held potential claims on the inventory, each had to be taken into account when deciding whether to accept or repudiate any given estate and its debts. Thus, the inventories not only include the marital histories of the decedents, but they also yield usually complete information on the size, composition, and stage in the life cycle of the households under consideration. Furthermore, for those individuals who can be linked to either a registered first marriage in Amsterdam or to a baptismal record, it is possible to calculate their exact age at death. This linkage process has been successful for more than three-quarters of the decedents, and for the remainder we can estimate the approximate age at death based on the ages and number of their surviving children.

The provision for evaluating the estates of former orphans fortuitously ensured that some inventories were also made for married women, even a few whose first husbands were still alive, and for both single men and women who were not yet household heads. In fact, women form a slight majority (55 percent) of the decedents for whom we have information, and of those nearly 70 percent were widows. The strong representation of women in these records, combined with the presence of never-married individuals of both sexes, offers a rare opportunity to study a much more diverse population than is usually possible using probate inventories available from the notarial records. In particular, it allows us to pose questions about the influence of gender and social and marital status in shaping the bequeathing strategies of individuals in mid-eighteenth-century Amsterdam.

It is worth noting that this collection of probate inventories offers one more unusual and fortunate characteristic concerning the recording of debts. Notarial inventories are typically silent on the issue of claims against the estate of the deceased. Debts left unpaid at the time of death are not, of course, the property of the deceased—although they are often inextricably connected to that property—but of his or her creditors. We would expect them to appear only if a comparable inventory was fortuitously drawn up for the creditor at roughly the same time. Admittedly the omission of debts would not be a serious defect for the study of material culture itself, but it poses a significant problem for those who wish to use probate inventories to map out wealth distributions, social hierarchies, and intergenerational transfers. The relationship between total assets and debt is complex. As both Margaret Spufford and Alice Hanson Jones have argued for early modern England and the American colonies respectively, debt can sometimes be an indication of poverty, but more often those who were most encumbered were also those with the greatest assets.[15] Thus ranking based on assets alone does not approximate even roughly to the ordering made on the basis of true net worth. Typical probate inventories alone cannot be used then, as was once hoped, to estimate wealth distributions, either within communities or across them. Nor can they be used to accurately assess the real value of estates being left to heirs at the time of death.

Fortunately, debts are not missing from the inventories used here. Because the orphanage was interested in the net cash value of an estate rather than in retrieving any particular possession or asset, its notaries and bookkeepers were meticulous in accounting for all moveable goods, which were almost always valued, for real estate, which was only sometimes valued but described when applicable, and for cash holdings, outstanding credits, and debts. Thus, the inventories drawn up by the orphanage are really a combination of what we would normally think of as the inventory proper and the administrative accounts of the estate, which could easily date well after the death of the decedent. Because the deceased's creditors had a stronger claim to the assets than did the municipal orphanage, or, for that matter, any of the family members standing to inherit, the bookkeeper could determine whether or not to repudiate an estate only if he had meticulously sought out all other possible claimants and determined accurately the resulting net value. We can be especially confident that this was the guiding principle in the bookkeeper's work as a great many of the inventories actually contain in the margins a record of the later sale of goods and the final dispersal of cash to the claimant parties, including where applicable the Burgerweeshuis itself. In those cases where the claims of creditors more than swamped the total value of an estate, the Burgerweeshuis simply repudiated its claim (as determined by the share that would otherwise have fallen to the child or children being placed in the orphanage) in order to avoid actual losses associated with paying off the outstanding debts.

## RESULTS

What can we learn about the ways in which the Burgerweeshuis operated and its function in helping preserve the economic viability of the family? Table 7.1 displays the basic composition of the inventoried population. As we would expect, the majority of households in the sample, amounting to 78 percent, were those of deceased parents leaving minor children in the care of the orphanage. Another 16 percent of the inventories belonged to orphans themselves, most of whom had already left the institution and entered adult occupations.[16] Finally, 6 percent of the inventories were drawn up at the death of a relative of a current orphan who had left that child (or children) as full or partial heirs to their estate. These relatives were most commonly grandmothers and aunts, less often grandfathers, and only occasionally an uncle or older sibling. Their only

**Table 7.1**
**Relationship of Decedents to the Orphanage**

|  | Males | Females | Total |
|---|---|---|---|
| Parents | 341 | 368 | 709 |
|     percent | 83.2 | 73.3 | 77.7 |
|     median household assets (guilders) |  |  | 68.5 |
| Former Orphan | 55 | 93 | 148 |
|     percent | 13.4 | 18.5 | 16.2 |
|     median household assets (guilders) |  |  | 63.8 |
| Relative of orphan | 14 | 41 | 55 |
|     percent | 3.4 | 8.2 | 6.0 |
|     median household assets (guilders) |  |  | 155.7 |

Source: Amsterdam Municipal Archives, Burgerweeshuis, G.A.A., p.a. 367, oud archief 652–63.

immediate connection to the orphanage was through the allocation of a share of their estate, or sometimes a formal bequest, to a current resident of the institution. Such allocations would normally occur only when the decedent had outlived some of his or her direct heirs, such as own-children or siblings, for in the absence of a specific bequest to a named individual, a share in an estate would pass to the next generation (that is, grandchildren or nieces and nephews) only when the direct heir of that share was already dead. Thus, we can think of the relatives of current orphans who appear in this sample as something of a demographically impoverished group. One-quarter of them had no other heirs than the child or siblings in the orphanage, while another 20 percent of them were survived by only their spouse and the orphaned child. Even among the remaining half that did show evidence of multiple nonspouse claimants to the estate, by far the most common division was between only two individuals.

Although only 55 inventories of relatives survive in this sample, they are nonetheless particularly interesting as they allow us to address the questions raised earlier regarding the transfers of wealth, for they represent one important mechanism by which these could be made. Not surprisingly, this is the subset of the inventoried population that enjoyed the strongest wealth profiles. Of all the individuals captured in this data, the relatives were the ones living with the least number of dependents (typically none) at the time of their deaths. Over half these relatives died with a positive net worth, compared with less than one-quarter of the parents in the sample. Moreover, only one of them was recorded by the bookkeeper as having had no recorded possessions whatsoever at death, whereas 127 parents were in that completely impoverished state.[17] While we might expect such demographically limited households to be less encumbered by debt than those of parents with minor children, the lower level of indebtedness was not the only thing driving the positive net worth of this group. As can be seen in the final rows of Table 7.1, the median value of the total household assets of the orphan relatives was nearly twice as high as for both other groups of decedents. Yet there is no reason to believe that the larger universe of potential orphan relatives was actually better off than the parent population because they were likely to have been different parts of the same extended families and would have generally shared common attributes of occupation and socioeconomic status. Rather, this suggests that the process of estate allocation to more distant heirs was most likely to come into play when the assets to be divided were greater than usual. Presumably the corollary to this was true as well: the estates of relatives that were obviously of no value may have been systematically ignored by the orphanage as not worthy of its time. Selection bias of this type might help to explain why transfers beyond the immediate parent-child relationship were not terribly common among the lower to middling Amsterdam citizenry. Considering that the Burgerweeshuis housed a steady population of upwards of 400 children throughout most of the eighteenth century, and the sample period covers more than 40 years, a total of only 55 deceased relatives leaving property to their orphaned kin is not many. Unfortunately, it is impossible to know whether this small number is a plausible reflection of a dearth of older kin from whom bequests might be forthcoming. An even more intriguing alternative explanation, which unfortunately cannot be explored given the absence of appropriate evidence, is that extended families actively tried to avoid bequeathing assets to kin children already in the Burgerweeshuis, knowing full well the assets would be tapped to pay for care the children were receiving anyway.

Regardless of what might have been the forces working to limit the number of better-situated households affiliated with the orphanage, there can be little doubt that the majority of this population had too few net assets at death to be in a position to even provide for the minimal care of the minor children they left behind, let alone to make a bequest to the next generation. As noted in Table 7.2 nearly 58 percent of the inventories recorded greater debts than assets, and a further 14.6 percent of the households were so impoverished that the bookkeeper did not bother to complete the inventory, remarking instead that they had "only some worthless old junk."[18] These were families that relied overwhelmingly on the labor power of their adult members, with very limited resources on which to fall back when the main wage earner died. Just under 28 percent of the total sample studied here left assets that could even cover their debts.

**Table 7.2**
**Distribution of Inventories by Net Worth**

|  | Males | Females | Total |
|---|---|---|---|
| Positive net worth | 109 | 143 | 252 |
| percent | 26.6 | 28.5 | 27.6 |
| median net worth (guilders) |  |  | 76 |
| Negative net worth | 251 | 276 | 527 |
| percent | 61.2 | 55.0 | 57.7 |
| median net worth (guilders) |  |  | −71 |
| Not inventoried | 50 | 83 | 133 |
| percent | 12.2 | 16.5 | 14.6 |

Source: See Table 7.1.

**Table 7.3**
**Incidence of Bequests by Household Assets**

|  | < 100 guilders | 101–200 guilders | 201–1000 guilders | >1000 guilders | Total |
|---|---|---|---|---|---|
| Bequest in record | 10 | 12 | 46 | 14 | 82 |
| percent of asset group | 1.7 | 11.5 | 25.7 | 35.0 | 9.0 |
| Total inventories | 584 | 109 | 179 | 40 | 912 |
| percent of total | 64.0 | 12.0 | 19.6 | 4.4 | 100 |

Source: See Table 7.1.

Moreover, the median net value of the positive estates was itself only 76 guilders—barely enough to cover the expenditure of the Burgerweeshuis for one child for even six months.[19] When we include those households whose debts exceeded their assets the median net value of all the fully inventoried estates in the sample drops to −23 guilders.

Given the paucity of financial resources outlined earlier, it is hardly surprising that such a small number—only 9 percent of the total inventories as noted in Table 7.3—record explicit evidence of any kind of intergenerational transfer, either in the form of a bequest given to the deceased or to someone else in his or her household prior to their death, or of a bequest left by the deceased to someone else. Consistent with this is the fact that the incidence of bequesting is strongly related to the financial status of the household. Estates valued at over 1,000 guilders before the subtraction of debts, which comprised less than 5 percent of the total, left evidence of bequesting in 35 percent of the time, whereas estates valued at less than 100 guilders, comprising nearly two-thirds of the sample, left evidence of bequeathing only 1.7 percent of the time. Even a modest increase in household assets to between 100 and 200 guilders raises the incidence of bequeathing to 11.5 percent.

Other ways of exploring the data to examine the influence of demographic profile on the likelihood that an individual would leave evidence of a bequest are shown in Tables 7.4 and 7.5. While the remarried parents in the inventory records were the most immediately obvious source of bequeathing through the legally mandated child support payment to the

**Table 7.4**
**Bequestors/Bequestees by Relationship to the Orphanage**

|  | Parent | Former Orphan | Relative of Orphan | Total |
|---|---|---|---|---|
| Bequest in record | 67 | 5 | 10 | 82 |
| percent of relationship group | 9.4 | 3.4 | 18.2 | 9.0 |
| Total inventories | 709 | 148 | 55 | 912 |
| percent of total | 77.7 | 16.2 | 6.0 | 100 |

Source: See Table 7.1.

**Table 7.5**
**Bequestors/Bequestees by Marital Status and Gender of Deceased**

|  | Married | Widower | Widow | Unmarried | All Men | All Women |
|---|---|---|---|---|---|---|
| Bequest in record | 49 | 12 | 16 | 5 | 53 | 29 |
| percent of marital group | 17.6 | 6.0 | 4.6 | 5.8 | 12.9 | 5.8 |
| Total inventories | 278 | 201 | 346 | 87 | 410 | 502 |
| percent of total | 30.5 | 22.0 | 37.9 | 9.5 | 45.0 | 55.0 |

Source: See Table 7.1.

Orphan Chamber in the name of their predeceased first spouse, the relative poverty of the parent group worked to keep its overall incidence of bequeathing much lower than that for the category of relatives of orphans, a group already identified as enjoying more secure financial positions. These rates were 9.4 percent and 18.2 percent, respectively. Marital status at death also serves as a strong indicator of ability to bequeath, with married persons at least three times more likely than any other group to have left evidence of an intergenerational transfer of wealth. Of course this group largely comprised the parents in the sample who had remarried, and as work elsewhere has shown, remarriage itself was an indicator of relative economic prosperity.[20]

Finally, male decedents were twice as likely to leave evidence of bequeathing as female decedents—12.9 percent of males compared with 5.8 percent of females. This finding is entirely consistent with the many other measures by which the inventories highlight the relatively stronger position of men in this strata of the Amsterdam economy than of women. First of all, the relatively higher rate of men than women in marital unions at the time of death, given the legal stipulation that only full orphans could be taken into the orphanage, is a reflection of their higher remarriage rates. The men in this sample were also twice as likely to have been running retail or artisanal shops at their deaths as were the women, while the latter were more likely to have died with no possessions worthy of record. These indicators point toward an environment of relative female economic disadvantage, over and above the general indigence of those associated with the orphanage in the first place.

Yet some puzzling questions remain. The most important of these is why so many of the inventories of remarried parents, both men and women, do not yield the evidence we would expect of the legally mandated provision for the children of a first marriage. This provision is the so-called *moeders-bewijs,* paid by fathers for their deceased wives, and the *vaders-bewijs,* for the reverse. Of the 709 parents recorded in this collection of inventories, 277 (or 39 percent) had remarried at some point in their adult lives. A small number of these (17) had either no children or at least no surviving children from their first marriage, so there is no reason to expect to find evidence of the *bewijs* in their inventories. Nonetheless, 260 individuals remain who should have been fully eligible and obligated to make this payment to the municipal Orphan Chamber at the time of their second marriage. Out of this number, the 49 cases (37 men and 12 women) that actually reveal such evidence seems paltry. To investigate this discrepancy further requires the collection of additional information available only in the municipal marriage registers. For it was in the margins of this document that the city clerk recorded the completion, or failure thereof, of the Orphan Chamber requirement alongside all remarriages where children were present from an earlier marriage. For a subperiod

**Table 7.6**
**Parental Bequeathing Patterns at Remarriage, 1748–1756**

|  | Bewijs in inventory & remarriage | Bewijs at remarriage only | No bewijs required at remarriage | Not in marriage register |
|---|---|---|---|---|
| Males | 9 | 22 | 13 | 3 |
| percent | 19.2 | 46.8 | 27.7 | 6.4 |
| median assets (guilders) | 323 | 48 | 29.8 | 139.5 |
| Females | 3 | 10 | 6 | 6 |
| percent | 12.0 | 40.0 | 24 | 24.0 |
| median assets (guilders) | 800 | 14.5 | 13.0 | 127 |

Note: This sample includes parents who died between January 1748 and July 1756 and who had remarried at least once, leaving minor children to the orphanage. The parents for whom no *bewijs* payment was recorded at the time of remarriage did not have minor children surviving from their previous marriages and therefore were not obliged to make such a payment.

Source: See Table 7.1.

between January 1748 and July 1756, all the parental decedents have been searched for in the city marriage registers in an effort to compile a complete record of their dates of marriage as well as the marginal notation regarding the status of their *bewijs* contributions. Of the 72 remarrying parents (25 women and 47 men) whose inventories were drawn up during this period, all but 9 (6 women and 3 men) have marital histories that can be fully traced in the city registers. Thus we can say with a fair degree of certainty that for the majority of the remarrying parents, the payment to the Orphan Chamber was in fact recorded as having been accomplished. With this more complete information, laid out in Table 7.6, much of the gender gap evidenced by the inventories disappears. Indeed, for both sexes, those out of compliance constitute roughly one-quarter of the total, although the much higher fraction of women who could not be linked to the marriage register could ultimately tip the balance back toward a greater rate of female default.

Just as we would expect, the few individuals whose *bewijs* obligations actually appear in their final inventories were the wealthiest of the entire group. And those individuals who either lacked surviving children at remarriage, or for whom the *bewijs* payment had disappeared from their final accounting, were substantially poorer. The median assets of those for whom marriage information is missing lie somewhere in between, confirming the most likely proposition that the missing category includes

individuals of both types. Once again it appears that the ability of individuals to fulfill even their legally obligatory bequests, let alone engage
in other kinds of voluntary intergenerational transfer, was greatly hampered by the severe financial constraints faced by many of those affiliated
to the orphanage.

Financial hardship is further evidenced by the fact that even among
those who did make the promise of a payment for their children, and
whose promise was still remembered officially at the time of their death,
it was, more often than not, as yet unpaid. Such cases show up in the
inventories as a debt against the estate of the deceased, with the children
as the ultimate creditors. Indeed, parental *bewijs* obligations were twice as
likely to remain as debts all the way to the grave as to show up as assets
held in reserve for the exclusive use of the children's upkeep. For even
among the relatively privileged individuals who had been able to remarry,
and had at least entertained the hope of keeping their promises made at
the moment of remarriage, the tying up of financial assets in the Orphan
Chamber, where they could not contribute to the productive potential of
the household, was too great a loss to actually sustain. The data in Table
7.7 suggest that other kinds of bequests might also end up in the inventories as debits rather than more logically as credits. The two cases of a
bequest made to a child of the deceased from outside parties, which are
nonetheless recorded as debts, as well as the case of Jacobus Wigman,
whose estate owed his surviving second wife, Jannetje Mast, two separate

Table 7.7
Incidence of Credits and Debits among Bequests

|  | Debit | Credit | Total |
|---|---|---|---|
| Bewijs payment | 34 | 17 | 51 |
| percent | 66.7 | 33.3 | |
| Bequest to deceased | 0 | 11 | 11 |
| percent | 0.0 | 100 | |
| Bequest to child of deceased from third party | 2 | 11 | 13 |
| percent | 15.4 | 84.6 | |
| Bequest to spouse of deceased from third party | 1 | 0 | 1 |
| percent | 100 | 0.0 | |
| Bequest from deceased to own child/grandchild | 0 | 2 | 2 |
| percent | 0.0 | 100 | |

Source: See Table 7.1.

debts totaling the enormous sum of 5,247 guilders, all point to this same conclusion. In each case, an outside bequest made to a member of the household other than the head was effectively intercepted by the head and absorbed for the economic needs of the household. The case of Jacobus Wigman is particularly interesting in this regard as he seems to have used the substantial inherited money his second wife brought into their union to finance his thriving cloth-shearing enterprise. And while the size of Jannetje's assets, and the extent of Jacobus's debts were anything but typical for the majority of the population affiliated with the orphanage, their case is not difficult to reconcile with that of their much poorer peers. Jacobus himself had one surviving child from his first marriage when he married Jannetje in May 1746. However, by the time of his death in June 1753, no record remains of the *bewijs* payment he had promised back in 1746 for the eventual care of his orphaned daughter Joanna. His may well have been one of those cases that were the lifeblood of a common early modern urban myth: the hardworking but financially failing artisan whose enterprise is rescued by a well-placed second marriage to a widow with inherited assets. One cannot help but wonder what relations were like between the stepmother Jannetje, who was destined to get her sizable inheritance back (as well as an additional 1,000 guilders in cash that she had brought to the marriage and managed to keep separate from Jacobus's final accounting!) and Joanna, who at the death of her father found herself in an orphanage with no hope even of claiming her legitimate portion from her own mother.

## CONCLUSION

Every one of these families, disrupted as they were by premature parental death, must have had some story of hardship to tell, and presumably one of strained relations as well. For people who relied almost entirely on the earning capacity of their labor and that of their immediate household members, there was no feasible way to ensure the financial security of dependents following death. Urban magistrates could attempt to mitigate the problem through legislation enforced at a moment of bureaucratic contact between ordinary citizens and their government, that is, when men and women desired to remarry, but they could not change the underlying economic realities that so severely constrained the options of these families. In some sense, the physical presence of the Burgerweeshuis was itself testimony to a recognition of that fact. Moreover, these families clearly did what they could in the way of voluntary bequests across generations and along lines of collateral kin. Household items and clothing were widely recycled; even tiny amounts of cash, sometimes as little as four guilders, were carefully set aside and marked off as inheritance portions for grandchildren, nephews, and nieces; daughters were treated equally with sons whenever *bewijs* payments were actually made on be-half of predeceased parents; and finally food, lodging, and nursing care during illness were widely shared. This latter phenomenon is in fact well documented in the inventory records because extended family members were very careful to charge as debts against the estates of the deceased the time and money spent providing such human services, particularly during the final illness preceding death. While this practice may at first appear to be mercenary and contrary to the sacred bonds which ideally hold families together, it was in fact a perfectly legal way of ensuring that some assets that would otherwise have leaked outside the family to other creditors, and eventually to the orphanage itself, instead remained within the control of the family. Moreover, this practice confirms precisely the point with which this essay began: that the labor time of household care and social reproduction is indeed valuable and amenable to valuation. Nursing of the sick and the watching of their children, whether performed by a male, or indeed more commonly, a female relative or neighbor, were services widely understood to be worthy of compensation.

Clearly then, for the families that appeared in the inventory records of the orphanage, this institution was more than just a boon; it was a veri-table life vest. For most, if not quite all of them, the Burgerweeshuis was able to provide a much higher standard of care for their minor children than they had been able to do at home, and certainly better than in those households already missing one parent. Thus it is not surprising to find evidence of families that had somehow found ways to support their minor children up until the death of the second parent but that sent their children to the Burgerweeshuis as soon as they had been made eligible by that death. Thus, when the widower Dirk Sibinga died in the East Indies in 1768, his 12-year-old son Abraham was removed immediately from the care of the neighbors and good friends who had raised him since the death of his mother and placed into the Burgerweeshuis. Even more worthy of note is the case of Johannes Melters, who had been living with his grand-mother following the death of his mother, while his father was also in service in the East Indies. Following the death of his father at sea in 1763, his grandmother was only too happy to relinquish him to the care of the orphanage. Even if something on the order of the typical *bewijs* payment of 50 guilders (which was not actually required in this case, given that his father never remarried) had been left for him in the name of his deceased mother, it would not possibly have been enough to see him through the rest of his minority, let alone to set him up in a trade. Only a municipally supported and well-financed institution could offer him that.

When the orphanage is examined from the perspective of intergenera-tional resource transfers and the bequeathing strategies of individual fam-ilies, who themselves were often in crisis, it is not at all hard to reconcile the emergence of this new institutional form of care with the dynamic market economy of the urbanizing Dutch Republic. Rather than being evidence of the increasing affective poverty of the Protestant, urban, nuclear family over the early modern period, it is really a testament to the remarkable prosperity of the civic community as a whole. For the Burgerweeshuis provided a kind of social insurance that no middling family could have ever hoped to provide on its own: the guarantee that its children would be raised to adulthood, well fed, clothed, and appropriately educated, even if both parents were to die prematurely and the financial assets of the family become quickly and fully exhausted. Only a community with a strong appreciation for the real costs of social reproduction and a willingness and capacity to pay at least some of those costs collectively would be in a position to even build such an institution as the Burgerweeshuis. That the Dutch built scores of these institutions, along with old men's and women's homes, foundling hospitals, widow's courtyards, reform institutions, and hospitals for the sick, is of course a clear sign of their unprecedented commercial prosperity but also of their strong sense of collective responsibility for the cultivation of human capital in its most comprehensive sense. While the operations of the Burgerweeshuis did not absolve the family from its financial responsibilities concerning its orphaned relatives, it nevertheless contributed to the ability of households to transmit assets from one generation to another. Without this institution, and assuming that cultural norms prevented the abandonment of such children, families would have been burdened individually with far higher costs of social reproduction. In this sense, the Burgerweeshuis fulfilled the task of social reproduction in cases where individual responses were inadequate and as such confirmed Polanyi's argument about the relationship between social institutions and the development of market capitalism.

## NOTES

The research presented here has been undertaken with the generous support of the Whiting Foundation and the Levitan Prize at MIT. Early drafts of the work have benefited greatly from the comments of discussants and audience participants in sessions at the European Social Science History Conference and the Annual Meetings of the Social Science History Association. I am especially grateful to the editors, whose questions and comments have sharpened the argument considerably.

1. See Gary Becker, *An Economic Analysis of the Family* (Dublin: Economic and Social Research Institute, 1986).

2. See especially the scathing critique provided by Nancy Folbre, *Who Pays for the Kids? Gender and the Structures of Constraint* (London: Routledge, 1994). See also Marianne Ferber and Julie Nelson, eds., *Beyond Economic Man: Feminist Theory and Economics* (Chicago: University of Chicago Press, 1993) and Marilyn Waring, *Counting for Nothing: What Men Value and What Women Are Worth* (Toronto: University of Toronto Press, 1999).

3. For a review of the extensive literature on the care of children in early modern Europe see Anne McCants, *Civic Charity in a Golden Age: Orphan Care in Early Modern Amsterdam* (Urbana: University of Illinois Press, 1997).

4. See, for example, E. A. Wrigley and Roger Schofield, *The Population History of England, 1541–1871: A Reconstruction* (London: Edward Arnold, 1981), in which they conclude that England owed much of its economic prosperity to the social and economic checks that held fertility relatively low by early modern standards, preventing dependency ratios from soaring out of control and sapping the surplus capacities of adult labor power.

5. The most obvious early example of this type of literature comes from the Pentateuch of the Hebrew Bible, where the Israelites are exhorted to succor the widows and orphans (Deut. 24:17–22).

6. Quoted in J. T. Engels, *Kinderen van Amsterdam* (Amsterdam: Walburg Pers, 1989), 6.

7. The cost of the *poortergeld* was 8 guilders until 1624 and 14 guilders thereafter. In 1630, it rose to 30 guilders, and to 40 in 1633. Finally, it stabilized at 50 guilders in 1650.

8. This phenomenon can be seen very clearly in the contemporary documentation from the Arnhem *Burgerweeshuis*. There, despite repeated mention in the orphanage's ordinances of the rules governing the admission of the orphaned children of "notables," none seems to have ever actually resided in the institution. See J. P. Vredenberg, *Als Off Sij Onse Eigene Kijnder Weren: Het Burgerweeshuis te Arnhem, 1583–1742* (Arnhem: Gemeente Arnhem, 1983), 54.

9. See the discussion in A.C.J. de Vrankrijker, *Mensen, Leven en Werken in de Gouden Eeuw* ('S-Gravenhage: Martinus Nijhoff, 1981), 110–11.

10. For a discussion of the contrasting French case see Rachel Fuchs, *Abandoned Children: Foundlings and Child Welfare in Nineteenth-Century France* (Albany: State University of New York Press, 1984).

11. Karl Polanyi, *The Great Transformation* (Boston: Beacon Press, 1957), 33.

12. Fissell's work on eighteenth-century charity hospitals in Bristol has also shown that public relief there directly "substituted for the care of family and friends." See Mary Fissell, *Patients, Power, and the Poor in Eighteenth-Century Bristol* (Cambridge: Cambridge University Press, 1991), 101.

13. This and all other data for this paper are taken from the Amsterdam Municipal Archives manuscript materials of the Burgerweeshuis, G.A.A., p.a. 367, oud archief 652–63.

14. The total collection records close to 1,500 households, but the sample reported on here is composed of the 912 complete inventories that were drawn up between May 1740 and April 1782. These 912 inventories include 49,926 separate enumerations of household goods; 6,350 separate listings of debts outstanding; 676 credits outstanding; and 858 notations for goods at pawn (*lombard briefjes*).

15. Margaret Spufford, "The Limitations of the Probate Inventory," in *English Rural Society, 1500–1800: Essays in Honour of Joan Thirsk*, ed. John Chartres and David Hey (Cambridge: Cambridge University Press, 1990), 151–53 and Alice Hanson Jones, *Wealth of a Nation to Be: The American Colonies on the Eve of the Revolution* (New York: Columbia University Press, 1980), 141–45.

16. A few inventories exist for children still living in the Burgerweeshuis who had been left sufficiently large estates that had not been entirely consumed by the

cost of the child's care to date. These estates had to be inventoried again at the death of the child to determine what assets remained of the original estate left by their parents.

17. This category of individuals is the poorest in the total sample, despite the fact that their ostensible net worth was only zero and not negative, as was the case for those individuals whose estates recorded more debts than assets. For these 133 individuals the bookkeeper found nothing at all of any value in the household and would write something to that effect rather than making out the usual inventory of possessions and debts. It is impossible to ascertain what, if any, debts these individuals incurred.

18. G.A.A., p.a. 367, oud archief 652.

19. The municipality estimated the annual cost of care per child in the Burger-weeshuis to be 150 guilders at the close of the eighteenth century. See McCants, *Civic Charity*, 194.

20. Anne E. C. McCants, "The Not-So-Merry Widows of Amsterdam, 1740–1782," *Journal of Family History* 24 (1999): 441–67.

# CHAPTER 8

# Did Women Invent Life Insurance? Widows and the Demand for Financial Services in Eighteenth-Century Germany

*Eve Rosenhaft*

## INTRODUCTION

Over a quarter of a century ago, Jack Goody proposed that "transmission *mortis causa* is not only the means by which the reproduction of the social system is carried out [but] also the way in which interpersonal relationships are structured."[1] This proposition can be broadened to apply to all practices and institutions that have the maintenance of family welfare as their object. However, their discernible motivations and practical consequences are bound to vary as widely as the definitions of *family* and *welfare* vary over time and place. Sometimes the values that underpin the social system that property transmission serves to reproduce are implicit, or self-evident. However, when people set out to create new institutions of family welfare provision, it becomes necessary to articulate what relationships and qualities need to be fostered—who needs what, and who owes what to whom.

This chapter examines the creation of widows' funds in eighteenth-century Germany. Widows' funds represented a new institutional form of *postmortem* provision for dependants, providing pensions for widows on the basis of contributions made during their husbands' lifetimes. The chapter's main concern is with those women whose need provided the ostensible rationale for the funds. Its central proposition is that, far from being complacent objects of policy in the new institutions, women had their own demands that contributed to innovation and informed the transition from widows' funds to modern life insurance.[2] At the same time, reading the institutions in terms of a conversation between widows on the one hand and the promoters and managers of the funds on the other makes it possible to interrogate rhetorics of poverty and welfare and to draw out the implications of visions of the family that underpinned them. The schemes that were marketed to men as the only way to forestall penury were interesting to women as new ways of managing the assets they had.

## WIDOWS' FUNDS: ECONOMICS AND CULTURAL INNOVATION

The history of the growth of widows' funds is a complex one. They developed in many parts of Europe from the late seventeenth century onward. The most extensive and continuous development appears to have been in Protestant northern Europe, with Britain and the Netherlands leading the way, and the northern and western German and Scandinavian states following. The territorial center of gravity reflects the fact that everywhere the first impulses came from within the Protestant churches, as successive cohorts of clergy and church administrators faced up to the family and intergenerational responsibilities created by the abandonment of clerical celibacy. The first beneficiaries of widows' funds were thus the widows of clergymen. In Germany, clerical widows' funds came into being very early in the wake of the Reformation, but before the end of the seventeenth century they were normally motivated and sponsored by the church authorities and took the form of closed solidary societies with compulsory membership. In this sense, they could trace a longer historical pedigree and mimicked the beneficial funds that had been operated by guilds and corporations since the Middle Ages.[3] Increasingly, however, clerical widows' funds took on an independent dynamic that needs to be understood in terms of the cultural shifts that accompanied changes in social structure. First, clergymen began to form widows' funds themselves on the basis of voluntary association. Second, the funds started to open their membership to men from other occupational groups, notably the professional and service-oriented middle classes. This development began in Britain and the Netherlands, and the first generation of widows' funds were founded in Germany in 1700. This was the first of two phases of widows' funds development: the first ended around 1725; the second began in the 1750s and came to an end in the late 1780s.[4] This latter phase, which is the focus of this chapter, was one of spectacular growth, as well as of experimentation and innovation, as funds adopted the strategy of continuous recruitment from a growing number of individuals. This period of development ended with the collapse of several funds, and the public and expert discussions about how the funds might be rescued provided the context in which Germans began to think critically about applying statistically derived life expectancies to the calculation of pensions.

The first modern life insurance scheme in Germany thus emerged directly out of the crisis of the widows' funds.

The trajectory of development of widows' funds in eighteenth-century Germany echoes the growth of life insurance in Britain. There the foundation, rise, and fall of the first commercial life-insurance schemes coincided with the speculative boom of the first two decades of the century (ending in the disaster of the South Sea and Mississippi bubbles); the second period of development, which occurred around 1760, is less easily explained.[5] It has been suggested that the growth in widows' funds in Germany around 1700 reflects the adoption of rudimentary actuarial techniques that had been used in British and Dutch institutions.[6] Certainly, changes in recruitment practice in Germany, even in this early phase, were associated with the introduction of regulations about the age and health of potential members. However, on the basis of research to date it is not possible to identify clear paths of technology transfer between Britain or Holland and Germany at any stage over the course of the funds' development.

The international parallels are nonetheless a reminder that the institution of widows' funds had a significant cultural dimension. Their invention, and more particularly their popularization in Germany, cannot be explained as a simple reflection of economic conditions. To be sure, they were rooted in measurable material circumstances. Examination of their day-to-day operation reveals an adaptability to local circumstances, while everywhere their emergence reflected the growth of an urban, salaried, and professional middle class. In Germany, the consolidation of territorial states, the elaboration of regional administrative apparatuses, the increase in urban populations, and the expansion of university training for both professional and civil service occupations contributed significantly to the growth of a constituency for the widows' funds. At the same time, widows' funds need to be viewed as part of the explosion of institutional and cultural innovation that took place in the second half of the eighteenth century throughout Europe. This was associated with the growth of a reading public, the expansion of supraregional communications (notably through the proliferation of print media and the periodical press) and the intensified circulation of information, the rise of associational culture, and the emergence of consumerism in the principal urban centers.[7] Changes in the cultural infrastructure helped to transform the collective imagination, which in turn shaped the economic context. Popular financial speculation, whether it entailed involvement in the early bubbles or in the more measured (though, in Germany, very uneven) growth of the capital market in which the second generation of widows' funds participated, is a function of the combination of information, optimism, and readiness to take risks.[8] The widows' funds, whatever their origins, participated in an expanding market of services, practices, and ideas, which made them responsive to impulses from the public, sensitive to fashion and innovation, and also, as it turned out, risks. In this situation the search for new solutions to old problems often involved redefining the problems; meeting old needs gave way to the more creative and profitable business of formulating new needs. The following account represents an attempt to elucidate the dialectical relationship between the material circumstances of middle-class families and ideologies of family life in the operation, self-definition, and transformation of the widows' funds, placing an emphasis on the cultural logic of the institutions.[9]

## THE CALENBERG WIDOWS' FUND AND ITS PUBLIC

Most of the archival evidence on which the following discussion is based comes from the records of the Calenberg widows' fund (Calenbergische Witwen-Verpflegungs-Gesellschaft). The Calenberg, founded in 1766, was the most ambitious of the second wave of widows' funds. It was set up and administered by the Treasury Committee of the Landschaft, or estates general, of Calenberg, a duchy subject to the Hanoverian crown.[10] The promotion of widows' funds by state authorities was not uncommon in Germany because they seemed to offer the means to provide a degree of security for the growing numbers of civil servants at minimal direct cost to the state. By the second half of the century, it was the underpaid servants of the state who figured most prominently in the literature on widows' funds. The widely cited handbook published in 1772 by the reform minister Carl Daniel Küster envisioned each of these men trembling in horror at the prospect of his own death, "a death which will surrender his loved ones to poverty, expose them to contempt, and make them prey to the miserable want in which he daily sees widows and orphans helplessly sighing." For Küster, this was not a problem of private happiness alone but rather that a man's gnawing anxiety, he argued, "puts a brake on the whole machine of his activity," interferes with his work, and thus weakens the state.[11] Rulers thus had an acknowledged interest in promoting the new funds. The royal decree that formally called the Calenberg into being did not make this rationale explicit but named two policy concerns equally characteristic of the eighteenth-century state; the stated purpose of the fund was to provide for widows and orphans and to make it easier for men to start families, "since it contributes greatly to improving a country's wealth and happiness, when the enthusiasm of both the male and female sex for marriage, and thus the useful population, can be increased, and at the same time the impoverishment of many widows can be prevented."[12] A further motivation for the foundation of the Calenberg was not publicly stated at all; the duchy had incurred very significant debts in the Seven Years' War (1756–1763), and the estates looked to the widows' fund to generate much-needed capital.

The state's interest in drawing income from the Calenberg led to a financial arrangement that distinguished the Calenberg from its contemporaries among widows' funds. With a few notable exceptions, widows' funds invested their capital, either putting it away by depositing it with financial institutions or lending it out themselves at interest, and were able to use the interest income to support their operations. In the case of the Calenberg, whose capital was deposited in the State Treasury, the Landschaft claimed the interest for its own use. In lieu of interest income, the Landschaft underwrote the widows' fund with a guarantee of a large sum of cash.

The result of this arrangement was that the Calenberg was exceptionally heavily dependent on income from premiums, and hence on recruitment, to meet its costs. This meant that it took to extreme practices that were implicit in the operation of all the publicly recruited funds. In spite of being a state foundation, it became the most adventurous fund of its generation, gambling on growth, constantly juggling rates and systems of payment, and increasingly committing itself to maintaining a positive public image and attracting new custom through both formal and informal networks of communication.

The adventurous character of the Calenberg was apparent at the beginning in its recruitment strategy. It was the only German widows' fund that was open to members of all confessions and nationalities; other funds accepted only citizens or residents of the territory or region in which they were founded, but the Calenberg had subscribers from all over Europe. In other respects, it seemed carefully designed to limit risk. A subscriber could contract for a pension in multiples of 10 Reichstaler (Rtl), up to a maximum of 1000 Rtl. This was a larger sum than other funds would pay, but there were some safety mechanisms. The first was a kind of actuarial calculation. Here, the Calenberg founders felt secure in that they could draw on technologies and calculi already available. The model of an insurance fund had already been tried with success in the case of fire insurance. Extending this model to human life required only a reliable way of assessing risk, and this seemed to be provided by the mortality tables drawn up in the first half of the century.[13] Life expectancies derived from these tables were used to scale premiums according to the difference in age between husband and wife. The Calenberg founders also excluded very old men and required the presentation of a certificate of good health by new members, and in order to assess the maximum possible pensions bill, they used census data to identify the maximum number of widows that the fund might have to support at any one time.

Second, the Calenberg required that each subscriber deposit a capital sum equivalent to a year's pension. Although the interest generated by this capital could not return to subscribers or widows, the capital itself was repayable on the husband's death; in a sense it served as a guarantee of the first year's pension. Finally, premiums were collected twice a year after the pensions were paid out to existing widows and could be recalculated upward as the pensions' bill rose; in this sense, subscribers were not in fact paying toward their own widows' pensions but buying guaranteed pensions for their own wives by paying the pensions of other men's widows. However, in order to maintain subscriber confidence, a maximum level was fixed in advance beyond which premiums could not rise. A widow collected her pension twice a year as long as she remained unmarried. If she remarried, the pension lapsed; she could opt either to take a lump sum or to have the pension reinstated in case she was widowed again. Remarriage payments were funded by a mechanism that also had incentive purposes. In order to encourage men to join the fund as soon as they married, it was stipulated that anyone who joined more than six months after marrying had to pay an additional 5 percent of the capital deposit for each year that had elapsed between his marriage and his joining the fund. The capital built up from these "marriage interest" payments (*Heiratszinsen*) went to remarrying widows, thus, it was hoped, providing an incentive for men to marry them and for them to resign their pensions.[14]

The founders of the Calenberg thus did everything they could to appeal to the public, offering an attractive product at a low price with every appearance of security. For over a decade they were successful in this. By April 1767, after the first six months it had been declared open for subscriptions, the fund had accumulated the 200,000 Rtl stipulated as the minimum capital necessary to go into full operation. Between its founding and 1780, 5,180 men—each of them, by definition, with a wife—became members at one time or another, and at its peak in 1779–1780 the Calenberg had more than 3,700 married couples and more than 700 pensioner widows on its books.[15] Other widows' funds experienced similar growth, relative to their more limited territorial constituencies, so that in this period joining a widows' fund can be characterized as a mass phenomenon. Contemporary observers represented the desire to buy a pension or have a pension bought for oneself as a fashion craze. The pension certificates had become consumer items, commented some critics; every wife wanted one in order to keep up with her neighbors and female relatives![16] The number and variety of projects for widows' funds, originating with a range of individuals and institutions and devised for the assistance many different interest groups, also testifies to the extent to which they caught the popular imagination.

The relationship between the widows' funds and their public was a two-sided one. In the case of the Calenberg, the conversation began very early on. Members of the Calenberg estates themselves had touched off a new phase in the discussion of first principles in 1764 when they encouraged the Göttingen Scientific Society to offer a prize for the best suggestions on how to organize a widows' fund.[17] In the following months and years responses came thick and fast. These included advice and warnings from the academic and broader scholarly community, published in pamphlet form and in the scholarly periodical press or submitted confidentially in manuscript. But inquiries and suggestions also came from individual members of the middle-class public, and correspondence was particularly intense during the six-month period between the fund being announced and its going into full operation.

## DEFINING NEEDS, CONSTRUCTING FAMILIES: THE GENDER POLITICS OF THE CALENBERG

A number of the comments and suggestions sent in by members of the public addressed the question of who qualified to be members and beneficiaries of the fund, or who the fund was for. A key issue raised by some male correspondents was whether the new institution could be adapted to benefit dependants who were not married women. People asked whether it might not be possible to invest in a pension for an unmarried woman: "Your Excellency might say that this goes against policy, and hinders marriage. Correct. But what if only spinsters of 30 or 40 were allowed as beneficiaries?"[18] Why should a son not be allowed to join on behalf of his mother? Or maybe any man should be allowed to become a member of the fund "for the benefit of a minor female relative." And shouldn't specific and more generous provision be made for the orphans?[19]

These suggestions had no impact on the decisions of the founders of the Calenberg, which was conceived as a society of married men. The Calenberg regulations did allow the possibility that premiums might be paid toward a widow's pension by "the [beneficiary's] parents, the woman herself or a third party," but this was clearly seen as an exception, and one that involved particular risks. It was further set out in the regulations "that in such cases measures must be taken to ensure that the premium is paid in good order." Even in a case like this, only married women could be considered as beneficiaries, and the pension was payable only on the death of the husband. There were women among contributors to the Calenberg, but very few. Sara Elisabeth Schlaeger paid contributions in the name of her husband, a librarian, but kept it secret from him all his life; her lawyer explained that there were "not inconsiderable grounds" for this course of action but was too discreet to provide details.[20]

Avowedly founded to encourage marriage, the Calenberg at the same time promoted a particular vision of marriage. Its patriarchal character was underlined by the way in which the regulations governed the disposal of the documents that certified receipt of the capital sum and the pension rights of the widow. During his lifetime, a husband who had paid the capital deposit could treat the capital receipts (*Rezeptionsscheine*) like any other negotiable instrument; in particular, there was no bar on his giving, lending, or pawning of them. In fact it seems to have been common for men to raise the capital to pay into the widows' fund by offering the *Rezeptionsscheine* as collateral for a loan. In some cases, this took place with the express permission of the wife, who thereby made herself personally liable to pay the debt incurred.[21] Whoever had the *Rezeptionsscheine* in their possession when the husband died, whether widow or creditor, could claim the money.

Once widowed, however, the woman lost any power to dispose in a preemptive way over her income; she could do as she wished with the cash, but the *right* to a pension certified in the *Pensionsscheine* could be neither lent, nor given away, nor pawned. The pension was defined as *alimentum*, or maintenance. Like salaries and other kinds of maintenance payments, it could not be treated as alienable property; it was permanently attached to the person whose food, clothing, housing, and/or education it was designed to pay for. In the case of a married woman, *alimentum* was regarded in law as the obligation of the husband and was explicitly distinguished from any property that appertained to her as an individual within the marriage, such as the dowry.[22] This definition protected the material interests of the beneficiaries of such payments, who were in a position of relative weakness. But the Calenberg founders made clear in the notes on their original plan that the designation of a pension as *alimentum* was a discretionary decision made "in favour" of the husbands, that is, in fulfillment of their presumptive wishes.

This point was elaborated in the response of the Calenberg administrators to the case of Widow Behrens in Dannenberg. At the end of 1776 the Dannenberg authorities applied for a distraint on her pension, to prevent it being paid out to her. Widow Behrens herself consented to this application because she had formally written over all her property, including her pension rights, to her late husband's creditors. By "oath sworn on her own body" she had renounced every legal immunity, including that granted by the regulations of the widows' fund. The high court issued a "collegial request" to the fund administrators to permit Widow Behrens's pension to be paid to her creditors, but the administrators were adamant. The fund, they explained, had been

created to provide assurance for husbands that their widows would receive an income appropriate to their station with absolute reliability. . . . In this regard the *bonum publicum* requires that that assurance be maintained intact, and it is all the more necessary to reinforce it so that the widows themselves are never able, whether compelled by necessity or moved by lack of reflection, thoughtlessness, ignorance or anything else, to relinquish their maintenance payments, because many incidents in human life can bring a widow into circumstances in which, in order to gain an apparent momentary advantage, she will give up the prospect of enjoying a pension payment a half a year away, never thinking of the discomfort and suffering to which she will inevitably expose herself in the long run. . . . Incidents of this kind certainly make it harder for a husband to resolve to join the widows' fund. And it is not simply in the public interest, but also in that of the husband—quite apart from the promptings of marital affection—that as far as is within his power his widow should be provided for in such a way that she and any minor children may not perish but also that she can honor him after his death by living out her widowhood in a manner appropriate to her station.[23]

## "... *ALS EINE EXTRAORDINARIUM:*" WIDOW HENZE AND THE CALENBERG

The official self-definition of the Calenberg thus took women—wives or widows—into account solely as objects of policy, whose interests were subsidiary to those of civil society as embodied in male heads of household. This vision was manifestly in tension with the complex realities of partnership, collusion, or shared interest between husband and wife that are evident even in the examples cited earlier of women's participation in the management of the pension investment. Indeed, as has already been suggested, contemporary commentators often depicted the purchase of a pension as motivated by the wife or as a joint decision of the married couple.[24] From the beginning, the publicity that accompanied the founding of new widows' funds attracted the attention of women as well as men.

At least one of the letters that reached the Calenberg administrators in the months following the launch of their fund came from a woman. Writing directly to the chairman of the Treasury Committee, she identified herself only as Widow Henze and lived in the village of Stöcken just north of Hanover.[25] She wanted to join the fund and draw a pension in her own right, as an exceptional case. The phrase she used was *"als eine Extraordinarium"*—a moment of grammatical gender confusion that provided a suitable opening to what can best be described as an exercise in financial cross-dressing.

In light of the intentions that lay behind the widows' fund, Widow Henze's request was not only inappropriate, but positively impious. Her awareness of this shaped the material form of her letter as well as its contents. She made a point of saying that she had written it in her own hand, rather than following the normal practice of having business letters written by a copyist or notary; she wrote it herself so that no other person would know of its contents and "so that the noble committee should suffer no more applications of this kind." After begging her "indulgent patron" to let her be the first to "partake of this collected blessing," she sought to preempt reproach with the exaggeratedly pious, almost superstitious wish "that God may make that same [blessing] flow back abundantly on all those who contribute and add the years he has taken from my husband's life to the lives of all the husbands. But remove from all the wives the many years of widowhood that I have suffered, and so keep them together in wedded contentment for years to come."

But behind this modest conclusion stood an intelligent and self-confident woman. Widow Henze, having penned the letter herself, expressly asked indulgence for "all the womanly errors" it contained—the surest sign of a practiced letter writer.[26] Her handwriting is firm, regular, and legible, her spelling and punctuation relatively consistent for an eighteenth-century letter writer, and while her grasp of Latin gender may have been shaky, she was careful to observe the convention of educated orthography that dictated that words of romance derivation be written in Latin rather than German script. The ease with which she handled the business of letter writing can be explained by the fact that both her father and husband had been Protestant ministers, a circumstance which she set out in some detail in her bid to legitimate her claim to the Abbot's consideration. Her father was the pastor in Mandelsloh, her husband in Fischbeck—and although Fischbeck actually lay in the Duchy of Schaumburg, beyond the jurisdiction of the Calenberg estates, Widow Henze was quick to point out that Pastor Henze also had a Hanoverian village (Wehrbergen) in his parish.

Widow Henze was also well informed about the formal conditions for membership of the widows' fund. Her proposal to the Abbot was that in order to receive a pension of 100 Rtl a year, she would pay 185 Rtl into the fund. 100 Rtl of this represented the standard capital deposit equivalent to one year's pension. The remaining 85 Rtl represented "marriage interest"; in the spirit of the regulation, Widow Henze was offering to pay 5 Rtl for each of the 17 years since her own marriage.

Widow Henze's punctiliousness in applying to herself the rule about "marriage interest" is characteristic of the imaginative energy that went into her petition. Even more than the capital deposit (which would have been required of anyone investing in any pension fund), the "marriage interest" rule was directed at married men. In any case, as the published regulations stated, the "marriage interest" rule applied only to men who joined after the 200,000 Rtl founding capital had been accumulated. Widow Henze was writing three months before that point was reached. The very fact that paying the "marriage interest" was completely unnecessary is a sign of the symbolic value it had for Widow Henze. The money she offered gave material form to something which she also expressed verbally in her letter, namely the intention to take on the person of her dead husband as an economic actor. She described the payment of the 185 Rtl in these terms: "just as if my husband were still alive and paid a seventeen-year supplement." She also declared that she was prepared, "like any other member of the fund"—and that is, like any other husband—to pay premiums out of her pension income as soon as any member should die and a pension need to be paid to a new widow—"which God in his grace forbid!"

For her own part she was convinced that the fund could afford to pay *her* her first half-year's pension immediately after joining because she was sure to be the only pensioner for a long time, especially since God was bound to reward the administrators for their generosity to her by granting all the members long life. This was another superfluous gesture, for the immediate payment of the pension would be a matter of course if she were a "normal" widow, the relict of a member of the fund. And here, too, her attempt to rationalize the obvious can be read as further evidence of her unease at the very exceptional nature of what she was doing. In order to justify her receipt of a pension, she had to execute an uncomfortable maneuver: she had to bring her husband back to life in her own person and then kill him off—and to do that continuously. Indeed, she said as much when she promised to pay her premiums "as though my husband were still alive and I were, in a single person, one who pays in and one who enjoys a widow's share."

In the phrase adopted by Joan Scott to characterize many of her more famous contemporaries, Widow Henze was a woman "with only paradoxes to offer."[27] Her letter is characterized by both creativity and unease. Rhetorically at least, she accepted that as a woman without a man she had no claim to the consideration of the widows' fund, but she nevertheless hoped to claim the advantages of the new institution for herself, and this meant that she had to redefine both herself and, through the imaginative rewriting of the regulations, the institution. Exceptional as it is, the letter illustrates the way in which innovation opened up a space for negotiation in the articulation of social needs. It also invites the question of what prompted such an effort. What *did* widows need? The answer provided by further investigation of the circumstances of Widow Henze is significantly ambiguous and at odds with the image of widowhood that contemporary publicists invoked to explain the necessity for widows' funds.

## WIDOWS AND POVERTY

The explicit rationale for the creation of widows' funds was the expectation that in the absence of special provision, middle-class widows were doomed to destitution. The "miserable want" in which Küster saw middle-class widows and orphans "helplessly sighing" was insistently presented as the logical consequence of the situation of middle-class men. Dependent on fees and salaries rather than ownership of land or an artisanal trade, these men could not be sure of having anything to pass on when they died. In her letter, Widow Henze self-consciously mobilized these expectations about a widow's prospects to support her case. She reported that her husband had died four years after their marriage and left her with two daughters, aged 1 and 2½ years. The terms she used to characterize her situation in the succeeding 13 years were "much suffering, hardship and worry."

But even the little that she revealed about herself stands in some contradiction to the stereotype, as does the information that is available about her from other sources. The woman who signed herself "Widow Henze" was baptized Agnesa Dorothea Elisabeth Schmidt on July 23, 1723. In 1749 she married Johann Daniel Henze, who by that time was a missionary of some experience and the author of a volume of "improving songs for household use" and had just taken up appointment to his second parish.[28] Agnesa married relatively late by comparison with the average age for the brides of Protestant ministers.[29] But she made a relatively young widow, only 30 when Johann died. Still, she never remarried. And yet she was *not* poor and certainly not destitute. The sum of 185 Rtl which she was prepared to pay into the Calenberg widows' fund was more than some village pastors were paid in a year.[30] It was almost half as much as her husband's successor could expect as a cash salary. Although no pastor was actually expected to live from his salary alone, the comparison suggests that the capital sum to which Agnesa Henze had access was not inconsiderable by contemporary standards.

A look at the next generation of the family helps further to put the stereotype into perspective. Agnesa's elder daughter, Sophie Elisabeth, was married and widowed by the time she was 19. Her husband had been the pastor in the village of Heemsen, and within three months of his death she had married his successor. Heemsen was not a wealthy parish, and without knowing exactly what happened we are fairly safe in speculating that Sophie's early marriage and precipitate remarriage are signs that she and her mother were living in constrained circumstances.[31] Although not a brilliant match, Sophie's marriage was one considered "appropriate to her station." It was an achievement on Agnesa's part, especially after not getting the pension she applied for two or three years earlier.

Agnesa Henze's career exemplifies many of the tensions and ambiguities that underlay the rhetoric of widowhood and widows' poverty in the middle of the eighteenth century. Her documented circumstances belied any claim to destitution. However, she could plausibly appeal to another definition of poverty. This was the perception of poverty as a condition relative to the individual's status position and demarcated by socially determined structures of obligation. One of the standard lexica of the eighteenth century, Johann Heinrich Zedler's *Großes Universal-Lexicon*, explained that poverty (*Armuth*) might be either relative or absolute, noting that "poor" on its own could be applied "when someone does not possess what he requires to secure his sustenance and comfort, taking into account his station [*Stand*]." Absolute poverty usually required elaboration, in terms such as *blutarm* (dirt poor) or "in the extremity of poverty." In keeping with the broader educational purpose of a lexicon, the article went beyond definition to consider the philosophical and ethical implications of poverty, and in particular who owed assistance to whom. Its key conclusion was that "we are not obliged [to help] one and all, but certainly those with whom we stand in a specific connection," a duty that applied as much in the case of relative poverty as in that of destitution.[32] Amid melodramatic invocations of widows' helpless sighs, even Küster's handbook took it for granted that the fundamental problem was the reproduction of a middle-class lifestyle: "Where should a mother find money for schooling and clothes, when she doesn't even have enough tear-soaked bread to fill her stomach?"[33] As we have seen, it was concern for the husband's interest in the maintenance of respectability that actuated the Calenberg administrators.

Similarly, in the eighteenth century the lexical opposite of poverty, *Wohlstand*, had quite different connotations from its present meaning, "prosperity." It meant both well-being or welfare and a way of living or acting in accordance with shared social position.[34] It was in this sense that the term would be used by widows protesting at the reduction of their pensions after the collapse of the Calenberg: "What can comfort us in the sad feeling of our inability to squeeze the meanest, let alone a respectable [*anständigen*] living out of the scant remains of a widow's pension left to us? [If no help is forthcoming] instead of the intended maintenance of our *Wohlstand* we will be literally brought to our knees and spend the rest of our lives in gnawing misery, with nothing to look forward to but an early end."[35]

Status-specific definitions of poverty implied a potential double bind for middle-class widows. This can be illustrated by an example from the practice of an urban charitable foundation: The widow of a physician who petitioned for relief was acknowledged to be poor (*arm*), but as an "*Arme vom Stande*" (genteel poor) she was presumed to have resources not available to the real paupers. Failing such resources, she would however not be exempt from the key criterion for eligibility: only physical incapacity to work qualified a person for poor relief.[36] To take up paid work, though, would contravene the social code that applied to upper-class women and extended by convention to the service middle class.

## WIDOWS' SURVIVAL STRATEGIES

Just what strategies and resources were available to women in this situation remains a relatively underresearched area in German social history, by contrast with the now substantial literature on the situation of widows in artisan and even peasant households in the early modern period.[37] Much of the scholarly literature still echoes the widows' fund publicists in defining widowhood in terms of lack.[38] It is clear that maintaining a livelihood, let alone a middle-class lifestyle, was not a simple business. Remarriage was the preferred option, but an increasingly remote one. Over the course of the eighteenth century, the incidence of remarriage following the death of a spouse declined in all social groups in Germany. For women, the opportunities for remarriage diminished with age and number of children. What data there are on the middle classes suggest that in this social group women suffered disproportionately from the decline in opportunities to establish a new household. In the case of a man, the death of a spouse, or, less common but still possible in Protestant territories, divorce, was likely to be succeeded by a new marriage. Most widows remained widows, sometimes for the better part of their adult lives.[39]

Institutional provision was patchy and partial and often depended on local connections that members of the socially and geographically mobile middle classes lacked. From the sixteenth century onward, men and women of the urban patriciate began to provide for poor relations and their descendants by creating endowments (*Familienstiftungen*) whose interest income supported cash stipends for individuals or almshouses with reserved places. These were normally intended not for the immediate family of the testators and administrators, but for penurious distant relatives. Their benefits were available only to a minority of women, and by the middle of the eighteenth century, many *Familienstiftungen* in north Germany were overstretched by the etiolation of family connections, their income at risk from the vagaries of a backward regional economy. A middle-class widow might still make use of institutions of this kind by purchasing a place in an endowed almshouse, but this could require the drastic measure of writing over all her moveable property and thus denying any material inheritance to her children. It would also involve paying out a considerable amount of cash.[40] The widows of Protestant clergy, like Agnesa Henze, benefited from the year or half-year of grace, during which a pastor's widow could continue to live in his house, often on the basis of providing domestic and managerial services for his successor, but in practice this was a matter of convention rather than of right. In any case it was a temporary expedient, and more long-term provisions such as the building of separate housing for widows and the provision of an income from reserved glebe land, though frequently ordered by the church authorities, was almost as frequently evaded—not least because it involved real expense for the parish and the incoming minister.[41]

The widows of long-serving pastors were at least relatively well equipped by their education and practical experience in the ministry and their standing within the parish to earn a modest income after their husbands' death through activities in keeping with their station.[42] For the mass of middle-class widows there were two alternatives to demeaning labor. One was reliance on other family members. The presumption was that a widow's first port of call, for both material support and housing, would be her male relatives. Agnesa Henze's father, Johann Conrad Schmidt, was incumbent of the relatively well-endowed parish of Mandelsloh until his death in 1762, and she and her daughters may well have lived with him during his lifetime.

The second survival strategy for respectable widows was the management of cash. The normal situation envisaged by a range of eighteenth-century texts was that a respectable widow would be supported by the interest income from a capital sum. The sense in which widows themselves perceived this as a matter of course is reflected in another letter in the Calenberg files, this one from a woman of the generation of Agnesa's daughters. In 1796 Louise Barth, the widow of one of the Calenberg book-keepers, complained to the Treasury Committee of the Duchy. As was common in the public service, her husband had paid 6,000 Rtl into the state treasury at the time of his appointment, as security (*Kaution*) for the honest and competent execution of his duties. The committee had decided to reduce the interest payable on that sum from 4 to 3 percent. Louise Barth's letter combined pathos, the claim to justice, and financial canniness, as she reminded the members of the committee

that my husband left me with seven children, five of them still not out of school, and the interest on that capital which he saved up by industry and effort has to serve as far as it can to bring them up, since I have no other help except 50 Rtl from the widows' fund which I need for myself, and the loss of 60 Rtl which I am bound to suffer would be very hard on me, given how hard it is to get a good return on one's money these days.[43]

Like Agnesa Henze before her, Louise Barth invoked the stereotype of the poor widow while at the same time revealing the extent of her real resources. Her letter, though, intimates the effort that went into maintaining and managing those resources. If the middle-class widow can be seen as the prototype of the small investor, the expectation of living from investments presented the widow and her family with further problems: where to get the capital and, in Louise Barth's words, how to get a good return on it.[44]

Inheritance was an unreliable source of capital. The promoters of widows' funds were insistent on the contrast between the situation of middle-class widows and that of the wives of estate owners or even peasants, who had access to property in land. In practice, however, even the future of landed widows was not always secure. The drafters of a 1766 plan for a widows' fund for estate owners in the Duchy of Lüneburg set out two problems as its rationale: Most estates were entailed by agnatic succession, so that the widow stood to inherit nothing and her maintenance could be secured only by a prenuptial agreement. Such agreements (they maintained, perhaps surprisingly) existed only in "the fewest families," and where they did exist, price inflation since the marriage had severely reduced their value.[45] Middle-class families appear to have been more hardheaded about devising marriage contracts and testamentary arrangements to provide for widows, often circumventing legal stipulations that excluded widows from direct inheritance.[46] But these arrangements were no less subject to the effects of inflation after mid-century, and there remained the central problem that capital had to be accumulated before it could be passed on. The conventional solution to this problem lay in the wife's dowry, which commonly remained her property throughout the marriage and ought to have been available for investment on her husband's death. The size of the dowry, however, depended on how effective the bride's father had been at accumulating capital. Moreover, the dowry was subject to administration by the husband during his lifetime, and there was always the danger that it would be eroded by expenditure or encumbered by debt—necessary or unnecessary—by the time the widow needed to call on it.[47]

Once capital was secured, there remained the problem of what to do with it. With some exceptions in the main trading centers of Hamburg, Frankfurt, and Leipzig, the banking and credit system in Germany was underdeveloped before the end of the eighteenth century. As the case of Louise Barth indicates, city and state treasuries paid interest on capital deposits. As her case also shows, the return on an investment of this kind was not generous. The other source of interest income was personal lending. There were few institutional lenders of money, principally Jews and charitable foundations; the residents of north German towns relied on pawnshops and on other individuals for everyday credit. What evidence there is indicates that widows played a key role in local capital markets. In Göttingen in the first half of the century, a disproportionate number of lenders were women. Widows, including the widows of professors and officeholders disposing over large sums, were responsible for some 70 percent of the funds lent, most of them against collateral in the form of real estate.[48]

## THE VICISSITUDES OF MIDDLE-CLASS LIFE AND THE APPEAL OF THE WIDOWS' FUNDS

In this situation, widows' survival strategies were not alternative, but complementary, as both Agnesa Henze and Louise Barth remind us: Barring catastrophes it was possible to get along by careful management.[49] But what this meant was piecing together an income from different sources—literally making ends meet. What the widows' pleas for special consideration tended to obscure was the fact that men of the service middle classes faced the same kind of problem. The social group from which the widows' fund subscribers were drawn was caught in a permanent dilemma between the imperative to maintain status and the requirement to hustle to sustain an income appropriate to their status-defined needs.[50] Civil servants and municipal officials, like pastors, depended on accumulating fee-paying functions to supplement their cash salaries. There was no systematic provision for retirement or for pensions for themselves, let alone their widows. Indeed, there was very little to which they were entitled; nearly every benefit and every career move required petitioning, strategic placement, and self-promotion. For men as well as women, survival as respectable parties depended on the successful management of social relations—of patronage and mutual obligation—as well as the juggling of debts and a keen eye for financial opportunities. The spectacular sum of 6,000 Rtl on which Louise Barth depended had very likely been raised by her husband through loans and sureties, which in his lifetime would have incurred ethical as well as financial obligations.[51]

Under these circumstances, the attractions of widows' funds were multiple. One thing they provided was a supplement to the limited sources of credit available. Not only could membership policies or *Rezeptionsscheine* be used as collateral for loans from third parties, but it was also the case that some funds acted in effect as credit unions, making loans from their accumulated assets; at least one provided for the capital deposit (the counterpart to Agnesa Henze's 100 Rtl) to be treated as a loan payable in installments with interest.[52] This made it possible for a man to purchase guaranteed provision for his widow with no capital outlay at all, and even where, as in most funds, payment of the capital deposit could not be deferred, the pension subscribed for was greater than could be generated by the interest on that capital alone. The further promise of the widows' funds was thus a new degree of security and regularity, a relief from the need for shifts and stratagems in a key area of family life.[53] These were advantages that could be appreciated by both men and women who were married or looking to marry.

## WIDOWS' FUNDS AND MIDDLE-CLASS GENDER IDENTITIES

Had the widows' funds been conceived solely in terms of the material needs outlined previously, however, Agnesa Henze would not have had to engage in what I have called financial cross-dressing in her efforts to get a pension. The arguments of widows' fund publicists invoked images of absolute poverty to embellish their address to a more specific and rooted anxiety about maintaining and transmitting status. The fact that this rhetoric stood in direct contradiction to the evidence that women alone might cope in ways not so different from those of men signals the aspirational and transformative function of the new institutions. They served to redefine needs and offered to create new material relationships that would secure not only material survival but also social identities. The expansion and cultural self-assertiveness of the middle-class groups that the widows' funds were designed to serve were themselves key elements of social change in mid- to late-eighteenth-century Germany, and new institutions for the support of widows constituted part of the ideological project of bourgeois self-construction. The discursive practice of the widows' funds thus needs to be situated in the context of shifting and contested notions of gender roles and gender-specific personality within middle-class culture at large, in which the late eighteenth century was a watershed. Ideas about the nature and purpose of marriage were deeply implicated in this development.

There is some evidence that the real handicaps that middle-class women and widows suffered were themselves the consequence of changes in attitudes to both individuality and marriage. When widows'-fund publicists noted that the widows of middle-class men were particularly ill placed in the remarriage market, for example, they cited familiar reasons; without landed property, a business, or a trade, these women had nothing to offer potential suitors. This analysis characteristically ignored the ways in which the nature of middle-class occupations and the expectations of their occupants were changing. The Protestant clergy is a case in point. For the first two centuries after the Reformation, it had been the norm in the church, as in many trades, for a man entering his first job to marry the widow of his predecessor. The emergence of clerical widows' funds coincided with a decline in the willingness of clergymen to continue this practice; the legal sanction for it was abandoned in the middle of the eighteenth century.[54] This change of practice implies a new self-image of the masculine actor as someone trading the security of corporate obligation for the freedom to construct both his career and his private life as an independent agent, in the context of voluntary association or freely chosen relationships, and on the basis of personal qualification alone.[55]

Similarly, the exclusion of middle-class women from productive work and thus from visible economic agency was associated with incipient professionalization in other middle-class occupations, a process in which masculinization, the redefinition of qualification, and enhanced status were mutually reinforcing. Even in the eighteenth century it was not unheard of in practice for the wife of a civil servant to carry on her husband's occupation after his death.[56] In the households of scholars and practitioners of the so-called free professions—physicians and lawyers, and particularly the many who practiced without academic qualifications—the conditions for a wife carrying on the trade were not materially different from those of a master craftsman: home and workplace were the same, and wives had access to the tools of the trade and the knowledge that it required. It was at the point where academic qualifications became a *sine qua non* and the laboratory, study, or surgery moved out of the home— where the man's work became a profession and no longer a trade—that women became marginalized as practitioners.[57]

It was not a foregone conclusion, however, that the professionalization of occupations open to middle-class men would lead to middle-class women being assimilated to a model of genteel dependency. The presumption that respectable women could not engage in paid work was an ideologeme. It rested on constructions of middle-class masculinity and femininity and would be fully enforceable only when attributed differences between men's and women's capacity acquired the force of the self-evident, or came to be seen as natural. In the generation that produced the second wave of widows' funds, men and women were openly exploring the possibilities of higher learning and scientific qualifications for females in debate and in practice. The discursive practice of the funds thus needs to be understood as a contribution to an ongoing social negotiation.

In this context, part of the appeal of the widows' funds may have lain in the fact that they made it possible not only to imagine but to realize a particular vision of marriage. The very foregrounding of the needs of men's widows as distinct from those of children, who were historically privileged in testamentary arrangements and inheritance law, placed a new emphasis on the married couple as a nexus for the definition of socially significant identity. This was in keeping with a wider trend in middle-class culture toward representing marriage as a relationship freely entered into for life on the grounds of mutual attraction and affection alone. Detached from the taint of financial interest, or indeed any economic function, marriage became a context for the self-realization of both partners. And the man who could buy a pension for his bride with little or no capital could afford to marry for love.[58]

Paradoxically, perhaps, the vision of widows' helplessness, too, can be read as an artifact of wishful thinking. In the eighteenth century, any particular marriage was likely to be but an episode in the life history of a man or a woman.[59] The rhetoric of the widows' funds, by contrast, implied that the married state was the normal one and also that women were absolutely dependent in marriage. In practice, the regulations of the Calenberg, by seeking to enforce the husband's ethical interest after his death while denying independent agency to the widow, promised to produce marriages in which the bond between man and wife was truly as long as both their lives. Similarly, the promise that a husband's pension contributions could obviate the need for any other form of provision, such as the dowry or contractual settlement, was an implicit promise of the wife's absolute dependency. Venerable though it was, by the mid-eighteenth century the rhetoric of widows' absolute poverty had acquired a new discursive function. The widows' funds were not only premised on the helplessness of widows; the benefits they offered to women came at the price of enforcing that helplessness.[60]

## WOMEN, DEMAND, AND INNOVATION: FROM WIDOWS' FUNDS TO LIFE INSURANCE

Even in the 1760s, as we have seen, people had noticed that there were real women whose needs were not met by the widows' funds. The 1770s and 1780s witnessed a series of changes that, taken together, add up to the creation of modern life insurance institutions. The process was one of simultaneous crisis and innovation, both of which were conditioned by the way in which the widows' funds interacted with their public. The organizers of widows' funds were forced to reflect on the presumptions that underlay their practice. This involved an acknowledgment of women's own demand for financial services, which thereby became a spur to innovation and a touchstone for its effectiveness.

One of the principal contributors to the public discussion about widows' funds in the 1770s and 1780s acknowledged with a candor characteristic of the late enlightenment that the helplessness of middle-class widows was a social construct. The botanist and public administrator Georg Christian von Oeder wrote in a memorandum to his employer, the Duke of Oldenburg, in 1781:

We understand as "needy" any person who cannot manage to live from the interest on a small capital and who is incapable of earning their keep in any other way. This includes: . . . those who to be sure are healthy and could manage to earn their own bread, but who according to our constitution cannot submit themselves to work of that kind, among whom we reckon above all the unmarried daughters of civil servants and men *vom Stande*, and their widows. . . .[61]

The context in which Oeder wrote this is important. He had organized a widows' and orphans' fund for the duchy of Oldenburg and was trying to persuade the duke to allow the fund to be extended to provide life annuities (*Leibrenten*). The payment of a life annuity did not depend on the death of a breadwinner: people paid premiums or let someone else pay them on their behalf, in expectation of receiving a pension themselves in their own lifetime; this was how one might provide for oneself in old age, for example.[62] The buying and selling of life annuities was well established in eighteenth-century Europe; they were frequently issued by governments as a way of raising finance.[63] They appear to have been relatively little used in Germany, where they were widely regarded as morally questionable. Even otherwise liberal-minded German commentators placed life annuities at the opposite ethical pole from widows' pensions, arguing that they encouraged selfishness to the disadvantage of household finances and to the detriment of the sense of family obligation. Even Oeder himself insisted that his proposed life-annuity fund would not admit "any parents or husbands who would leave their heirs poor by using up capital to their own benefit."[64]

It is clear that what Agnesa Henze was looking for in 1766 was a kind of life annuity, even though she did not use the term. The Oldenburg widow Elisabeth Margaret Catharina Facke, on the other hand, knew exactly what she wanted. In April 1781, on the day after her fiftieth birthday, she wrote to the administrators of the Oldenburg widows' fund and declared herself "ready and willing . . . to put some capital into the fund against a life annuity" of 15 Rtl every six months for the rest of her life. Like Agnesa Henze, she had read the regulations and worked out exactly the capital investment required to generate the pension she wanted: 348 Rtl and 48 Mariengroschen. Unlike Agnesa, Elisabeth Facke apparently did not feel it necessary to excuse her financial know-how with pious invocations.[65]

According to Oeder, it was Elisabeth Facke's letter that prompted him to apply for permission to expand into the provision of life annuities. Oeder was a compulsive innovator, so this was very likely a convenient fiction. Nevertheless, both the letter and Oeder's willingness to cite it suggest that by the 1780s the grounds of the public conversation had shifted, a consequence of the growth of the widows' funds and also of their collapse.

By the mid-1770s, competition among the widows' funds had become intense. As the case of the Calenberg shows, widows' funds had always striven to attract subscribers by promising guaranteed substantial pensions while keeping premiums low. Their administrators had convinced themselves and continued to insist in public that systems of calculation based on mortality and census data provided a sound basis for realizing their promises. At the end of the 1770s a number of the funds proved critically unable to meet their pension obligations and had to be wound up or rationalized. The collapse and long-drawn-out reform of the Calenberg, which staggered on until about 1800 by closing its books to new members, slashing pensions, and raising premiums, was the most spectacular. Financial failure had been the fate of most widows' funds over the decades, but the number of people affected by the collapse of the Calenberg, and not least the fact that its subscribers and advisers included some of the leading academics and public figures in northern Germany, meant that this crisis generated intense public debate about why the funds had failed and whether they could be made to succeed. In this discussion, attention focused on the inadequacy of the actuarial calculations employed by the funds. It was clear at the very least that they had underestimated both how many widows they would have to support and how the cost of their pensions would relate to the number and ages of subscribing couples. This was a fruitful debate in terms of the progressive refinement of statistical methods and actuarial calculation, which could provide the basis for more effective life-insurance schemes. But what also became clear was that the widows' funds, each in its own way, had failed in their marketing strategy, keeping premiums artificially low in order to attract subscribers. The fund administrators became aware of this before the general crisis brought it to the attention of the public. But the more apparent it became that premiums would have to rise, the harder it was for the funds to face increasing them, since this would undermine trust and drive subscribers away.[66]

Even before the funds collapsed, then, the risks of making too many financial concessions to subscribers began to be recognized. As competition intensified, the emphasis instead was on widening the portfolio of services and opening up new subscriber groups. This involved moving away from the cameralistic and patriarchal premises of the early funds and their consequences: the instrumentalization of the pension as a way of encouraging marriage and the presumption of the sole agency of husbands. As we have seen, the idea that anyone but a married man might be allowed to buy a pension was never unthinkable, but in the 1760s the consensus was against it. The Prussian widows' fund, set up in 1775, was the first to offer pensions to unmarried women, although the presumption was still that most purchasers of pensions would be men and each pension had to be contingent on the life of a named man.[67] In response to this, the Calenberg administrators, already aware that their accounts would not bear close scrutiny, considered introducing provision for single women. They came to the conclusion that the change would involve too great a risk, not only operational (the danger that spinsters might live even longer than widows) but also moral, through the promotion of "celibacy and concubinage."[68] Georg Christian von Oeder was less timorous in his reading of the Berlin experiment, concluding that there was "no reason why only women should be pensionable, and those on whose life or death the pension depends should only be men . . . or in a word, why sex should have any place at all in a transaction or contract of this kind." He reported that in the 1760s he had dared to express this view only "among persons in authority, where there was no danger of prejudice."[69] By 1781, as we have seen, he was prepared to embark on the creation of life annuities for women on the basis that this was what they wanted.

Oeder also saw that the principle of giving women, among others, what they wanted was built into the operation of the new pension fund for which he was working as a consultant. This was the Hamburgische Allgemeine Versorgungs-Anstalt, or HAVA, which opened for business in 1778.[70] The HAVA was built on the ruins of Hamburg's old widows' funds, and its operating principles were developed in explicit response to the funds' failure. Unlike the widows' funds, the HAVA survived into the twentieth century, when it was absorbed by the Hansa life-insurance firm. It offered nine different categories of service, from a simple savings bank to a range of life annuities and death benefits on varying terms. Although life insurance organized on a large-scale commercial basis did not appear in Germany for another 50 years, the HAVA is generally regarded as the beginning of modern life insurance in Germany in terms of the principles and techniques it applied. Accounts of its innovative character generally emphasize the way in which Oeder pioneered the systematic application of actuarial techniques that were rooted in an informed analysis of mortality tables and a critical approach to statistical method.[71] In Oeder's own view, though, getting the numbers right was important because it made it possible to operationalize a vision of the relationship between parties to a pension agreement as a "transaction or contract" governed entirely by considerations of measurable risk. The determination that individual attributes and social or ethical purposes that fell outside such considerations should be excluded from the transaction was expressed in the phrase "a widows' fund is not a poor-box." This signaled a second self-conscious innovation, namely the abandonment of charitable and disciplinary practices that had characterized the widows' funds. The HAVA made no offer of grants-in-aid to members in good standing and imposed no sanctions on subscribers or pensioners for bad character or misbehavior.[72] The fact that the HAVA was open to women and, indeed, to any person to invest for the benefit of themselves or any other person, regardless of station, confession, place of residence or sex (a third key innovation) was in keeping with these same principles.[73]

The emergence of the HAVA out of the crisis of the widows' funds exemplifies a dialectical relationship between gender politics and technical innovation in financial services, each of them in turn implicated in changing definitions of family and welfare. The widows' funds were an innovation in their time. While promising to solve the problems of provision for middle-class family welfare, they also served to redefine those problems. Part of their appeal lay in their capacity to realize the aspirational fantasies of a middle-class constituency that was engaged in the project of defining itself, both culturally and in terms of the material conditions of life. The family whose welfare the old widows' funds offered to promote was a new kind of patriarchal family in which women's economic agency had no place and whose rationale was the intergenerational maintenance of a status that was permanently at risk. In practice, though, the conventions that militated against respectable women earning an income by labor meant that real middle-class women constituted a key market for financial services. They were aware of the new funds and looked for ways to gain advantage from them, even though, as in Agnesa Henze's case, the institutional discourse barely left room for them to establish a subject position. Insofar as the funds operated as businesses, relying on an expanding subscriber base, it was increasingly in their interest to take account of demand from people outside the founding constituency of married men. But it was in the nature of the product (life-contingent pensions) that expanded recruitment implied increased risk; this was one of the lessons of the crisis. Demand for services from and on behalf of unmarried women as well as widows—a key constituency of the wider public demand for life insurance—thus provided part of the rationale for the development of actuarial technologies that could facilitate unlimited expansion. Acknowledging this demand required the abandonment of patriarchal conventions. Moreover, the extension of financial services to women in their own right was the ultimate test of the effectiveness of the new system. If women did not literally invent life insurance, it is nevertheless the case that the modernity of actuarially self-conscious schemes for individual and family welfare stemmed from their capacity to accommodate women. It was in women's interests to have direct access to the means of looking after themselves and their dependants in an increasingly complex and uncertain world. Their needs thus constituted one of the impulses that transformed the institutional provision for personal and family security, from the preserve of societies for the promotion of marriage and the protection of husbands, to a technology which was, at least in theory, implicitly blind to the differences among individuals.

## NOTES

Research for this chapter was supported by grants from the British Academy and the German Academic Exchange Service. Aspects of the project have been presented to seminar and conference sessions in Bad Homburg, Montreal, Liverpool, and Amsterdam. I have benefited greatly from discussions there and also from conversations with Jürgen Schlumbohm, William J. Ashworth, and Hans-Cord Sarnighausen, as well as from the suggestions of the editors of this volume. A shorter version has been published as Eve Rosenhaft, "'. . . mich als eine Extraordinarium.' Die Witwe als widerstrebendes Subjekt in der Frühgeschichte der Lebensversicherung," in Udo Arnold, Peter Meyers, Uta C. Schmidt, eds., *Stationen einer Hochschullaufbahn: Festschrift für Annette Kuhn zum 65. Geburtstag* (Dortmund: Edition Ebersbach, 1999), 292–309.

1. Jack Goody, "Introduction," in Jack Goody, Edward Thompson, and Joan Thirsk, eds., *Family and Inheritance: Rural Society in Western Europe 1200–1800* (Cambridge: Cambridge University Press, 1976), 1.

2. On the history of life insurance in Germany see Ludwig Arps, *Auf sicheren Pfeilern: Deutsche Versicherungswirtschaft vor 1914* (Göttingen: Vandenhoeck and Ruprecht, 1965) and Peter Borscheid, *Mit Sicherheit leben: Die Geschichte der deutschen Lebensversicherungswirtschaft und der Provinzial-Lebensversicherungsanstalt von Westfalen* (Greven: Eggenkamp, 1989).

3. For developments in Germany from the Reformation see Bernd Wunder, "Pfarrwitwenkassen und Beamtenwitwen-Anstalten vom 16.–19. Jahrhundert,"

*Jahrbuch für historische Forschung* 12 (1985): 429–98. On European developments see James C. Riley, "'That your widows may be rich:' Providing for widowhood in Old Regime Europe," *Economisch- en sociaal-historisch jaarboek* 45 (1982): 58–76.

4. The first phase is the less well researched of the two. An example of the rise and fall of one of these funds is the history of the Christliche Gesellschaft zu Versorgung der Witwen und Waysen, founded in 1700 in Lüneburg. The records of this institution are kept in the Stadtarchiv Lüneburg, Rep. 102.

5. Geoffrey Wilson Clark, *Betting on Lives: Life Insurance in English Society and Culture 1695–1775* (Manchester: Manchester University Press, 1999).

6. Wunder, "Pfarrwitwenkassen und Beamtenwitwen-Anstalten," 458.

7. For a Europe-wide survey of these developments, see Peter Burke, *A Social History of Knowledge: From Gutenberg to Diderot* (Cambridge: Polity Press, 2000). For developments in Germany see, for example, Ralf Pröve and Norbert Winnige, eds., *Wissen ist Mach: Herrschaft und Kommunikation in Brandenburg-Preußen 1600–1850* (Berlin: Wissenschafts-Verlag, 2001); Margot Lindemann, *Deutsche Presse bis 1815* (Berlin: Colloquium, 1969); Richard van Dülmen, *Die Gesellschaft der Aufklärer* (Frankfurt a. M.: Fischer, 1986); Jürgen Habermas, *Strukturwandel der Öffentlichkeit* (Darmstadt and Neuwied: Luchterhand, 1962); and Heidrun Homburg, "Werbung—'eine Kunst, die gelernt sein will': Aufbrüche in eine neue Warenwelt 1750–1850," *Jahrbuch für Wirtschaftsgeschichte* (1997, part one): 11–52.

8. Beyond studies of individual institutions, the literature on the history of finance in Germany is very limited. However, it is clear that there was a great deal of regional variation. For an account of the growth of the capital market in a northwest German town see Norbert Winnige, "Vom Leihen und Schulden in Göttingen: Studien zum Kapitalmarkt," in *Göttingen 1690–1755: Studien zur Sozialgeschichte einer Stadt*, ed. Hermann Wellenreuther (Göttingen: Vandenhoeck and Ruprecht, 1988), 252–320.

9. The social and cultural implications of life insurance practice and the relationship between life insurance and the emergence of modern mentalities has been addressed most directly in research on British life insurance. See, in particular, Robin Pearson, "Thrift or Dissipation? The Business of Life Assurance in the Early Nineteenth Century," *Economic History Review* XXXXIII (1990): 236–54; Clark, *Betting on Lives;* and Geoffrey Wilson Clark, "Life Insurance in the Society and Culture of London, 1700–75," *Urban History* 24 (1997): 17–36. For a more general dicsussion see Lorraine Daston, *Classical Probability in the Enlightenment* (Princeton, N.J.: Princeton University Press, 1988).

10. On the history of the Calenberg widows' fund, see Reinhard Oberschelp, *Niedersachsen 1760–1820*, vol. 1 (Hildesheim: Lax, 1982), 230–37 and William Boehart, ". . . *nicht brothlos und nothleidend zu hinterlassen*" (Hamburg: Verein für Hamburgische Geschichte, 1985).

11. C. D. Küster, *Der Wittwen- und Waisenversorger, oder Grundsätze, nach welchen dauerhafte Wittwen- und Waisensocietäten gestiftet werden können: Zum nutzen·unbelehrter Leser, welche Aufseher oder Glieder dieser wohlthätigen Anstalten sind* (Leipzig: Junius, 1772), 3.

12. Verordnung, behuef der von Calenbergischer Landschaft anzulegenden Witwen-Verpflegungs-Gesellschaft (14 October, 1766), Niedersächsisches Hauptstaatsarchiv Hanover (HStAHann), Cal.Br. 23b, no. 579 (no pagination).

13. The letter of the Calenberg Treasury Committee to the Royal Government

setting out the general plan for a new widows' fund, 9 June 1766, named the tables of Johann Süßmilch as their principal guide to average life expectancy, but also made reference to the work of British, Dutch, and French demographers: HStAHann, Dep 7B, no. 327I: 33–54.

14. Verordnung, behuef der von Calenbergischer Landschaft anzulegenden Witwen-Verpflegungs-Gesellschaft, §16.

15. Nachricht von der Situation der Calenbergischen allgemeinen Witwen-Verpflegungs-Gesellschaft im 24ten und 25ten Termin (August, 1779), HStAHann, Hann 93, no. 3706: 358; Verzeichnis sämtlicher recipirten und verstorbenen Männer der Calenbergischen Witwenpflegegesellschaft nach dem Alter zur Zeit der Aufnahme (November, 1783), HStAHann, Dep 7B, no. 358: 208–64.

16. J. A. Kritter, *Sammlung wichtiger Erfahrungen bei den zu Grunde gegangenen Witwencassen* (Göttingen, 1780), 5–7; Johann Peter Süßmilch, *Die göttliche Ordnung in den Veränderungen des menschlichen Geschlechts, aus der Geburt, dem Tode, und der Fortpflanzung desselben erwiesen von Johann Peter Süßmilch—Dritter Teil . . . herausgegeben von Christian Jacob Baumann* (Berlin: Realschule, 1787), 465.

17. Johann David Michaelis, "Nöthige Aufmerksamkeit, die man bey Vorschlägen zu Einlegung guter Witwencassen beobachten muß," in Johann David Michaelis, *Vermischte Schriften*, vol. 2 (Frankfurt a. M.: Garbe, 1766–69), 99–117; Philipp Peter Guden's letter of 18 October 1779 to Georg Christoph Lichtenberg, Staats- und Universitätsbibliothek Göttingen, Cod. Ms. Lichtenberg III, no. 82, reprinted in Georg Christoph Lichtenberg, *Briefwechsel*, vol. 1, ed. Ulrich Joost and Albrecht Schöne (Munich: Beck, 1983), no. 622.

18. Unknown (signature illegible) to Hofgerichts-Assessor A. C. von Wüllen, 26 November 1766, HStAHann, Dep 7B, no. 326: 215–17; see also Pro Memoria (PM), J. C. Wackerhagen, Westerhofe, 13 November 1766, HStAHann, Dep 7B, no. 108.

19. PM Johann Friedrich Blau [?], Bremervörde, 18 November 1766, HStAHann, Dep 7B, no. 316: 22f; Superintendent Daniel Christoph Klee, Bremen, to Georg Ebel, 11 November 1766, HStAHann, Dep 7B, no. 316: 24f.

20. PM J. G. Hartmann, 10 Nov. 1783, HStAHann, Dep 7B, no. 358: 493f.

21. See, for example, the declaration of Luisa Maier, geb. Bassen, 5 July 1775, HStAHann, Dep 7B, no. 371: 318f.

22. Letter of the Calenberg Treasury Committee to the Royal Government, 9 June 1766, 47v. On *alimentum* see Johann Heinrich Zedler, *Großes Universal-Lexicon aller Wissenschaften und Künste*, vol. 1 (Halle and Leipzig: Zedler, 1732), 1218. In the Hanoverian lands, as in most of northwestern and western Germany and Württemberg, the property rights of married women were governed by a number of common law variants (*gemeines Recht*), inflected by local custom. This generally dictated that marital property was held in common but administered by the husband. In principle, wives were not qualified to act independently in business or legal affairs. However, in practice this varied, and in any case the stipulation that a wife must submit to her husband's disposition of property *as long as he had acted in good faith* meant that a wife's formal agreement was commonly sought in business dealings. See Ute Gerhard, *Gleichheit ohne Angleichung: Frauen im Recht* (Munich: Beck, 1990), 146; Silke Lesemann, *Arbeit, Ehre, Geschlechterbeziehungen: Zur sozialen und wirtschaftlichen Stellung von Frauen im frühneuzeitlichen Hildesheim* (Hildesheim: Bernward, 1994), 78–82; and Susanne Rappe, "Frauen in der agrarischen Gesellschaft des 17. und 18. Jahrunderts—dargestellt anhand ausgewählter Ge-

richtsakten des Amtes Dannenberg" (M.A. diss., University of Hanover, 1992), 29, 69. See also Susanne Weber-Will, "Geschlechtsvormundschaft und weibliche Rechtswohltaten im Privatrecht des preußischen Allgemeinen Landrechts von 1794," in *Frauen in der Geschichte des Rechts*, ed. Ute Gerhard (Munich: Beck, 1997), 451–59; David W. Sabean, "Allianzen und Listen: Die Geschlechtsvormundschaft im 18. und 19. Jahrhundert," in Gerhard, *Frauen in der Geschichte des Rechts*, 460–79.

23. Calenberg administration to Royal Government, 10 April 1777, HStAHann, Dep 7B, no. 366: 18–23. The Royal Government confirmed the administration's decision in this case: HStAHann, Dep 7B, no. 366: 7. The Behrens family was one of the leading Jewish families in the Hanoverian territories, although one whose wealth and influence had declined since the early eighteenth century. See Bernd Schedlitz, *Leffmann Behrens: Untersuchungen zum Hofjudentum im Zeitalter des Absolutismus* (Hildesheim: Lax, 1984). It is to be presumed that the widow in question, identified in the correspondence as a Jew, belonged to that same family. According to the correspondence, she had been abandoned by her male relatives, presumably because of her irresponsibility in burdening both her own and her husband's estates with debt. There is no evidence in the correspondence that the fact of her being Jewish influenced the decisions of the Calenberg administrators. On the situation of Jewish widows, see Rainer Sabelleck, "Soziale Versorgung von Angehörigen jüdischer Familien in norddeutschen Städten des späten 18. und frühen 19. Jahrhunderts," in *Familien und Familienlosigkeit. Fallstudien aus Niedersachsen und Bremen vom 15. bis 20. Jahrhundert*, ed. Jürgen Schlumbohm (Hanover: Hahn, 1993), 117–32 and Sabine Ullmann, "Poor Jewish Families in Early Modern Rural Swabia," in *Household Strategies for Survival 1600–2000: Fission, Faction and Cooperation*, International Review of Social History Supplements 8, ed. Laurence Fontaine and Jürgen Schlumbohm (Cambridge: Cambridge University Press, 2000), 93–113.

24. See Kritter, *Sammlung wichtiger Erfahrungen* and Johann David Michaelis, "Einige Zweifel und Erinnerungen, so mir bey der Calenbergischen Witwenpflege-Gesellschaft beygefallen sind," in Michaelis, *Vermischte Schriften*, 169–90.

25. Widow Henze to Georg Ebel, Abbot of Loccum, 31 December 1766, HStAHann, Dep 7B, no. 326 I: 135. On Ebel see *Siebenfacher Königl. Groß-Britannisch- und Chur-Fürstl. Braunschweig-Lüneburgischer Staats-Calender . . . 1765–68*. The addressee is not named in the letter; I am grateful to Marc Stöber for information on Ebel.

26. On the social function and public discussion of letter writing by women in eighteenth-century Germany, see Lorely French, *German Women as Letter Writers: 1750–1850* (London: Associated University Presses, 1996); Angelika Ebrecht, Regina Nörtemann, and Herta Schwarz, eds., *Brieftheorie des 18. Jahrhunderts* (Stuttgart: Metzler, 1990); and Melanie Archangeli, "Negotiating the Public Sphere Through Private Correspondence: A Woman's Letters of Liberty in Eighteenth-Century Germany," *German Life and Letters* 53 (2000): 435–49. As a begging letter, Widow Henze's bears comparison with British examples of the genre: Donna T. Andrew, "*Noblesse oblige*: Female Charity in an Age of Sentiment," in *Early Modern Conceptions of Property*, ed. John Brewer and Susan Staves (London: Routledge, 1996), 275–300. In relation to widows see Pam Sharpe, "Survival Strategies and Stories: Poor Widows and Widowers in Early Industrial England," in *Widowhood in Medieval and Early Modern Europe*, ed. Sandra Cavallo and Lyndan Warner (Harlow: Longman, 1999), 220–39. For a discussion of letters of this kind in a German

context, see Marlene Besold-Backmund, *Stiftungen und Stiftungswirklichkeit* (Neustadt a. d. Aisch: Degener, 1986), 220–28.

27. Joan W. Scott, *Only Paradoxes to Offer: French Feminists and the Rights of Man* (Cambridge, Mass.: Harvard University Press, 1996).

28. Biographical information is taken from Philipp Meyer, ed., *Die Pastoren der Landeskirchen Hanovers und Schaumburg-Lippes seit der Reformation* (Göttingen: Vandenhoeck and Ruprecht, 1941–53); Bernhard Koerner, ed., *Deutsches Geschlechterbuch, Bd. 89/Niedersächsisches Geschlechterbuch*, vol. 3 (Görlitz: Starke, 1936), 362; *Deutsches Biographisches Archiv* I/515 and II/562 (extracts from Johann Conrad Paulus, *Nachrichten von allen Hessen-Schamburgischen Superintendenten* [Rinteln: Bösendahl, 1786]; F. W. Bautz, *Biographisch-Bibliographisches Kirchenlexicon* [Hamm: Bautz, 1978], both with the spelling "Henzen"); and Evangelisches Kirchenbuchamt Hanover, Register Bodenwerder (baptisms), 1723, 11. According to the *Geschlechterbuch*, Agnesa died after 1773; no information could be found about her younger daughter.

29. On the marriage age in ministers' families, see Luise Schorn-Schütte, *Evangelische Geistlichkeit in der Frühneuzeit* (Gütersloh: Gütersloher Verlagshaus, 1996), 296, 537.

30. See the information on clerical incomes provided in Meyer, ed., *Die Pastoren der Landeskirchen*. In the parish of Fischbeck the minister's salary was about 400 Rtl in 1782. See also Schorn-Schütte, *Evangelische Geistlichkeit*, 230–35. Exact statements about income are problematic for this period because a minister's income consisted to a considerable extent of "unspecified takings" [*ungewisse Einnahmen*]—fees for services—and payments in kind. There was no consensus about how large a widow's pension should be in order to maintain respectability and support children. See Michaelis, "Nöthige Aufmerksamkeit," 102. In the Calenberg, pensions of over 100 Rtl for a pastor's widow were exceptional.

31. *Deutsches Geschlechterbuch*. The salary of the pastor in Heemsen was 123 Rtl in 1745 and 200 Rtl in 1790. See Meyer, *Die Pastoren der Landeskirchen*.

32. Zedler, *Großes Universal-Lexicon*, vol. 2, 1555–62.

33. Küster, *Wittwen- und Waisenversorger*, 3.

34. Zedler, *Großes Universal-Lexicon*, vol. 58, 82–92, 163.

35. Magdalena Elisabeth Gaden geb Tom (and 16 others) to Landschaft, Land- und Schatzräte, Schatz-Deputierte, 10 June 1783, HStAHann, Dep 7B, no. 379, 25–30.

36. Besold-Backmund, *Stiftungen*, 225–30, 241.

37. For a recent overview see Dagmar Freist, "Religious Difference and the Experience of Widowhood in Seventeenth- and Eighteenth-Century Germany," in Cavallo and Warner, *Widowhood in Medieval*, 164–77. On merchant women see Daniel A. Rabuzzi, "Women as Merchants in Eighteenth-Century Northern Germany: The Case of Stralsund 1750–1830," *Central European History* 28 (1995): 435–56. On widowhood and gender politics in artisan households see Merry E. Wiesner, "Guilds, Male Bonding and Women's Work in Early Modern Germany," *Gender and History* 1 (1989): 125–37; Lyndal Roper, *The Holy Household* (Oxford: Oxford University Press, 1989); Merry Wiesner-Hanks, "Ausbildung in den Zünften," in *Geschichte der Mädchen- und Frauenbildung I: Vom Mittelalter bis zur Aufklärung*, ed. Elke Kleinau and Claudia Opitz (Frankfurt a. M. and New York: Campus, 1996), 91–118; and Lesemann, *Arbeit, Ehre, Geschlechterbeziehungen*. On agrarian house-

holds see Rappe, "Frauen in der agrarischen Gesellschaft" and David W. Sabean, *Property, Production, and Family in Neckarhausen, 1700–1870* (Cambridge: Cambridge University Press, 1990). Still a useful survey is Ida Blom, "The History of Widowhood: A Bibliographic Overview," *Journal of Family History* 16 (1991): 191–210. See also Olwen Hufton, *The Prospect Before Her: A History of Women in Western Europe 1500–1800* (New York: Knopf, 1996), 221–54 and Merry E. Wiesner, *Women and Gender in Early Modern Europe* (Cambridge: Cambridge University Press, 1993), 73–78.

38. See, for example, Yves Aubry, "Pour une étude du veuvage feminin à l'époque moderne," *Histoire, économie et société* 8 (1989): 223–36, where widows are described as "the weakest members of society." Like contemporaries, historians find different ways of reading the same data. Stefan Brakensiek's account of the situation of officials' widows presents a career very similar to Agnesa Henze's as a story of humiliating dependency. See Stefan Brakensiek, *Fürstendiener—Staatsbeamte—Bürger* (Göttingen: Vandenhoeck and Ruprecht, 1999), 248.

39. Brakensiek, *Fürstendiener—Staatsbeamte—Bürger,* 248 and Johannes Wahl, "Lebensläufe und Geschlechterräume im Pfarrhaus des 17. und 18. Jahrhunderts," in *Evangelische Pfarrer: Zur sozialen und politischen Rolle einer bürgerlichen Gruppe in der deutschen Gesellschaft des 18. bis 20. Jahrhunderts,* ed. Luise Schorn-Schütte and Walter Sparn (Stuttgart: Kohlhammer, 1997), 54. See also Arthur Imhof, "Remarriage in Rural Populations and in Urban Middle and Upper Strata in Germany from the Sixteenth to the Twentieth Century," in *Marriage and Remarriage in Populations of the Past,* ed. Jacques Dupâquier, Etienne Hélin, Peter Laslett, and Massimo Livi-Bacci (London and New York: Academic Press, 1981), 335–45 and John Knodel and Katherine A. Lynch, "The Decline of Remarriage: Evidence from German Village Populations in the Eighteenth and Nineteenth Centuries," *Journal of Family History* 10 (1985): 34–59. On divorce, see Sylvia Möhle, *Ehekonflikte und sozialer Wande: Göttingen 1740–1840* (Frankfurt a. M. and New York: Campus, 1997).

40. Besold-Backmund, *Stiftungen,* 119. For an example of a *Familienstiftung* see Hermann von Dassel, "Die Lütke v. Töbingsche Stiftung," in *Berichte über das Geschlecht von Dassel,* vol. I, ed. Otto von Dassel (Chemnitz, 1894), appendix, 31–91. Despite being relatively wealthy, members of the von Dassel family, leading figures among the Lüneburg patriciate, purchased substantial pensions for their wives from the Calenberg widows' fund. I am grateful to Karin Hausen for drawing my attention to the role of *Stiftungen.*

41. Schorn-Schütte, *Evangelische Geistlichkeit,* 232, 322–25.

42. Schorn-Schütte, *Evangelische Geistlichkeit,* 323 and Wahl, "Lebensläufe und Geschlechterräume," 44.

43. Louise Barth to Treasury Committee, 30 March 1796, HStAHann, Dep 7B, no. 385: 7. On the use of security payments (*Kautionen*) in public service, see Brakensiek, *Fürstendiener—Staatsbeamte—Bürger,* 184, who notes that in late eighteenth-century Hessen-Kassel, officials' wives were required to share liability for the *Kaution.*

44. Buying a place in an almshouse was, of course, an investment of a kind. For a brief discussion on women as investors in early modern Europe see Wiesner, *Women and Gender,* 106–10. For nineteenth-century England, see David R. Green, "Independent Women, Wealth and Wills in Nineteenth-Century London," in *Ur-*

*ban Fortunes: Property and Inheritance in the Town, 1700–1900,* ed. Jon Stobart and Alastair Owens, (Aldershot: Ashgate, 2000), 195–222.

45. Verfassung einer willkürlichen Wittwen Versorgungs Casse für die welche in denen vier Cantons Fürstentums Lüneburg mit Stimme führenden Gütern angesessen sind oder daran ein Erb- oder Lehn-Recht haben, HStAHann, Dep 7B, no. 327 II: 493–508.

46. Brakensiek, *Fürstendiener—Staatsbeamte—Bürger,* 238.

47. Möhle, *Ehekonflikte und sozialer Wandel,* 92. The terms for dowry (*Mitgift, Brautgabe*) and widow's jointure (*Wittum*) seem to have been used interchangeably into the nineteenth century, although *Wittum* commonly referred to landed property. See Jacob L. K. Grimm and Wilhelm K. Grimm, *Deutsches Wörterbuch* (Leipzig: Hirzel, 1854–1960), entry for *Wittum.*

48. Winnige, "Vom Leihen und Schulden," 281–83, 299. See also Möhle, *Ehekonflikte und sozialer Wandel,* 94 and Karl Heinrich Kaufhold, "Die Wirtschaft in der frühen Neuzeit: Gewerbe, Handel und Verkehr," in *Geschichte Niedersachsens: Politik, Wirtschaft und Gesellschaft von der Reformation bis zum Beginn des 19. Jahrhunderts,* ed. Christine van den Heuvel and Manfred von Boetticher (Hanover: Hahn, 1998), 351–636, especially 564–74. On the banking functions of charitable foundations see Besold-Backmund, *Stiftungen,* 136–38. This accords with the more extensive evidence about women's economic activity in eighteenth-century England. See Amy Louise Erickson, *Women and Property in Early Modern England* (London: Routledge, 1993), 80–82, 194. On widows' key role as moneylenders in England, see also B. A. Holderness, "Widows in Pre-Industrial Society: An Essay Upon Their Economic Functions," in *Land, Kinship and Life-Cycle,* ed. Richard Smith (Cambridge: Cambridge University Press, 1984), 423–46.

49. Etienne François, "Unterschichten und Armut in rheinischen Residenzstädten des 18. Jahrhunderts," *Vierteljahrschrift für Sozial- und Wirtschaftsgeschichte* 62 (1975): 433–64, places widows and spinsters in the category *Unterschichten* (literally "lower stratum") but notes that on closer examination it appears that in understanding the social position of widows "the key factor was the occupation and position of the husband." According to his estimate no more than 40 percent of the 141 single women (including widows) living in Koblenz in 1795 counted as members of the *Unterschicht* (451).

50. In his account of the motivations behind the propensity of clergymen to insure their own lives in eighteenth-century England, Geoffrey Clark proposes that the underlying material problem was that clergymen were actually living beyond their means in an attempt to emulate more genteel lifestyles. See Clark, *Betting on Lives,* 167.

51. Compare with the way that Johann Augustin Kritter raised the money for his security deposit as treasury officer of the city of Göttingen. See Hans-Jürgen Gerhard, *Diensteinkommen der Göttinger Officianten 1750–1850* (Göttingen: Vandenhoeck and Ruprecht, 1978) and documentation in the Stadtarchiv Göttingen.

52. This was the case in the Lüneburg widows' fund of 1700. See *Ordnung der Christlichen Gesellschaft zu Versorgung der Witwen und Waysen* (Lüneburg: Stern, 1700). See also the list of those having a claim on the estate of Georg Heinrich Matthäi, Superintendent in Lüneburg, June 1723: Stadtarchiv Lüneburg, Rep. 102, vol. I, no. 12/3.

53. Compare James C. Riley's account of the appeal of the widows' funds, which

emphasizes the attraction of innovation rather than any change in underlying circumstances to explain their popularity; Riley, "'That Your Widows may be Rich,'" 36.

54. Wunder, "Pfarrwitwenkassen und Beamtenwitwen-Anstalten," 437.

55. Anthony J. La Vopa, *Grace, Talent and Merit: Poor Students, Clerical Careers and Professional Ideology in Eighteenth-Century Germany* (Cambridge: Cambridge University Press, 1988).

56. Heide Wunder, *"Er ist die Sonn', sie ist der Mond": Frauen in der frühen Neuzeit* (Munich: Beck, 1992), 137, provides examples of wives formally sharing or taking over official functions. In practice, the category of "civil servant" (*Beamte*) has proved extremely elastic in its gendered connotations in Germany since the eighteenth century. See, for example, Ursula Nienhaus, *Vater Staat und seine Gehilfinnen: Die Politik mit der Frauenarbeit bei der deutschen Post (1864–1945)* (Frankfurt a. M. and New York: Campus, 1995).

57. On the professions and the issue of academic qualification, see Beate Ceranski, "The Professionalization of Science and the Privatization of Women's Scientific Activity at the End of the Enlightenment," in *Formatting Gender: Transitions, Breaks and Continuities in German-Speaking Europe 1750–1850,* ed. Marion Gray and Ulrike Gleixner (Ann Arbor: University of Michigan Press, 2004); Beatrix Niemeyer, "Ausschluß oder Ausgrenzung? Frauen im Umkreis der Universitäten im 18. Jahrhundert," in Kleinau and Opitz, *Geschichte der Mädchenbildung und Frauenbildung,* 275–94; Ulrike Weckel, "Der Fieberfrost des Freiherrn. Zur Polemik gegen weibliche Gelehrsamkeit und ihre Folgen für die Geselligkeit der Geschlechter," in Kleinau and Opitz, *Geschichte der Mädchen,* 360–72.

58. See, for example, Justus Möser, "Schreiben einer betagten Jungfer an die Stifter der Witwenkasse zu **," in Justus Möser, *Patriotische Phantasien (Justus Mösers sämtliche Werke II)* (Berlin: Nicolai, 1842), 184–86. On the emergence of a new marriage ideal in the eighteenth century see, for example, Rebekka Habermas, *Frauen und Männer des Bürgertums* (Göttingen: Vandenhoeck and Ruprecht, 2000).

59. Brakensiek, *Fürstendiener—Staatsbeamte—Bürger,* 226, finds an average duration of 22 years for eighteenth-century marriages within his sample population.

60. In the years following the crisis of the Calenberg (discussed later in the chapter), some widows claimed that their husbands had foregone more familiar and reliable forms of provision in order to invest in the widows' fund. See Maria Elisabeth Petersen and others to the Treasury Committee, 22 February 1791, HStAHann, Dep 7B, no. 362 II: 211. The interaction between middle-class gender ideology and widows' poverty is addressed for nineteenth-century England by Cynthia Curran, "Private Women, Public Needs: Middle-Class Widows in Victorian England," *Albion* 25 (1993): 217–36. She argues that the ideology of female dependency led to a systematic blindness to actual poverty. Dietlind Hüchtker examines the function of the topos *poor woman* for the discursive construction of poverty in Berlin around 1800. See Dietlind Hüchtker, *Elende Mütter und liederliche Weibspersonen* (Münster: Westfälisches Dampfboot, 1998).

61. Unterthänigstes Pro Memoria, September 1781, Staatsarchiv Oldenburg (StAOld), Best. 31, no. 2–46–41: 81. On Oeder, see C. Haase, "Georg Christian von Oeders Oldenburger Zeit," *Oldenburger Jahrbuch des Oldenburger Landesvereins für Geschichte, Natur- und Heimatkunde* 64 (1965): 1–58. This fund did not continue long

as a pension fund, but it formed the basis of what would become the longest-surviving state savings bank in Germany.

62. A detailed account is provided by George Alter and James C. Riley, "How to Bet on Lives: A Guide to Life Contingent Contracts in Early Modern Europe," *Research in Economic History* 10 (1986): 1–53.

63. See, for example, Clark, *Betting on Lives*. On the national debt in Britain in the eighteenth century see P.G.M. Dickson, *The Financial Revolution in England: A Study in the Development of Public Credit, 1680–1756* (London: Macmillan, 1967).

64. For critical comment on the Oldenburg life annuity scheme, see the remarks of August Ludwig von Schlözer in *Schlözers Stats-Anzeigen*, vol. 2 (1782), 40.

65. Unterthäniges Pro Memoria [Oeder et al.], 15 May 1781; M. [Facke], 25 April 1781, StAOld, Best. 31, no. 2–46–41: 64. On the shifting relationship between piety, or notions of divine providence, and scientific calculation in relation to the origins of modern demography and actuarial science, see Jacqueline Hecht, "Johann Peter Süßmilch, point alpha ou omega de la science démographique naive?," *Annales de démographie historique* (1979): 101–33 and Herwig Berg, ed., *Die Ursprünge der Demographie in Deutschland: Leben und Werk Johann Daniel Süßmilchs* (Frankfurt a. M. and New York: Campus, 1986).

66. For an account of the crisis that emphasizes the gender politics of the public debate, see Eve Rosenhaft, "But the Heart Must Speak for the Widows: The Origins of Life Insurance in Germany and the Gender Implications of Actuarial Science," in Gray and Gleixner, *Formatting Gender*. It is not clear what role was played by macroeconomic conditions in the crisis. Continuing price inflation in the 1770s both prompted people to worry about the future and reduced the amount of money available for pension investments. The currency devaluations of the 1770s may have undermined general confidence in financial dealings. See Richard T. Gray, "Buying into Signs: Money and Semiosis in Eighteenth-Century German Language Theory," *The German Quarterly* 69 (1996): 1–14.

67. *Patent und Reglement für die Königlich Preußische allgemeine Wittwen-Verpflegungs-Anstalt* (Berlin: Decker, 1775).

68. Gründe für und wider die Aufnahme von Jungfern in einer Witwencasse, nach der Berlinischen Einrichtung (anonymous memorandum, 1776), HStAHann, Dep7B, no. 332 II: 473–80.

69. Anmerkung über die neue Königlich Preußische allgemeine Wittwen-Verpflegungs-Anstalt, StAOld, Best. 31, no. 2–46–41: 418–23.

70. On the Hamburgische Allgemeine Versorgungs-Anstalt, see Boehart, ". . . *nicht brothlos und nothleidend.*"

71. Boehart, ". . . *nicht brothlos und nothleidend.*"

72. See Georg Christian von Oeder's "Consideranda wegen einer zu errichtenden allgemeinen Wittwen-Casse," Hamburg-Mannheimer Versicherungs AG Hamburg, Archives (FAHM), Altbestand HAVA, F0001–00019, vol. 3, Ea, no. 1.

73. The only list of first-generation HAVA subscribers to have survived is that of the fund for the purchase of survivors' pensions where purchaser and beneficiary were not marriage partners. All purchasers in the first 47 years were men. See Versicherungs-Register, Tabelle D, FAHM, Altbestand HAVA, F0001–00057. Records of the life-annuities fund from the 1820s show a significantly higher proportion of female subscribers. See Versicherungs-Register, Tabelle D, FAHM, Altbestand HAVA, F0001–00016.

# CHAPTER 9

# Women without Gender: Commerce, Exchange Codes, and the Erosion of German Gender Guardianship, 1680–1830

*Robert Beachy*

## INTRODUCTION

When Frau Zanke, a Leipzig merchant's wife, invoked her "female" privileges in 1673 to evade creditors, she sparked a legal controversy about existing exchange codes that ultimately led to the establishment of women's commercial rights in Electoral Saxony. Issuing letters of credit in her own name, Frau Zanke worked together with her husband, who provided banking services in the Leipzig trade fairs. When the Zanke firm faced financial difficulties, however, Frau Zanke, no doubt with her husband's connivance, attempted to evade her own obligations by drawing on the prerogatives of gender guardianship (*Geschlechtsvormundschaft*). This German legal custom shielded married women's property from the control of their husbands, but with ambivalent effect. Assigned the legal status of children and placed under the guardianship of a third party (necessarily male, but not the husband), women were technically unable to sign enforceable contracts without their guardian's permission, which significantly restricted their commercial activities.[1] However, this economic incapacity also allowed women such as Frau Zanke to exploit female guardianship by evading liability and a creditor's grasp.[2]

Through her opportunism, however, Frau Zanke unwittingly drew attention to the potential conflict between gender guardianship and the evolving commercial codes of German central Europe. By the mid-seventeenth century, European merchants relied on bills of exchange as a means by which to enact financial transactions. This was an Italian practice that had slowly spread north of the Alps in the sixteenth century.[3] The frequent conflicts, bankruptcies, and fraud created through the use of these exchange letters required legal recourse. German officials therefore promulgated new exchange codes to regulate these commercial practices. In Electoral Saxony the market ordinance of 1669—which governed the Zankes' business—decreed the uniform application of exchange law without regard to estate: "no less for those not engaged in trade, whether noble or commoner, academic, or public officeholder."[4] This formulation was intended to prevent nonmerchants, including, students, aristocrats, and other elites, from shirking liability for debts incurred with exchange letters.

Absent from the regulation, however, was any reference to gender. Although German women—single, married, and widowed—had engaged in some commerce since the Middle Ages, this had rarely conflicted with gender guardianship.[5] However, it was the increased prevalence of exchange letters that created tensions because creditors could not easily take women merchants to court. Many creditors therefore believed that if women were allowed to enter exchange contracts, then they should be considered legally competent and therefore held liable for their debts. In short, it was thought that they should not be allowed to hide behind the privileges of gender guardianship. A traditionalist might respond, however, by arguing that if women were granted commercial rights, this would undermine the distinct and separate legal regimes that governed property ownership for men and women, and, potentially, liberate women from the constraints of traditional patriarchy.[6] From this perspective, was it not better to maintain gender guardianship and exclude women categorically from interregional trade and banking business? In response, commercial elites and their advocates argued, as we will see, that this jeopardized the viability of family firms, which wives and particularly widows frequently owned and managed. By raising these thorny questions, the Zanke case thus represented the direct confrontation of an Old Regime legal framework for protecting women with the needs and requirements of an expanding mercantile economy, which promoted the interests of a growing urban class of commercial and professional elites.

While early modern women in Western Europe faced a range of legal, corporate, and economic restrictions, German gender guardianship was ultimately unique. The English common-law doctrine of coverture, for example, provided none of the protections of gender guardianship: under common law, wives were reduced to the legal identity of their husbands and denied the ability to enter contracts, stand surety, or sign exchange bills. Exceptions were made for some married merchant women (especially according to the custom of London), who could acquire *feme sole* status and legal autonomy for conducting business. With the use of the law of equity in the seventeenth and eighteenth centuries, which provided an alternative to common law, married women, and particularly the wives of nonlanded, urban commercial and professional elites, began to exercise some control of their own property.[7] French law similarly placed married women and their property under the absolute authority of their husbands with the status of *femme couvert*. Similar to the English *feme sole*, the status of *marchande publique* granted certain married women the right to conduct a trade or business independently of their husbands.[8]

German gender guardianship then offers an intriguing case study of how early modern business practices shaped premodern exchange codes, which worked, in turn, to undermine restrictive protections for women. This confrontation of new exchange codes with gender guardianship illuminates the dual character of family businesses. On the one hand, the family represented a unit of economic organization, responsible for managing retail shops and long-distance commerce. But it was simultaneously a unit of consumption and social reproduction, and the conduct of business was therefore heavily influenced by the needs of husbanding the patrimony of future generations. Within the family firm structure, women thus played crucial roles, not only as accountants and helpmates, but also as active commercial agents and independent firm owners. This activity required the legal empowerment of mothers, daughters, and, most often, widows, who not only assisted in but also directed family enterprises. While recent scholarship has begun to note the activities of German businesswomen, little attention has been paid to the complex interrelationships of commerce, law, and state building and how the evolving legal status of women expressed this fascinating process.[9] Ultimately, the legal empowerment of businesswomen created an early impetus, completely overlooked by historians, for undermining the gender guardianship that was finally abolished throughout Germany in the course of the nineteenth century. In effect, the dual character of the family firm as both a commercial organization and a unit of consumption promoted the legal and economic independence of those women who functioned in both mercantile and domestic roles.

## THE CONFRONTATION OF GENDER
## GUARDIANSHIP AND COMMERCIAL LAW

With the late medieval and renaissance reception of Roman law, German jurists began codifying and promoting gender guardianship. Their fundamental assumption was that a woman was vulnerable and needed to be protected, not only from third parties, but, if married, also from her own husband. By the end of the sixteenth century, most German states and territories had established gender guardianship, including Electoral Saxony, which promulgated its own law in 1572.[10] After that time women required a third-party guardian who could guarantee their free will over and against the actions of their husbands. This was especially the case for any transaction that affected a wife's property. Thus despite potentially acting as administrator of his wife's property, a husband could not use or manipulate her assets without her consent. And while a husband's property was tacitly pledged as a protection of his wife's marriage portion, nothing of hers was pledged in return; creditors could not proceed against her property for his debts. Single women faced a similar set of restrictions, which likewise provided a safeguard against abuse or manipulation. The protection sanctioned by gender guardianship functioned as an instrument for preserving a woman's will through a neutral or supportive third party in a period when few women were even literate.[11]

Gender guardianship meant, however, that women, whether single, married, or widowed, were not legally competent and could not be treated as legal adults. Because they required third-party representation in court, their signatures did not suffice as proof of their intentions. Only through the intervention or presence of a third party could a woman pledge her property and validly make contracts. These restrictions proved an enormous handicap for business because any commercial transaction required the representation of a legal guardian. Of course, commerce relied increasingly on the use of exchange letters, which circulated on the basis of a mere signature. And because these exchanges implied liability and a binding contract between independent adults, only an unambiguous commercial code enforced by a court of law could guarantee their circulation.[12] Under the provisions of gender guardianship, however, women were excluded from independently assuming liability or risk, which posed a significant obstacle to issuing, accepting, or endorsing exchange bills.

Frau Zanke's attempt to evade her obligations had the effect of jeopardizing Leipzig's business reputation because, as will be shown, women controlled an increasing number of Leipzig firms. For civic elites concerned about the trade fairs, gender guardianship needed to be modified or abolished altogether if women were permitted commercial rights. The issue prompted Leipzig authorities into action. As a complicated legal issue, the matter required the expert advice of qualified jurists. City officials therefore commissioned nonbinding legal opinions from three Saxon institutions of academic jurors, which included the Leipzig *Schöppenstuhl* (Court of Jurors) and the law faculties of the Universities of Leipzig and Jena.[13] All three bodies interpreted the Saxon exchange ordinance of 1669 (cited earlier) to have universal application, which effectively overrode the prerogatives of gender guardianship. According to the opinion of the Leipzig *Schöppenstuhl*, which was the most influential of the three bodies, "women who issue exchange letters, are required to appear in person [before the court] and when unable to pay, are liable for any civil penalty."[14] In 1674 Saxon officials in Dresden confirmed this interpretation with an "Extension" of the 1669 ordinance. "Women who engage in commerce or issue exchange letters," the revised ordinance directed, "subject themselves to the law of the merchant community and are liable according to the Saxon exchange code." This "clarification," the directive continued, "should not only be issued in Leipzig but also publicized to merchants outside of Saxony."[15]

There is no doubt that the commercial empowerment of female merchants was considered a community and state interest. The jurists of the Leipzig law faculty and the *Schöppenstuhl*—directed, significantly, by the Leipzig Lord Mayor—belonged to a broad civic elite, including the city's most powerful traders. Since Leipzig academics frequently married into the wealthiest merchant families, the jurists unquestionably understood and promoted the city's commercial interests.[16] As the 1674 market "Extension" indicated, the decision was to be broadcast to outside merchants in order to bolster confidence in the strict enforcement of Saxon commercial law. In future, no visiting merchant should fear that a woman might successfully hide behind the protection of gender guardianship to disavow payment or a contract. This ruling, moreover, was never again contested. With more explicit wording, a new Saxon exchange code of 1682 confirmed the 1674 declaration: "if a single or married woman directs her own business without her husband, and issues exchange letters in her own name . . . her negotiations will be held liable under the ordinance."[17] Indeed, Saxon commercial law confirmed and reiterated the universal and uniform application of exchange law, without regard to gender or estate, well into the nineteenth century.

The Saxon response to Frau Zanke conformed, moreover, to a broad German development. Beginning in the seventeenth century, leading commercial centers issued local ordinances that explicitly authorized women's commercial rights. One of the oldest, the Hamburg Exchange Ordinance of 1603, guaranteed businesswomen the right to enter commercial contracts and credit relations, but without the oversight of husbands or male guardians. Other municipal codes prescribed women's commercial rights, including those enacted in Frankfurt (1662), Brunswick (1686), Naumburg (1693), Danzig (1701), Erfurt (1707), Bremen (1712), Breslau (1712), Vienna (1717), and Nuremberg (1722). These city codes formed a legal patchwork that shaped the commercial legislation of the German territorial states throughout the eighteenth and into the nineteenth century. Like the municipal ordinances, the commercial codes of Baden (1752), the Palatinate (1726), Württemberg (1759), Austria and Bohemia (1763), and Bavaria (1776) secured the commercial privileges of married, widowed, and single women merchants.[18] The Prussian *Allgemeines Landrecht* of 1794 confirmed the rights of women merchants—whether married or widowed—to pursue commerce independent of their husbands.[19]

If denied gendered legal protection from her creditors, Frau Zanke's personal defeat signaled a broad and largely overlooked trend of conceding women fundamental trade privileges. Sources provide little information on the immediate consequences for Frau Zanke; her husband's

1679 bankruptcy suggests, however, that the Zanke family firm faced intractable financial difficulties.[20] But for other women of commerce, the unqualified extension of exchange law clearly weakened the significance of gender guardianship. This important development reassured potential business partners that women were in fact liable and therefore potential trading partners. Commercial fraud, business failure, or honest disagreement might now be settled in court. Moreover, liability endowed women with exchange rights, the potential to assume signing privileges in a firm, and general access to mercantile markets and credit.

## LEIPZIG COMMERCE AND THE FAMILY FIRM

Frau Zanke's case would have had little significance if her business activity, as a woman, represented a rare exception. She was just one of scores of women, however, who participated in Leipzig's vibrant commercial culture, centered on three annual trade fairs. By the late seventeenth century, the Leipzig fairs attracted traveling merchants from all corners of Europe, bridging the manufacturing regions of the Atlantic economy with eastern Europe and Russia. As the principal market of the Saxon-Thuringian region, the city received privileges for new year, spring, and autumn fairs from the Holy Roman Emperors. These privileges circumvented guild restrictions and guaranteed "market freedom" (*Marktfreiheit*) to buy and sell without restriction, a concession that permitted visiting merchants and artisans, local burghers and merchants, as well as non-burgher residents—without regard to guild membership or estate—to trade merchandise in any volume.[21]

Leipzig's commerce thus supported a large and heterogeneous business community. The oldest of these groups, the Retailers' Guild, monopolized shopkeeping outside the fairs and the retail sale of most food staples, as well as hardware, articles of clothing, leather, furs, silks, and other luxury items. Guild membership with its retail and shopkeeping privileges required a six-year apprenticeship and Leipzig citizenship. But the guild also extended the retail privilege to members' widows as long they did not remarry outside the guild.[22] Leipzig's interregional commerce fostered a second group of non-guild merchants, whose business activities were restricted to the commissions, banking, and wholesale trades of the fairs. While many retailers, particularly senior members of the guild, engaged in interregional commerce, wholesalers often joined the guild simply to obtain the retail privilege. To avoid exclusion from retailing and maintain direct contact with the guild, larger wholesale, banking, and manufacturing firms often employed or partnered at least one guild member. The line distinguishing these groups was often and easily crossed, and ultimately, the family firm became the central institution for structuring both retail and long-distance exchange.[23]

Of course, unlike the merchant associations, the firm lacked a distinct legal or corporate identity until well into the nineteenth century. Nevertheless, the merchant community developed effective informal mechanisms for regulating these business units. City address books, published since 1701, included lists of active wholesale and retail merchants, as well as book and music publishers, and functioned as a register of "creditable" Leipzig businesses for the outside traders visiting the fairs.[24] A listing in the address book conferred the imprimatur of "good standing" from the Leipzig business community and guarded both local and outside merchants against insolvent traders or unscrupulous business practices. In 1774 the Leipzig Commercial Court bolstered this control with a registration ordinance requiring Leipzig merchants to register changes of firm name, ownership, or personnel, and to publish this information in the local newspaper.[25] While smaller retail merchants simply appeared in the commercial court, larger firms printed fliers, which were then distributed to business partners in Leipzig and abroad. These single-page sheets announced not only partnership or ownership changes. They also requested customers and creditors to honor the signatures of new partners or employees who acquired signing privileges (*Prokura*): the authorization to sign credit and commercial documents for the firm.

Full partnership, however, implied more than just several years of apprenticeship or faithful service. This step almost always required a substantial contribution to the firm's existing capital. Some entrepreneurial apprentices could amass a few thousand Thaler—a minimum for a modest retail shop—after a decade of hard work and clever trading. They were then in a position to join a larger business, establish a partnership with a peer, or set up an independent shop. But for struggling young merchants, full membership of a business association more often required an investment of capital that could be acquired only through inheritance, marriage, or some combination of both. After years and even decades of faithful service to the family firm, a merchant's son might receive no more than signing privileges. Following the death or retirement of a senior relative, however, usually a father or uncle, a son or nephew might inherit his paternity as a share of the firm and finally obtain partnership. From the biographies of Leipzig's merchant councilors, it is clear that marriage also provided the key to business opportunity.[26] Many young apprentices married a daughter of the firm owner or partner and then became a full partner in the business association on the strength of his wife's inheritance.

Because firm structures reflected patrimony and marital alliance, the family underpinned the business. In turn, the family firm received its sanction through a listing in address books, in the local Leipzig newspaper, and in the firm register of the Leipzig Commercial Court. Thus firms increasingly acquired a collective identity or biography. If a firm owner lacked sons who might continue the business, partners or sons-in-law would often retain the name of the senior partner upon his retirement or death. But because women controlled their own marriage portions and could claim exchange rights, and, as a retailer's widow, shopkeeping privileges, they often assumed a prominent managerial role, especially in mediating the transmission of firm control and patrimony between generations. The contingencies of death and the character of mercantile credit—which depended on the preservation of both firm capital and family patrimony—created a special niche for the merchant's widow, who maintained the reputation and ownership of the family firm. Reflecting complicated familial genealogies, firm appellations like "Comp.," "Sohn" or "Söhne" (son or sons), "Gebr." (brothers), "Erben" (heirs), and "Wittwe" (widow) grew increasingly common in the Leipzig address books through the course of the eighteenth century.

## WIDOWS AS MERCHANTS

This sociolegal context helps to explain the relatively extensive business activity of women—wives, daughters, and, especially, widows—in the long eighteenth century. As shown in Table 9.1, the number of retail and wholesale firms, or book and music publishers, with the appellation "Wittwe" who were listed in the Leipzig address books ranged as high as 10 percent. This figure, moreover, is representative of larger German commercial centers at the end of the eighteenth century, including Frankfurt, Hamburg, Augsburg, Nuremberg, Cologne, and Lübeck, where widows typically owned and managed up to 10 percent or more of retail and wholesale firms.[27] In Leipzig, the number of widows' firms in the last decades of the eighteenth century hovered just above 30, representing between 7 and 9 percent of all Leipzig businesses. In 1811 the number of widows' firms soared to 61, making up over 10 percent of the total number of businesses. Additionally, anywhere from 2 to 16 firms were labeled "Erben" (estate) in a given year, and widows were shareholders and active participants in at least a handful of these. Virtually any firm, moreover, including those with titles like "Comp.," "Söhne" (sons), or "Gebr." (brothers) might have been partially owned by female family members, who contributed substantially but without acknowledgment. Of course, even without silent partnership or some formal financial share, wives and daughters were invariably involved in significant behind-the-scenes work and management. Therefore the 10 percent figure for firms with the appellation "Wittwe" offers at best a rough and minimal representation of women's involvement in Leipzig commerce.

One striking feature of Table 9.1 is the large number of retail firms owned by widows. Though the extension of the shopkeeping privilege to guild widows was an important factor, the difference in firm size between retail and wholesale businesses offers an equally compelling explanation.

**Table 9.1**
**Firm Titles in Leipzig Address Books**

|            | 1713 | 1723 | 1732 | 1747 | 1755 | 1764 | 1770 | 1781 | 1791 | 1800 | 1811 | 1821 | 1830 |
|------------|------|------|------|------|------|------|------|------|------|------|------|------|------|
| R/Widows   | 4    | 7    | 3    | 20   | 21   | 20   | 26   | 31   | 27   | 37   | 50   | 41   | 28   |
| W/Widows   | 0    | 1    | 2    | 3    | 1    | 1    | 5    | 3    | 3    | 3    | 9    | 0    | 0    |
| BM/Widows  | 0    | 0    | 1    | 2    | 0    | 1    | 1    | 2    | 2    | 0    | 2    | 0    | 1    |
| R/Estates  | 0    | 1    | 1    | 0    | 10   | 9    | 7    | 6    | 6    | 0    | 1    | 5    | 12   |
| W/Estates  | 0    | 0    | 2    | 3    | 1    | 2    | 5    | 0    | 0    | 1    | 0    | 0    | 0    |
| BM/Estates | 3    | 4    | 4    | 2    | 5    | 3    | 3    | 2    | 2    | 3    | 1    | 0    | 3    |
| Retailers  | 55   | 144  | 183  | 209  | 221  | 194  | 266  | 235  | 230  | 233  | 318  | 501  | 554  |
| Wholesalers| 89   | 99   | 103  | 151  | 180  | 130  | 144  | 103  | 123  | 157  | 151  | 0    | 0    |
| Book/Music | 16   | 16   | 15   | 25   | 20   | 15   | 15   | 20   | 23   | 48   | 58   | 63   | 96   |
| Total Firms| 167  | 272  | 314  | 415  | 459  | 375  | 472  | 402  | 416  | 482  | 590  | 610  | 694  |

Key to abbreviations: R: Retailer, W: Wholesaler, BM: Book/Music Dealer.

Note: This table is drawn from the address books of 1713, 1723, 1732, 1747, 1755, 1764, 1770, 1781, 1791, 1800, 1811, 1821, and 1830. Firms owned by widows are listed with the appellation "verw." Until 1817 the address books listed wholesalers and members of the Retailers' Guild separately, and beginning in 1818 they were listed together. For 1821 and 1830, therefore, wholesalers and retailers are counted together and listed under "retailers."

The largest city firms were almost always banking and wholesale businesses, which often consisted of three or more partners representing as many families. They additionally employed up to half a dozen apprentices. The retail firms, in contrast, rarely exceeded three partners and involved fewer families. Especially for these smaller firms, widows played an important role as experienced managers who might ease the transition from older to younger firm partners.

There is no question, however, that some women engaged in interregional trade, directing prominent, wealthy firms. In 1782 the childless Christiane Henriette Findeisen reported her husband's death to the Leipzig Commercial Court and registered the firm as "Johann Gottfried Findeisen Wittwe." This established not only the widow's firm ownership but also her shopkeeping privilege, since her husband had belonged to the Retailers' Guild. For over 30 years Widow Findeisen controlled and directed the firm, maintaining both a wholesale trade in colonial goods and a retail custom from the family shop. In 1783, the year following her husband's death, Widow Findeisen hired her sister's son, Friedrich Gottlob Litzkendorf, as a firm apprentice. At the beginning of 1794 she entered a business association with the brothers Johann Gottlob and August Friedrich Schröter and re-registered the firm as "Findeisen Wittwe und Gebr. Schröter." For unexplained reasons, the three partners chose not to continue their association, and when the six-month trial contract (*Associatäts-Contract*) ended in June 1794, Widow Findeisen created a new partnership with her nephew apprentice, Litzkendorf, and renamed the firm "Findeisen Wittwe und Comp." As part owner of the firm, Litzkendorf acquired signing privileges (*Prokura*) and, like his aunt, endorsed business and credit documents in the firm's name. In 1808 Findeisen's house was valued at 30,000 Thaler and the firm's assets at 50,000 Thaler.[28] While the wealthiest Leipzig banking firms held assets exceeding 500,000 Thaler, the sum of 80,000 Thaler certainly represented a substantial fortune; "Findeisen Wittwe und Comp." clearly belonged to the upper echelon of city wholesale firms.[29]

Unlike the childless Findeisen, widows more often managed family firms to preserve the patrimony of underage children. When Johann Andreas Pohlentz died in 1801, his widow, Anna Magdalena, announced her intention to manage the family's manufacture of oilcloth (*Wachstuch Fabrik*) in order to support her four small children. While the details of Widow Pohlentz's business are unknown, her use of the word *Fabrik* suggests that she manufactured textiles with at least a small number of paid employees. Not until 1817 did she enter into a partnership with Christian Friedrich Kretschmann. And when she finally died in December 1822, just months before the six-year contract expired, she left her share of the business to her two sons, Moritz and Adolph, who were able to buy out Kretschmann and continue the business in their own names under the firm title "Gebr. Pohlentz" ("Pohlentz Brothers").[30]

Even merchant widows with adult sons often assumed control of a family enterprise until death or retirement. From the date of her husband's death in 1800 until her own retirement in 1818, Catharina Mainoni actually expanded the family import business in silk wares. After managing the firm for two years, Mainoni engaged the services of her brother, Carl Franz Rossi, until her oldest sons, Johann Jacob and Dominik, entered the business as partners in 1807. During the French occupation of Leipzig, Widow Mainoni installed one son in a trading post in Lyon to purchase the firm's silk supplies directly. A second retail outlet was set up several years later in Frankfurt. Upon her retirement in 1818, Widow Mainoni thanked her customers and business associates for their "continuing trust" and announced the entry of her youngest son, Heinrich Joseph, as director of the retail outlet in Leipzig. The widow assured her business public that "the capital of the firm and its branches would remain undiminished."[31]

In some cases, mothers and daughters managed family firms across generations. After the death of Johann Christoph in 1772, Johanna Regina Anders directed her husband's exchange and forwarding business for a dozen years before entering a partnership with her son-in-law, Carl Christian Abraham Schroeder. In 1796, Schroeder publicized the death of his mother-in-law, explaining, "out of thankfulness to my predecessors, I continue the business under the name 'Anders Wittwe und Schroeder'." When Schroeder died in 1800, his widow Rahel Elisabeth (née Anders) assumed his position and granted signing privileges to the apprentice, Johann Christian Holzapfel. Rahel Elisabeth directed the firm until 1824, when she retired and turned the management over to Holzapfel, who was still listed as the owner of the firm "Anders Wittwe" in Leipzig's 1840 address book.[32]

Unlike Widows Pohlentz, Mainoni, Anders, and Schroeder, however, most women assumed firm management for only interim periods, until their own sons were old enough to enter the business. After the death of her husband, Johann Friedrich Geier, in February 1811, Johanna Christiana appeared in the Leipzig Commercial Court with the legal representative of her three underage children. In a published flier, she announced, "I assume the assets and liabilities of my late husband and continue his business on my own account in the interests of my dependent children."[33] The husband of the Widow Geier had shared his trade in French and Saxon textiles with a partner, Friedrich Ludwig Moltrecht, but Moltrecht left the firm in 1810 to establish his own business in Hamburg. In 1814, Moltrecht returned to Leipzig to enter a partnership with Widow Geier's eldest son, Gustave Friedrich. In the published flier from May 1814, she informed her customers and business associates that "with the trust and confidence that my son is fulfilling his duties along the path of his dear father, I am moved by the thought that he will make himself worthy of your esteem and goodwill."[34] Three years later, in 1817, the younger Geier, Gustave Friedrich, announced Moltrecht's departure from the firm and his independent management of the family business.[35]

Many widows also shared control with children who had already reached their majority. Elisabeth Thiele assumed the direction of the family tobacco firm together with her oldest son Carl Lebrecht after her husband's death in January 1808.[36] Similarly, Johann Rosina Heucke, following the loss of her husband in December 1802, announced the reorganization of the family firm under the name "Johann Franz Heucke seel. Wittwe & Comp." with her older son, Johann Franz, and her husband's apprentice, Adam Gotthilf Witzel, as shareholders and partners.[37] Johann Rosina Wapler also shared firm management with her son, but only after a trial arrangement with her deceased husband's apprentice. With the death of her husband in 1786, Widow Wapler assumed her husband's position in a partnership with Ernst August Schumann, an apprentice who had worked for the firm for 10 years before receiving full partnership shortly before her husband's death. Though Wapler's oldest son, Traugott Heinrich, still shared her address in the family house—347 Hain Street—he conducted a separate trade in furs and leather goods. In 1790 Widow Wapler ended her association with Schumann and announced the entry of her second son, Christian Heinrich, who took over the business in his own name when his mother retired in 1798.[38]

Women were also active in Leipzig's publishing industry. One of the city's most important eighteenth-century houses, the Weidmann *Verlag,* was owned—if not successfully managed—by Widow Weidmann, who chose a brilliant firm director when her own efforts failed. Following her husband's death in 1743, Maria Luise Weidmann nearly ruined the once-flourishing business before finally ceding management in 1746 to Philipp Erasmus Reich, a dynamic entrepreneur who not only made Widow Weidmann's publishing business one of Leipzig's largest, but also reformed the industry in central Europe.[39] Although more modest in means, another widow, Catharina Wilhelmina Haug, was successful in augmenting the publishing list left by her husband. In 1784 Widow Haug registered her ownership and management of the Haug *Verlag* under "Haugs Wittwe." Despite the burden of caring for two infant daughters, born in 1783 and 1784 just before her husband's death, Widow Haug expanded her husband's business by acquiring the list of a bankrupt house in Dessau. This lucrative acquisition included publishing rights to several early works of Johann Gottfried Herder. In 1789 Widow Haug married Johann Ambrosius Barth, who developed the Barth publishing house, which became renowned in the nineteenth century for its publications in the physical and natural sciences.[40]

Despite the literary conceits of publishing, Widows Weidmann and Haug shared a number of characteristics with all of Leipzig's female shopkeepers, wholesale agents, and manufacturers. As members—wives, mothers, daughters—of commercial families, they made significant and often unacknowledged contributions to family-based firms, which endowed them with exceptional skills and expertise. With significant property rights, these women were also able to influence decisions concerning enterprises that were often financed through their marriage portions or inheritances. But even without necessarily asserting their rights or interests, many businesswomen simply assumed a managerial position to maintain a custom or shop for underage children. This commercial activity was fostered, moreover, through the liberal widows' privilege of the Retailers' Guild and the explicit concessions of Saxon exchange law. Despite the restrictions of German guardianship, therefore, female commercial agents enjoyed most of the prerogatives of their male counterparts. In this fashion, the interests of the family firm—reflecting those of civic elites throughout central Europe—clearly defeated gender-based legal restrictions.

## COMMERCIAL REFORM AND THE ELIMINATION OF FEMALE GUARDIANSHIP

Female commercial agents represented, of course, no more than a tiny fraction of those German women who otherwise remained subject to the restrictions *and* protections of gender guardianship. This state of affairs persisted in most of Germany until well into the nineteenth century. This overwhelming majority included not only the wives and daughters of non-mercantile groups—artisans, academics, and bureaucrats, for example—but also the women of mercantile families who never actively engaged in commerce. Here again, however, the effect of gender guardianship was ambivalent. The usually successful attempts by insolvent merchants to withhold family assets from their creditors reveal the exploitation of gender guardianship. Thus for bankrupts, gender guardianship remained an important hedge against complete ruin. For legitimate creditors, however, gender guardianship increased losses by allowing debtors to shield property behind their wives' privilege. As such, it became a prominent target of critics and reformers.

The codification of German, and, specifically here, Saxon bankruptcy law offers a clear illustration of the efforts to close these loopholes. The occasion for drafting and promulgating the first full-blown Saxon bankruptcy law came in 1723 with the spectacular failure of a prominent Leipzig merchant and city councilor. When the wholesale trader, Gottfried Winckler, fled Leipzig rather than face his creditors, city officials drafted a new code, which the Saxon Elector-King promulgated as law in 1724. In an effort to restore business confidence and reassure outside traders who patronized the Leipzig fairs, local business and civic leaders established a set of guidelines to guarantee the most equitable settlement of the bankrupt's remaining estate. The new law was intended to prevent the bankrupt from hiding assets while guaranteeing a fair and proportional settlement of the remaining capital among all the merchant's creditors.

However, because gender guardianship prevented a merchant from pledging his wife's property as collateral without her express consent—requiring in turn the third-party approval of her sexual guardian—this property generally remained outside the creditors' grasp. Even if a handsome dowry had permitted a merchant to open or expand a firm or simply conferred the reputation of a significant working capital, as long as the wife never signed exchange letters herself, her dowry remained protected. After tabulating a bankrupt's remaining estate, officials prioritized repayment of the wife's marriage portion, and only what remained after this might be divided among the unfortunate creditors. As a result, insolvent merchants routinely emerged from a bankruptcy settlement with the sum of their wife's dowry, while creditors might at best receive 50 percent or less of their claims.

The estate of Gottfried Winckler, the merchant whose insolvency inspired the 1724 law, offers a perfect example. While business creditors received about 10 percent of their claims, or 8,233 from a debt of more than 80,000 Thaler, Winckler's wife, Dorothea Sophie (and their children who survived her death at the end of 1724) received most of her marriage portion, or 17,000 of 18,010 Thaler.[41] The authors of the new bankruptcy ordinance understood and regretted this inequity, but there was little they could do short of eliminating gender guardianship altogether. One striking gesture, however, was a paragraph in the bankruptcy law that encumbered a wife's marriage portion if it were proven that her ostentatious lifestyle had contributed to her husband's commercial failure. The 1724 code stated, "if a wife causes the bankruptcy through extravagance, through dishonest dealings, or otherwise colludes with her husband, she forfeits any claims for herself."[42] If rarely proven or imposed, this provision represented an initial effort to limit the protection of gender guardianship. The new bankruptcy ordinance also warned against fraudulent efforts to conceal property by bestowing expensive gifts, either property, jewels, or cash. In the event of bankruptcy, any recent transfers of property from husband to wife would fall under scrutiny of the bankruptcy lawyers, who could legitimately remove such valuables from the wife's formal possession. Even if difficult to enforce, the 1724 law did attempt to redress the common abuse of withholding property from creditors by presenting it as the wife's marriage portion.

Efforts to strengthen bankruptcy law and limit the protections of gender guardianship can be observed throughout the eighteenth and into the nineteenth century. In the wake of the Seven Years' War (1756–1763), which wrought economic havoc in Leipzig and Saxony, city and state officials embraced a range of measures to restore commerce and manufacturing. One such project was the drafting of a new bankruptcy code. The "stricter" (*geschärftes*) ordinance of 1766 repeated the earlier warnings to extravagant or deceitful wives who might scheme with their husbands in defrauding a creditor. This time the law introduced the threat of punishment, including torture and incarceration—and not only for the bankrupt, as before—but also for his wife.[43] The impact of the law was probably negligible—the proverbial dog with more bark than bite. The settlement of at least one later bankruptcy, again, the costly and scandalous failure of a city councilor, Johann Christoph Richter, appears to have conformed to older patterns. Announcing his insolvency in 1793, Richter ended up paying his creditors only 25 percent of an outstanding debt of over 140,000 Thaler.[44] Yet his last will and testament, dated 1804 and executed after his death in 1807, left more than 100,000 Thaler in cash and property to his five surviving children.[45] While it is unclear from the sources how Richter accumulated this sum within a decade of his own insolvency, the chances that he recouped his earlier fortune in commerce are slim, given that he was forced to resign from several Leipzig associations and lost his standing in the local business community. Richter's wife more than likely played some role by helping to manipulate their respective assets to secure this sizable inheritance for their children.

Legal scholars of the eighteenth and early nineteenth centuries were well aware of the legal dodges and financial manipulations facilitated by gender guardianship, especially in cases of fraud and bankruptcy.[46] The ultimate abolition of gender guardianship was therefore a question of time and political will. When Saxony abolished gender-based legal discrimination in a piecemeal fashion from 1828 to 1838, it joined a group of more than a dozen German cities and territories that followed a similar course in the same period.[47] The elimination of gender guardianship was as ambivalent in effect, however, as its initial introduction had been in the sixteenth century. On the one hand it represented a type of legal emancipation for single women, who gained formal economic independence. At the same time its repeal intensified the subjection of married women to their husbands, and obviously so, as gender guardianship was initially intended primarily for the protection of married women. With the elimination of gender guardianship, in effect, a bankrupt's creditors could make claims more easily on his wife's marriage portion. According to the Leipzig University law professor, Christian Gottlieb Haubold, the abolition of gender guardianship had a dramatic effect because a married woman's property now fell under the administration of her husband and could therefore be seized as surety in the event of his bankruptcy.[48] As David Sabean has recently demonstrated for Württemberg in the nineteenth century, bureaucratic reformers argued that gender guardianship hindered the growth of credit markets, slowed the commercialization of real estate, and damaged business by enabling fraud. But the bureaucrats were latecomers to this debate and merely adopted the perspective of local mercantile elites. In other words, for the same reasons that Leipzig jurists had supported local merchants in extending exchange privileges to women in the late seventeenth century and worked to strengthen and reform bankruptcy law in the eighteenth, German bureaucrats in the nineteenth now opted to eliminate gender guardianship altogether.[49]

## CONCLUSION

Both the timing and geography of the development traced in this essay suggest a number of larger patterns. The expansion of Europe's mercantile economy in the late seventeenth century reinforced the commercial privileges of German businesswomen, at least those imbricated in the network of European interregional trade. Accordingly, the first German merchant communities to promote the legal capacity of businesswomen were those in Hamburg (1603), Frankfurt (1662), and Leipzig (1674). We might certainly expect a similar pattern throughout continental Europe.[50] Within the Holy Roman Empire, this pattern was reproduced in the eighteenth century at the level of the German territorial states, which issued territorial commercial codes exempting businesswomen from gender guardianship.

The case of Leipzig's Frau Zanke underlines a second significant characteristic of this development: namely, the role of local business practices in shaping law. While traditional German scholarship has characteristically privileged the agency of the early modern state, the piecemeal dismantling of gender guardianship outlined here suggests that law was less a cause than a result of locally specific social and economic processes.[51] In response to Frau Zanke's alleged fraud—facilitated by her protective gender guardianship—Leipzig merchants and jurists, local or nonstate actors, promoted the universal application of exchange law, regardless of gender or estate, for any business transacted in the city. This signaled a broader trend led by Germany's commercial centers and only later followed by German territorial rulers. The significant actors in this development (again!) were neither bureaucrats nor state-employed mercantilists. Rather, merchants, city officials, and jurists with strong local business ties inaugurated and promoted reforms, which included granting women commercial privileges and elaborating bankruptcy regulation.

That German women of commerce generally enjoyed the same commercial rights in the late seventeenth century as they did 150 years later seems clear. At the same time, married women may have actually lost a measure of independence with the elimination of gender guardianship, which left them less recourse than before in countering their husbands. This represents anything but an unambiguous trajectory of progressive empowerment, therefore, and clearly counters any straightforward plotting of either the decline or progress of women's economic opportunities. Indeed, neither of the two broad narratives that have structured much of the economic history of women have much application here. One story line blames early modern merchant capitalism for the marginalization of middle-class women.[52] The account of the modern era charges industrial capitalism for the degradation of working women and the exclusion of elite women from any active economic engagement.[53]

More recent scholarship suggests that there were, in fact, few significant changes or genuine discontinuities in women's legal positions before the twentieth century, when women first gained political rights and equal protection before the law.[54] As an alternative to older historiographic templates, then, this suggests a useful approach for assessing the peculiar arc of German guardianship. In short, the family unit provided the crucial institution for mediating interests. Initially, women played a central role in family firms, which structured the interregional commerce of central Europe. In this capacity, women required both the legal independence to control property and exchange privileges to manipulate credit instruments and transfer capital. Perhaps the most striking feature in this story, then, is the disparate influences of market forces on the independence and agency of women. The expansion of Europe's mercantile economy actually reinforced the commercial privileges of German businesswomen, constructing them as women without gender. But the commercialization of property and the growth of corporate capitalism in the nineteenth century—to the extent that they weakened the importance of family business firms—likewise influenced commercial elites to strengthen male authority within the family unit.

## NOTES

1. For a discussion of gender and the decline of guardianship in Sweden see the chapter in this volume by Ann Ighe.

2. Frau Zanke's husband, Hieronymous, whose name also appears as "Zange" in the sources, was a textiles trader and a commercial agent in the Leipzig fairs. His firm was taxed at a value of 100,000 Florins in 1659, making him one of Leipzig's wealthiest merchants. See Gerhard Fischer, *Aus zwei Jahrhunderten Leipziger Handels-Geschichte 1470–1650* (Leipzig: F. Meiner, 1929), 178 and Johann Georg Friedrich Franz, *Pragmatische Handlungs Geschichte der Stadt Leipzig* (Leipzig: J. S. Heinsius, 1772), 273–77.

3. The best overview is Raymond De Roover, *L'evolution de la lettre de change XIVe–XVIIIe siècles* (Paris: A. Colin, 1953); on the Holy Roman Empire see Jürgen Schneider, "International Rates of Exchange: Structures and Trend of Payments Mechanism in Europe, Seventeenth to Nineteenth Century," in *The Emergence of a World Economy 1500–1914*, ed. Wolfram Fischer (Wiesbaden: F. Steiner, 1986), 143–70; Jürgen Schneider, "Messen, Banken und Börsen (15.–18. Jahrhundert)," in *Banchi pubblici, banchi privati e monti di pietà nell'Europa preindustriale: Amministrazione, tecniche operative e ruoli economici*, vol. 1, ed. Dino Puncuh and Giuseppe Felloni (Genoa: Società Ligure di Storia Patria, 1991), 135–69; and Siegbert Lammel, "Die Gesetzgebung des Handelsrechts," in *Handbuch der Quellen und Literatur der neueren europäischen Privatrechtsgeschichte, vol. 2: Neuere Zeit (1500–1800)*, ed. Helmut Coing (Munich: C. H. Beck, 1976), 629–31.

4. Saxon statutes-book *Codex Augusteus oder neu vermehrte Corpus juris Saxonici*, vol. 2. (Leipzig: J. F. Gleditsch, 1724), 2017.

5. On women's economic activity in the Middle Ages, see Margret Wensky, *Die Stellung der Frau in der stadtkölnischen Wirtschaft im Spätmittelalter* (Cologne: Böhlau, 1980) and the essays in Barbara Vogel and Ulrike Weckel, eds., *Frauen in der Ständegesellschaft: Leben und Arbeiten in der Stadt vom späten Mittelalter bis zur Neuzeit* (Hamburg: R. Krämer, 1991).

6. Consider the eighteenth-century debates about sexual guardianship outlined in David W. Sabean, "Allianzen und Listen: Die Geschlechtsvormundschaft im 18. und 19. Jahrhundert," in *Frauen in der Geschichte des Rechts: Von der Frühen Neuzeit bis zur Gegenwart*, ed. Ute Gerhard (Munich: C. H. Beck, 1997), 460–79.

7. Susan Mendelson and Patricia Crawford, *Women in Early Modern England* (Oxford: Oxford University Press, 1998), 38–42, 330–34; Susan Staves, *Married Women's Separate Property in England, 1660–1833* (Cambridge, Mass.: Harvard University Press, 1990), 27–32; and Leonore Davidoff and Catherine Hall, *Family Fortunes: Men and Women of the English Middle Class, 1780–1850* (London: Routledge, 2002), 200–201, 275–79.

8. Barbara Diefendorf, "Women and Property in *ancien régime* France: Theory and Practice in Dauphiné and Paris," in *Early Modern Conceptions of Property*, ed.

John Brewer and Susan Staves (London: Routledge, 1995), 170–93 and Julie Hard-wick, *The Practice of Patriarchy: Gender and the Politics of Household Authority in Early Modern France* (University Park, Penn.: Penn State University Press, 1998), 47–48. For discussion of the situation in Sweden, see the chapters by Ann Ighe and Kirsti Niskanen elsewhere in this volume.

9. Surveys addressing women's premodern business activities include Bonnie Anderson and Judith Zinsser, *A History of Their Own*, vol. 1 (Cambridge: Cambridge University Press, 1988), 392–406, 424–30; Heide Wunder, *"Er ist die sonn', sie ist der Monde": Frauen in der Frühen Neuzeit* (Cambridge, Mass.: Harvard University Press, 1997), 125–30; Merry Wiesner, *Women and Gender in Early Modern Europe* (Cambridge: Cambridge University Press, 1993), 96–97, 106–10; and Olwen Hufton, *The Prospect Before Her: A History of Women in Western Europe* (London: Vintage, 1995). For the German context see Robert Beachy, "Business was a Family Affair: Women of Commerce in Central Europe, 1680–1870," *Histoire sociale—Social History* 34 (2002): 307–30; Daniel Rabuzzi, "Women as Merchants in Eighteenth-Century Northern Germany: The Case of Stralsund, 1750–1830," *Central European History* 28 (1995): 435–56; Kristina Klausmann, "'Dann manche Kramers-Frau in ihrem Laden-Stul'–weibliche Handelstätigkeit in Frankfurt vom 17. Bis zum beginnenden 19. Jahrhundert," in *Brücke zwischen den Völkern—Zur Geschichte der Frankfurter Messe, vol. 2: Beiträge zur Geschichte der Frankfurter Messe*, ed. Patricia Stahl, Roland Hoede, and Dieter Skala (Frankfurt a.M: Ausstellung im Historischen Museum der Stadt, 1991), 280–90; Eva Labouvie, "In weiblicher Hand: Frauen als Firmengründerinnen und Unternehmerinnen (1600–1870)," in Eva Labouvie, ed., *Frauenleben–Frauen leben: Zur Geschichte und Gegenwart weiblicher Lebenswelten im Saarraum (17.–20. Jahrhundert)* (St. Ingbert: Röhrig, 1993), 88–131.

10. For a broad introduction to German gender guardianship and the impact of Roman law on the independent property rights of married women see Ernst Holt-höfer, "Die Geschlechtsvormundschaft: Ein Überblick von der Antike bis ins 19. Jahrhundert," in Gerhard, *Frauen in der Geschichte des Rechts*, 390–451.

11. The Saxon law appears in *Codex Augusteus*, vol. 2: 88–89.

12. See Schneider, "International Rates of Exchange," 143–70; Schneider, "Messen, Banken und Börsen," 135–69; and Lammel, "Die Gesetzgebung des Handelsrechts," 629–31.

13. The best account of the Leipzig *Schöppenstuhl* is Ernst Boehm, "Der Schöppenstuhl zu Leipzig und der sächsische Inquisitionsprozess im Barockzeitalter," *Zeitschrift für die gesamte Strafrechtswissenschaft* 60 (1941): 217.

14. Franz, *Pragmatische Handlungs Geschichte*, 277; for excerpts of the legal briefs see 273–77.

15. See "Rescript/Churf. Johann Georgens des II. Zu Sachsen, dass das Leipziger Marckt Rescript . . . auf die Weiber, so Kauffmannschafft treiben, extendiret seyn solle, den 8. April An. 1674," in *Codex Augusteus*, vol. 2, 2019.

16. For a social profile of Leipzig's academic and merchant elite in the late seventeenth century see Robert Beachy, "Reforming Interregional Commerce: The Leipzig Trade Fairs and Saxony's Recovery from the Thirty Years' War," *Central European History* 32 (1999): 431–52.

17. Quoted from the 1682 Leipzig Exchange Code in *Der Stadt Leipzig Ordnungen wie auch Privilegia und Statuta* (Leipzig: Fritsch, 1701), 66.

18. The texts of most exchange codes are published in Johann Gottlieb Siegel,

*Corpus Juris Cambialis*, 2 vols. (Leipzig: J.S. Heinsius, 1742) and in Carl Günther Ludovici, *Allgemeine Schatz-Kammer der Kauffmannschafft oder vollständiges Lexicon aller Handlungen und Gewerbe*, 5 vols. (Leipzig: J.S. Heinsius, 1741–43).

19. *Allgemeines Landrecht für die Preußischen Staaten von 1794* (Frankfurt a.M: A. Metzner, 1970), 476.

20. Frau Zanke's financial difficulties in 1673 marked the beginning of a downward spiral for the merchant family, and the failure of the Zanke firm in 1679 coincided with a rash of local bankruptcies. See a contemporary report from Leipzig merchants, including a list of bankruptcies, in StadtA Leipzig, XLV.G.6b, Commissions Acta, fols. 36r–136v.

21. The starting point for research on the Leipzig fairs remains Ernst Hasse, *Geschichte der Leipziger Messen* (Leipzig: S. Hirzel, 1885). The most recent study is Nils Brübach, *Die Reichsmessen von Frankfurt am Main, Leipzig und Braunschweig (14.–18. Jahrhundert)* (Stuttgart: F. Steiner, 1994).

22. On the Retailers' Guild see Karl Biedermann, *Geschichte der Leipziger Kramer-Innung* (Leipzig: O. Leiner, 1881), which includes the 1695 version of the Guild ordinance, 16–26.

23. On the Wholesalers' Association and its relationship to the Retailers' Guild see Beachy, "Reforming Interregional Commerce," 431–52.

24. The Leipzig address books published in the first half of the eighteenth century were incomplete and appeared erratically until 1751, after which they were published annually (with a hiatus from 1757 to 1763 during the Seven Years' War).

25. StadtA Leipzig: Ha VI 1a, Prot d Hd, vol. 5, fols. 386v–393; Handelsgericht, no. 27 "Errichtung eines Regulativs wegen der Handlungs Firmen."

26. This description is based on the author's detailed prosopography of the 220 Leipzig Councilors who held office between 1680–1830, 78 of whom were simultaneously merchants. These family biographies are based on published and serial archival sources. See Robert Beachy, "The Soul of Commerce: Credit and the Politics of Public Debt in Leipzig, 1680–1830" (Ph.D. diss., University of Chicago, 1998).

27. Beachy, "Business was a Family Affair."

28. See the property tax register, StadtA Leipzig, XLI B.124, "Tabellarische Uebersicht des Werths sämtlicher Privat-Grundstücke in der Stadt." For estate values see StadtA Leipzig, XLI.7/2 "Verzeichniß. . . ."

29. "Findeisen Wittwe und Comp." at 375 Katharinen Street was still registered as an active firm in 1818 and appeared in the Leipzig address books for the last time in 1819. Though it remains unclear whether she retired or possibly died before 1819, the appellation *Wittwe* in the firm title and the business address suggest her continued ownership and control. See StadtA Leipzig: Firmenbuch, vol. 1, nos. 154, 155; Neue Folge, vol. 1, no. 332; Ha VI 1a "Protocollbuch der Handelsdeputierten," vol. 16, fol. 216; and *Leipziger Adress-Buch:* (1764): 97, 108; (1770): 128, 142; (1772): 132; (1777): 137, 138; (1787): 103, 116; (1794): 98; (1802): 104; (1813): 104, 109; (1819): 107, 118.

30. StadtA Leipzig, Firmenbuch, vol. 1, no. 273; vol. 2, no. 14; vol. 4, no. 34; and Neue Folge, vol. 3, nos. 280–81.

31. StadtA Leipzig, Firmenbuch, vol. 1, no. 305; vol. 3, nos. 193, 237; and vol. 4, n. 63.

32. StadtA Leipzig, Firmenbuch, vol. 1, no. 200; vol. 2, no. 44; Neue Folge, vol.

4, no. 188; *Leipziger Adress-Buch:* (1764): 96; (1766): 96; (1770): 128; (1772): 129; (1782): 112; (1787): 116; and (1840): 118.

33. StadtA Leipzig, Firmenbuch, vol. 2, nos. 35, 142 and vol. 3, nos. 18, 53.

34. StadtA Leipzig, Firmenbuch, vol. 3, no. 148.

35. StadtA Leipzig, Firmenbuch, vol. 4, no. 40.

36. StadtA Leipzig, Firmenbuch, vol. 2, nos. 169–70.

37. StadtA Leipzig, Firmenbuch, vol. 2, no. 22.

38. StadtA Leipzig, Firmenbuch, vol. 1, nos. 97, 231–32; and *Leipziger Adress-Buch:* (1787): 114; (1799): 99.

39. Adalbert Brauer, *Weidmann 1680–1980: 300 Jahre aus der Geschichte eines der ältesten Verlage der Welt* (Zürich: Weidmann, 1980), 40–41; Hazel Rosenstrauch, *Buchhandelsmanufaktur und Aufklärung: Die Reformen des Buchhändlers und Verlegers Ph. E. Reich (1717–1787)* (Frankfurt a.M: Buchhändler-Vereinigung, 1986).

40. See Johann A. Barth, *Johann Ambrosius Barth in Leipzig 1780–1930* (Leipzig: C. G. Röder, 1930), 16–40.

41. On Dorothea Sophie's dowry see StadtA Leipzig, II. Sektion, W. 376IA, fols. 16v–17v. On the final bankruptcy settlement see StadtA Leipzig, II. Sektion, W. 501, fols. 5–16.

42. *Fortgesetzter Codex Augusteus* (Leipzig: J. F. Gleditsch, 1772), 2380. For the full text of the 1724 ordinance see 2374–82.

43. The 1766 law is in *Codex Saxonicus,* vol. 1 (Leipzig: Reclam, 1842), 955–65.

44. StadtA Leipzig, LXII. R. 5a, fols. 32v–33v, 41v.

45. StadtA Leipzig, LXII. R. 12, fols. 11–18.

46. See the commentary of Saxon legal scholar Christian Gottlieb Haubold together with a bibliography of eighteenth- and nineteenth-century legal critiques of gender guardianship in Christian Gottlieb Haubold, *Lehrbuch des königlich-sächsischen Privatrechts,* vol. 1 (Leipzig: Hahn, 1847), 148–51.

47. For the Saxon law see *Codex Saxonicus,* vol. 2, 274–76, 1046–47 and Haubold, *Lehrbuch,* 154–58. On Germany in the first half of the nineteenth century see Holthöfer, "Die Geschlechtsvormundschaft," 438–42.

48. Haubold, *Lehrbuch,* 71, 74–79.

49. David Sabean identifies a debate among state officials in the second half of the eighteenth century, and although he underlines the exemption of women merchants from restrictive sex-based discrimination, he neglects the earlier influences of merchant and civic elites in framing this discussion and the precedent set by local exchange codes. See Sabean, "Allianzen und Listen," 460–79.

50. Impressionistic evidence comes from the commercial centers of both Lyon and Amsterdam, where local seventeenth-century commercial ordinances released businesswomen from traditional legal and economic restraints. See Diefendorf, "Women and Property," 175; Simon Schama, *The Embarrassment of Riches: an Interpretation of Dutch Culture in the Golden Age* (New York: Knopf, 1987), 407.

51. For a critique of this more traditional approach see Robert Gordon, "Critical Legal Histories," *Stanford Law Review* 36 (1984): 57–125.

52. Examples of this scholarship include essays in Marilyn Boxer and Jean Quataert, eds., *Connecting Spheres: European Women in a Globalizing World, 1500 to the Present* (Cambridge: Cambridge University Press, 1987).

53. The most articulate and emphatic statement of this view is Davidoff and Hall, *Family Fortunes.* Consider as well the essays in Boxer and Quataert, *Con-*

*necting Spheres* and Bonnie Smith, *Women of the Leisure Class: the Bourgeoises of Northern France in the Nineteenth Century* (Princeton, N.J.: Princeton University Press, 1981).

54. Amanda Vickery, "Golden Age to Separate Spheres? A Review of the Categories and Chronology of English Women's History," *The Historical Journal* 36 (1993): 383–414.

# CHAPTER 10

# Minors, Guardians, and Inheritance in Early Nineteenth-Century Sweden: A Case of Gendered Property Rights

*Ann Ighe*

## INTRODUCTION

The emergence of the "woman question" in Swedish political debate can be dated to the first half of the nineteenth century. Concern was expressed about restrictions imposed on unmarried women to run a business or trade independently, which, it was argued, made it extremely difficult for them to make a living on their own.[1] This situation not only affected the welfare of unmarried women themselves but also had an impact on their families and kin, who were frequently expected to provide for them but who did not always have the means to do so. In contemplating reform, a number of formidable institutional obstacles had to be overcome. In the context of many Swedish towns, women's economic capacity was curtailed by the highly gendered regulations and controls over crafts and trades exercised by urban guilds and corporations. However, a more significant set of restrictions was the legal rules that made single women minors in the eyes of the law, regardless of their age, which severely limited their possibilities to earn an independent living.[2] The aim of this chapter is to explore the debates and legal changes concerning the minority status of unmarried women and to examine the impact they had on family welfare and relationships.

Throughout the eighteenth and nineteenth centuries, the regulations concerning guardianship in Sweden were part of the law of inheritance.[3] This stipulated that guardians were to be appointed for all orphaned children primarily to oversee the disposal and management of their inherited property. However, while males gained majority status when they reached the age of 21, there was no designated age at which females were released from guardianship, and unless they married, being a minor could prevail for a lifetime. Once married, women were formally released from guardianship, but even within marriage husbands assumed many of the functions of the previous guardian, and so in reality most women found that their status had changed little. This is not to argue that married women were completely subservient to their husbands. There were some restrictions on the capacity of husbands to act on behalf of their wife or to meddle in her affairs. For example, a husband required the consent of his wife in matters concerning the disposition of their common property. Even here, however, the restrictions were set by the claims of the wife's family of birth, or lineage, rather than by the woman herself. As in many other European societies at the time, it was not until widowhood that women were able to enjoy a degree of legal independence. It is something of a sad paradox that the theoretical independence of widowhood was often accompanied by extreme social vulnerability.[4]

These institutional arrangements of gendered and generational property rights had been formally codified in medieval times. However, their transformation and partial decline in the nineteenth century is the focus here, particularly the institutional reforms that led to unmarried women's emancipation from legal and economic minority. This was achieved gradually between 1858 and 1863, when single women were given general legal and economic "majority" at the age of 25. In the case of married women, similar economic rights were not secured until later. Their formal emancipation was achieved as a result of new marriage laws and the granting of universal suffrage in the years 1919–21.[5]

One way to tease out the changing functions of guardianship would be to examine the way in which it was related to the ownership and use of property. What kind of property came with guardianship? What was the institutional setting concerning the market for property? In this chapter, these questions are touched upon but not explored in detail. The development of the legal framework is primarily considered in order to identify the changing capacities of actors within the institutional setting of guardianship. The second approach, and the one explored in detail here, is to focus on the actors—the minors and guardians—and the changing sets of capacities that they were allowed to possess. That is, what were the restrictions, duties, and rights that were connected with guardianship and minority? *Who* had the right to do *what* with the property concerned? Questions of this kind help us address the relationships between changes in the legal system and transformation in the economic, social, and political spheres.

## ECONOMIC INSTITUTIONS AND SOCIAL CHANGE

In every society economic relations and transactions take place within a variety of institutional settings, of which guardianship is but one example. According to the economic historian Douglass North, economic institutions constitute "the rules of the game" and the "organization of the players" in society.[6] They provide the basis and context through and within which economic processes operate. North's work mostly focuses on institutions that enable firms and economic actors to reduce market transaction costs. According to this view, the existence of a large number of socially regulated and embedded institutions, such as guardianship and inheritance as well as craft guilds and other types of corporations, could be explained as less-costly ways of conducting economic exchange than pure market transactions.[7]

While this "new institutional theory" is sometimes posited as an alternative to a neoclassical approach to explaining economic activity, its underlying propositions are recognizably neoclassical, particularly the implicit assumption of methodological individualism. A shift in relative prices is considered to be the main factor behind alterations in human behavior and, thus, for historical change. Basically, changes in relative prices are assumed to reflect technical and demographic shifts as well as varying degrees of resource scarcity. Economic actors strive to maximize their utility in relation to altered circumstances of this kind, and this leads to a more-or-less gradual change in the institutional framework. At any given time, the actors' ability to react to changing prices will be restrained or facilitated by the existing institutions.

Another source of change may be a shift in "preferences." This is the "conceptual box" into which ideological changes are frequently stuffed. However, shifts in preferences or ideologies change gradually, and new ones are shaped and framed in relation to those that preceded them. This issue lies at the core of "path dependency," a concept that emphasizes the constraining nature and the evolutionary continuity of institutional change. Through these insights, neo-institutional economic historians have tried to grasp the persistence of institutions that, at least in theory, might seem to contradict the prevailing economic logic within in any given historical setting.

In the context of the analysis of "modern" economies and societies, by which is meant the emergence and dominance of market processes and individual property rights, historians of institutional change have rarely examined who actually constituted the modern individual capable of participating in exchange and exercising those rights. In particular, few have considered explicitly the role of gender, itself an institutional structure that has a significant impact on the ways in which economic and social relations are conducted.[8] North's treatment of institutions, for example, pays scant attention to gender issues. Yet when investigating the history of economic change it is clear that a gender order is evident, made up of various institutional arrangements, from legal rulings to the unwritten codes of everyday life.[9] The historical essence of this gendered institutional order is the subordination of females in relation to males.[10] However, the picture is more complex than just men's domination and women's subordination, and historians have begun to acknowledge the varied, complex, and contingent patterning of the gender order in past societies.

This chapter focuses on institutions as well as actors, drawing on critiques of both new institutional and neoclassical theory. During the nineteenth century, as liberal discourse sought to constitute the modern individual as a free economic agent and as market transactions came to dominate economic activity, so the restrictions imposed by guardianship in relation to property rights came to be seen as increasingly anachronistic, from the perspective of both guardians and minors. For the former, guardianship added to transaction costs by restricting their capacity to act in an economically rational way. For the latter, although liberal discourse favored an abstract notion of the individual, it was clearly based on an assumption of male supremacy; women, who formed the majority of minors, were not seen as possessing the capacity to act as free economic agents. This was becoming increasingly untenable in the context of an urbanizing and commercializing economy where there were growing numbers of single females who needed to make a living. The point at which these pressures coincided marked the start of a process of institutional change, which is the focus of this chapter.

## GUARDIANSHIP AND PROPERTY RIGHTS

The institution of guardianship was highly gendered, endowing some actors with specific rights while imposing certain restrictions on others. These rights were mainly concerned with the maintenance and control of inherited capital, making guardianship a central instrument for property transmission over the generations. An important task for a guardian was to protect minors from material and other losses that might be caused by the breakup of a family following the death of a key member, and in so doing he—for it was primarily a male—took over the role of welfare provider for the bereaved minor. The law provided minors with a more limited set of capacities over their property rights compared with the ones vested in a guardian. To understand these complex issues it is necessary to outline the gendered positions that minors and guardians occupied in the institutional structure.

## Guardians

The legal code on guardianship of 1734 required that guardians possess some specific qualities, of which "legal competence" was the most significant. There were essentially two types of guardianship. First, there was that which emanated from being a parent. In such instances fatherhood was the normal prerequisite for becoming a legally competent guardian. A different kind of conditional guardianship applied to mothers, which was usually activated by the death of the father. This is not to say that while the father was living a mother lacked authority over her children or matters concerning their welfare. However, the law assumed that only one person in each household would be in overall control of affairs. Even when a widowed mother became a guardian, her legal competence was still limited in the sense that she could act only with the "advice" of her deceased husband's male next of kin or an appointed male guardian. In the case of remarriage, a clear gendered difference between the position of the father and the mother applied. A widowed *and* remarried father was expected to take advice from the mother's male next of kin. In this case, the interests of lineage modified the father's power. A remarried widow was able keep her children in her "house and bread" if she wanted to but was not allowed to continue as their formal guardian. This did not mean that the stepfather automatically became the new guardian. On the contrary, the intention was usually that someone connected with the original father's lineage should take on guardianship in order to protect the children's property from this new male authority.

Second, there were those guardians who were appointed by a court. Guardianship could be conferred upon an individual by one of a number of courts that made up the Swedish judicial system: *Häradsrätter,* for the peasant majority in the countryside; *rådhusrätter,* for the burghers of the urban areas; *konsistorier,* for priests and scholars; and *hovrätter,* for the nobility. In appointing guardians, courts generally used a hierarchical definition of kinship that was similar to the successive order of inheritance. Priority was given to the next male relative at every level or circle of kin. The clear parallels between the law of inheritance and that of guardianship were probably not a coincidence. Being a potential heir to the property of a ward would function as a barrier against abuse and as an incentive not only to keep, but also to improve, the value of the capital in trust.[11] An interesting but contrasting principle to this, stemming from Roman law, can be found in early modern Tuscany, where the rule was that guardians could never expect to inherit from their wards. This rule has been interpreted as a form of protection for wards because guardians would otherwise have had an obvious incentive to kill them in order to get hold of an inheritance.[12]

In the Swedish case, the law of guardianship had long served to protect the legitimate property interests of the respective lines of kinship. However, this key principle had been in decline over the early modern period. One clear manifestation of this was expressed in the *Förmyndareordningen,* or Act of Guardianship, of 1669.[13] This act was, in some respects, a contrast to—or at least a step toward a balancing of—the medieval tradition, where the authority of the father and the preservation of the lineage were the most important organizing principles of guardianship. It bestowed primacy on both the parents' testamentary power to appoint guardians of their own choice for their children. The act presupposed that representatives from both the mother's and the father's side would be appointed, although the evidence presented here for Göteborg suggests that this was unusual. These appointments were to be valid no matter what position in the family lineage the guardian occupied and, indeed, would still hold if the guardian were unrelated to the parents. Furthermore, the act stated that kinsmen should not have the power to appeal against the appointment of non-kin and demand for themselves the position of guardian based on their own relationship to the parents. When there was no acceptable appointment made by the parents and no kinsmen were available or suitable, the courts appointed someone else who filled the general requirements of the role. With the new law of 1734, which further wrenched the institution of guardianship from the clutches of family lineage, the minimum requirement for the number of guardians was reduced to a single individual. Although joint guardianship was still allowed, it became an exception. Between 1845 and 1861, new legislation reinforced and further developed the control of public authorities over the guardians.[14] This was achieved partly by establishing specific local bodies to regulate guardianship and partly by tightening the demands on the guardian to keep records of his activities.

### Minors

The position of minority was normally expected to be of a temporary nature. However, the possible points of change in a minor's position were highly gendered. In the Swedish language the general term for *majority* or *coming of age—myndighet—*has no direct connotations with age at all. Instead, the word *myndighet* was, and is, more-or-less synonymous with the word *authority.*

The new legal code of 1734 established that a male's coming of age occurred at his twenty-first birthday (under the previous law males were assumed to attain majority upon their fifteenth birthday). There was no corresponding point at which females were recognized to have come of age. However, females were allowed to marry and to freely dispose of their earnings at the age of 15. The bequeathing of property was also allowed for "sensible maids." For women, marriage was a way out of their father's sphere of authority because at that point the husband assumed the functions of the previous guardian.[15] As was noted earlier, it was not until widowhood that married women found themselves in a position that was closer, but still not equivalent, to that of a male head of household. Nevertheless, to attain majority was not entirely impossible for unmarried women. By making an application to the king for exemption from guardianship, they could be declared as capable of tending to their own business. However, even royal intervention did not provide unmarried women with the same legal rights over property and the disposition of real estate as men.

Insanity or a general incapacity to tend to one's own business were valid legal grounds for being put under a new guardianship or for having to remain in legal minority. In view of women's continuous status as a minor, either under the guardianship of their husband or another male relative, this issue mostly affected men. This could pose a problem for women because legal incapacity and gender ideology meant that should a husband become unfit to perform his duties or responsibilities, the wife could not easily step into his shoes. Thus a potential contradiction occurred whereby a woman might have been required to act in the capacity of a guardian for her insane or otherwise incapacitated husband but did not have the legal authority to do so.

## WOMEN'S ECONOMIC RIGHTS AND SOCIAL CHANGE IN SWEDEN

As an institution deeply embedded in the structure of Swedish society, the nature of guardianship was shaped by wider economic, social, and political changes. From a broader perspective it appears to be the case that women's ability to function as independent economic actors was more highly developed in urbanized and economically advanced countries such as Britain and Germany.[16] Unmarried English women could act as *feme sole* traders and thereby had the means to manage their property. However, they did not have direct access to its political, or representational, functions. By contrast, in Sweden, which at this time lagged behind such countries, women's legal rights were far more circumscribed. Under Swedish law unmarried women were formally enclosed in the realm of the family and heavily dependent on the consent and benevolence of others.

These differences can best be understood in the context of experiences of urbanization. The share of the Swedish population that lived in urban areas did not exceed 10 percent until the middle of the nineteenth century.[17] Compared with other parts of central and western Europe, this rural dominance—or urban backwardness—is one of the specific features of the Swedish historical experience. It has been estimated that around

11.9 percent of the European population was urbanized in 1800. The figure for Scandinavian countries, however, was 6.2 percent, whereas 20.8 percent of the population of Britain lived in urban areas, along with 12.9 percent in France and 9.4 percent in Germany.[18]

The early nineteenth century was a period of demographic expansion in Sweden, where slowly accelerating urbanization was accompanied by falling rates of marriage and consequently an increase in the number and share of unmarried persons. This change in marriage rates was most notable among the middle and higher social strata, and, as Table 10.1 shows, it was more of an urban than a rural phenomenon.[19] Obviously, not all women who were unmarried at the age of 15 remained single for the rest of their lives, and the table also reflects a rise in the ages of marriage. Nevertheless, the unmarried women's share of the urban population continued to rise.

The economic and social situation for unmarried women was far more complicated than it was for men. In debates on women's rights and their supposed true nature—on their position in society and the possibilities open to them—the growth in the number of single females was viewed as a major problem.[20] When it comes to the emancipation of adult and unmarried women from their status as minors, the standard explanation is that this demographic expansion, coupled with falling marriage rates, resulted in large numbers of women who were either pauperized or depen-

**Table 10.1**
**Unmarried Women over 15 Years of Age as Percentage of All Women over 15 Years of Age**

|      | Stockholm | Other urban areas | Rural areas |
| ---- | --------- | ----------------- | ----------- |
| 1805 | 46.7      | 41.0              | 34.8        |
| 1810 | 47.2      | 42.6              | 35.4        |
| 1815 | 48.8      | 44.1              | 35.6        |
| 1820 | 49.4      | 44.4              | 35.4        |
| 1825 | 50.0      | 44.1              | 33.1        |
| 1830 | 51.8      | 46.0              | 33.3        |
| 1835 | 55.7      | 47.1              | 34.5        |
| 1840 | 57.4      | 49.4              | 37.3        |
| 1845 | 57.5      | 50.2              | 38.2        |
| 1850 | 57.4      | 50.7              | 38.8        |
| 1855 | 57.3      | 50.9              | 38.6        |

Source: Figures taken from Sten Carlsson, *Fröknar, mamseller, jungfrur och pigor: Ogifta kvinnor i det svenska ståndssamhället* (Uppsala: Studia historica Upsaliensia 90, 1977) 27, Table 6.

dent on relatives. The strict regulations over business and trade that were part of the guild system and the mercantilist economic policies that had dominated Sweden since the eighteenth century also restricted women's economic activity. Moreover, it has been argued that the falling rate of marriage was most prominent among the small but influential middle classes and the nobility and that this promoted and shaped political solutions to the "woman problem."[21] Shocking pictures of formerly respectable unmarried bourgeois women, or even the nobility, living in dire poverty and, in the worst cases, driven into prostitution, were painted in the public discourse. To cope with this problem, it was argued that more trades and professions should be opened to unmarried women, an argument that, because of the relatively diverse nature of urban economies, was more easily applicable to towns and cities than it was to rural places.[22] In particular, it was felt that shopkeeping and the running of small businesses ought to be open to these women, just as these activities were becoming increasingly open to the emerging white-collar sector. It is true that at a local level adjustments to and exemptions from some of the regulations that prevented women from engaging in economic activity can be found. However, overall their ability to participate in business and other forms of moneymaking was still severely limited.

Minors and guardians could, of course, be found all over the country, in rural areas as well as towns and cities. However, in view of the disproportionate share of women in urban areas, it was in towns and cities that the problems concerning guardianship were most acute. It is also clear that insofar as there were specific urban economies and social landscapes, Swedish towns and cities were also characterized by a particular gender order that, at least to some extent, diverged from that which could be found in surrounding agrarian communities. One example of this was that the law stipulated that for a married couple all their urban property was to be jointly owned, although it could not be disposed of jointly.[23] In rural areas there was a clearer distinction between the rights of ownership accruing to the husband's and wife's respective lineage. It is important to note that it is the location of the property, not the residence of the owner, that is the key distinction here. Similar differences existed with respect to inheritance where the law prescribed equal shares for women and men inheriting property in towns, while the rules for property located in the countryside granted the sons a double share in the estate compared with daughters.[24]

How did the different property regimes that existed in town and country impact on the gendered dimensions of guardianship in an urban community? The gendered urban property regime was a combination of the equal shares of inheritance with unequal rights to disposition. If rights to trade and professions are taken into account as a kind of property, it would also be necessary to consider the fact that generally, only sons and widows could inherit and use these rights in any active sense.[25] As legal and economic minors, daughters might work with their mothers or possibly pass on rights to a husband, but they were seldom capable of using them independently for their own means. The relationship between women and property in Swedish towns is therefore confused. On the one hand, it could be assumed that compared with the countryside a larger share of inherited property was passed on to daughters. On the other hand, following the falling rates of marriages over the first half of the nineteenth century, the demand for guardians would likely have been higher. The outcome of this was that while women in urban areas who inherited property were likely to have become economically independent, they were, because of the later age of marriage and because many of them remained single, equally likely to have been legally dependent on their guardians.

It was not until the 1840s onward, when urban populations began to grow significantly, that reforms were enacted. Driven by the tensions between political liberalism on the one hand and economic contingency on the other, debates centered on the disjuncture between women's economic independence and their legal status as minors. Reforms guaranteeing equal shares of inheritance for women and men were passed in 1845.[26] Some advocates of these reforms argued in explicitly gendered terms that this was a matter of justice between sons and daughters. However, the impact of such legal changes was limited because both unmarried and married women still did not have the right to actively dispose of property. The established explanation for the passing of this law interprets the reform as part of a wider effort to increase the mobility of landed property.[27] More recently, Maria Ågren has argued that the reforms should be analyzed together with the changes in the regulations for bequeathing property that were passed in 1857. Collectively, these brought about an increase in a testator's right to freely dispose of property.[28] Reforms gave single females outside widowhood the authority to dispose of property rather than the more-or-less passive, or at least dependent, right of ownership.

## AN URBAN CASE STUDY: GÖTEBORG 1777–1802

In Swedish urban society, obtaining civic citizenship was the same as being granted the rights to carry on a specific trade. However, it brought obligations as well as rights, such as the payment of taxes or undertaking the role of guardian. But was guardianship—the responsibility for and managing of the property of minors—an asset or a liability for the guardian? Was a minor's property something from which guardians could profit? To some extent these questions can be answered with reference to the legal requirements surrounding guardianship in an urban context. It is clear that the law forbade a guardian from selling the real estate of minors, except in cases where destitution was feared. However, the sale of moveable property to finance the support of wards was permitted. This was particularly important in towns where arguably such property was of greater significance compared with rural areas. Furthermore, a guardian was not allowed to buy the property of his own ward. Even though he was entitled to a small rate of compensation for his responsibilities—proportionate to the value of the estate—it was never the law's intention to make this a source of profit but merely one of compensation for efforts expended. In practice, however, the formal regulations that governed the conduct of guardians allowed them considerable freedom to act independently. For example, although it was actually stipulated that the guardian was expected to lend money from the estate at interest, it was anticipated that he himself should be considered the first choice as borrower. An understanding of these issues can be gained from the analysis of guardianship arrangements in late eighteenth-century Göteborg.

The city of Göteborg, founded in 1619, was one of many towns established during Sweden's early modern imperial age.[29] During the first part of the seventeenth century its main function was that of a garrison town, but its economy soon came to be dominated by trade and shipping. Such was the town's success that by 1750 it was Sweden's second-largest city, although its population of about 10,000 was dwarfed by Stockholm's, which numbered more than 60,000.[30] In this mercantile economy, not surprisingly, merchants and merchant capital were extremely influential. In the Napoleonic wars at the start of the nineteenth century, Göteborg's importance increased because it remained one of the few open ports in northern Europe. By contrast, the decades after 1814 are commonly pictured as years of stagnation. The demographic expansion was modest but noticeable, and by 1850 the population was at least 26,000.[31] Göteborg's strategic position in matters of trade, both domestic and foreign, meant a considerable flow of capital and goods. The significance of commercial capital combined with years of economic turbulence—as shown in the increased frequency of bankruptcies—provides an interesting backdrop for the study of guardianship, as these processes transformed property relations and continuously opened up and closed off different opportunities for investment and wealth accumulation.

In Göteborg the special register of guardianships established in court provides a brief quantitative picture of the scope of guardianship arrangements. In the years between 1777 and 1802, 769 new guardianships were established. The court also appointed *gode män*—"good men" (a more limited form of guardianship) in an additional 179 cases. This type of guardianship was usually economic in scope and was often of a more temporary character. Good men could, for example, be appointed in cases of bankruptcy or in cases of the division of an inheritance while one of the parents remained the guardian over the ward. All in all, this means that there were 948 appointments. Often these appointments related to more than one ward, as a single guardian was frequently chosen to look after the affairs of a group of siblings. Over time, the same person could be appointed to more than one guardianship, so the numbers of appointments inevitably exceeds the number of guardians.

What was the balance between males and females among the wards? Unfortunately, in 203 cases there is no record of either the number or the sex of the wards. This leaves us with 745 cases comprising 1,134 minors where the distribution between the sexes can be analyzed. Not surprisingly, given the gendered definitions of minority status, there was a preponderance of females among the wards: 702 (or 62 percent) were female, and 432 (or 38 percent) were male. If we distinguish between the appointment of guardians and good men, the gender difference becomes slightly more accentuated. In terms of guardianship, 65 percent of the persons allocated a guardian were female, leaving 35 percent male. Among those for whom a good man was appointed, 47 percent were female and 53 percent were male.

Court rolls provide a much more detailed picture of guardianship, particularly in relation to the key actors involved and their occupational background. While it might be imagined that the sources pose interesting questions about the agency of the unmarried women and widows involved, an analysis of all cases between 1776 and 1782 indicates that for the most part they were predominantly concerned with relations between men. Over this period, all the guardians that were appointed were men. This means that even though widows had a conditional, but legal, right to be guardians over their own children, they were never formally appointed by the court. The professional or occupational title of the guardian was given in the register, and these titles have been grouped into nine categories, as shown in Table 10.2. The categories reflect both social stratification at the time and the economic sectors to which the various professions belonged. The court demanded that the guardian be a citizen of Göteborg and a propertied individual. Even though these criteria were not officially a feature of the law, failure to fulfill these two characteristics was used as grounds to reject proposed guardians. Moreover, changes in either one of them might lead to a termination of the guardianship.

One of the questions that this evidence raises is the extent to which guardian relations were hierarchical or horizontal in character. Of course, the relation between the guardian and his ward might be assumed to be hierarchical by definition, but there is range of different possible kinds of relationships between guardians and minors. This could include a situation where full paternal authority over and responsibility for orphaned children is assumed or instances where a guardianship was little more than a legal formality—a deal struck between a woman and a male relative or friend.

In terms of understanding the social functions of guardianship, it is

Table 10.2
Guardians by Occupation, Göteborg, 1777–1802

|  | Number | Per cent |
| --- | --- | --- |
| Industrialists | 14 | 1.7 |
| Civil servants (judicial) | 51 | 6.1 |
| Merchants | 204 | 24.3 |
| Clerics | 17 | 2.0 |
| Civil servants (clerks) | 88 | 10.5 |
| Shopkeepers | 59 | 7.0 |
| Artisans | 332 | 39.5 |
| Skilled workers | 38 | 4.5 |
| Laborers | 38 | 4.5 |
| Total | 841 | 100.0 |

Source: GLA: Göteborgs Rådhusrätt och Magistrat intill 1900, Liggare över för-mynderskapsmål, 1777–1802 Dlll 1

useful to consider the professional status of the ward's deceased parent or the previous guardian and compare it with that of the newly appointed guardian. This can serve as a proxy for understanding the relations between households. Unfortunately, the sources are much more incomplete when it comes to this matter. Information on the profession of the previous guardian (usually the natural father of the ward) is given in only 41 per-cent of the cases.[32] It is likely that Table 10.3 mostly includes guardianships over children, as opposed to adults, although this would need to be verified via the court rolls. In this table the first two columns show the distribution of professional titles among the previous guardians, and the last two columns show the number of cases where the previous and newly appointed guardian belonged to the same occupational group.

The figures in Tables 10.2 and 10.3 illustrate several points. Merchant households were more common as a source of guardians than they were as the origin of wards. At the other end of the social scale, households headed by laborers provided more minors than guardians. These trends are to be expected as it would have been surprising if the practice of guardianship did not reflect the prevailing social hierarchy. Table 10.3 also suggests that it was among artisans and the merchants that guardians and minors were likely to come from the same professional background. As these two occupational groups were well defined—socially, politically, and economically—and were trades with considerable heritable potential, this should not come as a surprise. The point here is that guardianship was clearly rooted in the networks of social relations that formed this

Table 10.3
Occupations of Previous and New Guardians, Göteborg, 1777–1802

| | Occupation of previous parent/guardian | % of total guardians | Occupation of new guardian | % of new guardians with same occupation as previous parent/guardian |
|---|---|---|---|---|
| Industrialists | 9 | 2.7 | 3 | 33.3 |
| Civil servants (judicial) | 9 | 2.7 | 3 | 33.3 |
| Merchants | 43 | 13.1 | 30 | 69.8 |
| Clerics | 9 | 2.7 | 2 | 22.2 |
| Civil servants (clerks) | 29 | 8.8 | 5 | 17.2 |
| Shopkeepers | 38 | 11.6 | 12 | 31.6 |
| Artisans | 118 | 36.0 | 78 | 66.1 |
| Skilled workers | 33 | 10.1 | 8 | 24.2 |
| Laborers | 40 | 12.2 | 13 | 32.5 |
| Totals | 32 | 100 | 154 | 47.0 |

Source: GLA: Göteborgs Rådhusrätt och Magistrat intill 1900, Liggare över förmynderskapsmål, 1777–1802 DIII 1

urban community and, consequently, was a part of locally embedded property relations.

These points have several implications. At least at the start of the period in question, it seems to have been common practice in Göteborg for guardians to transform money inherited by minors into a mortgage for their own house. This is one reason that a potential guardian's status as a house owner seems to have been valuable information in the court cases, even though the law did not, as such, demand proprietorship. The mortgage was often established in court, sometimes specified and confirmed at the same time as the guardian was appointed. It is therefore likely that the suspension of guardianship could create severe problems for a financially stretched guardian whose house was underwritten by guardianship capital. Yet in a period when banking institutions and financial products remained limited and rudimentary, capital was frequently raised through such personal relationships. An example of this can be found in 1782, when two men—both artisans and citizens of the town—were engaged in a dispute over the guardianship of a girl, Johanna Westerlund, and her inherited money. Master Johan Schliebe, who lived with Johanna as her stepfather, demanded that the court transfer the guardianship from Master Olof Kruse to himself, a demand that Kruse resisted. There is no suggestion in the sources that the dispute hinged upon Schliebe's fitness as a guardian. Rather, it seems as if it was the court's demand on Kruse to repay the entire amount of Johanna's inheritance that constituted the problem.[33]

There were clear differences in the economic meaning of a guardianship in relation to the value and nature of the inheritance to be held in trust. Examples can be found of women who themselves applied to have a guardian appointed in order to get hold of relatively small sums of money they had inherited. There are also examples of men who were nominated as guardians but who made strong efforts to avoid the commitment, presumably because the sums involved were so trifling compared with the duties the role entailed. Because guardianship was viewed as a civic duty, even if it was also recognized to be a burdensome liability, the court sometimes used its power to force these men to assume the position, whether they were related to the minor or not.

## REFORMING THE LAW OF GUARDIANSHIP: A DISEMBEDDING PROCESS?

By the mid-nineteenth century, however, these institutional arrangements were under pressure from several quarters. Driven by the liberal discourse of possessive individualism, there was an ongoing political debate on these matters in the Swedish parliament (the *riksdag*), where the individual interests of minors and guardians were viewed in opposition to each other. In particular, the individual interests and capacities of un-married women stimulated debate and eventually became the main focus of reform.

In debating the issue of guardianship, two lines of argument can be distinguished, promoting different, but not altogether antagonistic, inter-ests. On the one hand, there was a widely held view that the security and legal rights of minors and their inheritance had to be reinforced. Propo-nents of this view argued that the ruthlessness and selfishness of some guardians meant that the institution of guardianship, designed to ensure the welfare of children, all-too-often failed to protect their interests. There-fore, the regulation of guardians was not just viewed as a key element in promoting the security of property transmission over generations but was also regarded as a matter of honor and responsibility. Reformers argued that new and extended powers of surveillance by public institutions were required to ensure that guardianship continued to function in the interests of the child. A second viewpoint claimed that the responsibilities of guard-ianship were designed in a way that actually violated guardians' economic freedom. More discretionary rights for the guardians were therefore needed. Once again, it was envisaged that this situation could be remedied through institutional regulation, separating the economic and the welfare aspects of guardianship.

Debates on the reform of guardianship point toward a process that can be interpreted in terms of Karl Polanyi's notion of disembedding.[34] Po-lanyi's claim was that in most known human societies, exchange and eco-nomic relations have been highly embedded in different types of social relations. However, during the liberal economic wave that accompanied industrialization of the western world, there emerged powerful forces that sought to disembed market transactions from the grip of social relations.[35] Guardianship is a good example of such a set of highly embedded prop-erty relations, where gendered hierarchies, familial responsibilities, and lineage interests created an institutional web restraining both minors and guardians. In the course of reform, the traditional rights and duties of a guardian were reshaped according to the process of disembedding out-lined earlier. Significantly, so too was the dependent position of women. The growing tendency of women to petition the monarchy for exemption from minority status is a clear example of their attempts to refashion gen-der roles.

### Applications to the King

One way that women could gain majority status was to apply for royal permission. At least since the early eighteenth century, unmarried women and underage men had been able to apply to the king for a *myndighets-förklaring*, a "declaration of majority."[36] It is important to note, however, that women who attained majority in this manner were still more restricted in their economic capacities than men or widows. But the declaration could enhance the possibilities of living by themselves and working independently. This procedure of applying to the king required applicants to make a case as to why they should be given a declaration of majority. Approval was also needed from the guardians and, preferably, the parish priest and the local court.[37]

In most cases applicants seem to have been driven by economic motives, that is, a declaration of majority was needed for economic reasons, even though we can assume that some women wanted to attain majority status for personal satisfaction and a sense of independence. In truth, little research has examined applications in detail. However, it is possible to identify three major reasons why minors applied to the king. First, majority was frequently sought in order to escape from, or to avoid the establishment of, a guardianship over an inherited estate. This was something that might be desired by young male heirs as well as young and unmarried female descendants. In families where the preservation of lineage or patrimony was of less concern, unmarried women with a claim on family property may have been keen to run their own lives and relieve their male relatives from the duties of guardianship. Second, in a number of cases, the applications were made by women who were in business and who wanted to be accepted as independent economic actors in all relevant matters. Third, applications came from women who were without inherited property and who simply wanted to avoid domestic service and the legal demand that they should be employed and become a part of someone else's household. Figure 10.1 shows a clear increase in the number of applications to the king over the period between 1750 and 1850. Between these dates the population of Sweden doubled whereas the number of applications grew eightfold. As a result it can be argued that the growth in applications reflects the increasing importance of these different reasons for seeking majority status.

It is apparent from sporadic cases in the historical literature, as well as from the names that appear in the actual records, that the nobility—both males and females—dominate applications in the eighteenth century. The likely motivation here is the first reason identified earlier: the desire to gain access to inherited estate and to release guardians from the responsibilities of their role. In the nineteenth century, the evidence suggests that the nobility became less important compared with growing numbers of peasants and women from the lower and middling strata of urban areas who made applications.[38] Significantly, no men can be found in any of the chosen years after 1810. These applications are certainly not to be seen as *the* reason why pressure for the reform of guardianship emerged. Collectively the applicants were small in number, yet they did challenge the prevailing legal system. Moreover, the relative growth in numbers and

**Figure 10.1**
**Number of Majority Applications to the King, 1750–1850 (selected years)**

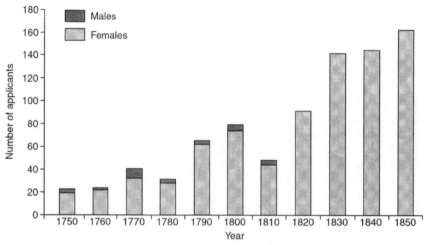

the apparent shift in the social and gender backgrounds of applicants suggest some pressure for change from below. If this assumption is correct, then the second and third reasons for women applying to the king for majority status—in order to escape from the constraints of guardianship and secure economic independence—must have been growing in importance.

### Gender, Economic Change, and the Reform of Guardianship

Debates in the *riksdag* concerning reform of the guardianship regulations reflected several important issues in nineteenth-century Swedish society.[39] Discussion here focuses on three key themes within this debate: the position of minors, the rights and duties of guardians, and the way in which such responsibilities conflicted with changing notions of individual agency.

Debate on women's minority status within guardianship hinged on the issue of whether they could be deemed economically and legally competent. Several contributors argued that since unmarried women were competent to run their own lives, so too should they be able to conduct businesses. By contrast, the majority held the view that this would be unacceptable. Women's legal status was also an issue discussed by the Swedish Juridical Association (Svenska Juridiska Föreningen) at its annual meeting in 1850. Here, the status of spinsters in relation to civil law was the main focus of discussion. As in the *riksdag*, there were those in favor of a general declaration of majority status for unmarried women. Opponents, however, argued that such a move would contradict both the Bible and the basic principles of nature. They believed that it would not be in the interest of women, suggesting that to remove them from the comfortable position of dependency would harm their well-being. Giving women the capacity to act as independent economic agents would force them to give up their true female nature and, it was argued, would consequently encourage sharper falls in the marriage rate.[40] Other contributors to the debate occupied a third position. They accepted the principle that unmarried women should be granted majority status but argued that in the real world these women were raised for domestic life, had an inferior education, and could therefore become easy prey for ruthless men.[41] There was also a discussion about the fact that in some instances women could attain majority at an earlier age than men, namely through widowhood, an anomalous position that some perceived as unjust.[42]

The lengthy debates by male representatives concerning a woman's place roughly mirrored party political distinctions between liberal and conservative members of parliament. But the disagreements were not always over the place of women; their domesticity, emotional superiority, and greater delicacy were widely held ideals that transcended party differences. It was the means by which such a gender order might be realized that was the line of demarcation. The conservative argument promoted the rationality of old, well-defined, and gender-specific rules. The liberal standpoint suggested that a sound gender order would emerge even if the legal framework lost parts of its rigidity.

Discussion about guardianship did not simply revolve around the status and position of women as minors. Indeed, the rights and duties of guardians were also frequent topics of discussion, as was the question of whether the guardian's first priority and obligation was to preserve or enhance the property of his wards. Various recommendations for reform were made in relation to these separate issues, only some of which are relevant to the discussion here. One key issue that emerged during the debates was the feeling that for guardians themselves, the obligations were too many and too restrictive, particularly in relation to their right to alienate a minor's property. In a way, it was argued that guardians, just like minors, faced a restrictive form of dependency that hampered their ability to operate as economic agents. Parliamentary reformers were certainly not arguing that guardians should have the right to abuse and dissipate the inheritance of innocent orphans; rather, they expressed disquiet about the way that the institutional arrangements confused the social, financial, and civic responsibilities incumbent on guardianship.

The key to understanding this line of discussion rests on the disposition of property as a defining characteristic of political citizenship. The concerns discussed earlier need to be understood in the context of an emergent bourgeois society in which to become a citizen was, in liberal discourse, to be able to function as an independent economic and political agent—preferably with as few restrictions as possible on the freedom to act. The establishment of individual rights to, and management over, property was an integral part of this process, albeit one that was confined primarily to men.[43] The established institution of guardianship was part of an older, household-based social order in which patriarchal authority entailed parallel patriarchal responsibilities.[44] However, in the liberal discourse of political citizenship, some of these responsibilities were increasingly at odds with the desire to manage or dispose of property without restriction.

Changes in the form of capital and nature of market relations arising from the increasingly impersonal character of economic life in nineteenth-century Sweden were also important factors in understanding pressures to reform the law of guardianship. For example, the older regulations concerning guardianship afforded inherited capital special protection in the case of a guardian's bankruptcy or indebtedness.[45] If a guardian went bankrupt, the capital of his wards was the first to be distrained. Banks or other lenders had no choice but to wait in line. Understandably, it was the banks that were most concerned by this issue, and the rights of creditors to capital held through guardianship was a focus of continuous debate from the 1820s to the 1850s.[46] In terms of neo-institutional theory, this concern might be understood as a matter of transaction costs.[47] The share of more impersonal market transactions—exchange that was not rooted in a local and firmly socially embedded context—was growing over this period. This created new or increased costs for information when actors undertook transactions and called for new forms of institutional arrangements to minimize these costs. For banks no less than for guardians, the existing rules imposed unacceptable costs on market transactions.

### The Reform of Guardianship

Debate and discussion of the law of guardianship eventually led to reform. Changes took place, both in respect of the legal regulation of the activities of guardians and in relation to gender and the institution of guardianship itself. With regard to the former, legislation passed in 1861 recast the rights of guardians, although the practical impact of this change is open to question. The status of minority also changed, and in 1884 the twenty-first birthday became the common age limit for attaining majority for unmarried women and men. By establishing a general limit for female majority, unmarried women also gained the franchise for local elections, albeit based on property holding. Marriage continued to imply a kind of minority for women up to 1921, at which time universal suffrage was introduced in Sweden. Citizenship and the rights to dispose of property went hand in hand.[48]

Furthermore, in the 1920s new legislation concerning guardianship—

now considered as a legal issue pertaining to parenthood rather than inheritance—removed gendered restrictions on who could act as a guardian. Restrictions were also removed with respect to the appointments of an *överförmyndare*—the chief guardian of a district. However, it was not until 1949 that married parents were formally put on an equal footing as guardians of their children. This legal time lag was the result of the continuation of specific gendered rules concerning the disposition of property. Only in 1949 was the special authority and responsibility of married men in relation to family property removed. It is therefore something of a paradox that although the institution of marriage allowed women—as mothers and widows—to assume the position of guardian in the eighteenth and nineteenth centuries, it also became a key reason for continuing female subordination in respect to guardianship in the twentieth century. While women were gaining access to a range of civic duties elsewhere in the public sphere, marriage continued to restrict their capacity as guardians.

## CONCLUSION

In understanding the relationships among gender, family, and property ownership, the institutional arrangements of guardianship were simultaneously a bearer of symbolic meaning and a framework for everyday human interaction. Within the *riksdag*, groups of reformers, chiefly belonging to burghers, peasants, and the nobility, regarded the social embeddedness of guardianship—its entanglement with the social structures of gender, family, and community—to be a problem and a liability. This embeddedness was cast as an obstacle to the free agency of individuals in what was thought of as an era of growing political and economic individualism. Indeed, the resulting reforms were part of a raft of legislation in the middle of the nineteenth century that transformed Swedish economy and society. Yet this was not the only impulse for reform, and there were always voices whose view of the world was different and who argued that the law of guardianship should focus more on protecting the interests of minors and on preserving traditional family structures. It was, of course, at the local level where these tensions in the law of guardianship were played out. Here reality met rhetoric in the everyday activity of making a living.

The most important changes that the institution of guardianship underwent—from the medieval and early modern legislation up to the twentieth century—were of two different but interrelated kinds. First, there was a relative disembedding of property relations from familial obligations. Second, there was a redefinition of the positions of minor and guardian within the institutional structure. Most significantly for this chapter, there was an "ungendering" of both minority and guardianship. Women were increasingly recognized as having the capacity for independent economic agency. Through this a situation developed where an increasing share of the population reached the status of functional—legal, economic, and eventually political—majority. At the same time the patriarchal responsibilities and powers of men were reduced. In short, the reform of the law of guardianship was part of a redefining of the Swedish gender order. It was also part of a shift in the focus and provision of family welfare that, over the course of the twentieth century, became increasingly regulated by public institutions.

## NOTES

This chapter draws upon work for a doctoral thesis investigating the shaping, extent, and functioning of the institution of guardianship in Sweden, c. 1770–1863. The research is being undertaken in the Department of Economic History at Göteborg University, Sweden.

1. Debates over women's rights to engage in trade and commerce were the subject of Gunnar Qvist, *Kvinnofrågan i Sverige 1809–1846: Studier rörande kvinnans näringsfrihet i de borgerliga yrkena* (Göteborg: Scandinavian University Books, 1960). The guild system was abolished in 1846 and the freedom of trade finally established in 1864. However "old" the guild system might have been, its importance peaked in Sweden during the eighteenth and early nineteenth centuries.

2. The relationship between early modern Swedish guilds and gender is explored by Martin Wottle, "Det lilla ägandet: korporativ formering och sociala relationer inom Stockholms minuthandel 1720–1810," (Ph.D. diss., Stads-och kommunhistoriska institutet, Stockholm, 1997).

3. For the period in question, inheritance was regulated by the legal code of 1734 (1734 års lag, Ärvdabalken). This code was part of a set of statutes that provided the Swedish realm with a coherent body of laws. In reality, many of the laws set down at this time were subject to frequent amendment. Changes were especially common in the fields of commerce and industry; see Martin Melkersson, *Staten, ordningen och friheten: en studie av den styrande elitens syn på statens roll mellan stormaktstiden och 1800-talet* (Uppsala: Studia Historica Upsaliensia, 1997). Differences between town and country relating to civil and commercial laws continued into the nineteenth century.

4. See, for example, Sandra Cavallo and Lyndan Warner, eds., *Widowhood in Medieval and Early Modern Europe,* (Harlow: Pearson, 1999); Lourens van den Bosch and Jan Bremmer, eds., *Between Poverty and the Pyre: Moments in the History of Widowhood* (London: Routledge, 1995).

5. A discussion of the reform of Swedish marriage law can be found in the chapter in this volume by Kirsti Niskanen.

6. Douglass C. North, *Institutions, Institutional Change and Economic Performance* (Cambridge: Cambridge University Press, 1990).

7. For a brief discussion of this see Douglass C. North, "Markets and Other Allocation Systems in History: The Challenge of Karl Polanyi," *Journal of European Economic History* 6 (1977): 703–16 and Bo Gustafsson, "Some Theoretical Problems for Institutional Economic History," *Scandinavian Economic History Review* XLVI (1998): 5–31.

8. Ann Ighe and Linda Lane, "Institutionell stabilitet: Om svårigheten i att omförhandla ett genuskontrakt," in *Kvinnovetenskapens vadan och varthän*, ed. Eva Borgström and Anna Nordenstam (Göteborg: Göteborg University, 1996), 108–19.

9. Joan Scott examines the way that gender operates at different analytical levels; see Joan Scott, *Gender and the Politics of History* (New York: Columbia University Press, 1988).

10. Ulla Wikander, *Delat arbete, delad makt: om kvinnors underordning i och genom arbete* (Uppsala: Uppsala Papers in Economic History 28, 1991).

11. A *ward* is another term for a minor.

12. Giulia Calvi, "Widows, the State and the Guardianship of Children in Early Modern Tuscany," in Cavallo and Warner, *Widowhood in Medieval and Early Modern Europe*, 212–13.

13. Förmyndareordningen was the first act to treat guardianship as a specific matter. It is a comparatively lengthy document that retained its status as a subsidiary legal source after the new code of 1734.

14. Svensk Författningssamling (The compilation of Swedish Laws) no. 9, 1845.

15. The legal competence of married women has been extensively discussed. For the Swedish case see Gudrun Andersson Lennström, "Makt och myndighet. Kring 1686 års lagkommission och kvinnans vardagsmakt," in *Sprickor i muren. Funktion och dysfunktion i det stormaktstida rättssystemet*, ed. Gudrun Andersson Lennström and Marie Lennersand (Uppsala: Opuscula Historica Upsaliensa 14, 1994), 3–87; Gudrun Andersson, "Tingets kvinnor och män: Genus som norm och strategi under 1600-och 1700-tal," (Ph.D. diss., Uppsala University, 1998); and Åsa Karlsson Sjögren, "Kvinnors rätt i stormaktstidens Gävle," (Ph.D. diss., Umeå University, 1998).

16. Ursula Vogel, "Property Rights and the Status of Women in Germany and England," in *Bourgeois Society in Nineteenth-Century Europe*, ed. Jurgen Kocka and Alan Mitchell (Oxford: Berg, 1993), 241–69.

17. Lars Nilsson, *Den urbana transitionen: Tätorterna i svensk samhällsomvandling 1800–1980* (Stockholm: Stadshistoriska institutet, 1989).

18. Figures are taken from Paul Bairoch, Jean Batou, and Pierre Chèvre, *La population des villes européennes de 800 à 1850* (Genève: Publications du Centre d'histoire économique internationale de l'Université de Genève, 1988). The Scandinavian countries are treated as a group here, but it should be noted that the proportion of the population that was urban was higher in Denmark and Norway than in Sweden.

19. Sten Carlsson, *Fröknar, mamseller, jungfrur och pigor: Ogifta kvinnor i det svenska ståndssamhället* (Uppsala: Studia Historica Upsaliensia 90, 1977) and Qvist, *Kvinnofrågan i Sverige*.

20. This concern was expressed in other parts of Europe. See, for example, David R. Green, "Independent Women, Wealth and Wills in Nineteenth-Century London," in *Urban Fortunes: Property and Inheritance in the Town, 1700–1900*, ed. Jon Stobart and Alastair Owens (Aldershot: Ashgate, 2000), 195–222.

21. Qvist, *Kvinnofrågan i Sverige*.

22. Qvist, *Kvinnofrågan i Sverige*.

23. Karlsson Sjögren, "Kvinnors rätt i stormaktstidens Gävle" and Maria Sjöberg, "Kvinnans sociala underordning—en problematisk historia: Om makt, arv och giftermål i det äldre svenska samhället," *Scandia* 63 (1997): 165–90.

24. This gendered difference also applies when the older generation inherited from the younger one, such as when parents inherited from their children. As an estate of the realm, the clergy were excluded from this and granted the privilege of dividing their estate equally.

25. On the meanings and definitions of property among the urban petite bourgeoisie, especially in the nineteenth century, see Geoffrey Crossick, "Meanings of Property and the World of the Petite Bourgeoisie," in Stobart and Owens, *Urban Fortunes*, 50–78.

26. Previous legislation regarding rural areas guaranteed women one-third and men two-thirds of inherited property.

27. Qvist, *Kvinnofrågan i Sverige*.

28. Maria Ågren, "Fadern, systern och brodern: Maktförskjutningar genom 1800-talets egendomsreformer," *Historisk tidskrift* 4 (1999): 683–708.

29. Bertil Andersson, *Från fästningsstad till handelsstad 1619–1820* (Göteborg: Nerenius and Santérus, 1996).

30. Andersson, *Från fästningsstad*, 126; Johan Söderberg, Ulf Jonsson, and Christer Persson, *A Stagnating Metropolis: The Economy and Demography of Stockholm 1750–1850* (Cambridge: Cambridge University Press, 1991).

31. This figure does not include Majorna, an important suburban area, which was incorporated later. See Martin Fritz, *Från handelsstad till industristad 1820–1920* (Göteborg: Nerenius and Santérus, 1996), 24.

32. Lack of information on the previous guardian is most frequent when the minor is an adult.

33. GLA: Göteborgs Rådhusrätt och Magistrat intill 1900, Liggare över förmynderskapsmål, 1777–1802, DIII 1, mål 820918, 40.

34. Karl Polanyi, *The Great Transformation* (Boston: Beacon Press, 1957).

35. This might seem to be a linear view of history. However, Polanyi went on to interpret the emergence of welfare states as a kind of "re-embedding" process.

36. The king was required to countersign and approve the rulings in such cases. In reality this was done by the *justitierevisionen*, a division of the Supreme Court.

37. It has been argued that this procedure provided women of the upper strata of Swedish society with an advantage. See Qvist, *Kvinnofrågan i Sverige*.

38. Patronymic surnames were still the most common among the rural population whereas family names were more common among the urban population. Noble family names are quite easily distinguished.

39. The Parliament of Estates was an institution stemming from the early seventeenth century where "the four estates of the realm"—the nobility, clerics, burghers, and peasants—were represented (though by no means proportionally to their share of the population). This was the principle for representation up to 1866.

40. The debates, with summaries and reservations, were published in the first issue of the *Journal of the Swedish Juridical Association: Juridiska föreningens tidskrift* (Stockholm: Första häftet, 1850).

41. See the commentary from the parliament's legal committee (*lagutskottet*) on the proposal made to grant spinsters majority status from the age of 25. Sveriges Rikes Ständers Protokoll, Bihang 1844–45, Saml 7:1, no. 10, 4.

42. See Sveriges Rikes Ständers Protokoll, Borgareståndets protocoller 1809, Band II, 1101f, where it was argued that widows under 21 should be considered

as minors. These discussions suggest a shift from the primacy of civil status (and hence gender) toward age as qualification for rights and duties.

43. See the discussions on gender, citizenship, and individualism in Joan Scott, *Only Paradoxes to Offer: French Feminists and the Rights of Man* (Cambridge, Mass.: Harvard University Press, 1996). See also the chapter by Kirsti Niskanen that appears elsewhere in this volume.

44. For a discussion of the transformation of nineteenth-century Swedish society from a household- to a market-based economic system and its relationship to gender, see, for example, Anita Göransson, "Kön som analyskategori i den ekonomiska historien: Några linjer och resultat," in Borgström and Nordenstam, *Kvinnovetenskapens vadan och varthän*, 49–65 and Anita Göransson, "Mening, makt och materialitet: Ett försök att förena realistiska och poststrukturalistiska positioner," *Häften för Kristiska Studier* 4 (1998): 3–26.

45. 1734 års lag, Handelsbalken, cap 17, § 8.

46. See the statements made by the *riksdag's* committee on banking (Banco-Utskottet), Sveriges Rikes Ständers Protokoll, Bihang, Saml. 6, no. 40, 677–85.

47. North, *Institutions.*

48. See the chapter by Kirsti Niskanen elsewhere in this volume.

# CHAPTER 11

# Marriage and Economic Rights: Women, Men, and Property in Sweden during the First Half of the Twentieth Century

*Kirsti Niskanen*

## INTRODUCTION: WOMEN'S ECONOMIC RIGHTS

In most western societies, struggles over married women's property rights have constituted an important component in the long social process whereby women have gradually come to obtain economic equality with men. In Sweden, in relation to their economic status, married women formally gained equality with men under the Marriage Act of 1921. This act abolished male guardianship and provided all women with the right to manage and control their own property.[1] Drawing upon the concept of "economic citizenship," the aim of this chapter is to discuss the development of Swedish women's economic rights within the context of marriage. In doing so this research incorporates Alice Kessler-Harris's work on economic citizenship, defined here as a right to participate in the economic life of a society.[2] The chapter will discuss the various ways in which women's economic citizenship was defined during the first part of the twentieth century, taking as a starting point the formulation of the Marriage Act of 1921.

Scholars who have used the concept of economic citizenship have usually focused on economic inequalities between men and women in the labor market.[3] In this chapter the idea is widened so that it also embraces other economically significant civil rights; above all, the right to own and manage property. There is a consensus among contemporary economic historians that legislation regarding labor, property, and contracts defines the limits of participation in the market economy.[4] Female involvement in the labor market has accordingly been a central focus of researchers concerned with the changing fortunes of women in twentieth-century Swedish life. However, in spite of the fact that the study of property rights has long had a prominent place in economic history, historians have seldom addressed the issue of how the gendered construction of property rights constrained women's opportunities to participate in the capitalist market economy as independent agents. Until 1921, married women had few property rights as their husbands legally assumed control over family assets and economic decision making. The new Marriage Act aimed to abolish male economic domination in the family.

The main purpose of this chapter is to examine the extent to which the Marriage Act really did contribute to the creation of economic equality between married women and men in Sweden during the first part of the twentieth century. Rather than focus on the legislation as such, it will concentrate on the social relations of property, the way that divisions of property at divorce reflected prevailing gender understandings, and notions of economic agency in specific, historical situations. In line with other chapters in the book, the main focus is on property relations within the context of marriage and the family.

Because economic relations and power structures in families are frequently considered to be private affairs, they have often been hidden in the historical evidence and therefore concealed from historians. However, by studying divorce proceedings, where private affairs are inevitably made public, it is possible to gain insights into property relations within a marital and familial context. The dissolution of a marriage usually led to the parallel dissolution of jointly held property. Upon divorce, goods would be distributed between the two parties and in order to accomplish this, an estate inventory was made. These inventories provide a detailed glimpse of property ownership within marriage. In the judicial proceedings accompanying the separation, the social relations relating to this property are also revealed, and in the court reports they are handed down to posterity.

This chapter consists of three sections. It begins by discussing the relationships between citizenship and economic citizenship and examines the Marriage Act of 1921 in the context of family legislation and the complex transitional rules that diluted the practical effects of the new law in its early phases of implementation. This section concludes with a discussion of the source material and some methodological considerations. The second part of the chapter examines divorce patterns in two administrative districts of Sweden between 1920 and 1950. After surveying the general trends, it analyzes in detail the division of property in middle-class marriages, exploring how this impacted women's economic citizenship. The final section illustrates the main arguments through a specific case study relating to the divorce proceeding of Lars and Ellinor Eriksson, who separated in the 1940s, which is used to tell a particular story about economic citizenship.[5] Their case demonstrates how the regulations of the new Marriage Act were interpreted through discourses of male bread-winning and male rights to marital property. This points to the continuing durability of traditional gender ideologies and experiences in shaping women's economic citizenship in early twentieth-century Sweden.

## CITIZENSHIP, THE LAW, AND MARRIED WOMEN'S ECONOMIC RIGHTS

Sociological understanding of the concept of citizenship owes a good deal to Thomas H. Marshall's famous lectures on the subject delivered at Cambridge in 1949.[6] Marshall's tripartite model of civil, political, and so-cial citizenship contains several elements that deal with basic economic rights. Civil citizenship, in terms of personal freedom, incorporates, among other things, the right to own property, enter contracts, work, and carry on business. Social citizenship, on the other hand, includes the right to education as well as other elements bound up with the formulation of social and tax legislation. Finally, political citizenship encompasses the exercise of political power in a society, including, for example, the right to vote. Using class as an analytical variable, Marshall described the de-velopment of the different elements of citizenship as an evolutionary so-cial process. He believed there was a connection between the leveling out of class distinctions and the way that citizenship had developed in western society from the eighteenth to the twentieth centuries. Eighteenth-century rights of citizenship, such as personal freedom, were a require-ment for the growth of political citizenship and materialized into rights of franchise during the nineteenth and early twentieth century. Access to social citizenship in the modern welfare state (in the form, for example, of social insurance) required, in its turn, that political citizenship be brought into being. Full citizenship in the postwar welfare state was thus a product of the emergence of all three types of citizenship over the pre-vious three centuries.

Marshall expressed himself mainly in gender-neutral terms. Typically for the period, and not at all surprisingly, his notion of citizenship was based on the male experience.[7] However, if Marshall's model is broken down in terms of gender, these different forms of citizenship can be seen to have developed at different rates and in different ways for men and women. There have been, and still are, great variations in the way women's social and economic rights have developed in different countries, de-pending, for example, on when women obtained the right to vote, how legislation has dealt with property relations in marriage, and the oppor-tunities women have had to participate in the labor market. Anne-Lise Nagel, who has studied the Norwegian situation, shows, for example, that when civil and political citizenship were brought into being at the start of the twentieth century, new social rights were established that had a strong male profile.[8] Similarly, Alice Kessler-Harris has recently used the concept of economic citizenship to analyze how gender-specific access to paid work, and thereby to economic independence, has affected requirements for women's economic and political citizenship in the United States during the twentieth century.[9]

### The Reform of Marriage and Property Law in Sweden

Drawing upon Marshall's model, the reform of the Marriage Act in 1921 can be seen as part of the development of economic citizenship in Sweden. It was one key reform among a broader reshaping of family legislation that took place in the early decades of the twentieth century. The divorce laws had been modernized in 1915 and, in connection with the Marriage Act, a law concerning children in marriage and a new law on the inheritance rights of marriage partners had also been introduced. The modernization of family legislation was the result of a joint Scandinavian legislative effort. Similar reforms were carried out in the other Nordic countries between 1909 and 1929, apart from Finland, where the liberalization of the divorce laws was not achieved until the late 1940s.[10]

By international standards, the Nordic family laws were progressive. Generally speaking, married women in western and central Europe did not achieve economic equality with men until after the Second World War, while the liberalization of the divorce laws was not achieved until the 1970s and 1980s.[11] The fact that as early as the 1920s married women achieved the same formal economic rights as men, and that the divorce law was modernized so that disagreement between the spouses was acknowledged as a valid reason for divorce—irrespective of who bore the fault for the breakup of the marriage—has led a number of Scandinavian researchers to speak of a distinctive Nordic marriage model. Their hypothesis is that the progressive Nordic marriage laws have been an important precursor for the emergence of the universal Nordic welfare state.[12] David Bradley has suggested that the reform of marriage legislation in Scandinavian countries was the result of the influence of a social-democratic political culture that emphasized issues of equality. However, it should be noted, as Bradley himself acknowledges, that the new family legislation in Scandinavia was enacted before the social-democratic parties consolidated their hold on political power.[13] What causal links there might be between these early changes in family law, divorce, and marital property relations, on the one hand, and the wider socioeconomic, political, and demographic changes, on the other, is still an open question. The main issue here is with the more restricted question of the impact of the reforms on gender relations and economic citizenship.

From this standpoint, the reform of the Marriage Act was an explosive business. The new law meant not only the introduction, in a formal sense, of economic equality in marriage, but also a decisive shift in the balance of gender power—the establishment of a new gender order. The unrestricted right of men to exercise power and control within the family was now at an end. According to the new law, married women and men had equal decision-making rights over family finances. They also had a mutual duty to support the family with equal powers over the raising and education of children. Moreover, special regulations on marital rights, discussed later, made spouses responsible to each other for the management of economic resources during marriage.

Modernization of family legislation should be placed in relation to the democratization of society in general.[14] Swedish women acquired the right to vote in 1921. Political democracy and the new marriage laws meant that women now, in most respects, had the same civil rights as men. Even if this formal equality was light years away from actual equality, women's new citizenship status had a transformative impact on marital relationships. Women were able to speak for themselves in a court of law on the same terms as men, and marriage partners could bring legislative actions against each other, pertaining, for example, to conflicts over property or the care of children, or relating to maintenance contributions upon the breakup of marriage. They could also make legal agreements with each other during marriage, something that had not been possible under the old jurisdiction. The changes touched on what was innermost in the nature of marriage and altered the most intimate relations between the sexes.

In Swedish historical research the new Marriage Act has rightfully been seen as a milestone in women's emancipation.[15] What has often been forgotten, however, is that the new law was introduced with one key limitation: it would be valid only for marriages entered into after 1920. For older marriages, transitional rules were created. According to these, male guardianship was generally abolished but was retained in relation to economic rights and powers within the marriage. These transitional rules meant that part of the traditional regime that defined property rights in terms of the older Marriage Act of 1734 survived as an element of Swedish marriage laws up until 1950. It was only at that comparatively late point that the transitional regulations were done away with. The consequence of this was that in relation to economic issues, large groups of married women—as many as 30–40 percent during the interwar period—were treated as minors. The law protected the prevailing system of control over property in existing marriages: the husband had the sole right to administer both his own and the couple's joint property as well as the wife's own separate property. The only exception to this was that separate property that had been acquired by the woman after the start of 1921 was to be administered by the wife personally. Male rights of management were of most practical significance in marriages where there was established property to be looked after, such as among business and farming families.

During the 1920s and 1930s, then, when it came to married women's rights Sweden had two parallel legal systems and ways of regulating property. In terms of political and economic citizenship this was a paradoxical situation. In marriages where the older Marriage Act prevailed, women were political citizens—they could vote—but they did not control or administer their own property. In marriages that had been entered into under the new law, women were, at least on the face of it, political and economic subjects enjoying the same conditions as men. The remainder of this chapter will study Swedish divorce cases to examine in greater detail the nature and extent of women's economic citizenship within this shifting legal context. First, however, it is necessary to consider the sources and methods used in this study.

### Source Material and Some Methodological Considerations

As indicated earlier, this chapter draws upon records of divorce proceedings. The number of divorces in Sweden increased when the new divorce law came into force in 1916, from approximately 1,100 per year in the period from 1916 to 1920, to more than 5,500 per year between 1936 and 1940.[16] Nevertheless, in the 1930s and 1940s such marital separations were still rare, particularly outside large towns. To understand how the division of property took place in connection with divorce, 23 cases involving middle-class families are examined in detail. These form part of a larger selection of judicial separation cases in two administrative county districts in central Sweden: Tiunda Administrative County District in the province of Uppland, and Mora Administrative County District in the province of Dalarna. Tiunda lies just outside the medium-sized city of Uppsala and during this period had a mixed economic structure, with agriculture, trade, and industries. Mora was part of an agricultural and small-business region, known for having a strong, independent peasant culture. The reason for focusing on middle-class marriages is twofold. First, with little property to divide, divorces in working-class marriages were usually routine procedures. Aside from registration of the divorce itself, such proceedings have generated little documentary source material. Second, the aim is to capture bourgeois attitudes to, and understandings of, property and gender in ordinary middle-class peoples' lives.

The use and value of legal documents as source material for historical research is open to discussion. For example, is it possible to draw general conclusions about marriage relations in situations as unique as divorce cases? Several historians have drawn upon divorce documents to study changing marriage relations. Lynn Abrams, for example, has examined marriage separation in Prussia during the early nineteenth century, while

Lawrence Stone and James Hammerton have researched marriage and divorce in early-modern and nineteenth-century England, respectively.[17] These studies reveal that a qualitative investigation of divorce documents gives a picture of the conflicts and tensions characteristic of marriage relations at particular, historically specific moments. Divorce proceedings, as Lynn Abrams suggests, reflect a situation where people were able to articulate their expectations of marital behavior. As a result, they provide a valuable window on the way that marriage relations were broadly constructed and understood by contemporaries. This observation informs the approach adopted in later sections of this chapter. The aim is not to establish the "truth" about the marital relations of the couples that have been researched, or indeed the "truth" about people's marital relations in general. Instead, the focus of the later sections of the chapter is largely at the level of discourse. It is concerned with the speech and rhetoric contained in the reports of court proceedings. In particular, it concentrates on those parts of the proceedings that deal with the relationships between gender, ownership, property, and access to material resources.

The narratives and rhetoric in court proceedings are adapted, with the assistance of the legal representatives of the respective parties, to the provisions of the Marriage Act in terms of the way marriage should work and, in relation to divorce law, with the grounds on which the marriage might be dissolved. Divorce legislation thus formed a platform from which women and men were enabled, during the court proceedings, to express their perceptions of marital problems and ideals. The individual stories that emerge from the court proceedings are therefore seen as fragments from a larger social narrative on gender relations.

## MARRIAGE, DIVORCE, AND WOMEN'S ECONOMIC RIGHTS

Before examining these social narratives in detail, some consideration of the overall patterns of divorce cases in Tiunda and Mora is helpful in establishing some general trends. The cases investigated are divided into two groups: divorces pertaining to older marriages from the time of the old Marriage Act, and those relating to marriages entered into after the reforms in 1921. It was an explicit aim of the new Marriage Act to improve the economic and social situation of married women. Comparison between the two groups of cases, therefore, gives an indication of changed attitudes to the institution of marriage and the conditions for increased equality for married women opened up by the new law.

An initial interesting observation in relation to the divorce patterns concerns the length of marriages, outlined in Table 11.1. The new Marriage Act involved a secularization and individualization of marriage so that it no longer formed a sacrament with a religious basis. Instead it was rec-

Table 11.1
Length of Marriage at the Time of Judicial Separation: Tiunda and Mora
Administrative County Districts, Sweden, 1921–50

| Length of marriage, years | Marriages under the old Marriage Act (until 1920) % | | Marriages under the new Marriage Act (1921–1929)% | |
|---|---|---|---|---|
|  | Tiunda | Mora | Tiunda | Mora |
| < 10 | 18 | 13 | 53 | 24 |
| 10-19 | 44 | 29 | 40 | 52 |
| 20-29 | 30 | 46 | 7 | 24 |
| 30 > | 8 | 13 | 0 | 0 |
| Total (N) | 50 | 24 | 73 | 33 |

Note: N = 180

Source: Judicial Separation Registers, Tiunda Administrative County District and
Mora Administrative County District 1921–50. Uppsala Provincial Record Office.

ognized as a voluntary union between two individuals that could be dissolved.[18] When the phase of the marriage in which the judicial separation
took place is examined, changes in attitudes toward marriage, as well as
regional differences in divorce patterns in the two administrative counties,
can be discerned.[19] After the new Marriage Act, the share of separations
increased in marriages that had lasted for less than 10 years in both regions. In Tiunda the number of judicial separations tripled in this group,
while in the agricultural district of Mora the number doubled. A decrease
in the number of separations is evident in marriages in Tiunda that had
lasted between 10 and 19 years, while separations in long marriages
(longer than 20 years) showed a sharp decrease. Mora administrative
county has a more traditional divorce pattern, with the majority of judicial
separations taking place in relationships lasting longer than 10 years. In
older marriages this was the dominant pattern.

A picture of the significance that the new divorce law had for women
emerges from Tables 11.2 and 11.3. In the majority of divorce cases, husbands and wives applied jointly for judicial separation; a trend that increased markedly for marriages that had been entered into after 1921. In
the older marriages, the partners sought judicial separation jointly in approximately half the cases (roughly 40–50 percent), while in the marriages
under the new act, this proportion was considerably higher (roughly
60–70 percent). As Table 11.3 reveals, however, the more interesting trend
is that the overwhelming majority of separate applications (roughly 70–80
percent) were sent in by women.

How, then, can these patterns to be interpreted? To begin with, it should

Table 11.2

Applications for Judicial Separation in Tiunda and Mora Administrative
County Districts, Sweden, 1921–50

| Applications submitted | Marriages under the old Marriage Act (until 1920) % | | Marriages under the new Marriage Act (1921–1929)% | |
|---|---|---|---|---|
| | Tiunda | Mora | Tiunda | Mora |
| Joint applications | 40 | 54 | 63 | 72 |
| Separate applications | 60 | 46 | 37 | 28 |
| Total (N) | 8 | 24 | 196 | 104 |

Note: N = 374

Source: Books of Judgments, Tiunda Administrative County District and Mora
Administrative County District 1921–50. Uppsala Provincial Record Office.

Table 11.3

Applications for Judicial Separation in Tiunda and Mora Administrative
County Districts, Sweden, 1921–50 (Separate Applications Only)

| Applications submitted from | Marriages under the old Marriage Act (until 1920) % | | Marriages under the new Marriage Act (1921–1929)% | |
|---|---|---|---|---|
| | Tiunda | Mora | Tiunda | Mora |
| The woman | 73 | 82 | 67 | 72 |
| The man | 27 | 18 | 33 | 28 |
| Total (N) | 30 | 11 | 72 | 25 |

Note: N = 138

Source: Judicial Separation Registers, Tiunda Administrative County District and
Mora Administrative County District 1921–50. Uppsala Provincial Record Office.

be recognized that judicial separations did not always lead to the dissolution of a marriage. Judicial separation, together with the accompanying
division of the joint property, was sufficient to dissolve the husband's right
of administration. It is probable that women in older marriages used judicial separation as a means of achieving financial independence and in
doing so to protest against the patriarchal exercise of power. Indeed, the
active role that women seemed to take in initiating judicial separations
under the new law would appear to contradict the way feminists at the
time envisaged the effects of liberal divorce legislation. Female activists

had been ambivalent toward the question when it was debated at a Nordic women's conference in 1914. They believed that liberalization of the law would, in the first place, favor men, who were generally more interested in divorce than women.[20] The findings presented here appear to indicate that divorce was something that women were also actively interested in. Consequently, there was a gap between middle-class feminist notions of marriage as a support institution and the needs expressed by ordinary women in a divorce situation.

### The Regulation of Property under the Old Marriage Act

Previous research has examined property relations in divorces concerning marriages under the older act.[21] An important dividing line was cases in which the woman brought her own real estate into the marriage and those in which the woman had no property. The research concerned farming couples and revealed that women who entered marriage with their own property were generally in a stronger position than when the couple's finances relied entirely on the husband's assets. Even if women in such relationships could not generally manage or control their own property while they were married, possession of personal assets gave them freedom of action once the divorce law had been liberalized. Thus, in spite of the fact that women, relatively speaking, had fewer economic opportunities than men, the ownership of property gave some of them the opportunity of making at least some choices, including, for example, leaving the marriage.[22]

It was, of course, a different matter in the vast majority of marriages, where economic relations between the spouses were asymmetrical. Women often ended up as hostages in relationship conflicts, particularly if the children were still minors. The maintenance contributions that men were ordered to pay for the children were generally very low. This reflected the fact that the gender order in a divorce situation worked in a hierarchical and normative way. The unspoken norm in agrarian marriages was that the woman's demands for maintenance, for both the children and herself, should not affect the husband's finances to any appreciable extent because this could be regarded as an encroachment on his property rights.

### The Regulation of Property under the New Marriage Act

By the early decades of the twentieth century, when reformation of Swedish family law commenced, the vulnerable position of married women had already been under discussion for many years, both in the Nordic countries and in the remainder of western Europe.[23] As suggested above, one of the aims of the 1921 Marriage Act was to improve the situation of married women by making them less economically dependent on men or, in other words, by creating conditions for the economic citizenship of women.

A new and revolutionary feature of the reform was the way in which the mutual duties of family support and maintenance were defined. The law now prescribed that women's work in the home was just as important financially for the support of the family as men's work outside it, thereby recognizing that unpaid domestic work was just as valuable as paid work. A more profound change in terms of equality, however, consisted of the way in which the property situation was regulated in the new Marriage Act.[24]

Another important part of the new law dealt with the right to the marital property. In the older law this right had been concerned with the right to joint property, which meant that when the marriage ended, for example, through death or divorce, the joint property of the couple (managed by the man) was divided equally between the partners. In the 1921 Marriage Act the concept of marital property gained a new meaning. Each partner had his or her own separate property, administered by each partner, and he or she was responsible for his or her own debts and credits. Marital property was now concerned with the right to the other person's property.[25] It implied, in the first place, that on the breakup of a marriage the property of both parties was pooled and shared out equally between the two. In the second place, marital property implied that each partner had a duty, during marriage, to administer the property so that he or she did not damage the other partner's financial interests. Spouses had some limited authority over, and control of, the other partner's method of administering assets. The result was, as David Bradley has pointed out, a combination of economic independence and solidarity. The important change, compared with the old law, was that married women were freed from their husband's control. The intention of this change was that women should avoid the situation where formal theoretical equality before the law in practice created inequality between the spouses.[26]

### Rhetoric and Reality: Divisions of Property in Practice

This new formulation of marital property was much discussed, and in popular speech a stock phrase was invented that summarized people's criticisms and misgivings: "Under the old Marriage Act women could 'marry property.' Under the new law they can 'divorce it.'" But was this really so? Marital property regulations under the new act may have ensured formal equal rights for women, but in relation to the way the law actually operated, they continued to create inequalities because the economic and social conditions under which women and men themselves lived were not equal. Regulation of marital property was an attempt to compensate for the fact that women and men often started their married lives from unequal economic starting points and that women, in most cases, had fewer assets than men. The reasoning of the law-drafting committee was based on the premise that women would, at least, not be penalized for marrying, as they had been under the old law when they lost their economic right of authority on marriage.[27] In practice, the property regulations of the new Marriage Act scarcely implied any great change in marital property relations, at least not during the decades immediately after it came into operation. Ideas of what was the "right" and "natural" division of labor between the sexes and the complex discourses that surrounded the legislation meant that property division on divorce, even under the new Marriage Act, was often asymmetrical. Table 11.4 demonstrates how property was divided among middle-class families as the result of divorce. In order to facilitate comparison between the old and the new Marriage Acts the figures include couples who married under both statutes.

While the number of cases dealt with is small, several interesting points emerge from this table. First, it shows that, in four of the eight marriages that came under the old Marriage Act, the assets were divided more or less equally, with approximately half of the property being given to each partner. In one case the husband sold his smallholding, and the assets

**Table 11.4**
**Division of Property in Middle-Class Divorce Cases: Tiunda and Mora Administrative County Districts, Sweden, 1921–50**

|  | Marriages under the old Marriage Act (until 1920) | Marriages under the new Marriage Act (1921–1929) |
|---|---|---|
| Fair division | 4 | 4 |
| Unfair division | 1 | 7 |
| No division | 3 | 2 |
| No information | 0 | 2 |
| N | 8 | 15 |

Note: N = 23. The social affiliation of the investigated couples has been decided according to the husband's occupation. Occupations within the following categories have been classified as middle-class trades: clerical professions, entrepreneurs, leaseholders, farmers, and officers. The cases considered in the Table make up 28 percent of the divorces in middle-class marriages that had been entered into under the old Marriage Act and 18 percent of the divorces in marriages that had been contracted after 1921.

Source: Books of Judgments, Tiunda Administrative County District and Mora Administrative County District 1921–50. Uppsala Provincial Record Office.

were divided equally between the woman and the man; in another case the couple had sold their property jointly and divided the cash assets, though it is not clear from the proceedings which of them brought the property into the marriage. In both these cases the marital partners split the burden of maintenance by sharing the care of the children. In a third case the man was forced against his will into a more-or-less equal division of the couple's property on moral grounds. He had been unfaithful, left his wife and children, and moved to another area with his new partner. The wife, who took care of the three young children, had a moral advantage both in the district court and in the local community. The man gave in to this, revoked his demands to remain in the marital home, and agreed to share the assets and pay maintenance contributions for the upkeep of the children. Finally, in the fourth case, both the husband and the wife had inherited property separately. They were in their sixties and got divorced upon the woman's initiative after nearly 40 years of marriage. Their separation was an example of how women in older marriages could—since they were unable to administer their property within marriage—use judicial separation as an instrument for regaining control of it. Finally, in one case among the group of older marriages, the property was divided unequally between the partners. The couple were of retirement age, and divorce meant the legal formalization of a separation that had taken place 15 years earlier. The woman received a portion of cash on divorce, while the man kept his business, the property on which his finances were based. In the case of three marriages the couple had no property to divide.

Second, Table 11.4 shows that in marriages which had been entered into after 1921, the property was divided fairly between partners in 4 of 11 judicial separations. In 3 of these the assets were so small—furniture, everyday items, and other movables—that there was no conflict of interests between the spouses. In the fourth case it is unclear whether one can say that the woman "divorced money." The couple were domiciled in Uppsala, and the husband was a sea captain, 12 years older than his wife. They had married in 1930 and applied for judicial separation 7 years later. They had 3 children, the eldest of whom was 6 years old and the youngest only a few months, when the order for separation came through in June 1937. According to an agreement between them, the husband was given care of the children and took upon himself the responsibility for their maintenance and upbringing. The marital estate consisted of the husband's property, and this was divided equally between the two partners. The man had significant assets, valued at more than 150,000 Swedish crowns, comprising for the most part of claims on his relatives. It is impossible, because of the lack of information in the Book of Judgments, to tell whether the woman really did have access to half the husband's property. Similarly, the proceedings do not divulge the real cause of the separation.

Third, Table 11.4 shows that in seven of the separations relating to marriages entered into after 1921, the division of property between partners was unequal. One of these cases stood out from the rest in that the assets were the separate property of the woman. The couple concerned had run a smallholding. They married in 1930, had one child, and applied for judicial separation in 1936. The case is interesting as it shows how the legal protection of women who had their own property was improved under the new Marriage Act. This woman had administered her property herself and sold the farm when the separation became a reality. She obtained care of the daughter of the marriage while retaining control over her property because it was not marital estate.

In the remaining six cases the women had little or no property, while their husbands possessed considerable wealth. In all these marriages the greater part of the man's property comprised fixed assets, notably land and real estate. In one case, the couple had drawn up a prenuptial agreement and applied jointly for a judicial separation after a union of 18 months. They had no joint assets. The woman obtained care of the child, along with an annual maintenance payment of 480 Swedish crowns. She was also awarded an income of 240 crowns per year for herself, as long as she could produce a doctor's certificate proving that she had back problems. The maintenance, which was not tied to the cost-of-living index, was relatively low and corresponded in 1944 to approximately 25 percent of a female clerk's annual salary.

In the other five cases the men were, once again, businessmen: a builder, a brewery tenant, the owner of a firm of haulage contractors, a manufacturer, and a farmer. Common to all these cases was the fact that the right to the marital estate, which should have provided the woman the right to obtain part of the husband's property, was eliminated. In the agrarian marriage the farm was the husband's separate property upon which the woman had no marital right. On divorce, after nine years of marriage, she obtained care of the couple's two children, who were nine and five years old, and received an annual provision of 600 crowns each for their maintenance. The woman was not granted any maintenance contributions for herself. In the other cases the couples had agreed to do away with the marital right. The crux of the agreement in all cases was that the woman relinquished her claim over the man's property; that the man remained in the joint home; and that the woman abandoned any claim for maintenance for herself. One of the couples was childless. In three cases in this group the woman had been pregnant when the couple married. The maintenance contributions, which were paid to the children, were relatively low. In two cases the woman received a lump sum in cash as compensation.

In summary, this detailed investigation of the division of assets in divorce cases suggests there is no justification for claiming that women "divorced" property or, in another words, that they gained economically from divorce, as some critics of the new marriage law had suggested during debates in the 1920s. The reality of the operation of the divorce laws was that married men frequently ended up paying maintenance contributions for children that were relatively low compared with their total assets, leaving the economic burden of supporting children on the shoulders of the women. This meant that women's economic citizenship remained firmly rooted in the family.

Divorces were still during the 1930s and 1940s sensational events, particularly outside the big towns. Even if every marriage that collapsed had its own story and its own specific conditions, it is reasonable to assume that divorce cases—just because they were so exceptional—provided powerful indications to local communities as to the economic and social rights that were bound up with the marriage and the roles of wife and husband. For married women the message was clear. Both the Marriage Act and prevailing gender understandings were based on the idea that women were, in the first place, supported through marriage. Women were not regarded as individuals economically in the same way as men, and their economic citizenship was tied up with the family.

## A STORY OF ECONOMIC CITIZENSHIP: ERIKSSON V. ERIKSSON

The complex ways in which the law reflected normative expectations of female and male behavior can best be understood in the context of a detailed case study. Ellinor and Lars Eriksson had married in 1930, when she was 23 and he was 25.[28] At that time they had already known each other for several years. Eighteen months before their marriage Ellinor had given birth to their first child, a boy, and their second child, a girl, was born 4 years into the marriage. After 12 years of wedded life Ellinor sought a judicial separation. She alleged that the relationship between herself and Lars had been "less good" over a period of years because of her husband's addiction to alcohol and his "unreasonable jealousy." The divorce process dragged on for more than 2½ years, from August 1942 to April 1944, and the case ended in the dissolution of the marriage and a divorce settlement. According to the terms, Ellinor relinquished all pretensions to marital rights concerning the couple's joint property, which for the most part consisted of the man's marital estate: a craft factory, land, forest, and other assets.

This settlement can shed light on the concept of economic citizenship and can be interpreted as a story of how they both came to obtain certain economic rights once their marriage was at an end. Several questions arise:

what were the economic discourses and gender understandings that led to the agreement between Ellinor and Lars and that produced their story? What were the links between Ellinor's and Lars's story and the wider social world? How did Ellinor and Lars come to produce their special individual stories? What does their story tell about marital property relations in the interwar years? And, finally, what social role might Ellinor's and Lars's story play? How might their story of economic citizenship work to conserve a prevailing social order? Or might it be used to resist or transform it?[29]

### Discourses of Work, Marital Property Rights, and Male Breadwinning

The beginning of this marital conflict, as presented in the district court, dealt with the provisions of the Marriage Act, whereby both partners had mutual duties of support. The proceedings also concerned the rights of one partner to the other's property in the case of divorce. Ellinor accused her husband of having neglected his breadwinner duties. Lars's concern was over the rights Ellinor was trying to claim in his property. He argued that she hoped, through divorce, to obtain half the couple's wealth. What, then, had happened?

At the time of the court case both Lars and Ellinor were self-employed. They had begun their marriage by running his family farm. According to Ellinor, she had been in charge of the byre and the fox farm (breeding for pelts), which her husband ran as a sideline. During the summer she had sometimes employed extra hands to help her; during the winter months, however, she looked after the household and her side of the farmwork on her own, despite the fact that she was not well and had difficulty in coping with the physical demands of the work. After six years of farming, the couple moved to a nearby market town. There, Lars operated a leather factory, which he ran successfully with a business partner, while Ellinor opened a ladies' hairdressing salon, which she ran with the help of one or two assistants. The court heard how she had been forced to start her business because her husband was mean with the housekeeping money. She maintained that Lars had scarcely given her any contributions for food or clothes in recent years on the pretext that she, as a hairdresser, "could well look after herself."

During the first hearing Lars's legal representative contested all Ellinor's accusations. Lars's tactics during the case were to try to stop the couple being given an order for judicial separation. He persistently maintained that the marriage was a happy one and tried to prove that Ellinor was influenced by her friends and had psychological problems that were driving her desire for a divorce. Witness after witness appeared during the subsequent court sessions, all of whom praised Lars, confirming that he was fair and well behaved, that his finances were in good shape, and that he could not be accused of addiction to alcohol, even if he took a glass or two in the company of good friends. The witnesses also assured the court that he was a good father and employer.

A common discourse shared by everyone in this court case was that marriage was a support institution for Ellinor. This pervasive gendered understanding of marriage came out in her application; in what was said by Lars, his legal representatives, and the witnesses; and in the way the judge and jury ruled in the case. Ellinor's accusations against Lars centered on the claim that he had neglected his duty of supporting her. She alleged this to be the reason for her opening a hairdressing salon rather than wanting an income of her own or being interested in running a business. Lars, for his part, reiterated his assurances that he had been generous to his wife and spoiled her. He saw himself as the breadwinner and perceived his wife's economic activities as complementing his own income. He stated that Ellinor "could well earn some pin money" through her business. Both partners corroborated the other's perception of the "right" economic relation between the two, and other witnesses returned to the same story of the man as the breadwinning partner and the woman as the dependant. Ellinor's father, for example, acted as a witness against his daughter and told her that she ought to understand the advantages she had gained from marriage. Her father thought that Ellinor "had been spoilt, probably even before her marriage, and that she had not rightly understood that one should be happy and content to be in such a relatively sound economic position, with a good husband and two healthy children." Ellinor's sister, on the other hand, supported her, providing two conflicting alternatives: she said she understood that marriage meant economic security for her sister but that she spoke on behalf of all her brothers and sisters in saying that they would rather see Ellinor in a state of extreme poverty, if she got divorced, than observe the way Lars "plagued and tormented their sister year in and year out in the most sadistic way, thanks to his jealousy, which had no grounds and must be regarded as incurable." Those employed in Ellinor's hairdressing salon were not questioned about her qualities as a businesswoman but were asked instead about the way Lars had looked after his family. They confirmed Ellinor's accusations that Lars was mean with the housekeeping money. Revealingly, in contrast, employees of Lars who appeared in the court were questioned about his competence as a businessman. Such proceedings are indicative of the understandings of men's and women's economic citizenship that were implicit to the operation of the law and middle-class marriages more generally.

Moreover, the interpretations of those taking part in the case about the economic relationship between Ellinor and Lars show the contradictions in the discourse that were built into the new Marriage Act. The regulation on duties of mutual support, which meant that the woman's domestic work was in principle equal to the man's work outside the home, had been introduced in order to give women a more equal economic and social position in marriage. By declaring that household work was of economic significance and obliging the man to give the woman housekeeping money, the law defined married women as economically involved, and thereby independent, economic citizens. Through their political citizenship and new status within marriage women now had the same abstract rights as men. At the same time, however, the Marriage Act confirmed that the economic relation between the spouses was unequal.[30] The law enabled Ellinor to define herself as an individual and maintain that she had economic rights in marriage. However, the same law enabled Lars to maintain that he was the real breadwinner of the family, and thereby the only economic actor to be reckoned with. By starting from an abstract principle—that the woman's work in the home was in principle equally as important as the man's work—but not defining how or to what extent the woman really contributed to her family's support through household work, the law simply reaffirmed existing economic inequalities in marriage. Both the court and those participating in the proceedings were at the mercy of their gendered understandings of marital relationships and economic competencies. Through these discourses they interpreted and applied the law, and although the law itself established an abstract principle, it had not provided any clues as to how this should have been applied.

Another issue raised during the court case was the meaning of marital rights. The economic relation between Ellinor and Lars was asymmetrical. According to the tax returns, Lars had brought fixed as well as movable assets to the marriage, to a value of approximately 58,000 Swedish crowns.[31] Ellinor's assets were insignificant: she owned a fifth of the property that she and her brothers and sisters had inherited from their mother, her share of which was taxed at 650 crowns. She also owned furniture and other items in her hairdressing salon, valued at approximately 2,000 crowns, her clothes, and some jewelry. Everything belonging to the couple was marital property, which was to be divided equally between the two.

At the first court session Lars outlined his view of the impending division of property. He maintained that Ellinor hoped to obtain half their joint property if the divorce went through but argued that she "lacked any sense of his rights in the matter" and hoped for a large amount of maintenance for herself and the children. He used the children as a means of blackmailing her and stated that if the court were to make an order for judicial separation against his will, then he would insist that he take on the care of the children: "It would be more than fair, if it were to come to judicial separation, that (she) should realize how it felt to be parted from the children." The conflict about property, as defined by Lars, was the main question during the court hearings in 1942, and also in the sequel, which ended in a financial agreement between the partners in April 1944.

Ellinor's legal representative replied to Lars by handing in a seven-page written petition in which she spoke out about the circumstances of her marriage. She said that she had been pregnant prior to the wedding and had married her husband "in order to make her son legitimate." She also maintained that the couple had already talked of divorce over a number of years but that Lars had always taken the view that her demands for maintenance were unreasonable. The conflict continued, but the county district court made an order for judicial separation in November 1942. Ellinor was allowed to remain in the family home and was given care of the children. She was also awarded a maintenance payment to the tune of 2,400 crowns per annum for herself and the children. This, however, was a third less than the 3,300 crowns that she had requested. Lars, for his part, did not wish to agree to the separation and appealed to the Court of Appeal (*Svea hovrätt*). The appeal was rejected, however, and the separation came into force in February 1943.

According to the law, a judgment for separation was always followed by an estate inventory and division of the joint property, which normally took place within three months of the judge's decision. In this case the inventory was drawn up in April 1943, but the division of the joint property did not take place until November. In the settlement, Lars bought Ellinor out: she received 17,000 crowns in cash on condition that she relinquish all rights to the couple's home. She also obtained the personal property and the items in her hairdressing salon and took on the debts for her own business. Including deductions for debts, she received in total some 15,000 crowns. According to the agreement reached in connection with their divorce in April 1944, she obtained care of their 10-year-old daughter, Margareta, and undertook not to make demands for her maintenance. Lars kept all the real estate, including Ellinor's portion that she had inherited from her mother, and all the personal property and furniture and household equipment that the couple had kept in their three different homes (their flat, the farm, and Lars's log cabin). He also obtained care of their son, Anders, and undertook sole responsibility for his support and education.

### The Story of Lars and Ellinor in Relation to the Wider Social World

How did the discourses of male breadwinning and male property rights implicit in this divorce case result in gendered economic citizenship? Put another way, what were the economic consequences of these discourses for Ellinor and Lars and their two children? Let us first think about Lars's situation. He was 39 years old and together with a partner ran a leather factory. Having invested in the business, he had also accumulated a number of debts. The cash lump sum he paid to Ellinor and his daughter, therefore, was a setback to his finances, but he kept intact all the productive capital (land, forest, and buildings) that might yield a good return in the future and possibly even increase in value. He could presumably offer Anders, who was then 15 years old, a higher standard of living and better educational opportunities than Ellinor could give her daughter.

Ellinor was 36 years old. She was able bodied and had obtained a cash lump sum of 15,000 crowns as well as the movables in her hairdressing salon. The alternatives for her were to continue running the salon or find a paid job. Her daughter Margareta was then 10 years old, went to school, and presumably did not need to be looked after during the day. If we think of the fact that Ellinor was to support her daughter until she was 18, the cash sum would have corresponded to a maintenance contribution of 1,875 crowns per year. In 1944 this was between 60 and 70 percent of a female clerk's or shop assistant's annual income.[32] With an average wage and the cash contribution, it ought to have been possible for Ellinor to be economically independent, establish a self-supporting household, and maintain herself and her child. From this point of view she was in a better economic position than many other women in similar situations. The cash sum, calculated in terms of an annual maintenance contribution, was also at a level that the administrative district court, in connection with the judicial separation a year earlier, had regarded as corresponding to her needs and those of the child, as well as reflecting Lars's financial capacity.[33] However, at the same time, if Ellinor did not invest the money it would quickly lose its value. Five years later the yearly sum of 1,900 crowns corresponded to roughly 40 percent of a female clerk's wages, falling in 1952, when Margareta was 18 years old, to approximately 30 percent. Why, then, did Ellinor not fight for her legal rights to get half the marital estate rather than accepting an economic settlement that favored Lars more than her?

### The Production of Individual Stories

The right to marital property was a key feature of the new Marriage Act and was intended as a means by which the weaker party in marriage could be protected. As suggested earlier, it was also envisaged as compensation for the fact that women and men often entered marriage in different economic situations. However, this was not an issue that arose in the proceedings concerning Ellinor's and Lars's court case. Lars viewed the right to marital property as an interference with his own property rights and no one—neither Ellinor, her legal representative, nor members of the administrative county district court—questioned this interpretation. Not once did Ellinor or her lawyer touch upon the property situation in the marriage, except when they rejected Lars's accusations that she was greedy. Lars produced his individual story of the economic relations within the marriage on a patriarchal understanding of gender relations.

The patriarchal gender order worked on many levels. Ellinor presented her story in a judicial context that, except for some of the witnesses, was "one gendered." Her lawyer, the judges, and the jury were all men, and this was something that she, more-or-less consciously, had to consider. Her aim was to obtain a divorce, make provisions for the care of the children, and get reasonable maintenance so that she could support herself and the children. Lars's view that Ellinor's demands were unreasonable was something with which the court could not agree. However, there was in this case, as with others, strong consensus that the capital forming the basis of a man's livelihood and business should, as far as possible, be unaffected by the woman's demands for maintenance for herself and the children. This is hardly surprising. The primary consideration was that men keep their economic citizenship intact, and both men and women shared this gendered understanding of property rights. Women in divorce cases were generally careful not to challenge male authority in case they lost the sympathy of the judge and jury. For the woman, the court case was a balancing act between public expectations of subservient female behavior and her own need to maintain her rights within the framework of a patriarchal gender order. She tipped that balance at her peril.

## CONCLUSION: FORMAL ECONOMIC EQUALITY IN MARRIAGE—GENDER DIFFERENCES IN LIFE CHANCES

For the majority of women, the new Marriage Act of 1921 involved a shift in gender relations and proved advantageous. For the first time, both men and women had mutual rights and duties in marriage. Married women obtained the same formal economic privileges as men as well as the power to influence the upbringing and education of children. The reformed divorce law, which was a part of the Marriage Act, also made it easier for all concerned to end unfulfilling marriages.

The Marriage Act set the formal framework for marital relations, and from it also emanated the norms and values that decided how the law worked and how it was applied in concrete social situations. There was, however, an inbuilt tension in the act between the theoretical equality that followed from women's equal citizenship rights and the inequalities that were grounded in women's and men's unequal access to economic resources. I have used formal equality, as it was expressed in the law, as a point of reference for a discussion of gender inequality in the division of property within the marriage. Formal equal rights, as has been demonstrated in this study, were dependent on individual women's and men's unequal possibilities to achieve the rights in question. The complex discourses surrounding marital property relations continued to define women's rights to own and manage property differently from men. Such discourses were shaped by established patriarchal understandings of the economic and social roles of women. These emphasized the dependence of married women on a male breadwinner; affirmed women's roles as family maintainers and caregivers; and stressed the sanctity of male productive property. Ultimately, therefore, while the Swedish Marriage Act was instrumental in establishing the notion of economic equality for women, the operation of the law defined women's economic citizenship in ways that were fundamentally different from those of men. Real equality was therefore suppressed by the deadweight of historically embedded discourses and the uneven structures of access to economic resources and wealth-making possibilities.

## NOTES

1. The initial steps toward equality between women and men in Sweden can be traced to the nineteenth century. From the 1840s the range of opportunities widened for women to carry on manufacturing and trading activities. In 1845 equal inheritance rights were established for boys and girls. Unmarried women were granted privileges in 1856 and 1863 that enabled them to maintain and control their own property. From 1874 married women obtained the right to dispose of income gained from their own work and from their own property. Through marriage decrees or by virtue of gifts or stipulations in wills, this property could be placed beyond the bounds of the husband's administration. Women's access to education, jobs, and professions was gradually extended between the 1860s and 1920s, and in 1939 a law was introduced that forbade employers to fire women on grounds of marriage or pregnancy. For an account of this growing equality see Ida Blom and Anna Tranberg, Nordisk lovoversikt: Viktige lover for kvinnor ca. 1810–1980 (Oslo: Nordisk ministerråd, 1985), 181–204.

2. Citizenship is defined here both as rights (for example, the right to work, rights over property, and rights of contract) and obligations (for example, the obligation to pay tax). The definition of economic citizenship used in this chapter is taken from Alice Kessler-Harris, who employs the term to "suggest the achievement of an independent and relatively autonomous status that marks self-respect and provides access to the full play of power and influence that defines participation in a democratic society." See Alice Kessler-Harris, In Pursuit of Equity: Women, Men and the Quest for Economic Citizenship in 20th Century America (Oxford: Oxford University Press, 2001), 12.

3. Kessler-Harris, In Pursuit of Equity; Alice Kessler-Harris, "Gender Identity: Right to Work and the Idea of Economic Citizenship," Schweizerische Zeitschrift für Geschichte 46 (1996): 411–26; and Gunnela Björk, Att förhandla sitt medborgarskap: Kvinnor som kollektiva aktörer i Örebro 1900–1950 (Lund: Arkiv förlag, 1999), 20, 296–97.

4. See, for example, Douglass C. North, Institutions, Institutional Change and Economic Performance (Cambridge: Cambridge University Press, 1990).

5. For a discussion of "a sociology of stories" see Ken Plummer, *Telling Sexual Stories: Power, Change and Social Worlds* (London: Routledge, 1995), 18–31.

6. Thomas H. Marshall and Tom Bottomore, *Citizenship and Social Class* (London: Pluto Press, 1992, originally published 1950).

7. Marshall mentions in passing that civil rights are absolutely necessary in a competitive market economy and that the basis of a person's civil rights is his (sic) status as an individual. It is obvious that Marshall thought of the economic citizen, the person functioning in a market economy, as a man: "civil rights were indispensable to a competitive market economy. They gave each man, as part of his individual status, the power to engage as an independent unit in the economic struggle." Marshall and Bottomore, *Citizenship and Social Class*, 20–21.

8. Anne-Hilde Nagel, "The Development of Citizenship in Norway: Marshall Remodelled," in *Women's Politics and Women in Politics: In Honour of Ida Blom*, ed. Sølvi Sogner and Gro Hagemann (Oslo: Cappelen Akademisk Forlag, 2000), 197–215.

9. Kessler-Harris, *In Pursuit of Equity*; Kessler-Harris, "Gender Identity"; Björk, *Att förhandla*.

10. A new marriage code was enacted in Denmark in 1925 and in Norway in 1918/1927. Iceland and Finland introduced similar reforms in 1923 and 1929, respectively. The divorce legislation, in its turn, was liberalized in Norway in 1909, in Sweden in 1915, in Denmark in 1922, in Iceland in 1921, and in Finland in 1948. Åke Malmström, *Betänkande med förslag om upphävande av den äldre giftermålsbalken*, Statens offentliga utredningar, 43 (Stockholm: Statistiska centralbyrån, 1947), 11–15 and David Bradley, *Family Law and Political Culture: Scandinavian Laws in Comparative Perspective* (London: Sweet and Maxwell, 1996), 9–12, 29–34. The social and political process by which the Nordic marriage legislation was modernized is currently the subject of a major comparative research project. For an outline of the project, see the introduction to Kari Melby, Anu Pylkkänen, Bente Rosenbeck, and Christina Carlsson Wetterberg, eds., *The Nordic Model of Marriage and the Welfare State* (Copenhagen: Nordic Council of Ministers, 2000), 13–26.

11. Bradley, *Family Law and Political Culture*, chapter 1 and Bente Rosenbeck, "Det nordiske samarbeide, kvindebevægelse og ægteskabslovgivning," in *Køn, religion og kvinder i bevægelse*, ed. Anette Warring (Roskilde: Konferencerapport fra det VI Nordiske Kvindehistorikermøte, 2000), 250–70.

12. Rosenbeck, "Det nordiske samarbeide"; Kari Melby, "Det nordiske ekteskap? Ekteskapslovreform i Norden 1909–1929: Likestillingskontrakt eller husmorskontrakt?" in Warring, *Køn, religion og kvinder i bevægelse*, 234–49.

13. Bradley, *Family Law and Political Culture*, 19–28.

14. Melby, "Det nordiske ekteskap?" 234; David Bradley, "Family Laws and Welfare States," in Melby et al., *The Nordic Model of Marriage*, 37–67.

15. Gunnar Qvist, *Konsten att blifva en god flicka* (Stockholm: LiberFörlag, 1978), 162–211; Anita Göransson, "Gender and Property Rights: Capital, Kin and Owner-Influence in Nineteenth- and Twentieth-Century Sweden," *Business History* 35 (1993): 11–32.

16. Sveriges offentliga statistik, *Befolkningsrörelsen 1931–1940* (Stockholm: Statistiska centralbyrån, 1940), 15–16. The increase in the number of dissolved marriages was a general trend in western Europe and the United States after the First World War. See Roderick Phillips, *Putting Asunder: A History of Divorce in Western Society*

(Cambridge: Cambridge University Press, 1988), 516–33 and Lawrence Stone, *Road to Divorce: England 1530–1987* (Oxford: Oxford University Press, 1990), 381–401.

17. Lynn Abrams, "Whores, Whore-Chasers, and Swine: The Regulation of Sexuality and the Restoration of Order in the Nineteenth-Century German Divorce Court," *Journal of Family History* 21 (1996): 269–71, 277; Lynn Abrams, "Companionship and Conflict: The Negotiation of Marriage Relations in the Nineteenth Century," in *Gender Relations in German History: Power, Agency and Experience from the Sixteenth to the Twentieth Century*, ed. Lynn Abrams and Elisabeth Harvey (London: University College London Press, 1996), 101–20; Lynn Abrams, "The Personification of Inequality: Challenges to Gendered Power Relations in the Nineteenth-Century Divorce Court," *Archiv für Sozialgeschichte* 38 (1998): 41–55; James A. Hammerton, *Cruelty and Companionship: Conflict in Nineteenth-Century Married Life* (London: Routledge, 1992), 3–5, 170–76; Stone, *Road to Divorce*, 27–33; and Nancy Cott, "Eighteenth-Century Family and Social Life Revealed in Massachusetts Divorce Records," *Journal of Social History* 10 (1976): 21.

18. Bradley, *Family Law and Political Culture*, 3–12.

19. To enable a comparison of the length of marriage under the old act and in marriages contracted after 1921, only marriages contracted during the 1920s are included in the latter group.

20. Melby, "Det nordiske ekteskap?" 240–41.

21. A shortened English-language version of the study can be found in Kirsti Niskanen, "Marriage and Gendered Property Rights in Early Twentieth-Century Rural Sweden," in Melby et al, *The Nordic Model of Marriage*, 69–87. The study is published in its entirety in Swedish (with an English summary) in Kirsti Niskanen, "Husbondeväldets röst: Äktenskap, egendom och kön under första delen av 1900-talet," in *Kvinnor och jord: Arbete och ägande från medeltid till nutid*, ed. Britt Liljewall, Kirsti Niskanen, and Maria Sjöberg (Stockholm: Nordiska museets förlag, 2000), 131–58.

22. See also Carol M. Rose, *Property and Persuasion: Essays on the History, Theory, and Rhetoric of Ownership* (Boulder Colo.: Westview Press, 1994), 253–57.

23. Rosenbeck, "Det nordiske samarbeide." For a discussion of the English context see Lee Holcombe, *Wives and Property: Reform of the Married Women's Property Law in Nineteenth-Century England* (Toronto: University of Toronto Press, 1983). Hammerton, in his analysis of middle-class marriage in England, gives examples of the economic, social, and emotional background upon which the English discussion on marriage legislation is based. See Hammerton, *Cruelty and Companionship*, 6, 71–163.

24. Bradley, *Family Law and Political Culture*, 10.

25. Bradley calls this "a system of deferred universal community." See Bradley, *Family Law and Political Culture*, 10.

26. Bradley, *Family Law and Political Culture*, 11. The Swedish law-drafting committee discussed the different ways of regulating property relations in marriage. The English "Married Women's Property Act" of 1882 was based on the principle of total differentiation of property in marriage. Equality between partners on a formal level was thereby introduced into the law. Similar proposals had also been presented in the *riksdag* (Swedish parliament) as early as the 1870s. The Swedish law-drafting committee stated, however, that total separation of the property of marital partners would, from the woman's point of view, be even more economi-

cally disadvantageous than the property regulations of the old Marriage Act. The committee argued that the English system of separate ownership would not improve the economic situation of women while they were married. They suggested that women would lose their right, on the dissolution of the marriage, to the portion of the assets that had been procured during marriage, to which they had often creatively, if indirectly, contributed by their work in the household. See Bihang till riksdagens protokoll år 1920: Andra samlingen, andra avdelningen, första bandet: Lagberedningens förslag till giftermålslbalk mm, 175–84. See also Holcombe, *Wives and Property*, 230–34.

27. Bihang till riksdagens protokoll år 1920, 175–84.

28. This section is based on the following source material: Books of Judgments, Mora Administrative County District: 1942, 1944, Uppsala Provincial Record Office. The places and names of the persons involved have been altered.

29. This approach of analyzing court cases as a form of "sociological story telling" is inspired by Plummer, *Telling Sexual Stories*, 24–26, 144–66.

30. See also Kari Melby's analysis of the Norwegian Marriage Act based on the concepts of "housewife's contract" and "equality contract." Melby, "Det nordiske ekteskap?" 241–47.

31. Books of Judgments, Mora Administrative County District: 1944, Uppsala Provincial Record Office.

32. A female clerk's salary in 1944 was, on average, 2,937 crowns per month, while a shop assistant's wage was around 2,626 crowns per month. See *Statistisk årsbok för Sverige 1950* (Stockholm: Statistiska cenralbyrån, 1950), 277 (tables 215 and 216).

33. The size of the maintenance contributions had been set at 1,200 crowns a year for the woman and 600 crowns per year for each child. This meant a total of 1,800 crowns for Ellinor and her daughter.

# Bibliography

Abrams, Lynn. "Companionship and Conflict: The Negotiation of Marriage Relations in the Nineteenth Century." In *Gender Relations in German History: Power, Agency and Experience from the Sixteenth to the Twentieth Century*, edited by Lynn Abrams and Elisabeth Harvey. London: University College London Press, 1996, 101–20.

Abrams, Lynn. "The Personification of Inequality: Challenges to Gendered Power Relations in the Nineteenth-Century Divorce Court." *Archiv für Sozialgeschichte* 38 (1998): 41–55.

Abrams, Lynn. "Whores, Whore-Chasers, and Swine: The Regulation of Sexuality and the Restoration of Order in the Nineteenth-Century German Divorce Court." *Journal of Family History* 21 (1996): 267–80.

Ago, Renata. "Giochi di squadra: Uomini e donne nelle famiglie nobili del XVII secolo." In *Signori, patrizi, cavalieri in Italia centro-meridionale nell'età moderna*, edited by Maria Antonietta Visceglia. Roma: Laterza, 1992, 256–64.

Ågren, Maria. "Caring for the Widowed Spouse: On the Use of Wills in Northern Sweden, 1750–1915." Unpublished paper.

Ågren, Maria. "Fadern, systern och brodern: Maktförskjutningar genom 1800-talets egendomsreformer." *Historisk tidskrift* 4 (1999): 683–708.

Allen, Michael Patrick. *The Founding Fortunes: A New Anatomy of the Super-Rich Families in America*. New York: Truman Talley, 1987.

*Allgemeines Landrecht für die Preußischen Staaten von 1794*. Frankfurt a.M: A. Metzner, 1970.

Alter, George, and James C. Riley. "How to Bet on Lives: A Guide to Life Contingent Contracts in Early Modern Europe." *Research in Economic History* 10 (1986): 1–53.

Amory, Cleveland. *Who Killed Society?* New York: Harper and Brothers, 1960.

Anderson, Bonnie, and Judith Zinsser. *A History of Their Own*, vol. 1. Cambridge: Cambridge University Press, 1988.

Anderson, Michael. *Family Structure in Nineteenth-Century Lancashire*. London: Cambridge University Press, 1971.

Andersson, Bertil. *Från fästningsstad till handelsstad 1619–1820*. Göteborg: Nerenius and Santérus, 1996.

Andersson, Gudrun. *Tingets kvinnor och män. Genus som norm och strategi under 1600- och 1700-tal*. Ph.D. diss., Uppsala University, 1998.

Andersson, Gudrun, and Maria Ågren. "Kvinnor och egendom under tidigmodern tid—forskningsläge och forskningsstrategier." *Scandia Band* 62 (1996): 25–54.

Andersson Lennström, Gudrun. "Makt och myndighet. Kring 1686 års lagkommission och kvinnans vardagsmakt." In *Sprickor i muren. Funktion och dysfunktion i det stormaktstida rättssystemet*, edited by Gudrun Andersson Lennström and Marie Lennersand. Uppsala: *Opuscula Historica Upsaliensa* 14 (1994), 3–87.

Andrew, Donna T. "*Noblesse oblige:* Female Charity in an Age of Sentiment." In *Early Modern Conceptions of Property*, edited by John Brewer and Susan Staves. London: Routledge, 1996, 275–300.

Archangeli, Melanie. "Negotiating the Public Sphere Through Private Correspondence: A Woman's Letters of Liberty in Eighteenth-Century Germany." *German Life and Letters* 53 (2000): 435–49.

Arps, Ludwig. *Auf sicheren Pfeilern: Deutsche Versicherungswirtschaft vor 1914*. Göttingen: Vandenhoeck and Ruprecht, 1965.

Arrizabalaga, Marie-Pierre. "Famille, succession, émigration au Pays-basque au XIXe siècle: Etude des pratiques successorales et des comportements migratoires au sein des familles basques." Ph.D. diss., Ecole des Hautes Etudes en Sciences Sociales, Paris, 1998.

Arrizabalaga, Marie-Pierre. "Female Primogeniture in the French Basque Country." In *The Logic of Female Succession: Rethinking Patriarchy and Patrilineality in Global and Historical Perspective*. International Research Symposium Proceeding, No. 19. Kyoto: International Research Center for Japanese Studies, 2003.

Arrizabalaga, Marie-Pierre. "The Stem Family in the French Basque Country: Sare in the Nineteenth Century." *Journal of Family History* 22 (1997): 50–69.

Ashford, Douglas E. *The Emergence of the Welfare States*. Oxford: Basil Blackwell, 1986.

Aubry, Yves. "Pour une étude du veuvage feminin à l'époque moderne." *Histoire, économie et société* 8 (1989): 223–36.

Augustins, Georges, and Rolande Bonnain. *Les Baronnies des Pyrénées, vol. 1: Maisons, mode de vie, société*. Paris: Ed. de l'Ecole des Hautes Etudes en Sciences Sociales, 1982.

Augustins, Georges, Rolande Bonnain, Yves Péron, and Gilles Sautter. *Les Baronnies des Pyrénées vol. 2: maisons, espace, famille*. Paris: Ed. de l'Ecole des Hautes Etudes en Sciences Sociales, 1986.

Bairoch, Paul, Jean Batou, and Pierre Chèvre, *La population des villes européennes de 800 à 1850*. Genève: Publications du Centre d'histoire économique internationale de l'Université de Genève, 1988.

Bardet, Jean-Pierre, Gérard Béaur, and Jacques Renard. "Marché foncier et exclusion en normandie. Premiers résultats d'une enquête sur la région de Vernon dans la seconde moitié du XVIIIe siècle." In *Les exclus de la terre en France et au Québec. Les exclus de la terre en France et au Québec, XVIIe–XXe siècles:La reproduction familiale dans la différence*, edited by Gérard Bouchard, John Dickinson, and Joseph Goy. Sillery: Septentrion, 1998, 193–202.

Barry, Norman. *Welfare*. Buckingham: Open University Press, 1999.

Barth, Frederik. *Balinese Worlds*. Chicago: University of Chicago Press, 1993.

Barth, Johann A. *Johann Ambrosius Barth in Leipzig 1780–1930*. Leipzig: C. G. Röder, 1930, 16–40.

Barthelemy de Saizieu, Tiphaine. "Partages égalitaires en Basse-Bretagne." *Terrains* 4 (1985): 42–49.

Barthelemy de Saizieu, Tiphaine. "Pratiques successorales et mobilité sociale: Exemples bretons." In *Famille, économie et société rurale en contexte d'urbanisation (17e–20e siècle): Famille, économie et société rurale*, edited by Gérard Bouchard and Joseph Goy. Chicoutimi-Paris: SOREP-Ecole des Hautes Etudes en Sciences Sociales, 1991, 57–66.

Beachy, Robert. "Business Was a Family Affair: Women of Commerce in Central Europe, 1680–1870." *Histoire sociale—Social History* 34 (2002): 307–30.

Beachy, Robert. "Reforming Interregional Commerce: The Leipzig Trade Fairs and Saxony's Recovery from the Thirty Years' War." *Central European History* 32 (1999): 431–52.

Beachy, Robert. "The Soul of Commerce: Credit and the Politics of Public Debt in Leipzig, 1680–1830." Ph.D. diss., University of Chicago, 1998.

Béaur, Gérard. "Investissement foncier, épargne et cycle de vie dans le Pays chartrain au XVIIIe siècle." *Histoire et Mesure* VI (1991): 275–88.

Béaur, Gérard. *Histoire agraire de la France au XVIIIe siècle: Inerties et changements dans les campagnes françaises entre 1715 et 1815*. Paris: SEDES, 2000.

Béaur, Gérard. "Land Accumulation, Life-Course and Inequalities among Generations in Eighteenth-Century France: The Winegrowers from the Chartres Region." *The History of the Family* 3 (1998): 285–302.

Béaur, Gérard. *Le marché foncier à la veille de la Révolution: Les mouvements de propriété beaucerons dans les régions de Maintenon et de Janville de 1761 à 1790*. Paris: Ecole des Hautes Etudes en Sciences Sociales, 1984.

Béaur, Gérard. "La transmission des exploitations: Logiques et stratégies. Quelques réflexions sur un processus obscur." In *Problèmes de la transition des exploitations agricoles (XVIIIe–XXe siècles). Nécessités économiques et pratiques juridiques*, edited by Gérard Bouchard, Joseph Goy, and Anne-Lise Head-König. Rome: Ecole française de Rome, 1998, 109–16.

Beck, Rainer. *Unterfinning: Ländliche Welt vor Anbruch der Moderne*. München: C. H. Beck, 1993.

Becker, Gary. *An Economic Analysis of the Family*. Dublin: Economic and Social Research Institute, 1986.

Berg, Herwig, ed. *Die Ursprünge der Demographie in Deutschland: Leben und Werk Johann Daniel Süßmilchs*. Frankfurt a.M. and New York: Campus, 1986.

Berkner, Lutz. "Inheritance, Land Tenure and Peasant Family Structure: A German Regional Comparison." In *Family and Inheritance: Rural Society in Western Europe 1200–1800*, edited by Jack Goody, Joan Thirsk, and Edward P. Thompson. Cambridge: Cambridge University Press, 1976, 71–95.

Berkner, Lutz. "The Stem Family and the Development Cycle of the Peasant Household: An Eighteenth-Century Austrian Example." *American Historical Review* 77 (1972): 398–418.

Berkner, Lutz, and Franklin Mendels. "Inheritance Systems, Family Structure and Demographic Patterns in Western Europe, 1700–1900". In *Historical Studies of Changing Fertility*, edited by Charles Tilly. Princeton, N.J.: Princeton University Press, 1978, 209–24.

Besold-Backmund, Marlene. *Stiftungen und Stiftungswirklichkeit.* Neustadt a.d. Aisch: Degener, 1986, 220–28.

Biedermann, Karl. *Geschichte der Leipziger Kramer-Innung.* Leipzig: O. Leiner, 1881.

Bingham, Sallie. "Biting the Hand: The Break-up of the Bingham Family Empire." *Radcliffe Quarterly* (June 1986): 32–33.

Bingham, Sallie. *Passion and Prejudice: A Family Memoir.* New York: Applause Books, 1989.

Bingham, Sallie. "The Truth About Growing Up Rich." *Ms.* 14 (June 1986): 48–50, 82–83.

Björk, Gunnela. *Att förhandla sitt medborgarskap: Kvinnor som kollektiva aktörer i Örebro 1900–1950.* Lund: Arkiv förlag, 1999.

Blom, Ida. "The History of Widowhood: A Bibliographic Overview." *Journal of Family History* 16 (1991): 191–210.

Blom, Ida, and Anna Tranberg. *Nordisk lovoversikt: Viktige lover for kvinnor ca. 1810–1980.* Oslo: Nordisk ministerråd, 1985, 181–204.

Boehart, William. "*. . . nicht brothlos und nothleidend zu hinterlassen.*" Hamburg: Verein für Hamburgische Geschichte, 1985.

Boehm, Ernst. "Der Schöppenstuhl zu Leipzig und der sächsische Inquisitionsprozess im Barockzeitalter." *Zeitschrift für die gesamte Strafrechtswissenschaft* 60 (1941): 155–249.

Bonnain, Rolande. "Droit écrit, coutume pyrénéenne et pratiques successorales dans les Baronnies, 1769–1836." In *Les Baronnies des Pyrénées, vol. 2: Maisons, espace, famille,* edited by George Augustins, Rolande Bonnain, Yves Péron, and Gilles Sautter. Paris: Ecole des Hautes Etudes en Sciences Sociales, 1986, 157–77.

Bonnain, Rolande, Gérard Bouchard, and Joseph Goy, eds. *Transmettre, hériter, succéder: La reproduction familiale en milieu rural, France-Québec, XVIIIe–XXe siècles.* Lyon-Paris-Villeurbanne: Presses Universitaires de Lyon, 1992.

Borscheid, Peter. *Mit Sicherheit leben: Die Geschichte der deutschen Lebensversicherungswirtschaft und der Provinzial-Lebensversicherungsanstalt von Westfalen.* Greven: Eggenkamp, 1989.

Boszormenyi-Nagy, Ivan, and Geraldine M. Spark. *Invisible Loyalities.* New York: Harper and Row, 1973.

Bouchard, Gérard, John A. Dickinson, and Joseph Goy, eds. *Les exclus de la terre en France et au Québec, XVIIe–XXe siècles: La reproduction familiale dans la différence.* Sillery: Septentrion, 1998.

Bouchard, Gérard, and Joseph Goy, eds. *Famille, économie et société rurale en contexte d'urbanisation (17e–20e siècle).* Chicoutimi-Paris: SOREP-Ecole des Hautes Etudes en Sciences Sociales, 1991.

Bouchard, Gérard, Joseph Goy, and Anne-Lise Head-König, eds. *Problèmes de la transmission des exploitations agricoles (XVIIIe–XXe siècles): Nécessités économiques et pratiques juridiques.* Rome: Ecole Française de Rome, 1998.

Bourdieu, Pierre. "Célibat et condition paysanne." *Etudes Rurales* 5–6 (1962): 32–135.

Bourdieu, Pierre. "La parenté comme représentation et comme volonté." In *Esquisse d'une théorie de la pratique, précédée de trois études d'ethnologie cabyle.* Paris: Seuil, 2000.

Bourdieu, Pierre. "Marriage Strategies as Strategies of Reproduction." In *Family and Society: Selections from the Annales Economies, Societes, Civilisations,* edited by Robert Forster and Orest Ranum. London: Johns Hopkins Press, 1976, 117–44.

Bourdieu, Pierre. *Masculine Domination.* Stanford, CA: Stanford University Press, 2001.

Bourdieu, Pierre. "What Makes a Social Class? On the Theoretical and Practical Existence of Groups." *Berkeley Journal of Sociology: A Critical Review* 32 (1987): 1–17.

Bourdieu, Pierre, and Luc Boltanski. "Formal Qualifications and Occupational Hierarchies: The Relationship between the Production System and the Reproduction System." In *Reorganizing Education: Management and Participation for Change,* edited by Edmund J. King. London: Sage, 1977, 61–69.

Boxer, Marilyn, and Jean Quataert, eds. *Connecting Spheres: European Women in a Globalizing World, 1500 to the Present.* Cambridge: Cambridge University Press, 1987.

Bradley, David. *Family Law and Political Culture: Scandinavian Laws in Comparative Perspective.* London: Sweet and Maxwell, 1996.

Bradley, David. "Family Laws and Welfare States." In *The Nordic Model of Marriage and the Welfare State,* edited by Kari Melby, Anu Pylkkänen, Bente Rosenbeck, and Christina Carlsson Wetterberg. Copenhagen: Nordic Council of Ministers, 2000, 37–67.

Brakensiek, Stefan. *Fürstendiener—Staatsbeamte—Bürger.* Göttingen: Vandenhoeck and Ruprecht, 1999.

Brauer, Adalbert. *Weidmann 1680–1980: 300 Jahre aus der Geschichte eines der ältesten Verlage der Welt.* Zürich: Weidmann, 1980.

Bremmer, J., and L. van den Bosch, eds. *Between Poverty and the Pyre: Moments in the History of Widowhood.* London: Routledge, 1995.

Brenner, Marie. *House of Dreams: The Bingham Family of Louisville.* New York: Knopf, 1988.

Bronfman, Joanie. "The Experience of Inherited Wealth: A Social-Psychological Perspective." Ph.D. diss., Brandeis University, 1987.

Brübach, Nils. *Die Reichsmessen von Frankfurt am Main, Leipzig und Braunschweig (14.–18. Jahrhundert).* Stuttgart: F. Steiner, 1994.

Bruce, Maurice. *The Coming of the Welfare State.* London: Batsford, 1961.

Brunel, Bernard. *Le Vouloir vivre et la force des choses: Augerolles en Livradois-Forez du XVIIe au XIXe siècle.* Clermont-Ferrand: Université Blaise-Pascal, Institut d'études du Massif Central, 1992.

Buquoy, Margarethe. "Die Armen auf dem Lande im späten 18. und frühen 19. Jahrhundert." *Bohemia* 26 (1985): 37–78.

Bürger, Erhard. "Bäuerliche Liegenschaftsübertragung und Vererbung im Gebiete der Tschechoslowakei." In *Die Vererbung des ländlichen Grundbesitzes in der Nachkriegszeit, vol. 2*, edited by Max Sering and Constantin von Dietze. München/Leipzig: Dunker, 1930, 109–58.

Burguière, André. *Histoire de la famille. vol. II*. Paris: Armand Colin, 1986.

Burguière, André, and François Lebrun. "The One Hundred and One Families of Europe." In *A History of the Family: vol II, The Impact of Modernity*, edited by André Burguière, Christiane Klapisch-Zuber, Martine Segalen, and Françoise Zonabend. Cambridge: Polity, 1996, 11–94.

Burke, Peter. *A Social History of Knowledge: From Gutenberg to Diderot*. Cambridge: Polity Press, 2000.

Calvi, Giulia. "Widows, the State and the Guardianship of Children in Early Modern Tuscany." In *Widowhood in Medieval and Early Modern Europe*, edited by Sandra Cavallo and Lyndan Warner. Harlow: Longman, 1999, 209–19.

Calvi, Giulia and Isabelle Chabot, eds. *Le ricchezze delle donne: Diritti patrimoniali e poteri famigliari in Italia (XIII–XIX sec.)* Torino: Rosemberg and Sellier, 1998.

Carlsson, Sten. *Fröknar, mamseller, jungfrur ochpigor: Ogifta kvinnor i det svenska ståndssamhället*. Uppsala: Studia Historica Upsaliensia 90, 1977.

Casson, Mark, and Mary Rose, eds. *Institutions and the Evolution of Modern Business*. London: Frank Cass, 1998.

Cavallo, Sandra. "Proprietà o possesso? Composizione e controllo dei beni delle donne a Torino (1650–1710)." In *Le ricchezze delle donne. Diritti patrimoniali e poteri famigliari in Italia (XIII–XIX sec.)*, edited by Giulia Calvi and Isabelle Chabot. Torino: Rosemberg and Sellier, 1998.

Cavallo, Sandra, and Lyndan Warner, eds. *Widowhood in Medieval and Early Modern Europe*. Harlow: Pearson,1999.

Ceranski, Beate. "The Professionalization of Science and the Privatization of Women's Scientific Activity at the End of the Enlightenment." In *Formatting Gender: Transitions, Breaks and Continuities in German-Speaking Europe 1750–1850*, edited by Marion Gray and Ulrike Gleixner. Ann Arbor: University of Michigan Press, 2004.

Cerman, Markus. "Bohemia after the Thirty Years' War: Some Theses on Population Structure, Marriage and Family." *Journal of Family History* 19 (1994): 149–75.

Cerman, Markus. "Central Europe and the European Marriage Pattern: Marriage Patterns and Family Structure in Central Europe, 16th–19th centuries." In *Family History Revisited: Comparative Perspectives*, edited by Richard Wall, Tamara K. Hareven, and Josef Ehmer. Newark: University of Delaware Press, 2001, 282–307.

Cerman, Markus. "Gutsherrschaft vor dem 'Weißen Berg': Zur Verschärfung der Erbuntertänigkeit in Nordböhmen 1380 bis 1620." In *Gutsherrschaftsgesellschaften im europäischen Vergleich*, edited by Jan Peters. Berlin: Akademie-Verlag, 1997, 91–111.

Cerman, Markus, and Hermann Zeitlhofer, eds. *Soziale Strukturen in Böhmen: Ein regionaler Vergleich von Wirtschaft und Gesellschaft in Gutsherrschaften, 16.–19. Jahrhundert*. Wien: Oldenbourg, 2002.

Chabrol, Guillaume-Michel. *Coutumes générales et locales de la province d'Auvergne*, vols. I and II. Riom: Dégouttes, 1784, vol. IX.

Chalmers, Thomas. *The Christian and Civic Economy of Large Towns*, vol. 1. Glasgow: Chalmers and Collins, 1821.

Chandler, David Leon, with Mary Voelz Chandler. *The Binghams of Louisville: The Dark History Behind One of the Country's Great Fortunes*. New York: Crown, 1987.

Chernow, Ron. *Titan: The Life of John D. Rockefeller, Sr.* New York: Random House, 1998.

Chesler, Phyllis, and Emily Jane Goodman. *Women, Money and Power*. New York: William Morrow, 1976.

Chester, Ronald. "Inheritance in American Legal Thought." In *Inheritance and Wealth in America*, edited by Robert K. Miller, Jr. and Stephen J. McNamee. New York: Plenum, 1998, 23–43.

Chiva, Isac, and Joseph Goy, eds. *Les Baronnies des Pyrénées: Anthropologie et histoire, permanences et changements*. Paris: Ecole des Hautes Etudes en Sciences Sociales, 1981.

Clark, Geoffrey Wilson. *Betting on Lives: Life Insurance in English Society and Culture 1695–1775*. Manchester: Manchester University Press, 1999.

Clark, Geoffrey Wilson. "Life Insurance in the Society and Culture of London, 1700–75." *Urban History* 24 (1997): 17–36.

Clausen, John A. *The Life Course: A Sociological Perspective*. New York: Prentice Hall, 1986.

Claverie, Elisabeth, and Pierre Lamaison. *L'impossible mariage: Violence et parenté en Gévaudan XVIIe, XVIIIe, XIXe siècles*. Paris: Hachette, 1982.

Clignet, Remi P. "Efficiency, Reciprocity, and Ascriptive Equality: The Three Major Strategies Governing the Selection of Heirs in America." *Social Science Quarterly* 76 (1995): 274–93.

Clignet, Remi P. "Ethnicity and Inheritance." In *Inheritance and Wealth in America*, edited by Robert K. Miller, Jr. and Stephen J. McNamee. New York: Plenum, 1998, 119–37.

*Codex Augusteus oder neu vermehrte Corpus juris Saxonici, vol. 2*. Leipzig: J. F. Gleditsch, 1724.

*Codex Saxonicus*, 2 vols. Leipzig: Reclam, 1842.

Cole, John, and Eric Wolf. *The Hidden Frontier: Ecology and Ethnicity in an Alpine Valley*. New York: Academic Press, 1974.

Collier, Peter, and David Horowitz. *The Rockefellers: An American Dynasty*. New York: Holt, Rinehart and Winston, 1976.

Collomp, Alain. *La Maison du père: Famille et village en Haute-Provence aux XVIIe et XVIIIe siècles*. Paris: Presses Universitaires de France, 1983.

Cookson, Peter W., Jr., and Caroline Hodges Persell. *Preparing for Power: America's Elite Boarding Schools*. New York: Basic Books, 1985.

Costa, Dora L. "The Evolution of Retirement: Summary of a Research Project." *American Economic History Review* 88 (1998): 232–36.

Cott, Nancy. "Eighteenth-Century Family and Social Life Revealed in Massachusetts Divorce Records." *Journal of Social History* 10 (1976): 20–43.

Crossick, Geoffrey. *An Artisan Elite in Victorian Society*. London: Croom Helm, 1978.

Crossick, Geoffrey. "Meanings of Property and the World of the Petite Bourgeoisie." In *Urban Fortunes: Propery and Inheritance in the Town, 1700–1900*, edited by Jon Stobart and Alastair Owens. Aldershot: Ashgate, 2000, 50–78.

Cunningham, Hugh, and Joanna Innes, eds. *Charity, Philanthropy and Reform: From the 1690s to 1850*. Basingstoke: Macmillan, 1998.

Curran, Cynthia. "Private Women, Public Needs: Middle-Class Widows in Victorian England." *Albion* 25 (1993): 217–36.

Daniels, Arlene Kaplan. "Gender, Class, and Career in the Lives of Privileged Women." In *Social Roles and Social Institutions: Essays in Honor of Rose Laub Coser*, edited by Judith R. Blau and Norman Goodman. Boulder, Colo.: Westview Press, 1991, 115–32.

Daniels, Arlene Kaplan. *Invisible Careers: Women Civic Leaders from the Volunteer World*. Chicago: University of Chicago Press, 1988.

Daston, Lorraine. *Classical Probability in the Enlightenment*. Princeton, N.J.: Princeton University Press, 1988.

Daunton, Martin, ed. *Charity, Self-Interest and Welfare in the English Past*. London: University College Press, 1996.

Davidoff, Leonore, and Catherine Hall. *Family Fortunes: Men and Women of the English Middle Class, 1780–1850*. London: Hutchinson, 1987; 2nd ed., London: Routledge, 2002.

de Haan, Henk. *In the Shadow of the Tree: Kinship, Property and Inheritance Among Farm Families*. Amsterdam: Het Spinhuis, 1994.

De Roover, Raymond. *L'evolution de la lettre de change XIVe–XVIIIe siècles*. Paris: A. Colin, 1953.

Dean, Mitchell. *The Constitution of Poverty: Towards a Genealogy of Liberal Governance*. London: Routledge, 1991.

Delille, Gérard. *Famille et propriété dans le Royaume de Naples (XVIe–XIXe siècle)*. Paris and Rome: Ecole française de Rome, 1985.

*Der Stadt Leipzig Ordnungen wie auch Privilegia und Statuta*. Leipzig: Fritsch, 1701.

Derouet, Bernard. "Le partage des frères: Héritage masculin et reproduction sociale en Franche-Comté aux XVIIIe et XIXe siècles." *Annales Economies, Sociétés, Civilisations*, XLVIII (1993): 453–74.

Derouet, Bernard. "Pratiques successorales et rapport à la terre: Les sociétés paysannes d'Ancien Régime." *Annales Economies, Sociétés, Civilisations*, XLIV (1989): 173–206.

Derouet, Bernard. "Transmettre la terre: Origines et inflexions récentes d'une problématique de la différence." *Histoire et Sociétés Rurales* 2 (1994): 33–67.

Derouet, Bernard. "La transmission égalitaire du patrimoine dans la France rurale (XVIe–XIXe siècles): Nouvelles perspectives de recherches." In *Familia, Casa y Trabajo: Historia de la Familia*, edited by F. Chacon Jiminez. Murcia: Universidad de Murcia, 1997, 73–95.

Dickson, P.G.M. *The Financial Revolution in England: A Study in the Development of Public Credit, 1680–1756*. London: Macmillan, 1967.

Diefendorf, Barbara. "Women and Property in *ancien régime* France: Theory and Practice in Dauphiné and Paris." In *Early Modern Conceptions of Property*, edited by John Brewer and Susan Staves. London: Routledge, 1995, 170–93.

DiMaggio, Paul, and Michael Useem. "The Arts in Class Reproduction." In *Cultural and Economic Reproduction in Education: Essays on Class, Ideology and the State*, edited by Michael W. Apple. London: Routledge and Kegan Paul, 1982, 181–201.

Ditz, Toby. *Property and Kinship: Inheritance in Early Connecticut 1750–1820.* Princeton, N.J.: Princeton University Press, 1986.

Domhoff, G. William. *The Higher Circles: The Governing Class in America.* New York: Random House, 1970.

Dupree, Marguerite W. *Family Structure in the Staffordshire Potteries, 1840–1880.* Oxford: Oxford University Press, 1995.

Duroux, Rose. *Les Auvergnats de Castille: Renaissance et mort d'une migration au XIXe siècle.* Clermont-Ferrand: Association des Publications de la Faculté des Lettres et Sciences Humaines de l'Université Blaise-Pascal, 1992.

Duroux, Rose. "La noria des exclus: Stratégie chez les migrants auvergnats en Espagne (XIXe siècle)." In *Les exclus de la terre en France et au Québec, XVIIe–XXe siècles. La reproduction familiale dans la différence,* edited by Gérard Bouchard, John Dickinson, and Joseph Goy. Sillery: Septentrion, 1998, 96–113.

Duroux, Rose. "The Temporary Migration of Males and the Power of Females in a Stem-Family Society: The Case of Nineteenth-Century Auvergne." *History of the Family* 6 (2001): 33–49.

Ebrecht, Angelika, Regina Nörtemann, and Herta Schwarz, eds. *Brieftheorie des 18. Jahrhunderts.* Stuttgart: Metzler, 1990.

Ehmer, Josef. "House and the Stem Family in Austria." In *House and the Stem Family in Eurasian Perspective: Proceedings of the 12th International Economic History Congress,* edited by Antoinette Fauve-Chamoux and Emiko Ochiai. Kyoto: International Research Center for Japanese Studies, 1998, 59–81.

Ehmer, Josef. "The 'Life Stairs': Aging, Generational Relations, and Small Commodity Production in Central Europe." In *Aging and Generational Relations over the Life Course,* edited by Tamara Hareven. Berlin: Walter de Gruyter, 1996, 53–74.

Ehmer, Josef. *Sozialgeschichte des Alters.* Frankfurt a.M.: Suhrkamp, 1990.

Ellis, William E. *Robert Worth Bingham and the Southern Mystique: From the Old South to the New South and Beyond.* Kent, Ohio: The Kent State University Press, 1997.

Engels, Friedrich. *The Origins of the Family, Private Property and the State.* London: Lawrence and Wishart, 1972 (originally published 1885).

Engels, J. T. *Kinderen van Amsterdam.* Amsterdam: Walburg Pers, 1989.

Erickson, Amy Louise. *Women and Property in Early Modern England.* London: Routledge, 1993.

Ernst, Joseph W., ed. *"Dear Father"/"Dear Son": Correspondence between John D. Rockefeller and John D. Rockefeller, Jr.* New York: Fordham University Press, 1994.

Fauve-Chamoux, Antoinette. "Les frontières de l'autorégulation paysanne: Croissance et famille-souche." *Revue de la Bibliothèque nationale* 50 (1993): 38–47.

Fauve-Chamoux, Antoinette. "Household Forms and Living Standards in Preindustrial France: From Models to Realities." *Journal of Family History* 18 (1993): 135–56.

Fauve-Chamoux, Antoinette. "Stratégies individuelles et politiques de reproduction familiale: Le perpétuel ajustement intergénérationnel des destins migratoires à Esparros (XVIIe–XXe siècles)." In *Marchés, Migrations et Transmission (XVIIIe–XXe siècles). Les stratégies familiales dans les espaces français, canadiens et suisse,* edited by Luigi Lorenzetti, Anne-Lise Head-König, and Joseph Goy. Bern: Petre Lang, 2004.

Fauve-Chamoux, Antoinette. "Les structures familiales au pays des familles-souches: Esparros." *Annales Economies, Sociétés, Civilisations* XXXIX (1984): 513–28.

Feigl, Helmuth. "Bäuerliches Erbrecht und Erbgewohnheiten in Niederösterreic." *Jahrbuch für Landeskunde von Niederösterreich* 37 (1967): 161–83.

Ferber, Marianne, and Julie Nelson, eds. *Beyond Economic Man: Feminist Theory and Economics.* Chicago: University of Chicago Press, 1993.

Finch, Janet, and Jennifer Mason. *Passing On: Kinship and Inheritance in England.* London: Routledge, 2000.

Finch, Janet, and Lynn Wallis. "Death, Inheritance and the Life Course." In *The Sociology of Death,* edited by David Clark. Oxford: Blackwell, 1993, 50–68.

Finlayson, Geoffrey. *Citizen, State, and Social Welfare in Britain 1830–1990.* Oxford: Clarendon Press, 1994.

Fischer, Gerhard. *Aus zwei Jahrhunderten Leipziger Handels-Geschichte 1470–1650.* Leipzig: F. Meiner, 1929.

Fissell, Mary E. *Patients, Power, and the Poor in Eighteenth-Century Bristol.* Cambridge: Cambridge University Press, 1991.

Flinn, Michael. *The European Demographic System, 1500–1820.* Brighton: Harvester 1981.

Folbre, Nancy. *Who Pays for the Kids? Gender and the Structures of Constraint.* London: Routledge, 1994.

Fontaine, Laurence, and Jürgen Schlumbohm. "Household Strategies for Survival: An Introduction." *International Review of Social History* 45, supp. 8 (2000): 1–17.

*Fortgesetzter Codex Augusteus.* Leipzig: J. F. Gleditsch, 1772.

Foster, George. "Peasant Societies and the Image of Limited Good." *American Anthropologist* 67 (1965): 293–315.

Foucault, Michel. *Discipline and Punish: The Birth of the Prison.* Harmondsworth: Penguin, 1977.

François, Etienne. "Unterschichten und Armut in rheinischen Residenzstädten des 18. Jahrhunderts." *Vierteljahrschrift für Sozial- und Wirtschaftsgeschichte* 62 (1975): 433–64.

Franz, Johann Georg Friedrich. *Pragmatische Handlungs Geschichte der Stadt Leipzig.* Leipzig: J. S. Heinsius, 1772.

Fraser, Derek. *The Evolution of the British Welfare State.* London: Macmillan, 1973.

Freist, Dagmar. "Religious Difference and the Experience of Widowhood in Seventeenth- and Eighteenth-Century Germany." In *Widowhood in Medieval and Early Modern Europe,* edited by Sandra Cavallo and Lyndan Warner. Harlow: Pearson, 1999, 164–77.

French, Lorely. *German Women as Letter Writers: 1750–1850.* London: Associated University Presses, 1996.

Friedan, Betty. *The Feminine Mystique.* New York: W. W. Norton, 1963.

Friedland, Roger, and Alexander F. Robertson, eds. *Beyond the Marketplace: Rethinking Economy and Society.* New York, Aldine de Gruyter, 1990.

Fritz, Martin. *Från handelsstad till industristad 1820–1920.* Göteborg: Nerenius and Santérus, 1996.

Fuchs, Rachel. *Abandoned Children: Foundlings and Child Welfare in Nineteenth-Century France.* Albany: State University of New York Press, 1984.

Gaunt, David. "The Property and Kin Relationships of Retired Farmers in Northern and Central Europe." In *Family Forms in Historic Europe,* edited by Richard Wall, Jean Robin, and Peter Laslett. Cambridge: Cambridge University Press, 1983, 249–79.

Gerhard, Hans-Jürgen. *Diensteinkommen der Göttinger Officianten 1750–1850.* Göttingen: Vandenhoeck and Ruprecht, 1978.

Gerhard, Ute. *Gleichheit ohne Angleichung: Frauen im Recht.* Munich: Beck, 1990.

Gervais, Diane. "La construction du consensus familial dans les successions inégalitaires du Lot au XIXe siècle." In *Transmettre, hériter, succéder: La reproduction familiale en milieu rural, France-Québec, XVIIIe–XXe siècles,* edited by Rolande Bonnain, Gérard Bouchard, and Joseph Goy. Lyon-Paris-Villeurbanne: Presses Universitaires de Lyon, 1992, 265–76.

Gonod, Philippe. "Les modalités du partage égalitaire: L'exemple du val de Saône aux XVIIIe et XIXe siècles." *Etudes Rurales* 137 (1995): 73–87.

Goody, Jack. "Dowry and the Rights of Women to Property." In *Property Relations: Reviewing the Anthropological Tradition,* edited by Chris Hann. Cambridge: Cambridge University Press, 1998, 201–13.

Goody, Jack. "Erbschaft, Eigentum und Frauen: Einige vergleichende Betrachtungen." In *Historische Familienforschung,* edited by Michael Mitterauer and Reinhard Sieder. Frankfurt a.M.: Suhrkamp, 1982, 88–122.

Goody, Jack. "Inheritance, Property and Women: Some Comparative Considerations." In *Family and Inheritance: Rural Society in Western Europe 1200–1800,* edited by Jack Goody, Joan Thirsk, and Edward P. Thompson. Cambridge: Cambridge University Press, 1976, 10–36.

Goody, Jack. "Introduction." In *Family and Inheritance: Rural Society in Western Europe 1200–1800,* edited by Jack. R. Goody, Joan Thirsk, and Edward P. Thompson. Cambridge: Cambridge University Press, 1976, 1–9.

Goody, Jack. "Strategies of Heirship." *Comparative Studies in Society and History* 15 (1973): 3–20.

Goody, Jack, Joan Thirsk, and Edward P. Thompson, eds. *Family and Inheritance: Rural Society in Western Europe 1200–1800.* Cambridge: Cambridge University Press, 1976.

Göransson, Anita. "Gender and Property Rights: Capital, Kin and Owner-Influence in Nineteenth- and Twentieth-Century Sweden." *Business History* 35 (1993): 11–32.

Göransson, Anita. "Kön som analyskategori i den ekonomiska historien: Några linjer och resultat." In *Kvinnovetenskapens vadan och varthän,* edited by Eva Borgström and Anita Nordenstam. Göteborg: Göteborg University, 1996, 49–65.

Göransson, Anita. "Mening, makt och materialitet: Ett försök att förena realistiska och poststrukturalistiska positioner." *Häften för Kristiska Studier* 4 (1998): 3–26.

Gordon, Robert. "Critical Legal Histories." *Stanford Law Review* 36 (1984): 57–125.

Gouldner, Alvin. "The Norm of Reciprocity: A Preliminary Statement." *American Sociological Review* 25 (1960): 161–78.

Goy, Joseph. "Transmission successorale et paysannerie pendant la Révolution française: Un grand malentendu." *Etudes Rurales* 110–112 (1988): 45–56.

Gray, Richard T. "Buying into Signs: Money and Semiosis in Eighteenth-Century German Language Theory." *The German Quarterly* 69 (1996): 1–14.

Green, David R. "Independent Women, Wealth and Wills in Nineteenth-Century London." In *Urban Fortunes: Property and Inheritance in the Town, 1700–1900,* edited by Jon Stobart and Alastair Owens. Aldershot: Ashgate, 2000, 195–222.

Green, David R., and Alan Parton. "Slums and Slum Life in Victorian England: London and Birmingham at Mid Century." In *Slums,* edited by Martin Gaskell. Leicester: Leicester University Press, 1990, 17–91.

Grimm, Jacob L. K., and Wilhelm. K. Grimm. *Deutsches Wörterbuch.* Leipzig: Hirzel, 1854–1960.

Gross, Stephen John. "Handing Down the Farm: Values, Strategies, and Outcomes in Inheritance Practices among Rural German Americans." *Journal of Family History* 21 (1996): 192–217.

Grossi, Paolo. *Il dominio e le cose: Percezioni medievali e moderne dei diritti reali.* Milano: Giuffré, 1992.

Grossi, Paolo. *Un altro modo di possedere: L'emersione di alternative di proprietà alla coscienza giuridica post-unitaria.* Milano: Giuffré, 1977.

Grulich, Josef, and Hermann Zeitlhofer. "Lebensformen und soziale Muster in Südböhmen im 16. und 17. Jahrhundert." *Jihočeský sborník historický* 66/67 (1997/98): 26–50.

Gunnela, Bjork. *Att förhandla sitt medborgarskap. Kvinnor som kollektiva aktörer i Örebro 1900–1950.* Lund: Arkiv förlag, 1999.

Gustafsson, Bo. "Some Theoretical Problems for Institutional Economic History." *Scandinavian Economic History Review* XLVI (1998): 5–31.

Guzzi, Sandro. "Antonomies locales et systèmes politiques alpins: La Suisse italienne au XVIIe et XVIIIe siècles." In *La découverte des Alpes,* edited by J.-F. Bergier and Sandro Guzzi. Basel: Schwabe and Company, 1992, 229–55.

Guzzi-Heeb, Sandro. "Marie-Julienne de Nucé, die Politik und die Religion: Elemente einer weiblichen Machtstrategie." *Traverse. Zeitschrift für Geschichte* 3 (2001): 132–40.

Haase, C. "Georg Christian von Oeders Oldenburger Zeit." *Oldenburger Jahrbuch des Oldenburger Landesvereins für Geschichte, Natur- und Heimatkunde* 64 (1965): 1–58.

Habakkuk, H. John. "Family Structure and Economic Change in Nineteenth-Century Europe." *Journal of Economic History* 15 (1955): 1–12.

Habermas, Jürgen. *Strukturwandel der Öffentlichkeit.* Darmstadt and Neuwied: Luchterhand, 1962.

Habermas, Rebekka. *Frauen und Männer des Bürgertums.* Göttingen: Vandenhoeck and Ruprecht, 2000.

Hajnal, John. "European Marriage Patterns in Perspective." In *Population in History,* edited by David Glass and David Eversley. London: Edward Arnold, 1965, 101–43.

Hajnal, John. "Two Kinds of Pre-Industrial Family Formation Systems." In *Family Forms in Historic Europe,* edited by Richard Wall, Jean Robin, and Peter Laslett. Cambridge: Cambridge University Press, 1983, 65–104.

Hammerton, James A. *Cruelty and Companionship: Conflict in Nineteenth-Century Married Life*. London: Routledge, 1992.

Hanlon, Gregory, and Elspeth Carruthers. "Wills, Inheritance and the Moral Order in Seventeenth-Century Agenais." *Journal of Family History* 15 (1990): 149–61.

Hann, Chris, ed. *Property Relations: Renewing the Anthropological Tradition*. Cambridge: Cambridge University Press, 1998.

Hardwick, Julie. *The Practice of Patriarchy: Gender and the Politics of Household Authority in Early Modern France*. University Park, Penn.: Penn State University Press, 1998.

Hareven, Tamara K. "A Complex Relationship: Family Strategies and the Processes of Economic and Social Change." In *Beyond the Marketplace: Rethinking Economy and Society*, edited by Roger Friedland and Alexander F. Robertson. New York: Aldine de Gruyter, 1990, 215–44.

Hareven, Tamara K. "Cycles, Courses, and Cohorts: Reflections on Theoretical and Methodological Approaches to the Historical Study of Family Development." *Journal of Social History* 12 (1978): 97–109.

Hareven, Tamara K. *Families, History and Social Change: Life-Course and Cross-Cultural Perspectives*. Boulder, Colo.: Westview Press, 1999.

Hareven, Tamara K. *Family Time and Industrial Time*. Cambridge: Cambridge University Press, 1982.

Hareven, Tamara K. "The Impact of the Historical Study of the Family and the Life Course Paradigm on Sociology." *Comparative Social Research* 2 (supp.) (1996): 185–205.

Hareven, Tamara K., ed. *Transitions: Family and the Life Course in Historical Perspective*. New York: Academic Press, 1978.

Harr, John Ensor, and Peter J. Johnson. *The Rockefeller Century*. New York: Charles Scribner and Sons, 1988.

Harris, Bernard. *The Origins of the British Welfare State: Society, State, and Social Welfare in England and Wales, 1800–1950*. Houndmills: Macmillan, 2004.

Harris, Olivia. "Households and Their Boundaries." *History Workshop Journal* 13 (1982): 143–52.

Hasse, Ernst. *Geschichte der Leipziger Messen*. Leipzig: S. Hirzel, 1885.

Haubold, Christian Gottlieb. *Lehrbuch des königlich-sächsischen Privatrechts*, 2 vols. Leipzig: Hahn, 1847.

Head-König, Anne-Lise. "Malthus dans les Alpes: La diversité de régulation démographique dans l'arc alpin du XVIe au début du XXe siècle." In *Quand la montagne aussi a une histoire: Mélanges offerts à Jean-François Bergier*, edited by Martin Körner and François Walter. Bern: Haupt, 1996, 361–70.

Hecht, Jacqueline. "Johann Peter Süßmilch, point alpha ou omega de la science démographique naive?" *Annales de démographie historique* (1979): 101–33.

Held, Thomas. "Rural Retirement Arrangements in Seventeenth-Century to Nineteenth-Century Austria: A Cross-Community Analysis." *Journal of Family History* 7 (1982): 227–54.

Hellinger, Bert. *Ordnungen der Liebe:. Ein Kurs-Buch mit B.H. Zweite überarbeitete und ergänzte Auflage*. Heidelberg: Cael Auer Systeme, 1995.

Hellinger, Bert, and Hunter Beaumont. *Touching Love*. Heidelberg: Cael Auer Systeme, 1999.

Higley, Stephen R. *Privilege, Power, and Place: The Geography of the American Upper Class*. Lanham, Md.: Roman and Littlefield, 1995.

Hirschon, Rene, ed. *Women and Property: Women as Property*. London: Croom Helm, 1984.

Hohkamp, Michaela. "Wer will erben?" In *Gutsherrschaft als soziales Modell*, edited by Jan Peters. München: Oldenbourg, 1995, 327–41.

Holcombe, Lee. *Wives and Property: Reform of the Married Women's Property Law in Nineteenth-Century England*. Toronto: University of Toronto Press, 1983.

Holderness, B. A. "Widows in Pre-Industrial Society: An Essay Upon Their Economic Functions." In *Land, Kinship and Life-Cycle*, edited by Richard H. Smith. Cambridge: Cambridge University Press, 1984, 423–46.

Holthöfer, Ernst. "Die Geschlechtsvormundschaft: Ein Überblick von der Antike bis ins 19. Jahrhundert." In *Frauen in der Geschichte des Rechts: Von der Frühen Neuzeit bis zur Gegenwart*, edited by Gerhard Ute. Munich: C. H. Beck, 1997, 390–451.

Homburg, Heidrun. "Werbung—'eine Kunst, die gelernt sein will': Aufbrüche in eine neue Warenwelt 1750–1850." *Jahrbuch für Wirtschaftsgeschichte*, part one (1997): 11–52.

Horáček, Cyril. "Das Ausgedinge: Eine Agrarpolitische Studie mit besonderer Berücksichtigung der Böhmischen Länder." *Wiener Staatswissenschaftliche Studien* 5 (1904): 1–96.

Horden, Peregrine. "Household Care and Informal Networks: Comparisons and Continuities from Antiquity to the Present." In *The Locus of Care: Families, Communities, Institutions and the Provision of Welfare Since Antiquity*, edited by Peregrine Horden and Richard H. Smith. London: Routledge, 1998, 21–67.

Horden, Peregrine, and Richard J. Smith, eds. *The Locus of Care: Families, Communities, Institutions and the Provision of Welfare Since Antiquity*. London: Routledge, 1998.

Hrdy, Sarah Blaffer, and Debra S. Judge. "Darwin and the Puzzle of Primogeniture." *Human Nature* 4 (1993): 1–45.

Hroch, Miroslav, and Josef Petraň. *Das 17. Jahrhundert: Krise der feudalen Gesellschaft?* Hamburg: Hoffmann und Campe, 1981.

Hüchtker, Dietlind. *Elende Mütter und liederliche Weibspersonen*. Münster: Westfälisches Dampfboot, 1998.

Hufton, Olwen. *The Prospect Before Her: A History of Women in Western Europe 1500–1800*. London: Vintage, 1995 and New York: Knopf, 1996.

Ighe, Ann, and Linda Lane. "Institutionell stabilitet. Om svårigheten i att omförhandla ett genuskontrakt." In *Kvinnovetenskapens vadan och varthän*, edited by E. Borgström and A. Nordenstam. Göteborg: Göteborg University, 1996.

Imesch, Dyonis. "Beiträge zur Geschichte und Statistik der Pfarrgemeinde Naters." *Zeitschrift für schweizerische Statistik* 44 (1908): 369–414.

Imhof, Arthur. "Remarriage in Rural Populations and in Urban Middle and Upper Strata in Germany from the Sixteenth to the Twentieth Century." In *Marriage and Remarriage in Populations of the Past*, edited by Jacques Dupâquier, Etienne Hélin, Peter Laslett, and Massimo Livi–Bacci. London: Academic Press, 1981, 335–45.

Inhaber, Herbert, and Sidney Carroll. *How Rich Is Too Rich?: Income and Wealth in America*. New York: Praeger, 1992.

Johnson, Barry W., and Martha Britton Eller. "Federal Taxation of Inheritance and Wealth Transfers."In *Inheritance and Wealth in America*, edited by Robert K. Miller, Jr., and Stephen J. McNamee. New York: Plenum, 1998, 61–90.

Johnson, Paul. "Risk, Redistribution and Social Welfare in Britain from the Poor Law to Beveridge." In *Charity, Self-Interest and Welfare in the English Past*, edited by Martin Daunton. London: University College London Press, 1996, 225–48.

Jones, Alice Hanson. *Wealth of a Nation to Be: The American Colonies on the Eve of the Revolution*. New York: Columbia University Press, 1980.

Judge, Debra S. "American Legacies and the Variable Life Histories of Women and Men." *Human Nature* 6 (1995): 291–323.

Kälin, Urs. *Die Urner Magistratenfamilien: Herrschaft, ökonomische Lage und Lebensstil einer ländlichen Oberschicht 1700–1850*. Zürich: Chronos, 1991.

Kann, Robert A., and David Zděnek. *The Peoples of the Eastern Habsburg Lands, 1526–1918*. Seattle: University of Washington Press, 1984.

Karlsson Sjögren, Åsa. *Kvinnors rätt i stormaktstidens Gävle*. Ph.D. diss., University of Umeå, 1998.

Kaser, Karl. *Macht und Erbe: Männerherrschaft, Besitz und Familie im östlichen Europa (1500–1900)*. Wien: Böhlau, 2000.

Katz, Michael, and Christoph Sachsse, eds. *The Mixed Economy of Social Welfare: Public/Private Relations in England, Germany and the United States, the 1870s to the 1930s*. Baden-Baden: Nomos, 1996.

Kaufhold, Karl Heinrich. "Die Wirtschaft in der frühen Neuzeit: Gewerbe, Handel und Verkehr." In *Geschichte Niedersachsens: Politik, Wirtschaft und Gesellschaft von der Reformation bis zum Beginn des 19. Jahrhunderts*, edited by Christine van den Heuvel and Manfred von Boetticher. Hanover: Hahn, 1998, 351–636.

Keckeis, Peter, ed. *Sagen der Schweiz. Wallis*. Zürich: Limmat Verlag, 1999.

Keller, Suzanne. "The American Upper-Class Family: Precarious Claims on the Future." *Journal of Comparative Family Studies* 22 (1991): 159–82.

Kendall, Diana. *The Power of Good Deeds: Privileged Women and the Social Reproduction of the Upper Class*. Lanham, Md.: Rowan and Littlefield, 2002.

Kennedy, Liam. "Farm Succession in Modern Ireland: Elements of a Theory of Inheritance." *Economic History Review* XLIV (1991): 477–99.

Kert, Bernice. *Abby Aldrich Rockefeller: The Woman in the Family*. New York: Random House, 1993.

Kertzer, David I., and Peter Laslett, eds. *Aging in the Past: Demography, Society and Old Age*. Berkeley Calif.: University of California Press, 1995.

Kessler-Harris, Alice. "Gender Identity: Right to Work and the Idea of Economic Citizenship." *Schweizerische Zeitschrift für Geschichte* 46 (1996): 411–26.

Kessler-Harris, Alice. *In Pursuit of Equity: Women, Men and the Quest for Economic Citizenship in 20th Century America*. Oxford: Oxford University Press, 2001.

Kidd, Alan. "Civil Society or the State? Recent Approaches to the History of Voluntary Welfare." *Journal of Historical Sociology* 15 (2002): 328–42.

Kirkhorn, Michael. "The Bingham Black Sheep." *Louisville Today* (1979): 36–41.

Klášterská, Alice. "Forma sociálního zabezpečení na vesnici v 18. a v první polovine 19. století (Forms of rural social insurance in the eighteenth and early nineteenth centuries)." *Historická demografie* 21 (1997): 95–132.

Klausmann, Kristina. "'Dann manche Kramers-Frau in ihrem Laden-Stul'–weibliche Handelstätigkeit in Frankfurt vom 17. Bis zum beginnenden 19. Jahrhundert." In *Brücke zwischen den Völkern—Zur Geschichte der Frankfurter Messe, vol. 2: Beiträge zur Geschichte der Frankfurter Messe*, edited by Patricia Stahl, Roland Hoede, and Dieter Skala. Frankfurt a.M: Ausstellung im Historischen Museum der Stadt, 1991, 280–90.

Knight, Louise W. "Jane Addams's Views on the Responsibilities of Wealth." In *The Responsibilities of Wealth*, edited by Dwight F. Burlingame. Bloomington, Ind.: Indiana University Press, 1992, 118–44.

Knodel, John, and Katherine A. Lynch. "The Decline of Remarriage: Evidence from German Village Populations in the Eighteenth and Nineteenth Centuries." *Journal of Family History* 10 (1985): 34–59.

Koerner, Bernhard, ed. *Deutsches Geschlechterbuch, Bd. 89/Niedersächsissssches Geschlechterbuch, vol. 3*. Görlitz: Starke, 1936.

Kok, Jan. "The Challenge of Strategy: A Comment." *International Review of Social History* 47 (2002): 473–77.

Kopczyński, Michal. "Old Age Gives No Joy? Old People in the Kujawy Countryside at the End of the Eighteenth Century." *Acta Poloniae Historica* 78 (1998): 81–101.

Kritter, J. A. *Sammlung wichtiger Erfahrungen bei den zu Grunde gegangenen Witwencassen*. Göttingen, 1780.

Küster, C. D. *Der Wittwen- und Waisenversorger, oder Grundsätze, nach welchen dauerhafte Wittwen- und Waisensocietäten gestiftet werden können: Zum nutzen unbelehrter Leser, welche Aufseher oder Glieder dieser wohlthätigen Anstalten sind*. Leipzig: Junius, 1772.

La Vopa, Anthony J. *Grace, Talent and Merit: Poor Students, Clerical Careers and Professional Ideology in Eighteenth-Century Germany*. Cambridge: Cambridge University Press, 1988.

Labouvie, Eva. "In weiblicher Hand: Frauen als Firmengründerinnen und Unternehmerinnen (1600–1870)." In *Frauenleben—Frauen leben: Zur Geschichte und Gegenwart weiblicher Lebenswelten im Saarraum (17–20 Jahrhundert)*, edited by Eva Labouvie. St. Ingbert: Röhrig, 1993, 88–131.

Ladurie, Emmanuel Le Roy. "Family Structures and Inheritance Customs in Sixteenth-Century France." In *Family and Inheritance: Rural Society in Western Europe 1200–1800*, edited by Jack Goody, Joan Thirsk, and Edward P. Thompson. London: Cambridge University Press, 1973, 37–70.

Ladurie, Emmanuel Le Roy. "Système de la coutume: structures familiales et coutumes d'héritage en France au XVIe siècle." *Annales Economies, Sociétés, Civilisations* XXVII (1972): 825–846.

Lamaison, Pierre. "La diversité des modes de transmission: une géographie tenace." *Etudes Rurales* 110–112 (1988): 119–75.

Lammel, Siegbert. "Die Gesetzgebung des Handelsrechts." In *Handbuch der Quellen und Literature der neueren europäischen Privatrechtsgeschichte, vol. 2: Neuere Zeit (1500–1800)*, edited by Helmut Coing. Munich: C. H. Beck, 1976, 629–31.

Langbein, John H. "The Twentieth-Century Revolution in Wealth Transmission." *Michigan Law Review* 84 (1988): 722–51.

Laslett, Barbara, and Johanna Brenner. "Gender and Social Reproduction: Historical Perspectives." *Annual Review of Sociology* 15 (1989): 381–404.

Laslett, Peter. "Familie und Industrialisierung: Eine starke Theorie." In *Sozialgeschichte der Familie in der Neuzeit Europas,* edited by Werner Conze. Stuttgart: Klett-Cotta, 1976, 13–31.

Laslett, Peter. "Introduction: The History of the Family." In *Household and Family in Past Time,* edited by Peter Laslett and Richard Wall. Cambridge: Cambridge University Press, 1972, 1–89.

Laslett, Peter. "Mean Household Size in England Since the Sixteenth Century." In *Household and Family in Past Time,* edited by Peter Laslett and Richard Wall. Cambridge: Cambridge University Press, 1972, 125–58.

Laslett, Peter, and Richard Wall, eds. *Household and Family in Past Time.* Cambridge: Cambridge University Press, 1972.

Laybourn, Keith. *The Evolution of British Social Policy and the Welfare State.* Keele: Keele University Press, 1995.

Le Play, Frédéric. *L'organisation de la famille selon le vrai modèle signalé par l'histoire de toutes les races et de tous les temps.* Paris: Téqui, 1871.

Le Play, Frédéric. *La réforme sociale.* Paris: H. Plon, 1864.

Lees, Lynn. *Exiles of Erin: Irish Migrants in Victorian London.* Manchester: Manchester University Press, 1979.

Lerner, Gerda. *Why History Matters: Life and Thought.* New York: Oxford University Press, 1997.

Lerner, Robert, Althea K. Nagai, and Stanley Rothman. *American Elites.* New Haven, Conn.: Yale University Press, 1996.

Lesemann, Silke. *Arbeit, Ehre, Geschlechterbeziehungen: Zur sozialen und wirtschaftlichen Stellung von Frauen im frühneuzeitlichen Hildesheim.* Hildesheim: Bernward, 1994.

Levi, Giovanni. *L'ereditá immateriale: Carriera di un esorcista nel Piemonte del Seicento.* Turin: Einaudi, 1985 (English edition: *Inhering Power: The Story of an Exorcist.* Chicago: University of Chicago Press, 1988).

Levi, Giovanni. "Famiglie contadine nella Liguria del Settecento." In *Centro e periferia di uno stato assoluto: Tre saggi su Piemonte e Liguria in età moderna,* edited by Giovanni Levi. Torino: Rosemberg and Sellier, 1985, 71–149.

Levi, Giovanni. *Das immaterielle Erbe: Eine bäuerliche Welt an der Schwelle zur Moderne.* Berlin: Wagenbach, 1986.

Lewis, Jane. "Family Provision of Health and Welfare in the Mixed Economy of Care in the Late Nineteenth and Twentieth Centuries." *Social History of Medicine* 8 (1995): 1–16.

Lichtenberg, Georg Christoph. *Briefwechsel,* vol. 1, edited by Ulrich Joost and Albrecht Schöne. Munich: Beck, 1983.

Lichtenstein, Marsha. "Upper Class Women and Potential for Social Change." *Humanity and Society* 16 (1992): 3–20.

Lindemann, Margot. *Deutsche Presse bis 1815.* Berlin: Colloquium, 1969.

Longhofer, Jeffery. "Toward a Political Economy of Inheritance: Community and Household Among the Mennonites." *Theory and Society* 22 (1993): 337–62.

Ludovici, Carl Günther. *Allgemeine Schatz-Kammer der Kauffmannschafft oder vollständiges Lexicon aller Handlungen und Gewerbe,* 5 vols. Leipzig: J. S. Heinsius, 1741–43.

Macfarlane, Alan. *The Origins of English Individualism: The Family, Property and Social Transition*. Oxford: Oxford University Press, 1978.

Mackenroth, Gerhard. *Bevölkerungslehre: Theorie, Soziologie und Statistik der Bevölkerung*. Berlin: Springer, 1953.

Maclean, Mavis, and Lenore J. Weitzman. "Introduction to the Issues." In *Economic Consequences of Divorce: The International Perspective*, edited by Lenore J. Weitzman and Mavis Maclean. Oxford: Clarendon Press, 1992, 1–12.

Macpherson, Colin B. *The Political Theory of Possessive Individualism: Hobbes To Locke*. Oxford: Clarendon Press, 1962.

Malmström, Åke. *Betänkande med förslag om upphävande av den äldre giftermålsbalken*, Statens offentliga utredningar, 43. Stockholm: Statistiska centralbyrån, 1947.

Marcus, George E. "'Elite' as a Concept, Theory, and Research Tradition." In *Elites: Ethnographic Issues*, edited by George E. Marcus. Albuquerque, N. Mex.: University of New Mexico Press, 1983, 7–27.

Marcus, George E. "The Fiduciary Role in American Family Dynasties and Their Institutional Legacy," In *Elites: Ethnographic Issues*, edited by George E. Marcus. Albuquerque, N. Mex.: University of New Mexico Press, 1983, 221–56.

Marcus, George E., with Peter Dobkin Hall. *Lives in Trust: The Fortunes of Dynastic Families in Late Twentieth-Century America*. Boulder, Colo.: Westview Press, 1992.

Marshall, Thomas H., and Tom Bottomore. *Citizenship and Social Class*. London: Pluto Press, 1992 [originally published 1950].

Maur, Eduard. "Das bäuerliche Erbrecht und die Erbschaftspraxis in Böhmen im 16. bis 18. Jahrhundert." *Historická demografie* 20 (1996): 93–118.

Maur, Eduard. *Gutsherrschaft und 'zweite Leibeigenschaft' in Böhmen: Studien zur Wirtschafts-, Sozial- und Bevölkerungsgeschichte (14.–18. Jahrhundert)*. Wien: Oldenbourg, 2001.

Mauss, Marcel. *The Gift*. London: Routledge, 1990 [first published as *Essai dur le Don*, 1925].

Mayor-Gay, Marcelle. "L'assistance publique en Valais de 1800 à nos jours." Travail de diplome, University of Lausanne, 1978.

McCants, Anne E. C. *Civic Charity in a Golden Age: Orphan Care in Early Modern Amsterdam*. Urbana: University of Illinois Press. 1997.

McCants, Anne E. C. "The Not-So-Merry Widows of Amsterdam, 1740–1782." *Journal of Family History* 24 (1999): 441–67.

McCarthy, Kathleen D., ed. *Lady Bountiful Revisited: Women, Philanthropy and Power*. New Brunswick, N.J.: Rutgers University Press, 1990.

McCrum, Ann. "Inheritance and the Family: The Scottish Urban Experience in the 1820s." In *Urban Fortunes: Property and Inheritance in the Town, 1700–1900*, edited by Jon Stobart and Alastair Owens. Aldershot: Ashgate, 2000, 149–71.

McNamee, Stephen J., and Robert K. Miller, Jr. "Estate Inheritance: A Sociological Lacuna." *Sociological Inquiry* 59 (1989): 7–29.

Medick, Hans, and David W. Sabean, eds. *Interest and Emotion: Essays on the Study of Family and Kinship*. Cambridge: Cambridge University Press, 1984.

Melby, Kari. "Det nordiske ekteskap? Ekteskapslovreform i Norden 1909–1929: Likestillingskontrakt eller husmorskontrakt?" In *Køn, religion og kvinder i bevægelse*, edited by Anette Warring. Roskilde: Konferencerapport fra det VI Nordiske Kvindehistorikermøte, 2000, 234–49.

Melby, Kari, Anu Pylkkänen, Bente Rosenbeck, and Christina Carlsson Wetterberg, eds. *The Nordic Model of Marriage and the Welfare State*. Copenhagen: Nordic Council of Ministers, 2000.

Melkersson, Martin. *Staten, ordningen och friheten: en studie av den styrande elitens syn på statens roll mellan stormaktstiden och 1800-talet*. Uppsala: Studia Historica Upsaliensia, 1997.

Menchik, Paul L. "Primogeniture, Equal Sharing, and the U.S. Distribution of Wealth." *The Quarterly Journal of Economics* 94 (1980): 299–316.

Menchik, Paul L. "Unequal Estate Division: Is It Altruism, Reverse Bequest, or Simply Noise?" In *Modeling the Accumulation and Distribution of Wealth*, edited by Denis Kessler and André Masson. New York: Oxford University Press, 1988, 105–16.

Menchik, Paul L., and Nancy J. Jianakoplos. "Economics of Inheritance." In *Inheritance and Wealth in America*, edited by Robert K. Miller, Jr., and Stephen J. McNamee. New York: Plenum Press, 1998, 45–59.

Mendelson, Susan, and Patricia Crawford. *Women in Early Modern England*. Oxford: Oxford University Press, 1998.

Merzario, Raul. *Adamocrazia: Famiglie di emigranti in una regione alpina (Svizzara italiana, XVIII secolo)*. Bologna: Il Mulino, 2000.

Meyer, Philipp, ed. *Die Pastoren der Landeskirchen Hanovers und Schaumburg-Lippes seit der Reformation*. Göttingen: Vandenhoeck and Ruprecht, 1941–53.

Michaelis, Johann David. "Einige Zweifel und Erinnerungen, so mir bey der Calenbergischen Witwenpflege-Gesellschaft beygefallen sind." In *Vermischte Schriften*, vol. 2, edited by Johann David Michaelis. Frankfurt a.M.: Garbe, 1766–69, 169–90.

Michaelis, Johann David. "Nöthige Aufmerksamkeit, die man bey Vorschlägen zu Einlegung guter Witwencassen beobachten muß," In *Vermischte Schriften*, vol. 2, edited by Johann David Michaelis. Frankfurt a.M.: Garbe, 1766–69, 99–117.

Michelet, Henri. "A St-Gingolph chez Marie-Julienne de Rivaz (1725–1791): Une famille d'autrefois." *Vallesia* 33 (1978): 443–66.

Millman, Marcia. *Warm Hearts and Cold Cash: The Intimate Dynamics of Families and Money*. New York: Free Press, 1991.

Mitterauer, Michael. *Familie und Arbeitsteilung: Historischvergleichende Studien*. Wien: Böhlau, 1992.

Mitterauer, Michael. "Formen ländlicher Familienwirtschaft im österreichischen Raum: Historische Ökotypen und familiale Arbeitsteilung im österreichischen Raum." In *Familienstruktur und Arbeitsorganisation in ländlichen Gesellschaften*, edited by Josef Ehmer and Michael Mitterauer. Wien: Böhlau, 1986, 185–323.

Mitterauer, Michael. *Grundtypen alteuropäischer Sozialformen: Haus und Gemeinde in vorindustriellen Gesellschaften*. Stuttgart: Bad Cannstatt, 1979.

Mitterauer, Michael. "Problemfelder einer Sozialgeschichte des Alters." In *Der alte Mensch in der Geschichte*, edited by Helmut Konrad. Wien: Verlag für Gesellschaftskritik, 1982.

Mitterauer, Michael. "Sozialgeschichte der Familie als landeskundlicher Forschungsgegenstand: Anwendungsmöglichkeiten historischer Personenstandlisten." In *Historisch-anthropologische Familienforschung: Fragestellungen und Zugangasweisen*, edited by Michael Mitterauer. Wien: Böhlau, 1990.

Mitterauer, Michael, and Reinhard Sieder. "The Reconstruction of the Family Life Course: Theoretical Problems and Empirical Results." In *Family Forms in Historic Europe*, edited by Richard Wall, Jean Robin, and Peter Laslett. Cambridge: Cambridge University Press, 1983, 309–45.

Mitterauer, Michael, and Reinhard Sieder. *Vom Patriarchat zur Partnerschaft: Zum Strukturwandel der Familie*. München: C. H. Beck, 1977.

Modigliani, Franco. "The Role of Intergenerational Transfers and Life Cycle Saving in the Accumulation of Wealth." *Journal of Economic Perspectives* 2 (1988): 15–40.

Moen, Phyllis, and Elaine Wethington. "The Concept of Family Adaptive Strategies." *Annual Review of Sociology* 18 (1992): 233–51.

Möhle, Sylvia. *Ehekonflikte und sozialer Wandel: Göttingen 1740–1840*. Frankfurt a.M. and New York: Campus, 1997.

Mooser, Josef. *Ländliche Klassengesellschaft 1770–1848: Bauern und Unterschichten, Landwirtschaft und Gewerbe im östlichen Westfalen*. Göttingen: Vandenhoek and Ruprecht, 1984.

Moriceau, Jean-Marc. *Les Fermiers de l'Ile-de-France: Ascension d'un patronat agricole (XVe–XVIIIe siècles)*. Paris: Fayard, 1994.

Moriceau, Jean-Marc, and Gilles Postel-Vinay. *Ferme, entreprise, famille: Grande exploitation et changements agricoles, les Chartier (XVIIe–XIXe siècles)*. Paris: Ecole des Hautes Etudes en Sciences Sociales, 1992.

Moring, Beatrice. "Family Strategies, Inheritance Systems and the Care of the Elderly in Historical Perspective—Eastern and Western Finland." *Historical Social Research* 23 (1998): 67–82.

Morris, Robert J. "The Middle Class and the Property Cycle During the Industrial Revolution." In *The Search for Wealth and Stability: Essays in Social and Economic History Presented to M. W. Flinn*, edited by T. Christopher Smout. Basingstoke: Macmillan, 1979, 91–113.

Möser, Justus. "Schreiben einer betagten Jungfer an die Stifter der Witwenkasse zu **." In *Patriotische Phantasien (Justus Mösers sämtliche Werke II)*. Berlin, 1842, 184–86.

Mulholland, Kate. "Gender Power and Property Relations Within Entrepreneurial Wealthy Families." *Gender, Work and Organization* 3 (1996): 78–102.

Nagel, Anne-Hilde. "The Development of Citizenship in Norway: Marshall Remodelled." In *Women's Politics and Women in Politics: In Honour of Ida Blom*, edited by Sølvi Sogner and Gro Hagemann. Oslo: Cappelen Akademisk Forlag, 2000, 197–215.

Nash, Alanna. "The Woman Who Overturned an Empire." *Ms.* 14 (June 1986): 44–46, 80–82.

Netting, Robert M. *Balancing on an Alp: Ecological Change and Continuity in a Swiss Mountain Community*. Cambridge: Cambridge University Press, 1981.

Nevins, Allan. *Study in Power: John D. Rockefeller, Industrialist and Philanthropist*. New York: Charles Scribner and Sons, 1953.

Nielsen, John. "After a Woman Is Scorned, a Publishing Family Cashes Out." *Fortune* 115 (January 5, 1987): 93.

Niemeyer, Beatrix. "Ausschluß oder Ausgrenzung? Frauen im Umkreis der Universitäten im 18. Jahrhundert." In *Geschichte der Mädchen- und Frauenbildung I: Vom Mittelalter bis zur Aufklärung,* edited by Elke Kleinau and Claudia Opitz. Frankfurt a.M. and New York: Campus, 1996, 275–94.

Nienhaus, Ursula. *Vater Staat und seine Gehilfinnen: Die Politik mit der Frauenarbeit bei der deutschen Post (1864–1945).* Frankfurt a.M. and New York: Campus, 1995.

Nilsson, Lars. *Den urbana transitionen: Tätorterna i svensk samhällsomvandling 1800–1980.* Stockholm: Stadshistoriska institutet, 1989.

Niskanen, Kirsti. "Husbondeväldets röst. Äktenskap, egendom och kön under första delen av 1900-talet." In *Kvinnor och jord. Arbete och ägande från medeltid till nutid,* edited by Britt Liljewall, Kirsti Niskanen, and Maria Sjöberg. Stockholm: Nordiska museets förlag, 2000, 131–58.

Niskanen, Kirsti. "Marriage and Gendered Property Rights in Early Twentieth-Century Rural Sweden." In *The Nordic Model of Marriage and the Welfare State,* edited by Kari Melby, Anu Pylkkänen, Bente Rosenbeck, and Christina Carlsson Wetterberg. Copenhagen: Nordic Council of Ministers, 2000, 69–87.

North, Douglass C. *Institutions, Institutional Change and Economic Performance.* Cambridge: Cambridge University Press, 1990.

North, Douglass C. "Markets and Other Allocation Systems in History: The Challenge of Karl Polanyi." *Journal of Economic History* 6 (1997): 703–16.

O'Rand, Angela M., and John C. Henretta. *Age and Inequality: Diverse Pathways Through Later Life.* Boulder, Colo.: Westview Press, 1999.

Oberschelp, Reinhard. *Niedersachsen 1760–1820,* vol. 1. Hildesheim: Lax, 1982.

Odendahl, Teresa. *Charity Begins at Home: Generosity and Self-Interest Among the Philanthropic Elite.* New York: Basic Books, 1990.

Odendahl, Teresa. "Women's Power, Nonprofits, and the Future." In *Gender and the Professionalization of Philanthropy: Essays on Philanthropy,* No. 19, edited by Teresa Odendahl and Marilyn Fischer. Indianapolis, Ind.: Indiana University Center on Philanthropy, 1996, 1–11.

Offer, Avner. "Between the Gift and the Market: The Economy of Regard." *Economic History Review* L (1997): 450–76.

Offer, John. "Idealist Thought, Social Policy and the Rediscovery of Informal Care." *British Journal of Sociology* 50 (1999): 467–88.

Ogilvie, Sheilagh, and Jeremy Edwards. "Women and 'Second Serfdom': Evidence from Early Modern Bohemia." *Journal of Economic History* 60 (2000): 961–94.

*Ordnung der Christlichen Gesellschaft zu Versorgung der Witwen und Waysen.* Lüneburg: Stern, 1700.

Orloff, Ann. "Gender and the Social Rights of Citizenship: The Comparative Analysis of Gender Relations and Welfare States." *American Sociological Review* 58 (1993): 303–28.

Orloff, Ann. "Gender in the Welfare State." *Annual Review of Sociology* 22 (1996): 51–78.

Ortmayr, Norbert. "'Oarbeits, sunst kemts ins Quartier': Alter und Armut am Land im frühen 20. Jahrhundert." In *'. . . und i sitz' jetzt allein': Geschichte mit und von alten Menschen,* edited by Helmut Konrad and Michael Mitterauer. Wien: Böhlau, 1987, 71–91.

Ostrander, Susan. *Women of the Upper Class*. Philadelphia, Penn.: Temple University Press, 1984.

Ostrawsky, Gertrude. "Die Zusammensetzung der Hausgemeinschaften in der Pfarre Maria Langegg im Dunkelsteinerwald, 1788–1875." Ph.D. diss., University of Vienna, 1979.

Ostrower, Francie. *Why the Wealthy Give: The Culture of Elite Philanthropy*. Princeton, N.J.: Princeton University Press, 1995.

Owens, Alastair. "Property, Gender and the Life Course: Inheritance and Family Welfare Provision in Early Nineteenth-Century England." *Social History* 26 (2001): 299–317.

Palazzi, Maura. "Female Solitude and Patrilineage: Unmarried Women and Widows During the Eighteenth and Nineteenth Centuries." *Journal of Family History* 15 (1990): 443–59.

Papataxiachis, Euthymios. "La valeur du ménage: Classes sociales, stratégies matrimoniales et lois ecclésiastiques à Lesbos au XIXe siècle." In *Espaces et familles dans l'Europe du Sud à l'âge moderne*, edited by Stuart Woolf. Paris: Ed. Maison des Sciences de l'Homme, 1993, 109–41.

Partch, Gottfried. *Das Mitwirkungsrecht der Familiengemeinschaft im älteren Walliser Recht (Laudatio parentum et hospiciumi)*. Genève: Librairie Droz, 1955.

*Patent und Reglement für die Königlich Preußische allgemeine Wittwen-Verpflegungs-Anstalt*. Berlin: Decker, 1775.

Pearson, Robin. "Thrift or Dissipation? The Business of Life Assurance in the Early Nineteenth Century." *Economic History Review* XXXXIII (1990): 236–54.

Pélaquier, Elie. *De la Maison du Père à la maison commune: Saint-Victor-de-la-Coste, en Languedoc rhodanien (1661–1789)*. Montpellier: Publications de l'Université Paul-Valéry-Montpellier III, 1996.

Perrenoud, Alfred. "The Coexistence of Generations and the Availability of Kin in a Rural Community at the Beginning of the Nineteenth Century." *The History of the Family* 3 (1998): 1–15.

Perrot, Michelle, and Anne Martin-Fugier. "The Actors." In *A History of Private Life: From the Great Fires of Revolution to the Great War*, edited by Michelle Perrot. London: Belknap Press, 1990: 95–338.

Pfister, Christian. *Bevölkerungsgeschichte und Historische Demographie, 1500–1800*. München: Oldenbourg, 1994.

Phillips, Roderick. *Putting Asunder: A History of Divorce in Western Society*. Cambridge: Cambridge University Press, 1988.

Phillips, Roderick. *Untying the Knot: A Short History of Divorce*. Cambridge: Cambridge University Press, 1991.

Pingaud, Marie-Claude. "Partage égalitaire et destins des lignées." *Annales de démographie Historique* 84 (1995): 17–33.

Pingaud, Marie-Claude. *Paysans en Bourgogne: Les gens de Minot*. Paris: Flammarion, 1978.

Pinker, Robert. *The Idea of Welfare*. London: Heinemann, 1979.

Pisano, Jean-Baptiste. "Wills as a Geography of Family Relations." In *The Art of Communication: Proceedings of the 8th International Conference of the Association for History and Computing, Graz, Austria, August 24–27, 1993*, edited by Gerhard Jaritz, Ingo Kropac, and Peter Teibenbacher. Graz: Akademische Druck-u Verlangsanstalt, 1995, 150–63.

Plakans, Andrejs. "Retirement, Inheritance, and Generational Relations: Life-Course Analysis in Historic Eastern Europe." In *Aging and Generational Relations over the Life Course*, edited by Tamara Hareven. Berlin/New York: Walter de Gruyter and Co., 1996, 140–57.

Plummer, Ken. *Telling Sexual Stories: Power, Change and Social Worlds*. London: Routledge, 1995.

Poitrineau, Abel. "Institutions et pratiques successorales en Auvergne et en Limousin sous l'Ancien Régime." *Etudes Rurales* 110–112 (1988): 31–43.

Polanyi, Karl. *The Great Transformation*. Boston: Beacon Press. 1957 [originally published New York: Farrar and Rinehart, 1944].

Poska, Allyson. "Gender, Property and Retirement Strategies in Early Modern Northwestern Spain." *Journal of Family History* 25 (2000): 313–25.

Poumarède, Jacques. *Les Successions dans le Sud-Ouest de la France au Moyen Age*. Paris: Presses Universitaires de France, 1972.

Procházka, Vladimír. *Česká poddanská nemovitost v pozemkových knihách 16. a 17. století*. Praha: ČSAV, 1963.

Pröve, Ralf, and Norbert Winnige, eds. *Wissen ist Macht: Herrschaft und Kommunikation in Brandenburg-Preußen 1600–1850*. Berlin: Wissenschafts-Verlag, 2001.

Psíková, Jiřina. "Rodové katastry uložené ve Státním oblastním archivu v Třeboni." *Historická demografie* 8 (1983): 75–80.

Putallaz, Pierre Alain. *Eugénie de Troistorrents et Charles d'Odet: Etude sur leur corréspondance inédite (1812–17)*, 2 vols. Lausanne: Payot, 1985.

Qvist, Gunnar. *Konsten att blifva en god flicka*. Stockholm: LiberFörlag, 1978.

Qvist, Gunnar. *Kvinnofrågan i Sverige 1809–1846: Studier rörande kvinnans näringsfrihet i de borgerliga yrkena*. Göteborg: Scandinavian University Books, 1960.

Rabuzzi, Daniel. "Women as Merchants in Eighteenth-Century Northern Germany: The Case of Stralsund, 1750–1830." *Central European History* 28 (1995): 435–56.

Raggio, Osvaldo. "Parentèles et espaces politiques en Ligurie à l'époque moderne." In *Espaces et familles dans l'Europe du Sud à l'âge moderne*, edited by Stuart Woolf. Paris: Edition Maison des Sciences de l'Homme, 1993, 143–63.

Ramella, Franco. *Terra e telai. Sistemi di parentela e manifattura nel Biellese dell'Ottocento*. Turin: Einaudi, 1984.

Rappe, Susanne. "Frauen in der agrarischen Gesellschaft des 17. und 18. Jahrunderts—dargestellt anhand ausgewählter Gerichtsakten des Amtes Dannenberg." M.A. diss., University of Hanover, 1992.

Razi, Zvi. "The Myth of the Immutable English Family." *Past and Present* 140 (1993): 3–44.

Reay, Barry. "Kinship and the Neighbourhood in Nineteenth-Century Rural England: The Myth of the Autonomous Nuclear Family." *Journal of Family History* 21 (1996): 87–104.

Riley, James C. "'That your widows may be rich:' Providing for Widowhood in Old Regime Europe." *Economisch- en sociaal-historisch jaarboek* 45 (1982): 58–76.

Roberts, David. *The Victorian Origins of the British Welfare State*. New Haven, Conn.: Yale University Press, 1960.

Rödel, Walter. "Die demographische Entwicklung in Deutschland 1770–1820." In

*Deutschland und Frankreich im Zeitalter der Französischen Revolution*, edited by Helmut Berding, Etienne Francois, and Hans-Peter Ullmann. Frankfurt a. M: Suhrkamp, 1989, 21–41.

Rolley, Francine. "Reproduction familiale et changements économiques: L'exclusion dans le Morvan du nord, XVIIe–XVIIIe siècles." In *Les exclus de la terre en France et au Québec XVIIe–XXe siècles: La reproduction familiale dans la différence*, edited by Gérard Bouchard, John Dickinson, and Joseph Goy. Sillery: Septentrion, 1998, 133–57.

Roper, Lyndal. *The Holy Household*. Oxford: Oxford University Press, 1989.

Rose, Carol M. *Property and Persuasion: Essays on the History, Theory, and Rhetoric of Ownership*. Boulder, Colo.: Westview Press, 1994.

Rose, Marsha Shapiro. "The Legacy of Wealth: Primogeniture Among the Rockefellers." *Journal of Family History* 27 (April 2002): 172–85.

Rose, Marsha Shapiro. "Southern Feminism and Social Change: Sallie Bingham and the Kentucky Foundation for Women." In *The New Deal and Beyond: Social Welfare in the South Since 1930*, edited by Elna Green. Athens, Ga.: University of Georgia Press, 2003, 239–58.

Rosenbeck, Bente. "Det nordiske samarbeide, kvindebevægelse og ægteskabslovgivning." In *Køn, religion og kvinder i bevægelse*, edited by Anette Warring. Roskilde: Konferencerapport fra det VI Nordiske Kvindehistorikermøte, 2000, 250–70.

Rosenfeld, Jeffrey P. "The Heir and the Spare: Evasiveness, Role-Complexity and Patterns of Inheritance." In *Social Roles and Social Institutions: Essays in Honor of Rose Laub Coser*, edited by Judith R. Blau and Norman Goodman. Boulder, Colo.: Westview Press, 1991, 73–89.

Rosenhaft, Eve. "But the Heart Must Speak for the Widows: The Origins of Life Insurance in Germany and the Gender Implications of Actuarial Science." In *Formatting Gender: Transitions, Breaks and Continuities in German-Speaking Europe 1750–1850*, edited by Marion Gray and Ulrike Gleixner. Ann Arbor: University of Michigan Press, 2004.

Rosenhaft, Eve. "'. . . mich als eine Extraordinarium.' Die Witwe als widerstrebendes Subjekt in der Frühgeschichte der Lebensversicherung." In *Stationen einer Hochschullaufbahn: Festschrift für Annette Kuhn zum 65. Geburtstag*, edited by Udo Arnold, Peter Meyers, and Uta C. Schmidt. Dortmund: Edition Ebersbach, 1999, 292–309.

Rosenstrauch, Hazel. *Buchhandelsmanufaktur und Aufklärung: Die Reformen des Buchhändlers und Verlegers Ph. E. Reich (1717–1787)*. Frankfurt a.M.: Buchhändler-Vereinigung, 1986.

Rosental, Paul-André. "Pratiques successorales et fécondité: L'effet du Code civil." *Economie et Prévision* 100–101, (1991): 231–38.

Rosental, Paul-André. "Les liens familiaux, formes historiques?" *Annales de Démographie Historique* 2 (2000): 49–81.

Rosental, Paul-André. *Les Sentiers invisibles: espace, familles et migrations dans la France du 19e siècle*. Paris: Editions de l'Ecole des Hautes Etudes en Sciences Sociales, 1999.

Ross, Ellen. "Survival Networks: Womens' Neighbourhood Sharing in London before World War I." *History Workshop Journal* 15 (1983): 4–27.

Rothman, Robert A. *Inequality and Stratification: Class, Color, and Gender.* Englewood Cliffs, N.J.: Prentice Hall, 1993.

Sabean, David W. "Allianzen und Listen: Die Geschlechtsvormundschaft im 18. und 19. Jahrhundert." In *Frauen in der Geschichte des Rechts: Von der Frühen Neuzeit bis zur Gegenwart,* edited by Ute Gerhard. Munich: C. H. Beck, 1997, 460–79.

Sabean, David W. *Kinship in Neckarhausen, 1700–1870.* Cambridge: Cambridge University Press, 1998.

Sabean, David W. *Property, Production and Family in Neckarhausen, 1700–1870.* Cambridge: Cambridge University Press, 1990.

Sabelleck, Rainer. "Soziale Versorgung von Angehörigen jüdischer Familien in norddeutschen Städten des späten 18. und frühen 19. Jahrhunderts." In *Familien und Familienlosigkeit. Fallstudien aus Niedersachsen und Bremen vom 15. bis 20.Jahrhundert,* edited by Jürgen Schlumbohm. Hannover: Hahn, 1993, 117–32.

Salamin, Daniel. *Pauvreté et assistance en Valais au XIXe siècle: Le cas de la communauté de Bagnes.* Mémoire: Université de Genève, 1976.

Sauermann, Dietmar. "Hofidee und bäuerliche Familienverträge in Westfalen." *Rheinisch-westfälische Zeitschrift für Volkskunde* 17 (1970): 58–78.

Schama, Simon. *The Embarrassment of Riches: An Interpretation of Dutch Culture in the Golden Age.* New York: Knopf, 1987.

Schedlitz, Bernd. *Leffmann Behrens: Untersuchungen zum Hofjudentum im Zeitalter des Absolutismus.* Hildesheim: Lax, 1984.

Schervish, Paul G. "Introduction: The Wealthy and the World of Wealth." in *Gospels of Wealth: How the Rich Portray Their Lives,* edited by Paul G. Schervish, Platon E. Coutsoukis, and Ethan Lewis. Westport, Conn.: Praeger, 1994, 1–17.

Schervish, Paul G. "The Moral Biographies of the Wealthy and the Cultural Scripture of Wealth." In *Wealth in Western Thought: The Case For and Against Riches,* edited by Paul G. Schervish. Westport, Conn.: Praeger, 1994, 167–208.

Schlögl, Rudolf. *Bauern, Krieg und Staat: oberbayerische Bauernwirtschaft und frühmoderner Staat im 17. Jahrhundert.* Göttingen: Vandenhoeck and Ruprecht, 1988.

Schlumbohm, Jürgen. "The Land-Family Bond in Peasant Practice and in Middle-Class Ideology: Evidence from the North-West German Parish of Belm, 1650–1860." *Central European History* 27 (1994): 461–77.

Schlumbohm, Jürgen. *Lebensläufe, Familien, Höfe: Die Bauern und Heuerleute des Osnabrückischen Kirchspiels Belm in proto-industrieller Zeit, 1650–1860.* Göttingen: Max Planck Institute for History, 1994.

Schlumbohm, Jürgen. "Micro-History and the Macro-Models of the European Demographic System in Pre-Industrial Time: Life-Course Patterns in the Parish of Belm (Northwest Germany), Seventeenth to the Nineteenth Centuries." *The History of the Family* 1 (1996): 81–95.

Schmid, G. "Hofgröße—Familiengröße—Vererbungsgewohnheiten. Eine Fallstudie über fünf Familien." In *Historische Demographie als Sozialgeschichte,* vol. 2, edited by Arthur Imhof. Darmstadt: Hessische Historische Kommission, 1975, 687–707.

Schneider, Jürgen. "International Rates of Exchange: Structures and Trend of Payments Mechanism in Europe, Seventeenth to Nineteenth Century." In *The Emergence of a World Economy 1500–1914*, edited by Wolfram Fischer. Wiesbaden: F. Steiner, 1986, 143–70.

Schneider, Jürgen. "Messen, Banken und Börsen (15.–18. Jahrhundert)." In *Banchi pubblici, banchi privati e monti di pietà nell'Europa preindustriale: Amministrazione, tecniche operative e ruoli economici*, vol. 1, edited by Dino Puncuh and Giuseppe Felloni. Genoa: Società Ligure di Storia Patria, 1991, 135–69.

Schofield, Roger. "Family Structure, Demographic Behaviour, and Economic Growth." In *Famine, Disease and the Social Order in Early Modern Society*, edited by John Walter and Roger Schofield. Cambridge: Cambridge University Press, 1989, 279–304.

Schöne, Bernd. *Kultur und Lebensweise Lausitzer Bandweber 1750–1850*. Berlin: Akademie-Verlag, 1977.

Schorn-Schütte, Luise. *Evangelische Geistlichkeit in der Frühneuzeit*. Gütersloh: Gütersloher Verlagshaus, 1996.

Scott, Joan W. *Gender and the Politics of History*. New York: Columbia University Press, 1988.

Scott, Joan W. *Only Paradoxes to Offer: French Feminists and the Rights of Man*. Cambridge, Mass.: Harvard University Press, 1996.

Sealander, Judith. *Private Wealth and Public Life: Foundation Philanthropy and the Reshaping of American Social Policy from the Progressive Era to the New Deal*. Baltimore, Md.: Johns Hopkins University Press, 1997.

Searle, Geoffrey R. *Morality and the Market in Victorian Britain*. Oxford: Clarendon Press, 1998.

Segalen, Martine. *Die Familie: Geschichte, Soziologie, Anthropologie*. Frankfurt a.M.: Campus, 1990.

Segalen, Martine. *Fifteen Generations of Bretons: Kinship and Society in Lower Brittany 1720–1980*. Cambridge: Cambridge University Press, 1981.

Segalen, Martine. *Quinze générations de Bas-Bretons: Parenté et société dans le pays bigouden Sud, 1720–1980*. Paris: Presses Universitaires de France, 1985.

Segalen, Martine. "Sein Teil haben: Geschwisterbeziehungen in einem egalitären Vererbungssystem." In *Emotionen und materielle Interessen: Sozialanthropologische und historische Beiträge zur Familienforschung*, edited by Hans Medick and David W. Sabean. Göttingen: Vandenhoeck und Ruprecht, 1984, 181–98.

Sharpe, Pam. "Survival Strategies and Stories: Poor Widows and Widowers in Early Industrial England." In *Widowhood in Medieval and Early Modern Europe*, edited by Sandra Cavallo and Lyndan Warner. Harlow: Longman, 1999, 220–39.

Shoemaker Robert B., and Mary Vincent, eds. *Gender and History in Western Europe*. London: Arnold, 1998.

Siddle, David. "Inheritance and Lineage Development in Peasant Society." *Continuity and Change* 1 (1986): 333–61.

Siddle, David. "Migration as a Strategy of Accumulation: Social and Economic Change in Eighteenth-Century Savoy." *Economic History Review* L (1997): 1–20.

Sieder, Reinhard, and Michael Mitterauer. "The Reconstruction of the Family Life Course: Theoretical Problems and Empirical Results." In *Family Forms in*

*Historic Europe*, edited by Richard Wall, Jean Robin, and Peter Laslett. Cambridge: Cambridge University Press, 1983, 309–45.

Siegel, Johann Gottlieb. *Corpus Juris Cambialis*, 2 vols. Leipzig: J. S. Heinsius, 1742.

Simmel, Georg. *The Philosophy of Money*. London: Routledge, 1990 [originally published 1907].

Sjöberg, Maria. "Kvinnans sociala underordning—en problematisk historia: Om makt, arv och giftermål i det äldre svenska samhället." *Scandia* 63 (1997): 165–90.

Slater, Philip. *Wealth Addiction*. New York: E. P. Dutton, 1980.

Smith, Bonnie. *Women of the Leisure Class: The Bourgeoises of Northern France in the Nineteenth Century*. Princeton, N.J.: Princeton University Press, 1981.

Söderberg, Johan, Ulf Jonsson, and Christer Persson. *A Stagnating Metropolis: The Economy and Demography of Stockholm 1750–1850*. Cambridge: Cambridge University Press, 1991.

Spufford, Margaret. "The Limitations of the Probate Inventory." In *English Rural Society, 1500–1800: Essays in Honour of Joan Thirsk*, edited by John Chartres and David Hey. Cambridge: Cambridge University Press, 1990, 139–74.

Sreenivasan, Govind. "The Land-Family Bond at Earls Colne (Essex) 1550–1650." *Past and Present* 131 (1991): 3–37.

Stack, Carol. *All Our Kin: Strategies for Survival in a Black Community*. New York: Harper Collins, 1974.

*Statistisk årsbok för Sverige 1950*. Stockholm: Statistiska cenralbyrån, 1950.

Staves, Susan. *Married Women's Separate Property in England, 1660–1833*. Cambridge, Mass.: Harvard University Press, 1990.

Štefanová, Dana. "Die Erbschaftspraxis, das Ausgedinge und das Phänomen der 'zweiten Leibeigenschaft' in den nordböhmischen Dörfern der Herrschaft Frydlant." In *Wiener Wege der Sozialgeschichte*, edited by Erich Landsteiner, Franz X. Eder, and Peter Feldbauer. Wien: Böhlau, 1997, 225–41.

Štefanová, Dana, and Hermann Zeitlhofer. "Alter und Generationenbeziehungen in Böhmen. Zum Ausgedinge in nord- und südböhmischen Dörfern 1650–1750." In *Das Alter im Spiel der Generationen: Historische und sozialwissenschaftliche Beiträge*, edited by Josef Ehmer and Peter Gutschner. Wien: Böhlau, 2000, 231–58.

Stone, Lawrence. *The Family, Sex and Marriage in England 1500–1800*. Harmondsworth: Penguin, 1979.

Stone, Lawrence. *Road to Divorce: England 1530–1987*. Oxford: Oxford University Press, 1990.

Stum, Marlene S. "'I Just Want to be Fair': Interpersonal Justice in Intergenerational Transfers of Non-Titled Property." *Family Relations* 48 (1999): 159–66.

Süßmilch, Johann Peter. *Die göttliche Ordnung in den Veränderungen des menschlichen Geschlechts, aus der Geburt, dem Tode, und der Fortpflanzung desselben erwiesen von Johann Peter Süßmilch—Dritter Teil . . . herausgegeben von Christian Jacob Baumann*. Berlin: Realschule, 1787.

Sveriges offentliga statistik. *Befolkningsrörelsen 1931–1940*. Stockholm: Statistiska centralbyrån, 1940.

Tanner, Albert. *Spulen—Weben—Sticken: Die Industrialisierung in Appenzell-Ausserrhoden*. Zürich: Junis Druck, 1982.

Tebbel, John. *The Inheritors: A Study of America's Great Fortunes and What Happened to Them.* New York: G. P. Putnam and Sons, 1962.

Thane, Pat. *Foundations of the Welfare State.* London: Longman, 1996.

Theibault, John. *German Villages in Crisis: Rural Life in Hesse-Kassel and the Thirty Years' War.* Atlantic Highlands, N.J.: Humanities Press, 1995.

Thompson, Edward P. "The Grid of Inheritance: A Comment." In *Family and Inheritance: Rural Society in Western Europe 1200–1800,* edited by Jack Goody, Joan Thirsk, and Edward P. Thompson. Cambridge: Cambridge University Press, 1973, 328–60.

Thompson, Edward P. "The Moral Economy of the English Crowd in the Eighteenth Century." *Past and Present* 50 (1971): 78–98.

Thompson, Edward P. "The Moral Economy Reviewed." In *Customs in Common,* by Edward P. Thompson. Harmondsworth: Penguin, 1993, 259–351.

Thorndike, Joseph J., Jr. *The Very Rich: A History of Wealth.* New York: Bonanza, 1976.

Tickamyer, Ann R. "Wealth and Power: A Comparison of Men and Women in the Property Elite." *Social Forces* 60 (1981): 463–81.

Tifft, Susan E., and Alex S. Jones. *The Patriarch: The Rise and Fall of the Bingham Dynasty.* New York: Summit, 1991.

Tilly, Charles, and Richard Tilly. "Agenda for European Economic History in the 1970s." *Journal of Economic History* 31 (1971): 184–98.

Tomes, Nigel. "Inheritance and Inequality within the Family: Equal Division among Unequals, or Do the Poor Get More?" In *Modeling the Accumulation and Distribution of Wealth,* edited by Denis Kessler and André Masson. New York: Oxford University Press, 1988, 79–104.

Traversat, Michel. *Les pépinières: Etude sur les jardins français et sur les jardiniers et les pépiniéristes.* Ph.D. diss., Ecole des Hautes Etudes en Sciences Sociales, Paris, 2001.

Ullmann, Sabine. "Poor Jewish Families in Early Modern Rural Swabia." In *Household Strategies for Survival 1600–2000: Fission, Faction and Cooperation,* edited by Laurence Fontaine and Jürgen Schlumbohm. *International Review of Social History,* supp. 8, Cambridge: Cambridge University Press, 2000, 93–113.

van den Bosch, Lourens, and Jan Bremmer, eds. *Between Poverty and the Pyre: Moments in the History of Widowhood.* London: Routledge, 1995.

van Dülmen, Richard. *Die Gesellschaft der Aufklärer.* Frankfurt a.M.: Fischer, 1986.

van Leeuwen, Marco. "Histories of Risk and Welfare in Europe during the Eighteenth and Nineteenth Centuries." In *Health Care and Poor Relief in Eighteenth and Nineteenth-Century Europe,* edited by Ole Peter Grell, Andrew Cunningham, and Robert Jütte. Aldershot: Ashgate, 2002, 32–66.

Velková, Alice. "Eingriffe des Staates in die Beziehung zwischen der Obrigkeit und den Untertanen und ihre Wirkung auf die Dorffamilie an der Wende des 18. zum 19. Jahrhundert." In *Untertanen, Herrschaft und Staat in Böhmen und im 'Alten Reich,'* edited by Markus Cerman and Robert Luft. München: Oldenbourg, 2004.

Viazzo, Pier Paolo. *Upland Communities: Environment, Population and Social Structure in the Alps since the Sixteenth Century.* Cambridge: Cambridge University Press, 1989.

Viazzo, Pier P., and Katherine A. Lynch. "Anthropology, Family History, and the Concept of Strategy." *International Review of Social History* 47 (2002): 423–52.

Vickery, Amanda. "Golden Age to Separate Spheres? A Review of the Categories and Chronology of English Women's History." *The Historical Journal* 36 (1993): 383–414.

Viret, Jérôme-Luther. *Valeurs et parenté: L'exemple d'Ecouen et de Villiers-le-Bel (1560–1685)*. Ph.D. diss., l'Université de Paris X-Nanterre, 1998.

Vivier, Nadine. "La transmission des patrimoines en Bretagne au XIXe siècle." In *Familles, terre, marchés: Familles, terre, marchés: logiques économiques et stratégies dans les milieux ruraux (XVIIe–XXe siècles)*, edited by Gérard Béaur, Christian Dessureault, and Joseph Goy. Rennes: Presses Universitaires Rennes II, 2004.

Vogel, Barbara, and Ulrike Weckel, eds. *Frauen in der Ständegesellschaft: Leben und Arbeiten in der Stadt vom späten Mittelalter bis zur Neuzeit*. Hamburg: R. Krämer, 1991.

Vogel, Ursula. "Property Rights and the Status of Women in Germany and England." In *Bourgeois Society in Nineteenth-Century Europe*, edited by Jürgen Kocka and Allen Mitchell. Oxford: Berg, 1993, 241–69.

von Dassel, Hermann. "Die Lütke v. Töbingsche Stiftung." In *Berichte über das Geschlecht von Dassel*, vol. I, edited by Otto von Dassel. Chemnitz: 1894, appendix, 31–91.

Vrankrijker, A. C. J. de. *Mensen, Leven en Werken in de Gouden Eeuw.* 'S-Gravenhage: Martinus Nijhoff, 1981.

Vredenberg, J. P. *Als Off Sij Onse Eigene Kijnder Weren: Het Burgerweeshuis te Arnhem, 1583–1742* Arnhem: Gemeente Arnhem, 1983.

Wahl, Johannes. "Lebensläufe und Geschlechterräume im Pfarrhaus des 17. und 18. Jahrhunderts." In *Evangelische Pfarrer: Zur sozialen und politischen Rolle einer bürgerlichen Gruppe in der deutschen Gesellschaft des 18. bis 20. Jahrhunderts,* edited by Luise Schorn-Schütte and Walter Sparn. Stuttgart: Kohlhammer, 1997, 36–55.

Wall, Richard. "Introduction." In *Family Forms in Historic Europe*, edited by Richard Wall, Jean Robin, and Peter Laslett. Cambridge: Cambridge University Press, 1983, 1–63.

Wall, Richard, Jean Robin, and Peter Laslett, eds. *Family Forms in Historic Europe.* Cambridge: Cambridge University Press, 1983.

Ward, Joe. "The Binghams: Twilight of a Tradition." *The Courier-Journal Magazine* (April 20, 1986): 16–38.

Waring, Marilyn. *Counting for Nothing: What Men Value and What Women Are Worth.* Toronto: University of Toronto Press, 1999.

Weber-Will, Susanne. "Geschlechtsvormundschaft und weibliche Rechtswohltaten im Privatrecht des preußischen Allgemeinen Landrechts von 1794." In *Frauen in der Geschichte des Rechts*, edited by Gerhard Ute. Munich: Beck, 1997, 451–59.

Weckel, Ulrike. "Der Fieberfrost des Freiherrn. Zur Polemik gegen weibliche Gelehrsamkeit und ihre Folgen für die Geselligkeit der Geschlechter." In *Geschichte der Mädchen- und Frauenbildung I: Vom Mittelalter bis zur Aufklärung,* edited by Elke Kleinau and Claudia Opitz. Frankfurt a.M. and New York: Campus, 1996, 360–72.

Wegge, Simone. "To Part or Not to Part: Emigration and Inheritance Institutions in Nineteenth-Century Hesse-Cassel." *Explorations in Economic History* 36 (1999): 30–55.

Weitzman, Lenore J. "Marital Property: Its Transformation and Division in the United States." In *Economic Consequences of Divorce: The International Perspective*, edited by Lenore J. Weitzman and Mavis Maclean. Oxford: Clarendon Press, 1992, 85–142.

Wensky, Margret. *Die Stellung der Frau in der stadtkölnischen Wirtschaft im Spätmittelalter.* Cologne: Böhlau, 1980.

Wetherell, Charles, and Andrejs Plakans. "Intergenerational Transfers of Headships over the Life Course in an Eastern European Peasant Community, 1782–1850." *The History of the Family* 3 (1998): 333–49.

Wiesner, Merry E. "Guilds, Male Bonding and Women's Work in Early Modern Germany." *Gender and History* 1 (1989): 125–37.

Wiesner, Merry E. *Women and Gender in Early Modern Europe.* Cambridge: Cambridge University Press, 1993.

Wiesner-Hanks, Merry E. "Ausbildung in den Zünften." In *Geschichte der Mädchen- und Frauenbildung I: Vom Mittelalter bis zur Aufklärung,* edited by Elke Kleinau and Claudia Opitz. Frankfurt a.M. and New York: Campus, 1996, 91–118.

Wikander, Ulla. *Delat arbete, delad makt: om kvinnors underordning i och genom arbete.* Uppsala: Uppsala Papers in Economic History 28, 1991.

Winnige, Norbert. "Vom Leihen und Schulden in Göttingen: Studien zum Kapitalmarkt." In *Göttingen 1690–1755: Studien zur Sozialgeschichte einer Stadt,* edited by Hermann Wellenreuther. Göttingen: Vandenhoeck and Ruprecht, 1988, 252–320.

Wottle, Martin. "Det lilla ägandet: korporativ formering och sociala relationer inom Stockholms minuthandel 1720–1810." Ph.D. diss., Stads-och kommunhistoriska institutet, Stockholm, 1997.

Wright, Erik Olin. *Class Counts: Comparative Studies in Class Analysis.* Cambridge: Cambridge University Press, 1997.

Wrigley, Anthony, and Roger Schofield. *The Population History of England, 1541–1871: A Reconstruction.* London: Edward Arnold, 1981.

Wunder, Bernd. "Pfarrwitwenkassen und Beamtenwitwen-Anstalten vom 16.–19. Jahrhundert." *Jahrbuch für historische Forschung* 12 (1985): 429–98.

Wunder, Heide. *"Er ist die Sonn', sie ist der Mond": Frauen in der frühen Neuzeit.* Munich: Beck, 1992; Cambridge, Mass.: Harvard University Press, 1997.

Young, Michael, and Peter Wilmott. *Family and Kinship in East London.* Harmondsworth: Penguin, 1962.

Yver, Jean. *Essai de géographie coutumière: Egalité entre héritiers et exclusion des enfants dotés.* Paris: Sirey, 1966.

Zedler, Johann Heinrich. *Großes Universal-Lexicon aller Wissenschaften und Künste,* vol. 1. Halle and Leipzig: Zedler, 1732.

Zeitlhofer, Hermann. "Besitztransfer und sozialer Wandel in einer ländlichen Gesellschaft der Frühen Neuzeit: Das Beispiel der südböhmischen Pfarre Kaplicky, 1640–1840." Ph.D. diss., University of Vienna, 2001.

Zelizer, Viviana A. *The Social Meaning of Money.* New York: Basic Books, 1994.

Zink, Anne. *L'heritier de lamaison: Géographie coutumière du Sud-Ouest de la France sous l'Ancien Régime.* Paris: Ecole des Hautes Etudes en Sciences Sociales, 1993.

# Index

# About the Contributors

**ROBERT BEACHY** is Assistant Professor of History at Goucher College in Baltimore, Maryland, United States. His forthcoming book, *The Soul of Commerce: Property, Politics, and Public Debt in Saxony, 1750–1850,* will be published by Brill Press.

**GÉRARD BÉAUR** is Directeur de Recherches at the Centre National de la Recherche Scientifique and Directeur d'Etudes and leader of le Centre de Recherches Historiques at the Écoles des Hautes Études en Sciences, Paris, France. He is the author of many books and articles on the social and economic history of France, including *Histoire agraire de la France au XVIIIe siècle* (SEDES, 2000). He is currently President of the Association Française des Historiens Economistes.

**ROSE DUROUX** is Emeritus Professor at the University of Clermont-Ferrand, France. Her research examines migration between France and Spain. She is author of *Les Auvergnats de Castille* (Association des Publication de la Faculté des Lettres, 1992) and editor of *L'Émigration: le retour* (Cahiers du CRLMC, 1999).

**DAVID R. GREEN** is a Senior Lecturer in Geography at King's College London. For the past five years he has been editor of the *London Journal* and has published widely in urban history.

**SANDRO GUZZI-HEEB** is a researcher based in Bern, Switzerland. He is currently completing a study funded by the Swiss National Science

Foundation on men, women, and family relations in the Swiss Alps, 1650–1850.

**ANN IGHE** teaches and researches in the Department of Economic History at Göteborg University, Sweden. She is currently working on her doctoral dissertation examining gender, property rights, and citizenship in Sweden, 1770–1860.

**ANNE E. C. MCCANTS** is Associate Professor of Economic History at the Massachusetts Institute of Technology, United States. She has published widely on the economic and demographic history of northwestern Europe in the early modern period and is author of *Civic Charity in a Golden Age: Orphan Care in Early Modern Amsterdam* (University of Illinois Press, 1997).

**KIRSTI NISKANEN** is Associate Professor in the Department of Gender Studies, Linköpings University, Sweden. She received her Ph.D. in Economic History from Stockholm University in 1995, and her current research interests focus on the history of economic thought and the relationships between gender and economics.

**ALASTAIR OWENS** is Lecturer in Geography at Queen Mary, University of London.

**EVE ROSENHAFT** is Reader in German Studies at the University of Liverpool, United Kingdom. She has published widely on labor, working-class culture, social policy, ethnic minorities, and gender history in modern Germany. She is currently engaged in research examining the origins of life insurance in eighteenth-century Germany.

**MARSHA SHAPIRO ROSE** is Associate Professor of Sociology at Florida Atlantic University, United States. She received her Ph.D. from Ohio State University, and her current research interests focus on American elites and the history of technological change in the twentieth century.

**HERMANN ZEITLHOFER** is a research assistant at the Department of History, University of Salzburg and also teaches at the University of Vienna, Austria. His research focuses on migration history, historical demography, and the history of the family and social structure. He is co-editor of *Soziale Strukturen in Böhmen: Ein regionaler Vergleich von Wirtschaft und Gesellschaft, 16.–19. Jahrhundert* (Oldenbourg, 2002).